HANDBOOK OF EMPLOYEE ENGAGEMENT

NEW HORIZONS IN MANAGEMENT

Series Editor: Cary L. Cooper, CBE, *Distinguished Professor of Organizational Psychology and Health, Lancaster University, UK*

This important series makes a significant contribution to the development of management thought. This field has expanded dramatically in recent years and the series provides an invaluable forum for the publication of high quality work in management science, human resource management, organizational behaviour, marketing, management information systems, operations management, business ethics, strategic management and international management.

The main emphasis of the series is on the development and application of new original ideas. International in its approach, it will include some of the best theoretical and empirical work from both well-established researchers and the new generation of scholars.

Titles in the series include:

Handbook of Employee Engagement

Perspectives, Issues, Research and Practice

Edited by

Simon L. Albrecht

School of Psychology and Psychiatry, Monash University, Australia

NEW HORIZONS IN MANAGEMENT

Edward Elgar
Cheltenham, UK • Northampton, MA, USA

Contributors

Simon L. Albrecht, School of Psychology and Psychiatry, Monash University, Melbourne, Victoria, Australia.

Arnold B. Bakker, Department of Work and Organizational Psychology, Erasmus University Rotterdam, Rotterdam, The Netherlands.

Shashi Balain, Centre for Performance-led HR, Lancaster University Management School, Lancaster, UK.

Karen M. Barbera, Valtera Corporation, Chicago, IL, USA.

Constant D. Beugré, College of Business, Delaware State University, Dover, DE, USA.

Uta K. Bindl, Institute of Work Psychology, University of Sheffield, Sheffield, UK.

Carmen Binnewies, Institute of Psychology Work and Organizational Psychology Unit, University of Mainz, Mainz, Germany.

Sonja Brouwers, Hay Group, Brussels, Belgium.

Richard Carter, Macquarie Graduate School of Management, Macquarie University, Sydney, New South Wales, Australia.

Helena D. Cooper-Thomas, Psychology Department, University of Auckland, Auckland, New Zealand.

Gabriel M. De La Rosa, San Mateo, CA, USA.

Peggy De Prins, University of Antwerp Management School, Antwerp, Belgium.

M. Auxiliadora Durán, University of Málaga, Spain.

Natalio Extremera, University of Málaga, Spain.

Taru Feldt, Department of Psychology, University of Jyväskylä, Jyväskylä, Finland.

Bettina Fetzer, University of Konstanz, Konstanz, Germany.

Steven Fleck, SHL Group Ltd, London, UK.

Marylène Gagné, The John Molson School of Business, Concordia University, Quebec, Canada.

Jennifer M. George, Jesse H. Jones Graduate School of Business and Department of Psychology, Rice University, TX, USA.

Eusebio Rial González, European Agency for Safety and Health at Work, Bilbao, Spain.

Marjan J. Gorgievski, Department of Work and Organizational Psychology, Erasmus University Rotterdam, Rotterdam, The Netherlands.

George B. Graen, Center for Strategic Management Studies, University of Illinois at Urbana-Champaign, IL (Ret.), USA.

Jamie A. Gruman, College of Management and Economics, School of Hospitality and Tourism Management, University of Guelph, Ontario, Canada.

Anne E. Herman, Kenexa Research Institute, Minneapolis, MN, USA.

Peter A. Heslin, Cox School of Business, Southern Methodist University, Dallas, TX, USA.

Charles L. Hulin, University of Illinois at Urbana-Champaign, IL, USA.

Ilke Inceoglu, SHL Group Ltd, London, UK.

Steve M. Jex, Bowling Green State University, Bowling Green, OH, USA

Dana L. Joseph, University of Illinois at Urbana-Champaign, IL, USA.

Miriam Joy, Be Learning, Sydney, New South Wales, Australia.

William A. Kahn, Boston University School of Management, Boston, MA, USA.

Ulla Kinnunen, Department of Psychology, University of Tampere, Tampere, Finland.

Neal Knight-Turvey, JRA (Aust) Pty Ltd, Brisbane, Queensland, Australia.

Brenda J. Kowske, Kenexa Research Institute, Minneapolis, MN, USA.

Peter H. Langford, Voice Project, Department of Business, Macquarie University, Sydney, New South Wales, Australia.

Heather K.S. Laschinger, School of Nursing, University of Western Ontario, London, Ontario, Canada.

Nicola Leighton, Psychology Department, University of Auckland, Auckland, New Zealand.

William H. Macey, Valtera Corporation, Chicago, IL, USA.

Anne Mäkikangas, Department of Psychology, University of Jyväskylä, Jyväskylä, Finland.

Saija Mauno, Department of Psychology, University of Jyväskylä, Jyväskylä, Finland.

John P. Meyer, Department of Psychology, The University of Western Ontario, London, Ontario, Canada.

Daisuke Miyanaka, Rating and Investment Information Inc., Tokyo, Japan.

Giovanni B. Moneta, London Metropolitan University, London, UK.

Loren J. Naidoo, Psychology Department, Baruch College, City University of New York, NY, USA.

Paul Nesbit, Macquarie Graduate School of Management, Macquarie University, Sydney, New South Wales, Australia.

Daniel A. Newman, University of Illinois at Urbana-Champaign, IL, USA.

Karina Nielsen, National Research Centre for the Working Environment, Copenhagen, Denmark.

Natalya M. Parfyonova, Human Resource Systems Group, Ontario, Canada.

Sharon K. Parker, UWA Business School, University of Western Australia, Crawley, Western Australia, Australia.

Dan J. Putka, Human Resources Research Organization (HumRRO), Alexandria, VA, USA.

Lourdes Rey, University of Málaga, Spain.

Joanne Richardson, Aston Business School, Aston University, Birmingham, UK.

Alan M. Saks, Centre for Industrial Relations and Human Resources, University of Toronto, Ontario, Canada.

Marisa Salanova, WONT Research Team, Department of Psychology, Universitat Jaume I, Castellón, Spain.

Wilmar B. Schaufeli, Department of Social and Organizational Psychology, Utrecht University, Utrecht, The Netherlands.

Charles A. Scherbaum, Department of Psychology, Baruch College, City University of New York, NY, USA.

Benjamin Schneider, Valtera Corporation, Chicago, IL, USA.

Lior M. Schohat, School of Political Sciences, University of Haifa, Israel.

Jesse Segers, Management Department, University of Antwerp, Belgium.

Akihito Shimazu, Department of Mental Health, University of Tokyo Graduate School of Medicine, Tokyo, Japan.

Paul Sparrow, Centre for Performance-led HR, Lancaster University Management School, Lancaster, UK.

Eran Vigoda-Gadot, School of Political Sciences, University of Haifa, Israel.

Michael A. West, Aston Business School, Aston University, Birmingham, UK.

Cristina de Mello e Souza Wildermuth, School of Education, Drake University, Des Moines, IA, USA.

Jack W. Wiley, Kenexa Research Institute, Minneapolis, MN, USA.

Jessica Xu, JRA (NZ) Ltd, Auckland, New Zealand.

Scott A. Young, Valtera Corporation, Chicago, IL, USA.

David Youssefnia, Critical Metrics, Seattle, WA, USA.

Preface

The idea of employee engagement has clearly captured the hearts and minds of many researchers and practitioners across the globe. An internet search of the term "employee engagement" will probably yield in excess of 1.5 million hits. The field continues to grow and to grow rapidly. The proliferation of published research papers, conference papers, practitioner articles, case studies, survey instruments, and internet commentary provides little support for the contention, as some have suggested, that engagement is a mere fad that will soon disappear from organizational discourse and practice.

My interest in employee engagement, and the impetus for this Handbook, grew out of a contract research project I was doing with a large international mining company. Like many other companies that focus on employee engagement, they hoped their genuine attempt to embed a high-engagement culture would result in higher productivity, a more positive organizational culture, and a more positive organizational reputation and profile. As the project unfolded, many varied and vexing questions were thrown up regarding how best to define engagement; how best to measure engagement; the relevance of academic definitions and measures to practice; what are the key drivers of engagement; do key drivers vary across employment levels; does engagement mean different things for individuals, teams, business units and the organization; and what techniques can best be used to develop individual, team and organizational engagement? These represent only some of the issues, challenges and opportunities associated with the study and practice of employee engagement in applied settings. Throughout the project I became convinced of the merit of a single resource to help researchers and practitioners critically evaluate and navigate the "state of play" of employee engagement.

The *Handbook of Employee Engagement: Perspectives, Issues, Research and Practice* has the ambitious goal of covering a broad range of topics relevant to both the science and the practice of employee engagement. The book is intended as a comprehensive collection of conceptual pieces and research studies aimed at summarizing the "state of play" from across the globe. It aims to help researchers and practitioners identify, understand and apply the key theories, models, measures, and interventions associated with employee engagement.

I am deeply indebted to the many eminent researchers and practitioners who so readily said "yes" when I invited them to contribute to the

Handbook. Any success for this book is down to the willingness of so many positive and switched-on people being prepared to apply their considerable minds to the topic and share their very considerable experience and insights. All chapters were double-blind peer reviewed by a specially convened review panel. Unfortunately not all chapters submitted for consideration successfully passed through to the final stage of the review process.

True to intent, a wide cross-section of internationally recognized practitioners and researchers are represented in the Handbook. You will find chapters from world-class researchers and scholars such as Arnold Bakker, Jennifer George, Bill Kahn, John Meyer, Sharon Parker, Alan Saks, Marissa Salanova, Wilmar Schaufeli, Ben Schneider, and Michael West, many of whom have made enormous contributions to the study and profile of employee engagement. Similarly you will find extremely interesting contributions from researchers and consultants working in world-renowned consulting organizations such as Kenexa, SHL Group Ltd, and Valtera Consulting and who have also made extremely important contributions to the conceptualization, measurement and practice of employee engagement.

It is testimony to the richness and complexity inherent in the study of employee engagement that, despite for the most part not directing individual authors to focus on particular topics, there is very little overlap in the 34 chapters that are represented in the Handbook. I simply asked authors to contribute what they thought would best add to an examination of "the state of play". In order to satisfy a broad but informed readership, I also asked contributors to pitch their contributions more at the level of a keynote conference paper rather than at the level of an individual research paper. I asked for conceptual pieces, empirical pieces, and case studies. I also asked authors to restrict their word count and wherever possible to include a well-developed section on practical applications. No doubt some of the contributors must have struggled to accommodate the rather strict limits on word count, the number of references and the depth of the arguments that they might ordinarily include in their research papers. I am sure the book is the stronger for their accommodation and discipline with respect to these requests. I am also very confident that the authors would be happy to respond to requests for any additional information relating to their chapter.

The structure of the Handbook
The Handbook is organized into six parts. Part I covers the key issues, definitions, theories, models and measures of engagement. Part II focuses on the key drivers, predictors or antecedents of engagement. Issues and

research surrounding the influence of job resources, leadership, trust, voice and individual differences on employee engagement are discussed. Part III focuses on key processes and dynamics which underpin and form part of the experience of engagement. Issues and research surrounding career crafting, fluctuations in engagement, affect, and flow are discussed. Part IV focuses on the influence that management and human resource systems, processes and practices have on employee engagement. Socialization practices, top leadership, team engagement and empowerment are also covered. Part V deals with cross-cultural issues and with the question of how generalizable conceptualizations and measures of engagement might be across different global contexts. Finally, Part VI deals with the questions of how engagement links to performance and of how best to build employee engagement in organizational contexts. A number of innovative and well-grounded intervention strategies are outlined.

It is my sincere hope that the *Handbook of Employee Engagement* will provide an important impetus to ongoing research and practice on employee engagement. There are many new insights, practical applications and areas for future research identified in the Handbook which, I am sure, will spur new questions, new perspectives, new research and new practice.

Simon Albrecht
March 2010

PART I

WHAT IS EMPLOYEE ENGAGEMENT? ISSUES, THEORIES, MODELS AND MEASUREMENT

1 Employee engagement: 10 key questions for research and practice
Simon L. Albrecht

Introduction

The concept of employee engagement has generated enormous interest in both academic and practitioner domains. Macey et al. (2009) recently commented: "rarely has a term . . . resonated as strongly with business executives as employee engagement has in recent years" (p. xv). In addition there has been a significant spike in the amount of academic research being published on employee engagement over the past 5–10 years. So much so that it is probably no longer the case that "Much of what has been written about employee engagement comes from the practitioner literature and consulting firms. There is a surprising dearth of research on employee engagement in the academic literature" (Saks, 2006, p. 600).

Despite the proliferation in engagement-related research, and despite enormous advances having been made about how best to understand and manage engagement, a number of fundamental issues remain unresolved. While there are no doubt many more than 10 such issues, the purpose of this chapter is to highlight 10 key issues or questions facing researchers and practitioners working in the field of work-related engagement. The 10 key questions are:

1. How do we define engagement and what are its key characteristics and constituents?
2. Is it "old wine in a new bottle"?
3. What theories can be used to explain engagement?
4. Can we have too much engagement?
5. Are there fluctuations in engagement across the working day and working week?
6. How do we measure engagement?
7. What are the key drivers of engagement?
8. What is its relationship with organizational outcomes and performance?
9. What can we do to maximize or optimize engagement in organizational settings?
10. What are the key areas for further research?

This chapter provides a very brief overview of some of the differing perspectives, conceptual complexities and empirical evidence associated with these 10 issues. The chapter is aimed at orienting readers who are not so familiar with the academic literature and helping them navigate through these issues as they arise throughout the Handbook. I provide only a high-level and brief overview of these key issues.

1. How do we define engagement and what are its key characteristics and constituents?

Ideally we need a clear and agreed definition of engagement in order to clearly understand what engagement is, how it differs from other constructs, what it is related to, and how it should be measured. However, within this Handbook and within the broader academic and practitioner domains, there are numerous definitions of employee engagement – too many to cover here – and there remains considerable debate about what engagement is and how best to define it.

Kahn (1990), one of the first to theorize about work-related engagement, described engaged employees as being fully physically, cognitively and emotionally connected with their work roles. More recently, Macey et al. (2009) defined employee engagement as "an individual's sense of purpose and focused energy, evident to others in the display of personal initiative, adaptability, effort, and persistence directed toward organizational goals" (p. 7). Perhaps the most widely cited definition of engagement is that offered by Schaufeli et al. (2002, p. 74), who defined engagement as "a positive, fulfilling, work-related state of mind that is characterized by vigor, dedication, and absorption". Schaufeli et al. (2006) emphasized the diffuse and state-like (versus trait-like or momentary emotion-like) nature of engagement, arguing that engagement is a "more persistent and pervasive affective–cognitive state that is not focused on any particular object, event, individual, or behavior" (p. 702).

Common to many definitions offered by researchers and practitioners is the idea that engagement is a positive work-related psychological state (reflected in words like enthusiasm, energy, passion and vigor) and that engagement is also a motivational state reflected in a genuine willingness to invest focused effort toward organizational goals and success. Bakker et al. (2008), for example, argued that engagement is best conceptualized and characterized by "a high level of energy and a strong identification with one's work" (p. 189). As already noted, Macey et al. (2009) argued that engagement is best characterized as "purpose and focused energy . . . directed toward organizational goals" (p. 7). Definitions of engagement, however cast, might therefore usefully reflect these two essential qualities: (i) a positive and energized work-related motivational state, and

(ii) a genuine willingness to contribute to work role and organizational success.

Definitions of engagement need to clearly differentiate engagement from constructs that are better conceptualized as antecedents or "drivers" of engagement (for example, organizational, job and personal resources). Similarly, engagement needs to be clearly differentiated from constructs and measures which are better conceptualized as outcomes of engagement (for example, task performance, discretionary behavior, proactive behavior, turnover intention). Fleck and Inceoglu (ch. 3, this volume) make a good case for clearly separating out engagement from its antecedents and consequences.

In summary, although it is unlikely that there will ever be universal agreement about a single definition and measure of engagement, it is important that measures of engagement reflect what is conceptually at the core of the construct. Definitions of employee engagement might usefully recognize that employee engagement is a positive work-related psychological state characterized by a genuine willingness to contribute to organizational success. It is hoped that the inclusion of these core qualities in definitions and measures will consolidate understanding of what engagement is, and reduce some of the "noise" currently associated with the construct. Measures which reflect these core characteristics should therefore provide opportunities for more interpretable and robust meta-analyses which will help us understand, with greater confidence, the strength and the direction of the relationships that engagement has with its properly conceptualized antecedents and outcomes.

2. Is engagement old wine in a new bottle?

To be of any practical value engagement needs to be shown to be different from other related organizational constructs such as job involvement, job satisfaction, commitment, discretionary effort, and turnover intention. A number of researchers and practitioners have tackled the question of whether engagement is nothing more than "old wine in new bottles" (for example, Hallberg & Schaufeli, 2006; Macey & Schneider, 2008a; Newman & Harrison, 2008). Schohat and Vigoda-Gadot (ch. 8, this volume) revisit the arguments, asking whether engagement represents "same lady – different dress?".

In the Handbook there are a number of differing perspectives with regard to this issue. Newman et al. (ch. 4), for example, argue in favor of engagement being conceptualized as part of a higher-order overarching job attitude or "A-factor" which encompasses affective commitment, job satisfaction, and job involvement. In part, they argue this on the basis of a strong correlation ($r = 0.77$) between engagement and the A-factor. In contrast, numerous other contributors to the Handbook conceptualize engagement as being a distinct construct and adopt Schaufeli et al.'s (2002) vigor, dedication and absorption conceptualization of engagement.

While readers of the Handbook will come to their own conclusions on the "old wine, new bottle" issue, and while clearly not fully resolved (see Newman et al., ch. 4, this volume), it needs to be noted that there is considerable research and theory which supports treating engagement as a unique and distinct construct. On the research side, Hallberg and Schaufeli (2006), using confirmatory factor analysis, showed that engagement, job involvement and organizational commitment are best considered as distinct yet related constructs. On the theoretical side, Inceoglu and Fleck (ch. 6, this volume) argue that job satisfaction and engagement are located in different areas of well-established theoretical models of job-related affect (for example, Warr, 1990; Russell, 2003). Inceoglu and Fleck argue that in contrast to engagement, which is characterized by activated, high-arousal, and positive feelings at work (for example, energy, enthusiasm and vigor), job satisfaction and organizational commitment are characterized by less activated positive feelings such as contentment and comfort.

It is probably worthwhile noting that some of the empirical overlap between measures of engagement and pre-existing measures of job satisfaction, job involvement and commitment may, in part, be attributable to imprecision in the pre-existing measures. There is ongoing debate in the literature as to the psychometric properties of various measures of job satisfaction, organizational commitment and job involvement (for example, Solinger et al., 2008). Additional large-sample confirmatory factor analytic studies are required to further refine existing measures of job satisfaction and job involvement before we can confidently assess the degree of overlap or redundancy among such constructs.

To summarize, it is important to acknowledge some overlap between engagement and other similar constructs such as organizational commitment, job involvement and job satisfaction. Each of these constructs refers to positive work-related psychological states, and therefore we would expect that they will be related. However, it also needs to be recognized that engagement is a unique construct which deserves the same theoretical and practical attention as other more established organizational constructs.

3.   What theories can be used to explain engagement?

> There is nothing more practical than a good theory.
> (Lewin, 1952, p. 169)

Within the Handbook, and within the broader literature, engagement has been linked to a broad range of theories. Such theories include conservation of resources (COR) theory (Hobfoll, 1989); self determination theory (SDT, Deci & Ryan, 1985); social exchange theory (SET, Blau, 1964); social identity theory (SIT, Tajfel, 1974); role theory (Kahn, 1990); broaden-and-build theory of positive emotion (Fredrickson, 2001); job characteristics theory (JCT, Hackman & Oldham, 1980); and the job demands–resources model (JD–R, Bakker & Demerouti, 2007).

There are various ways in which the key tenets of these theories can help explain the emergence and management of employee engagement. COR (see Bakker, ch. 19, this volume), for example, describes how employees strive to gain and protect resources and why they will perform more effectively when they have access to a range of individual and job resources. SDT (see Meyer et al., ch. 5, this volume) explains that the experience of employee engagement requires the satisfaction of basic psychological needs such as competence, autonomy and relatedness. SET describes how the provision of valued resources from an external party (for example, resources from the organization) results in employees developing a felt obligation to reciprocate with prosocial attitudes and engagement-related behaviors. The JD–R model, which is probably the most widely cited and widely used theoretical engagement model, shows how job resources (for example, autonomy, feedback, support) and personal resources (for example, self-efficacy, optimism, resilience) directly influence work engagement, which in turn influences outcomes such as in-role performance, extra-role performance, creativity and financial outcomes.

Without going too deeply into individual theories, the take-away message is that ongoing research and practice on employee engagement needs to be firmly grounded in well-established theories, frameworks and models. By so doing we shall not only be able to *describe* the relationships and effects we find, but also be able to *explain* the psychological processes which underpin the relationships and effects we find.

4.   Can we have too much engagement?
Generally, employee engagement is seen as positive and desirable, with high levels of engagement, evidenced for example by high scores on an engagement survey, expected to be associated with higher levels of employee well-being, increased proactivity, increased creativity and innovation, higher productivity, and better bottom-line results. However, should we therefore hope and expect employees to be fully engaged all of the time? Can too much engagement be a bad thing?

At the extremes, the answer to these questions is probably "yes". As noted by Macey and Schneider (2008b, p. 80) "people cannot expend their energy at the highest levels all of the time – there is a need for recovery to ensure continued employee well-being". Indeed a constant state of high-energy engagement may have negative individual and organizational consequences in terms of exhaustion and loss of creativity. George (ch. 21, this volume) argues compellingly that, particularly under conditions of ambiguity, uncertainty, and the need for creative solutions, sustained conscious engagement may have detrimental effects and that "alternating levels of high and low levels of engagement may lead to more desirable outcomes". Additionally and importantly, Halbesleben et al. (2009) provided empirical evidence to show that higher levels of engagement can result in higher levels of work interference with family and that this relationship is mediated by the performance of organizational citizenship behaviors (OCBs). Managers and individual employees will therefore need systems and supports in place to help them actively manage engagement and to mitigate the possibility of negative health, well-being and performance consequences associated with overexertion, over-engagement and workaholism (see Gorgievski & Bakker, ch. 22, this volume).

5.   Are there fluctuations in engagement across the working day and working week?

The idea that engagement may fluctuate across the working day and the working week has clear implications for how we think about and measure engagement. If engagement is thought to be highly labile, often fluctuating up and down by large amounts over the course of a day or week, we would need to research and measure engagement with a much clearer and "explicit focus on . . . microtime within-person variability [focused on] fluctuations in employee engagement within the context of transient events, experiences, and processes" (Dalal et al., 2008, p. 53).

While it is perfectly reasonable that we should expect to see and experience fluctuations in the intensity of employee engagement across the working day and across the working week, it also makes sense that over time employees will be able to resolve or "average" micro-level fluctuations into an overall evaluation of the extent to which they experience being engaged at work over a specified period of time. This averaging process is consistent with Schaufeli et al.'s (2002) definition of employee engagement as a pervasive positive psychological state, likely to persist over days and weeks. So while fluctuations in engagement no doubt exist, and are clearly worthy of ongoing research attention, these fluctuations should not fully compromise the confidence with which we can assess and aggregate individual employee engagement over the course of "the past few weeks", for instance. Perhaps in our research and in our practice we need to more clearly distinguish between momentary short-term experiences of "flow" (Csikszentmihalyi, 2000) and more persistent and enduring states of engagement (see Moneta, ch. 23, this volume).

6. How do we measure engagement?

Measures of engagement need to operationalize a theoretically defensible definition of engagement, need psychometric evidence in support of their validity and reliability, and need to have sufficient fine-grain focus to be of practical utility in organizational contexts (Macey & Schneider, 2008b).

Within the academic and practitioner literatures there are references to a wide range of measures of employee engagement. A large number of consultancies have their own proprietal measures. Measures of engagement can also be sourced in the academic domain (for example, May et al., 2004; Saks, 2006; Schaufeli et al., 2006). While a full review of the various measures is beyond the scope of this chapter, the reader is referred to Macey and Schneider (2008b), Newman and Harrison (2008), and Newman et al. (ch. 4, this volume) for discussion of the relative merits of some of the measures.

Bakker et al. (2008) argued, with good justification, that the Utrecht Work Engagement Scale (UWES; Schaufeli et al., 2002) is the most widely cited and widely used measure of engagement. The 9-item version (UWES-9, Schaufeli et al., 2006) is currently the most widely used version. The UWES has the advantages of being grounded in theory, of clearly reflecting core aspects of the correspondent definition (that is, vigor, dedication, and absorption), and of being validated in many different countries with the use of sophisticated statistical data analytic methods. Although Bakker et al. have argued that their hypothesized three-factor measurement model provides a superior fit to alternative models, Schaufeli and Bakker (2010) argued that an overall score for work engagement may sometimes be equally or more useful in empirical research than scores on the three separate dimensions of the UWES.

So, how best to measure employee engagement? I would argue that when measuring engagement it would be extremely useful to have agreement about common items or questions, which have a clear link to an agreed definition of the construct. Items similar to core items of the UWES-9 (for example, "at my work I feel full of energy", "I am usually very enthusiastic about my job", "I am often fully immersed in my job") in combination with items that also reflect a willingness to contribute to work role and organizational success (for example, "I am very motivated to do a good job for this organization", and "I feel a real sense of enthusiasm for what I help achieve in this organization") might sensibly be included in employee engagement surveys. Ongoing studies to evaluate and refine the convergent and discriminant validity associated with such items and scales will obviously be required.

7.   What are the key drivers of engagement?

This question is of key importance to practitioners and academics alike. If engagement is desirable in organizational contexts, practitioners in particular, will want to know which levers to pull and which buttons to press in order to manage and develop engagement. Drivers provide "the keys to taking action to increase engagement and performance" (Fleck & Inceoglu, ch. 3, this volume).

To identify key drivers we first we need to know the pool of potential drivers which are likely to be relevant in most organizational contexts. Second, we need to conduct analyses in varying contexts to determine which of the pool of drivers are most salient in each particular context. It may be the case, for example, that the importance rankings of key drivers of engagement in the healthcare sector are different from those in the manufacturing sector.

To identify the broader pool of potential drivers it is instructive to look at the results of meta-analyses. Meta-analyses use advanced statistical procedures to combine the results of individual studies and arrive at an overall best determination of the strength and direction of relationships between constructs of interest. The search for salient drivers should also be conducted with reference to reputable theoretical models and frameworks which help us understand the reason why the drivers relate to engagement.

Fortunately, a few meta-analyses and qualitative reviews have recently been published which identify the strongest and most reliable drivers of engagement (for example, Christian & Slaughter, 2007; Simpson, 2008; Halbesleben, 2010; Mauno et al., ch. 9, this volume). Halbesleben's (2010) meta-analysis, consistent with the JD–R model (Bakker & Demerouti, 2007), showed that feedback, autonomy, social support and organizational climate are consistently associated with engagement and or particular facets of engagement. Halbesleben's meta-analysis also showed that personal resources (for example, self-efficacy and optimism) are strongly related to engagement.

Mauno et al. (ch. 9, this volume) conducted a qualitative review of high-quality two-wave longitudinal studies aimed at determining what can be done to change levels of engagement over time. They showed that increases in employee experiences of job control and support at work consistently predict an increase in employee engagement over time. These findings therefore suggest in very practical terms some of the ways in which we can intervene to improve engagement over time. Interestingly, and again consistent with JD–R theorizing, Mauno et al. also reviewed research evidence which supports the idea of reciprocal causation between job resources and engagement, such that resources predict engagement and that engagement predicts resources.

Overall, a broad range of predictors of engagement have been identi-fied in the literature. Within the Handbook the predictors discussed and examined include demands, control and support (De La Rosa & Jex, ch. 10), voice (Beugré, ch. 14), trust (Schneider et al., ch. 13), person–job and person–organization fit (Fleck & Inceoglu, ch. 3), fairness (Laschinger, ch. 26), opportunities for development (Fleck & Inceoglu, ch. 3), leader-ship (Meyer et al., ch. 5; Segers et al., ch. 12), affect regulation, recovery and relaxation (Binnewies & Fetzer, ch. 20) and individual personality characteristics (Wildermuth, ch. 16). From a practical point of view, the challenge remains to derive and agree a coherent and comprehensive set of resources or drivers which can be applied across a broad range of organi-zational contexts. Agreement on a set of theoretically derived key drivers, appropriately measured, will allow us to consolidate in meta-analytic reviews the relative influence of the various key drivers of engagement. Appropriate statistical techniques will then need to be applied to survey data in order to identify which drivers are key in which particular organi-zational and cultural contexts. Scherbaum et al. (ch. 15, this volume) provide an overview of such appropriate statistical techniques. Shimazu et al. (ch. 30, this volume) and Wiley et al. (ch. 29, this volume) discuss how engagement also needs to be considered in cross-cultural contexts.

8.   What is its relationship with organizational outcomes and performance?

Is there good evidence to support the much-touted benefits of employee engagement? The answer to this question appears to be a "yes". Confining our attention to the academic literature, there is now increasing evidence showing robust relationships between employee engagement and a range of important organizational outcomes. Engagement, for example, has been shown to be associated with increased employee commitment (Hallberg & Schaufeli, 2006), in-role and extra-role behavior (Bakker et al., 2004), and service climate, employee performance and customer loyalty (Salanova et al., 2005). Xanthopoulou et al. (2009) in a recent diary study showed a clear link between daily levels of engagement and daily level financial returns for employees working in a fast-food restaurant.

Overall, verifying the influence that engagement has on a wide range of important individual, team and organizational outcomes remains an important ongoing challenge for both researchers and practitioners. Despite considerable progress on this issue, there is more to be done; particularly with regard to establishing the relationship between engage-ment and important individual employee, business unit and organiza-tional financial metrics (see Macey et al., 2009; Wiley et al., ch. 29, this volume for examples and discussion). For engagement to remain a valued organizational focus it will be important for both researchers and practitioners to demonstrate both financial and non-financial advantages associated with interventions aimed at improving employee engagement.

9.   What can we do to maximize or optimize engagement in organizational settings?

So, given the demonstrated advantages of engagement, as outlined above, what can we do to develop and improve employee engagement in organizational contexts? What do we need to do at a practical level in order to build and maintain employee engagement? In relation to these questions it needs to be noted that "Unfortunately to date only very few interventions to improve work engagement exist and have been tested" (Schaufeli & Salanova, ch. 33, this volume).

Irrespective of what key driver analyses might tell us about particular opportunities to develop employee engagement in particular contexts, it will be useful to classify engagement interventions in terms of organizational-, job- and individual-level interventions. Some combination of interventions across the various levels will probably be needed to develop, embed and sustain engagement in organizational settings.

If we first think of organizational-level interventions, tried and tested organizational development (OD) methodologies should be considered. Survey feedback processes, for example, could be used to create a culture or climate for engagement. Schneider (for example, Schneider et al., 1998) has long advocated that measures of organizational climate need to have a particular focus or referent (for example, climate for safety, climate for service, climate for innovation). The development of a "climate for engagement" or a "high engagement climate" might sensibly build on traditional models of organizational climate (for example, Koys & DeCotiis, 1991; Patterson et al., 2005) and focus on employee experiences of participation, autonomy, trust, safety, cohesion, support, fairness, feedback, recognition, and opportunities for growth and reward as a means to predict and develop employee engagement.

Aspiring toward a high-engagement climate requires that engagement becomes a central focus in organizational systems and processes. As such, employee opinion surveys, multi-rater feedback processes, performance development systems, performance management systems, leadership development programs, team development programs, mentoring and coaching programs, and induction and socializations processes will all need to have a central focus on engagement. Senior leadership commitment to engagement will also be essential and transformational leadership, empowering leadership, and coaching programs will likely prove foundational OD interventions in the pursuit of a vibrant and positive climate for engagement. Consistent with this system-level thinking, Schaufeli and Salanova (ch. 33, this volume) overview several organizational strategies that focus on assessing and evaluating employees; designing and changing workplaces; enhancing transformational leadership; work training; and career management. Wiley et al. (ch. 29, this volume) also overview a number of top-line system-level actions to help organizations embed engagement and "drive employee engagement levels higher". These include developing and implementing processes for selecting and promoting executive talent; developing and executing quality strategic plans; and widely inculcating enabling leadership processes.

If we next think of job-level interventions, traditional job design methodologies need to be considered. Given the considerable evidence suggesting that "active jobs" (see Karasek, 1979; Bakker, ch. 19, this volume), characterized by high levels of control, demands and support, are associated with employee engagement, jobs need to be designed so that employees experience meaning, significance, variety, autonomy, feedback, and challenge in their roles. Job enrichment, job enlargement, job rotations, secondments and special assignments are proven means by which jobs can be designed to facilitate optimum levels of engagement. As previously noted, it might also be useful to build opportunities for respite, recovery and unconscious processing into job roles (see George, ch. 21, this volume), probably through the provision of ongoing support systems and job autonomy.

If we next consider what to do at the individual level to facilitate and optimize personal resources important to employee engagement, we can design and deliver training, coaching, and developmental supports aimed, for example, at building positive affect, self-efficacy, resiliency, emotional intelligence and adaptive behavioral strategies (see Durán et al., ch. 17; Heslin, ch. 18; Binnewies & Fetzer, ch. 20; George, ch. 21; Schaufeli & Salanova, ch. 33; Carter et al., ch. 34; all this volume). Schaufeli and Salanova, for example, provide a very interesting overview of how positive psychology interventions, classified by behavioral, cognitive and volitional strategies, might be deployed in organizational contexts. Example behavioral strategies include developing signature strengths, expressing gratitude, and nurturing social relationships. Schaufeli and Salanova overview evidence in support of the effectiveness of each of these positive psychological intervention strategies. Carter et al. overview some very interesting theatre-based interventions which should prompt us all to think widely and creatively about how individual- and group-level engagement can be developed, nurtured and managed. Ongoing research, program design and program evaluation aimed at determining how best to adapt these individual-based strategies to different organizational contexts will of course be necessary.

Importantly, whichever strategies we implement in our attempts to enhance engagement in organizational contexts, there is a clear and ongoing need to systematically evaluate the effectiveness of such interventions across a range of different contexts. Cooper-Thomas et al. (ch. 7, this volume), for example, provide some useful perspectives on the need to conduct rigorous analyses of survey data in order to fully understand the nature of any changes in engagement that may or may not have occurred over time.

10.   What are the key areas for further research?

There are numerous and varied ideas for future research outlined in the Handbook. Perhaps overlaying these ideas is an important opportunity to consolidate and elaborate on what has already been achieved and agreed. Given there is a growing consensus that engagement can be defined in terms of high levels of energy and high levels of involvement in work (Bakker et al., 2008) and that the JD–R model (Bakker & Demerouti, 2007, 2008) provides a useful unifying theoretical platform to examine the nomological net around engagement, ongoing research which acknowledges and builds on this consensus will help the study of engagement advance in a way that is coherent, systematic and integrated.

Future research and theorizing might usefully be focused on elaborating the JD–R model to accommodate additional variables and additional complexity. Just as Parker et al. (2001) and Morgeson and Campion (2003) advocated elaborating traditional job design models, such as the job characteristics model (Hackman & Oldham, 1980), similar suggestions might be applied to core models underpinning engagement. Parker et al. argued for the inclusion external contextual factors such as "uncertainty of the environment, customer demands, the available technology, social and cultural norms, economic circumstances, the nature of the labour market, and political and labour institutions" (p. 419) in job design models. Similarly they argued for the inclusion of internal contextual factors such as "the style of management, technology, nature of the tasks, information systems, human resource practices, strategy, history, and culture" (p. 419). The JD–R model might similarly be expanded (perhaps more broadly conceptualized as an organization demands–resources model) to more explicitly acknowledge contextual factors such as organizational leadership, organizational strategy, organizational vision and values, organizational culture, organizational structure and human resources (HR) systems. Even though these contextual factors have an influence on engagement which is more distal relative to the more proximal influence of job resources such as autonomy, co-worker support, variety and feedback, they probably also serve to influence and condition employee experiences of job resources and the expression of personal resources. For example, with respect to organizational vision and values, Bindl and Parker (ch. 32, this volume) argue:

> [T]he more employees internalize and identify the values and goals of the organization they work in, the more likely they will feel engaged at work. Thus, organizational practices that effectively convey the values of the organization to all employees, and involve them with the goals of the organization, result in more engaged employees, and – ultimately – in more positive behaviors at work.

More broadly, the influence that senior leadership has on shaping organizational culture, organizational climate, and HR systems could usefully be embedded in a larger elaborated model.

At the more macro levels of analysis the influence of job insecurity, downsizing and the employment of contract staff could also usefully be further researched. George (ch. 21, this volume), for example, observed that "it would be useful to explore how reactions to adverse organizational events (for example, layoffs) differ depending upon whether employees were highly engaged in their jobs prior to the event". On a related theme, the main and moderating effects of environmental ambiguity and environmental uncertainty on the relationship between resources and engagement could usefully be examined (see George; Bindl and Parker; both this volume). Finally, researchers might also usefully examine the extent to which employee perceptions of their organization's record on corporate social responsibility and environmental responsibility influences engagement.

The Handbook suggests a number of job resources which might directly influence engagement and which might usefully be incorporated into an elaborated JD–R model of employee engagement. Voice (Beugré, ch. 14), trust, justice and the psychological contract (Schneider et al., ch.13), and person–organization and person–job fit (Fleck & Inceoglu, ch. 3) have been proposed to have a salient and direct influence on employee engagement. Additionally, the relative influence of resources such as organizational communication, communication about change, and process feedback might usefully be the subject of future research. More generally, the influence of the social context (for example, co-worker support, efficacy of supervisor, team engagement), recognizing the importance of social information-processing perspectives (Salancik & Pfeffer, 1978) and social networks (Monge & Contractor, 2001) may provide an additional and particularly rich vein of future research. As previously noted, some of these future research ideas might usefully come together under a research agenda aimed at identifying dimensions and measures of a "climate for engagement". On a related theme, additional research on "team climate for engagement" could usefully be conducted.

Further research on the extent to which individual difference factors influence engagement will also be of interest. Not only will it be important to determine if individual difference variables have any influence on engagement beyond that explained by contextual factors (this question clearly has implications for selection and development processes) but it will also be important to assess how individual difference variables serve to influence the relationships between resources and engagement and between engagement and outcomes. For example, further research might usefully examine which personality factors and which dimensions of PsyCap (Luthans & Youssef, 2004) have the most salient main and moderated influence on engagement. Indeed, on the question of salience, the extent to which the strength of the relationship between resources and engagement is influenced by the extent to which employees perceive engagement as important also provides an interesting area for future research.

A number of contributors in the Handbook noted increasing research interest in daily and momentary fluctuations in engagement. Binnewies and Fetzer (ch. 20), for example, note increased numbers of diary studies aimed at better understanding how day-specific engagement corresponds to or relates to more enduring state-like engagement. In a similar vein, Mauno et al. (ch. 9) advocate for the development of process-oriented models of engagement which map the phases of the development of employee engagement. Researchers will no doubt continue to come up with innovative ways, perhaps for example using social networking, texting, blog and twitter technologies, to collect data and knowledge on the development and dynamics of employee engagement. On this issue, further theorizing and research aimed at establishing the similarities and distinctions between day-specific and momentary work engagement and the experience of flow (Csikszentmihalyi, 2000) may also be helpful. Perhaps a more elaborated language for engagement-related constructs to better enable us to speak differentially about momentary, daily, weekly and longer, more state-like periods of engagement might usefully emerge.

More research also needs to be undertaken on the impact of engagement. While clear progress has been made in this area, additional research could usefully focus on the short-, medium- and long-term effects of individual engagement on a range of individual-level outcomes such as satisfaction, well-being, commitment, health, creativity and productivity. The effects of individual employee engagement on co-workers, supervisors, subordinates, partners, friends and family should also be the subject of ongoing research. More broadly, additional research is needed to establish the influence that engagement has on business-unit and organizational-level financial outcomes. Macey et al. (2009) have described the advantages and disadvantages of some alternative financial metrics which could usefully be employed in this endeavor.

Finally, the study of engagement needs to remain firmly focused on understanding the psychology or felt experience of engagement. By proceeding from well-established psychological theories we shall no doubt derive a clearer understanding of how to intervene to improve engagement at the level of the individual, the team, the business unit and the organization. As researchers and practitioners we need to be seen to be making a positive difference in organizational contexts. The ongoing challenge is to continue to merge good science and good practice.

George (ch. 21, this volume) argued that "[C]learly, there are many unanswered questions in the study of employee engagement", and so there are. The Handbook has probably delivered as many questions as it has answers. Hopefully, however, the Handbook will prompt fresh thinking and fresh questions which can be worked out in an ongoing upward spiral of high-quality research and high-quality practice to deliver practical and positive outcomes across the full range of job, organizational, sector and cultural contexts.

References

Bakker, A.B. & Demerouti, E. (2007), "The job demands–resources model: state of the art", *Journal of Managerial Psychology*, **22**, 309–28.

Bakker, A.B. & Demerouti, E. (2008), "Towards a model of work engagement", *Career Development International*, **13**(3), 209–23.

Bakker, A.B., Demerouti, E. & Verbeke, W. (2004), "Using the job demands–resources model to predict burnout and performance", *Human Resource Management*, **43**, 83–104.

Bakker, A.B., Schaufeli, W.B., Leiter, M.P. & Taris, T.W. (2008), "Work engagement: an emerging concept in occupational health psychology", *Work & Stress*, **22**, 187–200.

Blau, P.M. (1964). *Exchange and Power in Social Life*, New York: John Wiley.

Christian, M.S. & Slaughter, J.E. (2007), "Work engagement: a meta-analytic review and directions for research in an emerging area", Congress paper in 67th annual meeting of Academy of Management, Philadelphia, Pennsylvania, August 6.

Csikszentmihalyi, M. (2000), *Beyond Boredom and Anxiety: Experiencing Flow in Work and Play*, 2nd edn, San Francisco, CA: Jossey-Bass.

Dalal, R.S., Brummel, B.J., Wee, S. & Thomas, L.L. (2008), "Defining employee engagement for productive research and practice", *Industrial and Organizational Psychology*, **1**, 52–5.

Deci, E.L. & Ryan, R.M. (1985), *Intrinsic Motivation and Self-determination in Human Behavior*, New York: Plenum.

Fredrickson, B.L. (2001), "The role of positive emotions in positive psychology. The broaden-and-build theory of positive emotions", *American Psychologist*, **56**(3), 218–26.

Hackman, J.R. & Oldham, G.R. (1980), *Work Re-design*, Reading, RA: Addison-Wesley.

Halbesleben, J.R.B. (2010), "A meta-analysis of work engagement: relationships with burnout, demands, resources and consequences", in A.B. Bakker & M.P. Leiter (eds), *Work Engagement: Recent Developments in Theory and Research*, New York: Psychology Press, pp. 102–17.

Halbesleben, J.R.B., Harvey, J. & Bolino, M.C. (2009), "Too engaged? A conservation of resources view of the relationship between work engagement and work interference with family", *Journal of Applied Psychology*, **94**(6), 1452–65.

Hallberg, U.E. & Schaufeli, W.B. (2006), "'Same same' but different? Can work engagement be discriminated from job involvement and organizational commitment?", *European Psychologist*, **11**, 119–27.

Hobfoll, S.E. (1989), "Conservation of resources: a new attempt at conceptualizing stress", *American Psychologist*, **44**(3), 513–24.

Kahn, W.A. (1990), "Psychological conditions of personal engagement and disengagement at work", *Academy of Management Journal*, **33**(4), 692–724.

Karasek, R.A. (1979), "Job demands, job decision latitude, and mental strain: implications for job redesign", *Administrative Science Quarterly*, **24**(2), 285–308.

Koys, D.J. & De Cotiis, T.A. (1991), "Inductive measures of psychological climate", *Human Relations*, **44**, 265–85.

Lewin, K. (1952), *Field Theory in Social Science: Selected Theoretical Papers by Kurt Lewin*, London: Tavistock.

Luthans, F. & Youssef, C.M. (2004), "Human, social and now positive psychological capital management: investing in people for competitive advantage", *Organizational Dynamics*, **33**, 143–60.

Macey, W.H. & Schneider, B. (2008a), "The meaning of employee engagement", *Industrial and Organizational Psychology: Perspectives on Science and Practice*, **1**, 3–30.

Macey, W.H. & Schneider, B. (2008b), "Engaged in engagement: we are delighted we did it", *Industrial and Organizational Psychology: Perspectives on Science and Practice*, **1**, 76–83.

Macey, W.H., Schneider, B., Barbera, K.M. & Young, S.A. (2009), *Employee Engagement: Tools for Analysis, Practice, and Competitive Advantage*, Malden, MA: Wiley.

May, D.R., Gilson, R.L. & Harter, L. (2004), "The psychological conditions of meaningfulness, safety, and availability, and the engagement of the human spirit at work", *Journal of Occupational and Organizational Psychology*, **77**, 11–37.

Monge, P.R. & Contractor, N.S. (2001), "Emergence of communication networks", in F.M. Jablin & L.L. Putnam (eds), *New Handbook of Organizational Communication*, Newbury Park, CA: Sage, pp. 440–502.

Morgeson, F.P. & Campion, M.A. (2003), "Work design", in W.C. Borman, D.R. Ilgen & R. J. Klimoski (eds), *Handbook of Psychology: Industrial and Organizational Psychology*, Vol. 12, Hoboken, NJ: John Wiley & Sons, pp. 423–52.

Newman, D.A. & Harrison, D.A. (2008), "Been there, bottled that: are state and behavioral work engagement new and useful construct 'wines'?", *Industrial and Organizational Psychology*, **1**, 31–5.

Parker, S.K., Wall, T.D. & Cordery, J.L. (2001), "Future work design research and practice: towards an elaborated model of work design", *Journal of Occupational and Organizational Psychology*, **74**, 413–40.

Patterson, M.G., West, M.A., Shackleton, V.J., Dawson, J.F., Lawthom, R., Maitlis, S., Robinson, D.L. & Wallace, A.M. (2005), "Validating the organizational climate measure: links to managerial practices, productivity and innovation", *Journal of Organizational Behavior*, **26**, 379–408.

Russell, J.A. (2003), "Core affect and the psychological construction of emotion", *Psychological Review*, **110**(1), 145–72.

Saks, A.M. (2006), "Antecedents and consequences of employee engagement", *Journal of Managerial Psychology*, **21**, 600–619.

Salancik, G.R. & Pfeffer, J. (1978), "A social information processing approach to job attitudes and task design", *Administrative Science Quarterly*, **23**, 224–53.

Salanova, M., Agut, S. & Peiró, J.M. (2005), "Linking organizational resources and work engagement to employee performance and customer loyalty: the mediation of service climate", *Journal of Applied Psychology*, **90**, 1217–27.

Schaufeli, W.B. & Bakker, A.B. (2010), "Defining and measuring work engagement: bringing clarity to the concept", in A.B. Bakker & M.P. Leiter (eds), *Work Engagement: A Handbook of Essential Theory and Research*, New York: Psychology Press, pp. 10–24.

Schaufeli, W.B., Bakker, A.B. & Salanova, M. (2006), "The measurement of work engagement with a short questionnaire: a cross-national study", *Educational and Psychological Measurement*, **66**(4), 701–16.

Schaufeli, W.B., Salanova, M., González-Romá, V. & Bakker, A.B. (2002), "The measurement of engagement and burnout: a two sample confirmatory factor analytic approach", *Journal of Happiness Studies*, **3**, 71–92.

Schneider, B., White, S.S. & Paul, M.C. (1998), "Linking service climate and customer perceptions of service quality: tests of a causal model", *Journal of Applied Psychology*, **83**, 150–63.

Simpson, M. (2008), "Engagement at work: a review of the literature", *International Journal of Nursing Studies*, **46**, 1012–24.

Solinger, O.N., van Olffen, W. & Roe, R.A. (2008), "Beyond the three-component model of organizational commitment", *Journal of Applied Psychology*, **93**(1), 70–83.

Tajfel, H. (1974), "Social identity and intergroup behaviour", *Social Science Information*, **14**, 101–18.

Warr, P. (1990), "The measurement of well-being and other aspects of mental health", *Journal of Occupational Psychology*, **63**, 193–210.

Xanthopoulou, D., Bakker, A.B., Demerouti, E. & Schaufeli, W.B. (2009), "Work engagement and financial returns: a diary study on the role of job and personal resources", *Journal of Occupational and Organizational Psychology*, **82**, 183–200.

2 The essence of engagement: lessons from the field
William A. Kahn

Introduction

Engagement is an enormously appealing concept. We seem to intuitively understand what it means, and believe that it helps to explain something about how people are (or ought to be) at work. The problem, of course, is that many of us have different understandings of what engagement is. We all believe that it is a good thing to be engaged, particularly in contrast to being disengaged, which suggests absence. But we are just not exactly sure what engagement really looks like, except that it involves people working hard and caring about what they are doing. This seems like a good thing, for individuals, their organizations and its customers, and the quality of the work that gets done. Beyond that, there is much divergence in terms of what, exactly, engagement is. This divergence makes it difficult for us to agree on how to get more people engaged at work.

I have been thinking about, researching, and helping people and organizations with engagement for almost thirty years. I developed the concept of engagement to explain what traditional studies of work motivation overlooked – namely, that employees offer up different degrees and dimensions of their selves according to some internal calculus that they consciously and unconsciously make (Kahn, 1990). Traditional motivation studies implicitly assumed that workers were either on or they were off; that is, based on external rewards and intrinsic factors, they were either motivated to work or not, and that this was a relatively steady state that they inhabited (Hackman & Oldham, 1980). I believed that workers are more complicated. Like actors, they make choices about how much of their real selves they bring into their role performances (Kahn, 1992). They might fully and truly express themselves, to the extent their role allows, or they might not at all, with degrees in between. I believed that, rather than label workers as "motivated" or not, these movements into or out of role performances could change a great deal as various conditions shifted. I developed the engagement concept to capture that process. And I set out to determine the conditions that led workers to engage or disengage to varying degrees. In this chapter I share some of what I have discovered and have since expanded upon.

We know engagement mostly by what people actually *do*. The most clearly observable behaviors that suggest engagement are people's efforts. We believe that people are engaged when we see them working hard, putting in effort, staying involved. They truly show up for their work. They remain focused on what they are doing. They strive to move their work ahead. They put energy into what they are doing (Schaufeli & Bakker, 2004).

Yet engagement is not simply working hard. It is not simply about the vigor with which people work, their high levels of involvement. It is about putting ourselves – our real selves – into the work. This begins but does not end with effort. Our real selves show up when we say what we think and feel in the service of doing the work the best way that we know how. When we deeply care about what we are doing, and are committed to doing the best that we can, we feel compelled to speak rather than remain silent. We use our voices. This is part of engagement. It is what I referred to in 1990 when I initially defined engagement as the harnessing of people's selves to their work (Kahn, 1990). The self is crucial here. When we are engaged, we express that self, rather than defend or withdraw it from view. Self-expression is a matter of voice (Morrison & Milliken, 2000). The accountant tells her supervisor that she does not feel comfortable using a certain financial technique that seems to hide certain budgetary practices. The project manager tells a colleague that he is frustrated by the lack of communication across departments. The consultant tells a client that she feels like she is wasting her time and their money on a project that has no senior management support. These workers are expressing rather than hiding their thoughts and feelings.

When workers are present in their role performances, they also allow the full range of their senses to inform their work. They do not simply follow routines, which can require little of them other than simply showing up at work and putting in their time. They place their ideas, hunches and feelings at the disposal of the problems they are trying to solve. It matters that it is *these* specific individuals working on those problems. The line worker on the manufacturing floor senses that the wooden handles he creates on the lathe are smaller than usual in his hands. On a break he goes and checks the specifications on the machine, and discovers that the settings are wrong. The bank clerk senses something odd in the manner of someone making a large wire transfer, and takes an extra moment to examine paperwork that proves to be identity theft. These workers are bringing their full selves – a depth of awareness of which they may not even be fully aware – to bring to bear on their work.

So this is what engagement looks like. People are focused on their tasks. They stay with them. They show that they care about them. They work hard to accomplish them as best they can. They bring all sorts of data – their thoughts, feelings, hunches, experiences – into play as they go about their work. They say what they think and feel insofar as it advances the work. They fully inhabit their roles, not just do their jobs. They do not need to do this in a showy way, designed to make others stop and applaud them. They are just very present in doing their work (Kahn, 1992).

Engagement is not a simple matter. It requires a depth of intensity and focus that cannot be constantly sustained. Workers need intervals, moments of absence, of being away. They need space in which to re-charge before their next engagements. Such moments are necessary. But they are not entirely sufficient. People do not get engaged simply because they get enough breaks, like runners who train simply with intervals of running and resting. Engagement is a far more delicate phenomenon, trickier to create and sustain. My research involves understanding and helping to create the conditions that make it more likely that people will become and remain engaged in their work role performances. In my initial empirical work I identified three psychological conditions that must be met to the satisfaction of employees (Kahn, 1990). People are more likely to engage when they feel that it is *meaningful* to do so, when they sense that it is *safe* to do so, and when they are *available* to do so. These three conditions, taken together, shape how much of their selves people bring into task performances. Since that initial work I have conducted action research focusing on how leaders and members actually create or undermine these conditions (Kahn, 1998, 2001, 2005). In this chapter I share those lessons, grouped into three general questions that people need to answer affirmatively for themselves if they are to engage.

Does it matter?
People engage when they feel that, on balance, it matters to do so. This is, of course, partly about self-interest. We are more likely to engage when it is in our interest to do so: we are more likely to get the dividends that we want by investing as much of ourselves as possible in some situation. So a basic strategy in engaging others is to help align their interests, such that they very much want to do that which is their job to do. There are other lessons here.

We use our voices when they are likely to be heard
At the heart of engagement is the use of the voice, as the instrument by which we say what we think and feel, question others, describe options and inventions, dialogue. We use our voice when we feel that our words matter – that they will make a difference, change minds and directions, add

value, join us with others in something larger than ourselves (Morrison & Milliken, 2000). When this is not the case, we use our voice less. Deaf ears make us mute. We hold our tongue. We nod and do others' bidding. We disengage. The learning organization depends on the engaged voices of its members (Senge, 1990). Systems learn only when their members bring issues to one another's attention. Processes change only because people engage, offering data that requires the system to alter how it does its work. We can see this with any kind of mistakes that happen in organizations. People improve their practices by learning from near misses and errors – but only when members believe that their voice will be heard and their ideas valued. If not, they check out, shield themselves from blame, scapegoat others, and in other ways disengage. Organizational learning occurs only when people feel that their words matter.

We bring ourselves into roles that fit who we wish to be and whose tasks and boundaries are quite clear
People are more likely to engage when it is perfectly clear what, exactly, their roles are, and they like what those roles allow them to express about themselves (Tyler, 1999). Organizational roles, like theatrical ones, allow people to express parts of their selves. Certain roles allow us to be smart, creative, organized, caring, attentive, zany. We are more likely to engage when the role matches what we wish to be. And the role has to be clearly understood, such that there are clear boundaries between what we are and are not supposed to be doing. People are more likely to disengage when it is not clear what their tasks or authority is, relative to others, and what decisions are theirs to make.

We invest ourselves in roles that reward us in currencies that we value
Unavoidably, the meaning that we ascribe to our work is shaped by the rewards that we get from that work. Much organizational research over the years has explored the nature and impact of rewards on effort, motivation, and job performance (Hackman & Oldham, 1980). We thus know a great deal. Workers need to feel that there is a clear and fair relation between the work that they do and the extrinsic rewards – money, promotions, status, visibility – that they get (Kerr, 1975). They need a sense of intrinsic reward from the work that they do, that is, that the work feels good to do and complete, that they are recognized and valued by others, that what they do makes a difference in ways that matter to them (Deci, 1975). They need to feel that the measurement systems by which they are evaluated provide clear, sensible, and justifiable feedback and lead to fair outcomes. When these dimensions are missing, it makes it difficult for people to see the meaning in what they do.

We allow ourselves to engage with others when we find that our interactions matter

People can get meaning from the relationships that they create with one another at work. Our colleagues can help us get work done. They can offer personal support. They can provide mentoring. They can help us make sense of ambiguous situations. And they can help provide us with a sense of meaning. Our work lives matter to us more when we feel connected to others at work, and less when we feel isolated and alone (Dutton & Heaphy, 2003). Work has more meaning when we are joined with others – doing things together, spurring one another on, having fun, and learning about ourselves in relation with others. It becomes meaningful as well when we are treated with a certain amount of dignity, respect and appreciation by others with whom we work – particularly by supervisors and other figures of authority (Kahn, 1992). Good working relations enable us to play off one another, such that working together is better – more creative, interesting, productive – than working alone. When we are lucky enough to have such relations, it makes it more likely that we will engage ourselves within them (Kahn, 1998).

We engage in the context of systems that we find trustworthy, predictable, and sensible

People are more likely to engage when they have a clear sense of the direct relation between efforts and outcomes. We need to see that reward systems make sense – that people are rewarded for the extra parts of their selves that they invest in their roles, or held accountable for going about their work on automatic pilot (Kerr, 1975). We need to see that people who engage themselves get the resources to enable their efforts to matter, rather than a less obvious and more capricious system of resource allocation. Nothing creates cynicism more than our sense of injustice or outrage triggered by nonsensical rewards and outcomes (Senge, 1990). Leaders can be reluctant to truly reward excellence, and to hold others accountable for poor performance. Doing so weakens the possibility of engagement.

This first set of lessons suggests that people need to feel as if they matter, that their contributions have meaning. Each of us is more or less constantly performing some fleeting, pre-conscious calculus whose results lead us toward or away from truly engaging in the situations in which we find ourselves. This first set of lessons focused on one dimension of the calculus: how much we and others might gain through our engagements. The second set of lessons focuses on another dimension: how much we risk in doing so.

Is it possible?
People engage not only when it matters but when they feel that they can. This is partly about the sense that their voice will be absorbed, digested, and worked with in ways that are respectful and dignified. To engage is to present others with the gift of our real selves, to stand vulnerable amidst them. If others are careful with such gifts, we offer them more, and more freely. If they drop them, ignore them, or do not know how to open and use them, we take them back. The possibility of our engagement is also a matter of our organizations. There are particular lessons here as well.

We bring ourselves into forums in which we can safely join with others to identify and solve problems
Organizational learning requires places in which people are brought together and asked to engage with one another, in order to identify and solve problems (Senge, 1990). Such forums must be safe (Kahn, 2001): organization members must *know* that they can say what they think and feel, show what they know and do not know, be creative and think "out of the box", remain silent or jump around in excitement, or be whoever they are without penalty. Penalties come in different shapes and packages. They can be formal, in job performance reviews and the like, or informal, with sideway glances from co-workers, silence, or laughter (Harvey, 1988). We know when forums are safe or not. We know when it feels okay to be ignorant or dramatic and when it does not. It is that sense – that in some settings we shall be okay no matter what, and in other settings we are too vulnerable – that defines what is and is not safe, and ultimately, whether we shall engage.

We engage ourselves in difficult situations when we can address them openly and together
Organizational life is filled with difficult situations. A key project loses funding. A leader suddenly leaves the organization. A product that has been under development fails key tests. These are difficult moments, not just for the individuals involved but for all of those who identify with the project or group. It shakes them up, distracts them. People can then engage only when they have the chance to clear themselves, emotionally, from the debris of their daily work or difficult episodes in their units (Kahn, 2005). This means that they have to address them openly, with others. Groups need to get together to talk about their work and figure out what to do. They need forums in which to address difficult issues with one another, but more, to create connectedness among them that allows them to face further difficulties. That connectedness furthers engagement (Dutton & Heaphy, 2003).

We require healthy rules of engagement by which to manage our differences with others

When people engage at work, they are likely to come upon their differences with one another. Indeed, I would suggest that one hallmark of disengagement is the lack of expressed or observable differences (Harvey, 1988). When we go on automatic pilot, we do what we are told to do. We follow the routines in prescribed ways, just like the person to our left and to our right. We conform, without differing. When we engage, on the other hand, we do what we believe to be right. We say what we think and feel. We throw ourselves into and at our work, and perhaps into and at one another. We bump up against others. This can get messy. We can get into conflict. How our differences with others get handled has a lot to do with the extent to which we continue to engage (Smith & Berg, 1987). Different settings – units, divisions, organizations – have what I call "rules of engagement" that shape and constrain how differences and conflict are dealt with. There are productive and unproductive rules. *Productive rules*, for example, include the following: differences are embraced as opportunities for learning and creativity, allowed to surface and if necessary, to develop into conflicts; conflicts are framed around tasks, not individuals; people hang on to shared goals and interests rather than positions; and people examine their differences with respect, concern about process, and a sense of perspective. *Unproductive rules* include these: differences and possible conflicts are avoided, ignored, smoothed over, suppressed, laughed away, or in other ways disappeared; it becomes more important to "get along" than to productively engage differences and potential conflicts; and differences are framed in terms of right/wrong thinking that shuts down creativity. Productive rules create the possibility for us to safely engage; the others do not.

We engage in the context of systems that do not lock us into certain categories, identities, or roles

Engagement is, in part, the ability to bring all of who we are into our roles (Smith & Berg, 1987). We can be serious, funny, creative, emotional. We can draw upon our experiences as men or women, as Christians and Jews, as Asians and blacks and whites. The different aspects of ourselves are available to us, in appropriate ways, as we go about our work. We do not need to hide crucial parts of our identities, taking them off like hats and hanging them on hooks at work. This is disengagement, a pretending to be less than or different from who we are. We are more likely to engage, then, in settings in which the different parts of ourselves are welcome, insofar as they enable us to engage more deeply in our work. We usually have a pretty good sense of these settings. We say or do something that indicates some part of our identity – a reference to what we know as a woman or a Muslim – and gauge the reactions from others, looking to see if it is okay to bring those parts of ourselves in. If we sense that we are being categorized or dismissed, we are less likely to engage. We become parts of ourselves – and only parts of our energies are available to the organization.

Are we led?

Leaders at all levels of organizations can exert great influence on the extent to which members can become fully engaged at work. Individuals will make their own choices, of course, bringing themselves into or holding themselves back from their work. They are more or less personally available, due to circumstances and temperament. But they are also more likely to engage when it matters that they engage, and conditions make it possible for them to do so. It is to their leaders that they look to help make it matter, and to help make it possible for them to so do well and safely. This requires leaders to act in certain ways. There are lessons here as well.

We engage in relations with leaders who enable us to remain both separate and connected

There is an interesting facet associated with engagement: we are best able to venture forth and express ourselves completely when we know that we have a place to which to return should we run into trouble (Kahn, 2001). We thus need leaders and supervisors who can let us rest a bit, and offer coaching and insight when we need it. And these leaders need to also be able to leave us alone at times, let us make our decisions and learn our lessons. This is, in many ways, the difficult part of leadership: remaining close enough to others to give support as needed, and distant enough to let people take up their own adult responsibility for their work. If leaders fall off this balance, they risk abandoning or intruding upon others – making it less likely that they will wish to fully engage.

We engage in settings in which leaders hold fast to collaborative relations among groups, areas, and divisions

Organizations contain departments, areas, units, functions, disciplines, and professions. The relations among those groups can help create either engagement or disengagement. If those relations are rocky – competitive, hierarchical, disintegrated, blaming – workers are less likely to feel able to fully engage, for they fear getting caught in the crossfire. The system is marked by faultlines and booby-traps, and members must be extremely careful about what they say and do. Leaders must thus attend carefully to the nature of intergroup relations (Alderfer & Smith, 1982). If they are able to spread, reward, and sustain the message that the setting is marked by a sense of "we" (rather than "us" or "them") then their members can more safely engage and collaborate with one another (Smith & Berg, 1987). If leaders pit groups against one another, favor some groups over others, or fight their own battles through their groups, then members view one another as group representatives (Kahn, 2005). They implicitly simplify, stereotype and diminish one another. This is a recipe for disengagement. Leaders who hold fast to collaboration across groups and divisions make it both meaningful and possible for members to engage undisturbed.

Leaders who insist on learning about their organizations, employees and themselves help create cultures of engagement

We look to leaders, whether we want to or not. We look to see what they reward and what they sanction, and what they themselves do. We look for signals about what is accepted and what is not. For signals about how welcome our engagements are, we look to see how much our leaders truly wish to learn the truth of what happens, truths that might well include them. We are more likely to engage when our leaders are, at their core, curious. They very much wish to explore and examine what they see, to follow trails regardless of where they might lead, because they want to learn. These leaders are the ones who invite others to go along with them on the journeys of trying to figure things out. They make it matter, and make it possible, for others to engage. The opposite of curiosity is pathological certainty (Shapiro & Carr, 1993). People are pathologically certain when they are locked into specific ways of seeing the world. They dismiss all other possibilities. Others must join in their beliefs, or be dismissed in turn. We cannot help but disengage then, for what we really think and feel is likely to have no place. Leaders who insist on learning – who are curious – create ways for the hierarchy to support rather than shut down our engagements.

We engage in relations with leaders who validate and respect us

Engagement feeds upon itself. We first engage tentatively, testing the ice to see if it will hold some of our weight, and if it does, we commit more of ourselves, venturing further out, to the point that we are fully committed, trusting the ice to hold us. If our leaders welcome our engagements, and those engagements seem to matter and feel right, we are encouraged to do more. Here, too, leaders play a significant role (Kahn, 1992). Do they validate us when we fully engage? Do they take in and work with our ideas, taking them – and therefore us – seriously? Do they listen to us? Do they encourage us to create solutions and own them? Do they explain their reasoning to us, and ask us what we really think? Do they provide opportunities for us to influence our work? Do they, in effect, trust us? The answers to these questions are crucial. In every interaction – meetings, hallway conversations, written memos – employees are looking for their leaders' signals, for their answers to these unspoken questions. They determine the extent to which employees engage or not.

The nature of engagement

These lessons are relatively simple to write, even though they took me a number of years to do so simply and clearly. What I have learned, primarily, is that employee engagement is both very delicate and fragile, and quite resilient. The fragility of engagement is a function of how vulnerable we feel, and are, when we risk being fully present in a situation. The more of us that is truly in a moment, the more of ourselves that is on the line – the more that we care about how others respond and how effective we are. We are thus looking intently for signs that we ought to get out of there, draw ourselves back, like a soldier who senses he or she has walked into a trap and is about to get caught in a firefight. Employees have pretty sophisticated radars. They are looking around constantly for signals about whether their engagements matter, how safe they are, whether their leaders truly welcome and know what to do with them. If the signs are good, they will move themselves into the place. If the signs are not so good, they will step back. If the signs look bad, they will disengage. They will do this instantly, without notice. This is the fragility of engagement. Like a spell or an uneasy truce, it can be broken with a word, said just the wrong way at the wrong time.

I have also been struck by the resilience of employee engagement. I have worked with organizations that seemed, frankly, hopeless. Employees were cynical, at war with the administration and with one another. Disengagement was the norm. Workers were routinely calling in sick. Turnover was high. Factions were rampant. But engagement was not dead. There was a spark, and over time, it grew and grew, to the point that employees began again to more routinely identify with the organization, and care about its health and performance. This took some work, of course. Leaders needed to learn to dismantle the obstacles to engagement – structures, processes, and, for some, themselves – and create new patterns of interaction with and among employees. They had to create learning forums that were safe enough for employees to tell them the truth of their experiences. They had to create forums for themselves, in which they worked through – with some outside help – the implications of what they heard, and they had to figure out what to do about it. In the settings in which this occurred, employee engagement proved remarkably resilient. It blossomed, like a malnourished child suddenly fed and loved. People have a desire to engage. They have an instinctive drive to express who they are, and who they wish to be, and given half a chance at work, they will do so. This does not fully go away, although it might go underground for some time.

References

Alderfer, C.P. & Smith, K.K. (1982), "Studying intergroup relations embedded in organizations", *Administrative Science Quarterly*, **27**(1), 35–65.

Deci, W.L. (1975), *Intrinsic Motivation*, New York: Plenum.

Dutton, J.E. & Heaphy, E. (2003), "The power of high quality connections", in K.S. Cameron, J.E. Dutton and R.E. Quinn (eds), *Positive Organizational Scholarship*, San Francisco, CA: Berrett-Koehler, pp. 263–78.

Hackman, J.R. & Oldham, G.R. (1980), *Work Redesign*, Reading, MA: Addison-Wesley.

Harvey, J. (1988), *The Abilene Paradox and Other Meditations on Management*, San Francisco, CA: Jossey-Bass.

Kahn, W.A. (1990), "Psychological conditions of personal engagement and disengagement at work", *Academy of Management Journal*, **33**(4), 692–724.

Kahn, W.A. (1992), "To be fully there: psychological presence at work", *Human Relations*, **45**(4), 321–49.

Kahn, W.A. (1998), "Relational systems at work", *Research in Organizational Behavior*, **20**, 39–76.

Kahn, W.A. (2001), "Holding environments at work", *Journal of Applied Behavioral Science*, **37**(3), 260–79.

Kahn, W.A. (2005), *Holding Fast: The Struggle to Create Resilient Caregiving Organizations*, London: Brunner–Routledge.

Kerr, S. (1975), "On the folly of rewarding A while hoping for B", *Academy of Management Journal*, **18**(4), 769–83.

Morrison, E.W. & Milliken, F.J. (2000), "Organizational silence: a barrier to change and development in a pluralistic world", *Academy of Management Review*, **25**, 706–25.

Schaufeli, W.B. & Bakker, A.B. (2004), "Job demands, job resources, and their relationship with burnout and engagement: a multi-sample study", *Journal of Organizational Behavior*, **25**(3), 293–315.

Senge, P. (1990), *The Fifth Discipline*, New York: Doubleday.

Shapiro, E.R. & Carr, A.W. (1993), *Lost in Familiar Places*, New Haven, CT: Yale University Press.

Smith, K.K. & Berg, D.N. (1987), *Paradoxes of Group Life*, San Francisco, CA: Jossey-Bass.

Tyler, T.R. (1999), "Why people cooperate with organizations: an identity-based perspective", *Research in Organizational Behavior*, **21**, 201–46.

3 A comprehensive framework for understanding and predicting engagement

Steven Fleck and Ilke Inceoglu

Introduction

Employee engagement has rapidly entered the mainstream of the language and practice of human resources (HR) practitioners, organizational psychologists, and HR-oriented management consultants. In most cases, the term is taken to mean some or all of "involvement, commitment, passion, enthusiasm, focused effort, and energy" (Macey & Schneider, 2008, p. 4). Numerous studies that report strong relationships between engagement and important metrics of organizational performance such as profitability, revenue growth, earnings per share, and employee turnover (for example, Harter et al., 2002; ISR, 2006) have conferred legitimacy to the concept, and helped to fuel its growth in popularity.

Unfortunately, development of precise and agreed-upon definitions of the construct of engagement has lagged behind the rapid uptake of the construct in practice. Current definitions of engagement (both those offered by practitioners and those in academic publications) vary widely: they include defining it as a trait, a state, a set of behaviors, characteristics of the work environment, or a combination of these (Macey & Schneider, 2008).

There are substantial negative implications of such conceptual diversity both for research and for practice. From a research perspective, diverse conceptualizations make it difficult to accumulate a coherent body of research knowledge. From a practice perspective, it becomes problematic to make recommendations for actions when definitions of the construct in question are ambiguous.

This chapter reports on a model of engagement that was developed as an attempt to address some of these issues. One of the key aims of developing this model was to not only develop and offer a definition of engagement itself, but to also locate engagement in relation to its predictors and consequences.

Two principles form the core starting point for the logic of this model. First, engagement is defined as a state that people can be in when they perform their work. This means that the intensity of this state is likely to vary over time. Employees who are "highly engaged" today can feel less engaged tomorrow for a range of personal or situational reasons. Second, it is necessary to separate three areas that are often conflated when engagement is discussed. These are predictors of the state of engagement, the state of engagement itself, and the consequences of being in this state of engagement.

Deploying these principles may help resolve many of the problems that are associated with other definitional approaches to engagement. For example, behaviors such as working hard, performing extra-role contributions and professing an intention to stay with the organization are often included as parts of the construct of engagement. However, employees can display such behaviors because they feel compelled to do so by situational factors, such as fearing for the safety of their jobs. This in turn can lead measures of engagement to provide misleading information.

After administering an engagement survey (which includes such behaviors as indicators of engagement), an organization might be assured that levels of engagement are high. However, the organization cannot be sure of what motivational basis lies behind the employees' enthusiastic responses – if it is an external basis such as fear of employment insecurity, or an internal basis such as a positive, internalized, motivated state. Presumably, an organization would intuitively expect "engaged" employees to mean the latter, and assume that their engaged employees are keen to remain with and contribute to the organization for the long term. But if it is the former, then it may be surprised to find that as soon as the job market improves, a large proportion of their employees leave for better opportunities elsewhere. By treating engagement as a state, and separating the state of engagement from behaviors expected as a consequence of being in a state of engagement, such problems of ambiguity are avoided.

The model of engagement is presented in the diagram in Figure 3.1. The logic and key elements of the model are outlined briefly, and then the remainder of the chapter describes each element in more detail.

On the left-hand side of the figure are the "drivers of engagement". These are the characteristics, or features, of the work environment. A better fit on these features in terms of what employees want and what is available to them is predicted to be associated with higher levels of engagement, which is presented to the right of the "drivers". When employees are more engaged, they are in turn expected to perform more frequently a range of behaviors that are beneficial for the organization (such as exerting effort on their core job role, as well as going beyond this to contribute to the organization in other ways as well).

When employees perform such contributory behaviors, both they and their organization are more likely to experience secondary benefits. An

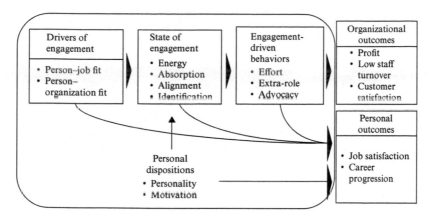

Figure 3.1 Model of engagement

organization where a larger proportion of employees more frequently engage in contributory/positive behaviors is more likely to see a positive impact on metrics such as revenue, profitability, turnover, and customer satisfaction. Employees themselves are more likely to experience higher levels of job satisfaction and affective well-being, and to find that they make more rapid career progression.

Finally, personal dispositions (such as personality and motivation constructs) of employees are expected to influence many elements of the model. For example, such dispositions are likely to affect a person's pattern of preferences for work environment features, they are likely to play a role in determining how frequently people become engaged, and existing research has established that they play a key role in understanding behavioral and affective outcomes such as effort, contextual performance, job satisfaction, and well-being.

Drivers of engagement: characteristics of the work environment
The characteristics, or features, of the work environment consist of the features of an employee's job role, and the features of the wider organization in which the job role is embedded. This means that the work environment shapes the experience employees have of their work, and can drive the employee towards becoming engaged, or they can push the employee towards disengagement. The work environment is therefore expected to play a critical role in determining employees' state of engagement. As Kahn (1990) highlights, it is "organizational (Hochschild, 1983) contexts that enhance or undermine people's motivation and sense of meaning at work" (p. 695).

A wealth of literature has shown that people's work environment – or more precisely, their perception of it – is related to their affective reactions to their work, such as job satisfaction and well-being (Hackman & Oldham, 1980; Warr, 2007). Kahn (1990) also stresses that the psychological experience of work is influenced by interpersonal, group, intergroup, and organizational factors (Adelfer, 1985), and that it is this experience that drives people's attitudes and behaviors (Hackman & Oldham, 1980). These are psychological conditions that give the employee a sense of fit with what Kahn terms the "preferred self" in a job role: "People who are personally engaged keep their selves within a role, without sacrificing one for the other" (p. 700).

The environmental features are therefore essential to understanding what makes employees engaged, and perhaps most importantly, they are the keys to taking action to increase engagement and performance. If we know which work environment features are affecting engagement in a particular context, then we know which levers to pull in order to change engagement.

The classification of the work environment used in this model of engagement was based on an extension of Warr's "Vitamin" model (1987, 2007). The vitamin model is rooted in the well-being literature and captures key aspects of the work environment (for example, opportunity for control and task variety) that are positively related to employee well-being and work satisfaction. After extending the constructs in the original vitamin model, 38 job features and 10 organizational job features were specified to predict engagement in the workplace (see Table 3.1). Furthermore, a person–environment fit approach (for example, Dawis, 2002; Cable & Edwards, 2004) was integrated into the logic and measurement approach of the model.

Table 3.1   High-level overview of characteristics of the work environment

Job-level features 38 features: 9 factors, 2–5 features per factor	Organization-level features 10 features
1. Challenge (6 features)	Wider influence
2. Ethics (4 features)	Vision
3. Competition (4 features)	Effective communication
4. Interaction (3 features)	Fairness
5. Career ambition (5 features)	Ethics
6. Personal impact (4 features)	Effective decision making
7. Supportive environment (6 features)	Customer orientation
8. Work setting (4 features)	Bureaucracy
9. Development (2 features)	Employee relations
	Cross-functional cooperation

When measuring the features of the work environment, for each feature, respondents are asked how much of it they would like in their ideal job/organization and to what extent they perceive this feature to be present. This approach is used to determine the fit between what employees want from their job and organization and what they actually have. This approach is similar to what other work has referred to as "complementary fit" (Cable & Edwards, 2004). Such work has demonstrated a relationship between the fit of employees' desires to the provision of supplies in the work environment to meet these desires, and their work-related attitudes (for example, Verquer, 2003; Kristof-Brown et al., 2005). We similarly expect that employees who experience better fit to the work environment will be more likely to enter a state of engagement.

State of engagement

Engagement is a psychological state that employees can be in when they are performing their work roles. To describe engagement, we use Kahn's conceptualization of engagement as a starting point, that "in engagement, people employ and express themselves physically, cognitively, and emotionally during role performances" (Kahn, 1990, p. 694).

When people are in an engaged state, they invest more of themselves in their work role – they are more likely to conduct their work with energy and enthusiasm. Schaufeli et al. define work engagement as a "positive, fulfilling work-related state of mind that is characterized by vigor, dedication, and absorption" (2006, p. 702).

When engaged, people are attached to their work role, and are absorbed by enacting it. They invest a lot of their personal energy into performing the role, as it is an important part of their identity. They have internalized the goals and aspirations of the organization as their own.

In contrast, when people are disengaged, they are only physically present at work. They do not deploy their emotions, energies, and passion in conducting their work. They are like empty shells, just going through the motions. People who are disengaged have little or no emotional attachment to their work role, do not care about the organization's goals, and rarely find themselves engrossed in their work. They are more likely to feel burned out (Maslach, 1982), apathetic or detached (Goffman, 1961) and perform tasks in a robotic manner without putting in effort (Hackman & Oldham, 1980).

Engagement can change over time, particularly in response to situational changes at work such as starting a new job, having more responsibility or being affected by structural changes in the organization. Engagement can also be influenced by factors outside the job such as having to deal with personal issues which can distract and deplete energy, or in the case of positive events, result in approaching work with more enthusiasm. Finally, an individual's level of engagement may also be affected by stable characteristics of the person (for example, generally being very energetic) as well as the physical, emotional and psychological resources available at a particular moment (Kahn, 1990). Engagement can therefore fluctuate to some extent but following Schaufeli et al.'s (2006) approach, engagement is not viewed as a momentary and very short-lived state, but as "a more persistent and pervasive affective-cognitive state that is not focused on any particular object, event, individual, or behavior" (p. 702).

In this model, engagement is seen as a higher-order construct, which is a compound of several more specific constructs that have a clear heritage in established streams of theory and research in the organizational behavior literature. Engagement is treated as a distinct construct in the sense that it is a novel recombination of established constructs, which describes an employee state that has criterion-relevant implications.

Four facets are used to describe the state of engagement in more detail, and these are located within a two-dimensional framework (see Table 3.2). The first dimension distinguishes between engagement with a job or task-related focus versus engagement with an organization focus. The job or task-related side of this dimension can be referred to as "job engagement". Facets in this area draw mainly on concepts and research from the field of job involvement (for example, Lawler & Hall, 1970; Kanungo, 1982). The organization-related side of the first dimension can be referred to as "organization engagement", and is rooted in the organizational

Table 3.2   Facets of state of engagement

	Cognitive	Affective
Job engagement	*Absorption* Employees lose themselves in their work, and experience a sense of engrossment when doing their work	*Energy* The energy employees draw from their work
Organizational engagement	*Alignment* Employees' views of the direction of the organization are aligned with the direction in which the organization is being taken	*Identification* The emotional bond between the employee and the organization

commitment literature (for example, O'Reilly & Chatman, 1986; Meyer et al., 1993). The second dimension delineates facets of engagement that have a stronger cognitive (thinking) versus affective (emotional, feeling) emphasis.

Job engagement: job-related facets of engagement
Job engagement is related to the construct of job involvement, which has been ascribed several different meanings in previous research (for a discussion, see Kanungo, 1982; Rich, 2006; Rich et al., 2010). Absorption and energy, the two job-related engagement facets in this model, are similar to definitions that regard job involvement as a state that is related to one's present job situation. In Kanungo's (1982) definition, for example, job involvement stems from a motivational framework and can be viewed on a continuum where alienation and involvement represent bipolar end points. Job involvement is therefore regarded as a state, describing an employees' psychological identification with his/her job. Similarly, Paullay et al. (1994) defined job involvement as "the degree to which one is cognitively preoccupied with, engaged in, and concerned with one's present job" (p. 225).

Job-related engagement features with a stronger affective emphasis
Energy refers to the sense of energy that employees draw from conducting their work, that is the degree to which they feel energized by their work. Employees who experience a strong sense of energy at work direct their motivational resources towards their work performance, rather than towards other activities (Baker et al., 2003; Cross et al., 2003; Quinn & Dutton, 2005).

Energy emphasizes the affective or emotional side of job-related engagement: emotions energize an individual physiologically and induce appropriate action (Wallbott & Scherer, 1989). As Rich (2006) points out, "the individuals' engagement in their role is not possible without an emotional connection" (p. 20).

Job-related engagement features with a stronger cognitive emphasis
Absorption refers to the extent to which employees lose themselves in their work and experience a sense of engrossment when conducting their work. When absorbed, people can feel as if time stands still. This construct is closely related to the concepts of "flow" (Csikszentmihalyi, 1975) and "timelessness" (Mainemelis, 2001). It has a stronger emphasis on thinking rather than feeling. Individuals who are absorbed in their work are so "cognitively involved" that they notice their surroundings only peripherally.

Organizational engagement: organization-related facets of engagement
Organizational engagement is closely related to the concept of organizational commitment. Organizational commitment has been defined as a
psychological state that characterizes the employee's relationship with the
organization, and has implications for his or her decision to continue or
discontinue membership in the organization (Allen & Meyer, 1990). Allen
and Meyer (1990; Meyer & Allen, 1991) conceptualized organizational
commitment in terms of three distinct components: affective commitment (emotional attachment to the organization), normative commitment
(perceived obligation to remain with the organization), and continuance
commitment (evaluation of costs and benefits associated with leaving
the organization). Of these three components, affective commitment has
shown higher correlations with job satisfaction, turnover and job performance (Meyer et al., 2002; Riketta, 2002) compared to the other two. In
our engagement model, there are two engagement facets that are closely
related to the organization: identification and alignment. Identification has
a stronger affective (emotional) emphasis, while alignment is more cognitive in nature.

*Organization-related engagement features with a stronger affective
emphasis*
Identification refers to the emotional bond an employee experiences with
the organization, and is also referred to as "affective commitment" (Allen
& Meyer, 1990). When employees experience a high degree of affective
commitment, the organization features prominently in their work-related
identity – characteristics of the organization are important for them in
defining who they are. Employees with a high level of affective commitment will have a strong sense of belonging to the organization, and place
great value on many of the intangible, symbolic, and relational aspects of
the organization.

Organization-related engagement features with a stronger cognitive emphasis
Alignment focuses on the congruence between employees' beliefs about
where the organization should be heading, what the goals and aspirations
of the organization should be, and the actual direction of the organization. The more strongly employees agree with the strategic decisions of
senior management, the more strongly their belief that the direction of the
organization will be aligned with the actual direction of the organization.
This process is more cognitive than affective as it involves an evaluation
in the first instance, which may then be followed by some affective state
(for example, feeling happy or not happy about the way the organization
is going).

The extent to which employees have a sense of alignment is likely to be related to how satisfied they feel about their job and especially the organization. It can also directly impact on their performance; as Kahn (1990) observed in his qualitative study, people's ambivalence about their fit with their organization and their purposes led to heightened insecurity and preoccupation, "leaving them little space, energy, or desire to employ or express themselves in moments of task performance" (p. 716).

Employee-level outcomes of engagement
When employees are engaged, a range of behaviors and cognitive and affective states are more likely to occur, such as investing more effort in one's work and experiencing higher levels of job satisfaction. In this model, we focus on three behaviors (effort, extra-role behavior, and advocacy), which are linked to types of outcomes that organizations tend to value most: general employee performance and portraying a positive image of the organization outside work. These three behaviors are predicted to be closely related to both the task- and the organization-related facets of engagement.

Effort
Employees who are engaged are likely to exert a lot of effort on their core tasks. Schaufeli et al.'s (2006) definition of their "vigor" facet of engagement alludes to this: "Vigor is characterized by high levels of energy and mental resilience while working, the willingness to invest effort in one's work" (p. 702). In contrast to Schaufeli et al.'s approach, we explicitly distinguish between the energy employees draw from their work and the energy (effort) they apply to their work.

Extra-role behavior
Engaged employees are also more likely to "go the extra mile" for the organization and show behaviors that go beyond the requirements of their job, such as taking the initiative to solve problems, or offering help to co-workers before being asked for it. This phenomenon has been extensively documented in previous research, sometimes under labels such as "organizational citizenship behavior" (Organ & Ryan, 1995) and "contextual work behaviors" (van Scotter & Motowidlo, 1996).

Advocacy
The behavioral contributions of engaged employees can also stretch beyond activities within the organization. Engaged employees are more likely to act as positive advocates for the organization when interacting with people external to the organization. Such advocacy behaviors can,

for example, focus on recommending the organization to potential customers as a trustworthy partner to do business with, or recommending the organization to potential job applicants as a great place to work.

Job satisfaction and longer tenure
Compared to disengaged employees, engaged employees are more likely to be satisfied with their job and with working for their organization, and are more likely to remain with the organization for a longer period of time. This extends beyond the identification (affective commitment) aspect of engagement itself. Engaged employees are also more likely to actively seek out ways to remain with the organization, even in situations where they face external or internal pressures that make leaving the organization an attractive option. Examples of such situations can include pressure from family to relocate, or restructuring of the organization that involves changes in the employee's job role.

Personal dispositions
Most elements of this model of engagement are likely to be, at some level, affected by constructs related to the personal disposition of employees. To properly understand and measure engagement, as well as its predictors and consequences, it is therefore necessary to take such personal disposition constructs into account.

The drivers of engagement indicate the work context, which – mediated by people's perceptions – create conditions in which employees personally engage and disengage (Kahn, 1990). Those perceptions may be influenced by more stable person-variables such as schemata, which are linked to personality and trait-motivation (Mischel & Shoda, 1998). Individuals with a high level of emotional stability are likely to experience higher levels of optimism and positive affect, compared to less emotionally stable individuals. Positive affect has been found to be related to job satisfaction (Judge & Ilies, 2002) and is likely to influence how employees perceive their work environment.

Personal dispositions also influence how people approach work and how likely they are to engage or disengage in all or some types of role performances, just as they shape people's abilities and willingness to be involved or committed at work (Kahn, 1990). Linked to this, personal dispositions will also have an impact on how people deal with situations where they experience misfit between what they would like in their job and what they perceive to be present. Simmering et al. (2003) found that conscientiousness was positively related to development (assessed through 360 ratings) but only when employees perceived misfit with respect to autonomy. Similarly, other motivation-related traits such as high achievement orientation (broad motives), self-efficacy (Bandura, 1977), persistence (Duckworth et al., 2007) or proactivity (Parker et al., 2006) may lead an individual to try to shape the experienced misfit into a positive outcome, which can result in job shaping and job enlargement.

Summary and conclusion

The model outlined in this chapter is an attempt to delineate the construct of engagement, and to locate engagement in relation to its antecedents and consequences. Using the logic of this model, we locate characteristics of the work environment as predictors of engagement, and various desirable employee behaviors and attitudes as consequences of engagement. We find that this approach enables us to resolve many of the ambiguities of interpretation that are often associated with organizational engagement surveys.

References

Adelfer, C.P. (1985), "An intergroup perspective on group dynamics", in J. Lorsch (ed.), *Handbook of Organizational Behavior*, Englewood Cliffs, NJ: Prentice-Hall, pp. 190–222.

Allen, N.J. & Meyer, J.P. (1990), "The measurement and antecedents of affective, continuance, and normative commitment to the organization", *Journal of Occupational and Organizational Psychology*, **63**, 1–8.

Baker, W., Cross, R. & Wooten, M. (2003), "Positive organizational network analysis and energizing relationships", in K.S. Cameron, J.E. Dutton & R.E. Quinn (eds), *Positive Organizational Scholarship: Foundations of a New Discipline*, San Francisco, CA: Berrett-Koehler, pp. 328–42.

Bandura, A. (1977), *Social Learning Theory*, New York: General Learning Press.

Cable, D.M. & Edwards, J.R. (2004), "Complementary and supplementary fit: a theoretical and empirical integration", *Journal of Applied Psychology*, **89**(5), 822–34.

Cross, R., Baker, W. & Parker, A. (2003), "What creates energy in organizations?", *MIT Sloan Management Review*, **44**(4), 51–7.

Csikszentmihalyi, M. (1975), *Beyond Boredom and Anxiety*, San Francisco, CA: Jossey-Bass.

Dawis, R.V. (2002), "The Minnesota theory of work adjustment", in S.D. Brown & R.W. Lent (eds), *Career Development and Counseling: Putting Theory and Research to Work*, Hoboken, NJ: Wiley, pp. 3–23.

Duckworth, A.L., Peterson, C., Matthews, M.D. & Kelly, D.R. (2007), "Grit: perseverance and passion for long-term goals", *Journal of Personality and Social Psychology*, **92**(6), 1087–101.

Goffman, E. (1961), *Encounters: Two Studies in the Sociology of Interaction*, Indianapolis, IN: Bobbs-Merrill.

Hackman, J.R. & Oldham, G.R. (1980), *Work Redesign*, Reading, MA: Addison-Wesley.

Harter, J.K., Schmidt, F.L. & Hayes, T.L. (2002), "Business-unit-level relationship between employee satisfaction, employee engagement, and business outcomes: a meta-analysis", *Journal of Applied Psychology*, **87**(2), 268–79.

ISR (2006), ISR Research Report, Chicago, IL, pp. 2–3.

Judge, T.A. and Ilies, R. (2002), "Relationship of personality to performance motivation: a meta-analytic review", *Journal of Applied Psychology*, **87**(4), 797–807.

Kahn, W. (1990), "Psychological conditions of personal engagement and disengagement at work", *Academy of Management Journal*, **33**(4), 692–724.

Kanungo, R.N. (1982), "Measurement of job and work involvement", *Journal of Applied Psychology*, **67**(3), 341–9.

Kristof-Brown, A.L., Zimmerman, R.D. & Johnson, E.C. (2005), "Consequences of individuals' fit at work: a meta-analysis of person–job, person–organization, person–group, and person–supervisor fit", *Personnel Psychology*, **58**(2), 281–342.

Lawler, E.E. & Hall, D.T. (1970), "Relationship of job characteristics to job involvement, satisfaction, and intrinsic motivation", *Journal of Applied Psychology*, **54**(4), 305–12.

Macey, W.H. & Schneider, B. (2008), "The meaning of employee engagement", *Industrial and Organizational Psychology*, **1**, 3–30.

Mainemelis, C. (2001), "When the muse takes it all: a model for the experience of timelessness in organizations", *Academy of Management Review*, **26**(4), 548–65.

Maslach, C. (1982), *Burnout: The Cost of Caring*, Englewood Cliffs, NJ: Prentice-Hall.

Meyer, J.P. & Allen, N.J. (1991), "A three-component conceptualization of organizational commitment", *Human Resource Management Review*, **1**, 61–89.

Meyer, J.P., Allen, N.J. & Smith, C.A. (1993), "Commitment to organizations and occupations: extension and test of a three-component conceptualization", *Journal of Applied Psychology*, **78**, 538–51.

Meyer, J.P., Stanley, D.J., Topolnytsky, L. & Laryssa, H. (2002), "Affective, continuance, and normative commitment to the organization: a meta-analysis of antecedents, correlates, and consequences", *Journal of Vocational Behavior*, **61**, 20–52.

Mischel, W. & Shoda, Y. (1998), "Reconciling processing dynamics and personality dispositions", *Annual Review of Psychology*, **49**(1), 229–58.

O'Reilly, C.A. & Chatman, J.A. (1986), "Organizational commitment and psychological attachment: the effects of compliance, identification, and internalization on prosocial behavior", *Journal of Applied Psychology*, **71**, 492–9.

Organ, D.W. & Ryan, K. (1995), "A meta-analytic review of attitudinal and dispositional predictors of organizational citizenship behavior", *Personnel Psychology*, **48**, 775–802.

Parker, S.K., Williams, H.M. & Turner, N. (2006), "Modeling the antecedents of proactive behavior at work", *Journal of Applied Psychology*, **91**(3), 636–52.

Paullay, I.M., Alliger, G.M. & Stone-Romer, E.F. (1994), "Construct validation of two instruments designed to measure job involvement and work centrality", *Journal of Applied Psychology*, **79**, 224–8.

Quinn, R. & Dutton, J. (2005), "Coordination as energy-in-conversation", *Academy of Management Review*, **30**(1), 36–57.

Rich, B.L. (2006), "Job engagement: construct validation and relationships with job satisfaction, job involvement, and intrinsic satisfaction", thesis, University of Florida.

Rich, B.L., Lepine, J.A. & Crawford, E.R. (2010), "Job engagement: antecedents and effects on job performance", *Academy of Management Journal*, **53**.

Riketta, M. (2002), "Attitudinal organizational commitment and job performance: a meta-analysis", *Journal of Organizational Behavior*, **23**(3), 257–66.

Schaufeli, W.B., Bakker, A. & Salanova, M. (2006), "The measurement of work engagement with a short questionnaire: a cross-national study", *Educational and Psychological Measurement*, **66**(4), 701–16.

Simmering, M., Colquitt, J., Noe, R. & Porter, C. (2003), "Conscientiousness, autonomy fit, and development: a longitudinal study", *Journal of Applied Psychology*, **88**(5), 954–63.

van Scotter, J.R. & Motowidlo, S.J. (1996), "Interpersonal facilitation and job dedication as separate facets of contextual performance", *Journal of Applied Psychology*, **81**(5), 525–31.

Verquer, M. (2003), "A meta-analysis of relations between person–organization fit and work attitudes", *Journal of Vocational Behavior*, **63**(3), 473–89.

Wallbott, H.G. & Scherer, K.R. (1989), "Assessing emotion by questionnaire", in R. Plutchik & H. Kellerman (eds), *Emotion: Theory, Research, and Experience – the Measurement of Emotions*, San Diego, CA: Academic Press, pp. 55–82.

Warr, P. (1987), *Work, Unemployment, and Mental Health*, Oxford: Oxford University Press.

Warr, P. (2007), *Work, Happiness, and Unhappiness*, London: Lawrence Erlbaum.

4 Job attitudes and employee engagement: considering the attitude "A-factor"

Daniel A. Newman, Dana L. Joseph and Charles L. Hulin*

Introduction

The employee engagement concept has faced scrutiny due to its near-redundancy with three classic job attitudes – job satisfaction, organizational commitment, and job involvement (Harter & Schmidt, 2008; Macey & Schneider, 2008; Newman & Harrison, 2008). We address this scrutiny in four steps. First, we distinguish the commonly-used *attitudinal engagement* construct (for example, Schaufeli & Bakker, 2003) from the less-well-known *behavioral engagement* construct (Harrison et al., 2006). Second, we present a higher-order attitude factor, or "*A*-factor", that underlies job satisfaction, affective commitment, and job involvement. Third, we conceptually and meta-analytically review the strong overlaps between this higher-order attitude factor and attitudinal employee engagement to show that engagement correlates $r = 0.77$ with the *A*-factor (that is, typical engagement measures are essentially redundant with the higher-order *A*-factor of job satisfaction, affective commitment, and job involvement). Finally, we use meta-analysis to extend Harrison et al.'s (2006) attitude–engagement model, showing that the *A*-factor robustly predicts a broad criterion of behavioral engagement ($r = 0.51$). We argue that the similarity between attitudinal employee engagement and the job attitude *A*-factor is a strength of engagement research and not a limitation; the overlap suggests the utility of attitudinal employee engagement (also called "state engagement" by Macey & Schneider, 2008) as a powerful predictor of a general work-behavior construct. At the same time, the substantial overlap suggests that little new is being brought to the table by engagement researchers; the "engagement" labeling of the general attitude factor is unlikely to lead to new conceptualizations or understanding of employees' reactions to the many characteristics of their work organizations.

Employee engagement: the construct and the measurement of the construct

The study of any construct requires that it be defined with sufficient precision to exclude irrelevant manifest variables and to include only those variables that reflect the construct. The definitional process is indeed a process and often involves fuzzy logic, wherein the probabilities of variables' belongingness to, or exclusion from, the construct can deviate from the extremes of 1.00 and 0.00. Such fuzzy logic neither invalidates the definitional process nor erects insurmountable roadblocks to progress. Rather, it reinforces the probabilistic nature of our constructs and their empirically established relations. In the case of employee engagement, the debate is still underway at the basic level of whether it should be regarded as a trait, a state, or a behavior (Dalal et al., 2008; Macey & Schneider, 2008).

This process of refining our definitions is necessary to allow researchers to proceed to the second step in the research process: measuring the construct with sufficient convergent and discriminant validity to support empirical studies with reasonable confidence. The outcome of the process will also determine whether we conclude that employee engagement is stable within individuals (that is, a trait), highly variable within individuals (that is, a state), or if we capitalize on both definitions by treating traits as density distributions of states (Fleeson, 2001). The within-person dynamics of conceptualizing employee engagement as a behavioral construct have not been explicated, although research suggests that behaviors in organizations are functions of within-person variation in affect levels (Miner et al., 2005; Dalal et al., 2009).

Despite progress toward definitional clarity, the measurement of new constructs often resembles the new clothing of the emperor. New constructs are often widely accepted until a brave soul points out that no one had bothered to weave the definitional "fabric" required of all constructs. As a result, new constructs often fail the requirements of discriminant validity (Campbell & Fiske, 1959) and are shown to be nearly redundant with existing measures of other, established constructs. Still, other measures that demonstrate adequate discriminant validity and internal consistency fail to show the expected relations with external measures or behaviors the construct was hypothesized to account for. Emotional intelligence, goal orientation, need hierarchies, growth need strength, job involvement, measures of satisfaction based on needs, and Protestant work ethic are but a few examples of constructs that garnered flurries of attention and adoption, even after empirical data revealed their conceptual or measurement deficiencies.

In this regard, the conceptual and measurement issues of employee engagement are little different from other constructs in the behavioral sciences. In fact, employee engagement typifies the development of many new constructs in organizational research: it enjoys great popularity among practitioners and yet is viewed with skepticism among researchers.

As a testament to this, employee engagement consulting practices have been implemented at or by the Gallup Organization, Towers Perrin, Hewitt Associates, Dell, Molson Coors Brewing Company, Caterpillar, Development Dimensions International, and Kenexa (see Vance, 2006). Meanwhile, a recent issue of *Industrial and Organizational Psychology* concerning employee engagement described the construct as "an umbrella term for whatever one wants it to be" (Saks, 2008, p. 40), a potential "repackaging of other constructs" (Macey & Schneider, 2008, p. 4), and "in a state of disarray" (Dalal et al., 2008, p. 52). In summary, whereas some believe that putting old wine in a new bottle may improve the taste, others argue it is still the same fermented grape juice.

The current chapter contributes to research and theory on employee engagement in three ways. First, we describe and provide large-scale empirical estimates supporting the existence of a broad attitude factor, or *A*-factor. Second, we conduct meta-analyses to estimate the utility of this *A*-factor for predicting a broad behavioral construct defined by the covariances among focal job performance, citizenship behavior, lateness, absence, and turnover. This extends the work of Harrison et al. (2006) by incorporating job involvement into the higher-order attitude factor. Third, we meta-analytically show employee engagement to be largely redundant with the *A*-factor. Results show that attitudinal engagement (as measured by traditional engagement surveys – that is, Schaufeli & Bakker's 2003 Utrecht Work Engagement Scale (UWES)) is indeed a "new blend of old wines" (Macey & Schneider, 2008, p. 10). This new blend is useful to practitioners because it strongly predicts a broad behavioral criterion. A crucial question we shall have to resolve is the extent to which we learn anything using employee engagement that we did not already know from our knowledge of the general job attitude.

The structure of job attitudes: an '*A*-factor' model
First, we note that the three most commonly studied job attitudes (job satisfaction, organizational commitment, and job involvement) substantially overlap among themselves. These overlaps are both conceptual and empirical. For instance, job satisfaction (that is, the favorable evaluation of one's work role; Smith et al., 1969) and affective organizational commitment (that is, feelings of attachment to one's company; Meyer & Allen, 1997) may be thought of as two reflections of a single concept that differ only in their conceptual targets – the work role versus the entire organization (Hulin, 1991). Job involvement, or one's psychological identification with work (Lodahl & Kejner, 1965), has a similar connotation of liking/being focused on one's work role. Not surprisingly, meta-analytic evidence has confirmed these conceptual overlaps: $\hat{\rho}_{satisfaction,\ commitment} = 0.60$

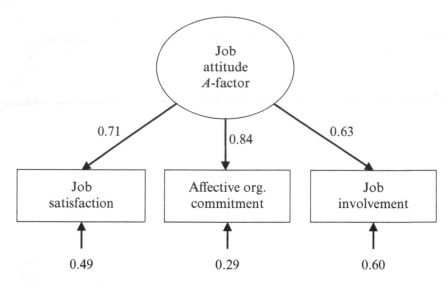

Note: Parameter estimates based on meta-analysis, harmonic mean N = 8,897.

Sources: Brown (1996); Meyer et al. (2002); Harrison et al. (2006).

Figure 4.1   The higher-order job attitude factor or A-factor

(k = 112 studies, N = 39,187; Harrison et al., 2006), $\hat{\rho}_{satisfaction, involvement}$ = 0.45 (k = 81 studies, N = 26,883; Brown, 1996), and $\hat{\rho}_{commitment, involvement}$ = 0.53 (k = 16 studies, N = 3,625; Meyer et al., 2002). In short, job satisfaction, affective organizational commitment, and job involvement exhibit important theoretical and empirical redundancy.

Figure 4.1 displays a conceptual model that interprets the relations among these attitudes to suggest a higher-order job attitude factor. Although these overlaps have been noted for some time (Brooke et al., 1988; Mathieu & Farr, 1991), they have not traditionally been interpreted as evidence for a higher-order attitude factor. The overall attitude model in Figure 4.1 was introduced by Harrison et al. (2006, p. 320), and labeled the "A-factor" model by Newman and Harrison (2008). In essence, the model notes that common job attitudes are intercorrelated, and this pattern of correlations reflects a higher-order job attitude concept (or "A") of which job satisfaction, organizational commitment, and job involvement are congeneric instantiations. Empirical estimates support the model, via large factor loadings (Figure 4.1).

Broad behavioral outcomes: the attitude–engagement model
In 1974, Fishbein and Ajzen reported that broad attitudes (for example, similar to an overall attitude toward one's work role) were very strong predictors of broad behavioral outcomes (that is, syndromes of behaviors that were similar in their positive or negative orientations toward the attitude object). This classic social psychological notion (broad attitudes predict broad behavioral criteria) has direct relevance for the contemporary study of employee engagement.

In particular, if one specifies a broad behavioral criterion that describes the overlap among job performance, organizational citizenship behavior, and withdrawal (that is, lateness, absence, and turnover), then, according to attitude theory, a broad job attitude should predict this criterion very strongly. Harrison et al. (2006) proposed such a behavioral criterion, which they defined as an employee's tendency to contribute rather than withhold desirable inputs from one's work role (they labeled this criterion *behavioral engagement*). Using meta-analysis, they showed that the attitude *A*-factor correlated $r = 0.59$ with the broad behavioral engagement criterion (ibid., p. 311; see Figure 4.2). We note that in Figure 4.2, (the attitude–engagement model), the term "engagement" describes a behavioral construct, not an attitude (Newman & Harrison, 2008).

To elaborate on the model in Figure 4.2, we briefly discuss the conceptual underpinnings of the broad behavioral criterion. The notion of "behavioral engagement" has roots in the work of March and Simon (1958), Fisher (1980), Hulin (1982), Organ (1988), Kahn (1990), and Viswesvaran (1993). Harrison et al. (2006) noted that commonly studied work behaviors exhibited a positive manifold, and they interpreted this overlap as indicating a single, underlying behavioral construct that mutually drives employee job performance, citizenship, and withdrawal behavior (see also Hanisch & Hulin, 1991; Hanisch et al., 1998; and Viswesvaran et al., 2005). This behavioral construct was labeled "behavioral engagement", because it captures the denotative "condition of being in gear" at work (*American Heritage Dictionary*, 2007; Newman & Harrison, 2008; cf. Macey & Schneider, 2008), and is the physical (as opposed to cognitive or emotional) referent of Kahn's (1990) notion of role engagement. It is believed that the broad behavioral engagement construct captures the common variance among those work behaviors deemed effective by most employers.

Method for estimating Figure 4.2
In order to empirically estimate Figure 4.2, a matrix of 28 meta-analytic correlations among job satisfaction, job involvement, organizational commitment, job performance, citizenship behavior, turnover, lateness,

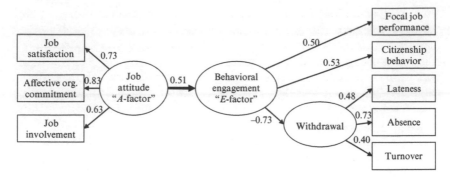

Note: RMSEA (root mean square error of approximation) = 0.067; NNFI (non-normed fit index) = 0.94; CFI (comparative fit index) = 0.96; SRMR (standardized root mean square residual) = 0.044; Harmonic mean N = 2,231. We also estimated this attitude–engagement model using Harrison et al.'s (2006, p. 311) original criterion specification, in which all five behaviors loaded directly onto the criterion factor (that is, no withdrawal construct), and there was a progression of withdrawal structure allowing correlated uniquenesses both from lateness to absence and from absence to turnover. Under this alternative specification, the goodness of fit was also adequate (RMSEA = 0.058; NNFI = 0.95; CFI = 0.97; SRMR = 0.035) and the latent attitude–engagement correlation was γ = 0.54. (None of the correlations involving any behavioral criteria include common source/common method estimates. Focal job performance correlations are corrected for Cronbach's alpha = 0.86, not interrater reliability = 0.52 (Viswesvaran et al., 1996, pp. 562–3).)

Figure 4.2   *The "attitude–engagement model" from Harrison et al. (2006), updated to include job involvement and the lower-order withdrawal construct*

and absenteeism was constructed. All meta-analytic estimates were corrected for attenuation in the predictor and the criterion. Of the 28 estimates in the meta-matrix, 24 correlations were taken from published sources, and four were estimated via original meta-analyses. Most of the published meta-analytic correlation estimates can be found in Harrison et al. (2006, p. 314; minimum N = 578), where correlations among criterion variables were not contaminated with common source bias. The correlation between job satisfaction and citizenship behavior was updated using Ilies et al.'s (2009, p. 951) non-common-source estimate (r = 0.24), and the correlations between affective commitment and both job performance and organizational citizenship behavior (OCB) were also altered to include exclusively non-common-source effects (r = 0.17 and r = 0.27, respectively; Meyer et al., 2002). Further, the job satisfaction–performance correlation from Judge et al. (2001) was re-attenuated and then corrected for criterion reliability of Cronbach's α = 0.86, rather than using Judge et al.'s more liberal correction for criterion interrater reliability of r_{yy} =

0.52 (see Viswesvaran et al., 1996, pp. 562–3). Thus, the final corrected job satisfaction–performance effect was $r = 0.23$, and not $r = 0.30$. Because job involvement was not included in Harrison et al.'s analyses, several correlations regarding job involvement were taken from Brown (1996, p. 245). Specifically, a sample-weighted average of reliability-corrected estimates based on Lodahl and Kejner's (1965) and Kanungo's (1982) job involvement scales was calculated for job involvement's relationships with absenteeism ($r = -0.13$) and general job satisfaction ($r = 0.45$). We chose to exclude all other measures of job involvement because the popular Lodahl and Kejner (1965) and Kanungo (1982) scales are believed to have greater construct validity than other measures of job involvement, which are typically home-made measures that exist for use in only one study. Finally an estimate of the relationship between job involvement and affective commitment ($r = 0.53$) was taken from Meyer et al. (2002, p. 33).

To complete the meta-matrix, several original meta-analyses were conducted involving the relationships of job involvement with job performance, citizenship behavior, turnover, and lateness (see Table 4.1). We used original meta-analyses of job involvement with job performance (to avoid including same-source – common-method-biased – studies) and with turnover (to avoid measures of involuntary turnover). To identify studies for inclusion, searches of the American Psychological Association's PsycINFO (1887–September 2009), Google Scholar, and Dissertation Abstracts International (1861–September 2009) were conducted for variations of the keywords: job involvement, job performance, task performance, organizational citizenship behavior, contextual performance, extra-role behavior, pro-social behavior, tardiness, lateness, promptness, turnover, and withdrawal. References of relevant published works and previous meta-analyses were also searched, and the bibliographies of all studies found were snowballed to increase our database of primary studies. Finally, recent conference programs were searched and several relevant authors were contacted to locate any unpublished manuscripts or raw data. This search identified 522 studies that were compared against several inclusion criteria.

First, the study had to report enough information to calculate a correlation between job involvement and job performance, citizenship behavior, turnover, or lateness. Second, the participants of the primary study had to be employed adults, excluding adult participants in laboratory settings. Third, in order to limit common-source bias, we excluded any correlations with relevant outcomes (that is, job performance, citizenship behavior, turnover, and lateness) if the independent and dependent variables came from a common source (for example, both variables were measured with self-report). Fourth, any study that did not report the sample size,

Table 4.1   Meta-analytic results for job involvement and employee engagement

	k	N	r	ρ	SDp	95% CI-L	95% CI-U	80% CI-L	80% CI-U
Job involvement results*									
Job performance	32	7,551	0.10	0.12	0.14	0.08	0.17	−0.05	0.30
Supervisor rated	22	5,490	0.08	0.09	0.15	0.03	0.16	−0.10	0.15
Self-report	7	1,643	0.18	0.22	0.03	0.15	0.28	0.18	0.25
Objective measure	3	418	0.12	0.13	0.00	0.07	0.19	0.13	0.13
Supervisor and objective (excludes self-report)	25	5,908	0.08	0.10†	0.14	0.04	0.15	−0.08	0.28
OCB	10	3,612	0.26	0.30	0.25	0.16	0.44	−0.01	0.62
Supervisor rated	6	2,828	0.21	0.24†	0.19	0.10	0.38	−0.002	0.48
Self-report	4	784	0.45	0.54	0.28	0.29	0.78	0.18	0.89
Turnover	7	2,922	−0.10	−0.12	0.00	−0.15	−0.09	−0.12	−0.12
Voluntary turnover measures only	4	824	−0.12	−0.14†	0.00	−0.18	−0.10	−0.14	−0.14
Lateness									
No self-reports of lateness	3	380	−0.06	−0.08†	0.00	−0.15	−0.004	−0.08	−0.08

Employee engagement results

	k	N	r	ρ	SDρ				
Job satisfaction	19	10,054	0.39	0.44	0.24	0.34	0.53	0.14	0.74
UWES only	12	5,300	0.49	0.54†	0.11	0.47	0.60	0.39	0.68
Organizational commitment	17	11,201	0.46	0.54	0.05	0.50	0.57	0.48	0.60
UWES only	14	9,522	0.46	0.53†	0.05	0.49	0.57	0.46	0.60
Job involvement	7	1,522	0.53	0.60	0.11	0.51	0.69	0.45	0.74
UWES only	6	1,331	0.54	0.61	0.14	0.49	0.72	0.43	0.79
Lodahl/Kanungo measures of job involvement only	6	1,331	0.54	0.61†	0.14	0.49	0.72	0.43	0.79

Note: † = estimates used in path models; * = estimates are based on Lodahl and Kejner (1965) and Kanungo (1982) measures of job involvement only; UWES = Utrecht Work Engagement Scale. k = number of effect sizes in the meta-analysis; N = total sample size in the meta-analysis; r = sample-size weighted mean correlation; ρ = correlation corrected for attenuation in the predictor and criterion; $SD\rho$ = standard deviation of the corrected correlation; 95% CI-U/L = upper/lower bound of confidence interval; 80% CI-U/L = upper/lower bound of credibility interval. A list of primary studies included in the meta-analyses can be obtained from the authors.

did not report individual-level effects, or was not independent of other samples was excluded. Finally, any studies measuring relevant outcomes through intentions (for example, turnover intentions, performance intentions) rather than actual behavior were excluded. These inclusion criteria resulted in final database of 40 studies (k = 44 independent samples and total N = 11,164).

The current meta-analyses followed Hunter and Schmidt's (2004) procedures, and all original estimates were corrected for unreliability in the predictor and criterion. Because local estimates of criterion reliability were not available for correlations involving lateness, an estimate of criterion reliability was taken from Hattrup et al. (1998; α = 0.86). Objective measures of performance (for example, sales performance) were considered to be perfectly reliable, as were measures of turnover.

Overlap between employee engagement and the attitude *A*-factor
Why is the current conceptualization of employee attitudes and behavior (Figure 4.2) relevant to employee engagement? We shall demonstrate that employee engagement is correlated close to unity with the attitude *A*-factor. This means that an employee engagement scale can be thought of as a brief, direct measure of the *A*-factor. As such, employee engagement can be expected to predict broad behavioral criteria very strongly (r = ~0.5).

Engagement as an indicator of the A-*factor*
Conceptually, "*A*" is the shared content among commitment/affective attachment, job satisfaction/liking, and job involvement. This conceptual content is similar in meaning to the shared aspects of job dedication, vigor, and absorption articulated in the definition of employee engagement (Schaufeli & Bakker, 2003). Indeed, every item in the popular UWES is paralleled by a nearly identical item from a well-known measure of job satisfaction, organizational commitment, job involvement, or job affect (Newman & Harrison, 2008, p. 33; for example, the engagement item, "To me, my job is challenging", is semantically identical to the Job Descriptive Index item, "challenging", see Smith et al., 1969).

In addition to this conceptual overlap between employee engagement and the *A*-factor, we assessed the empirical overlap. In order to do this, we constructed a meta-analytic correlation matrix of the relationships among engagement, affective commitment, job satisfaction and job involvement. In addition to the meta-analytic correlations described under Figure 4.1, several original meta-analyses were conducted to assess the relationships of engagement with job satisfaction, job involvement, and organizational commitment.

To identify studies for inclusion in the original meta-analyses, searches of the American Psychological Association's PsycINFO (1887–September 2009), Google Scholar, and Dissertation Abstracts International (1861–September 2009) were conducted for keywords: engagement, job involvement, satisfaction, and commitment. References of relevant published works and recent conference programs were searched, and relevant authors were contacted to locate any unpublished manuscripts or raw data. This search identified 739 studies which were examined for congruence with several inclusion criteria: the study had to report enough information to calculate a correlation, the participants had to be employed adults, and any study that did not report the sample size, did not report individual-level effects, or was not independent from other samples was excluded. Second, only studies that used the more construct-valid job involvement measures from Lodahl and Kejner (1965) or Kanungo (1982) scales were included. Third, reverse-scored measures of disengagement were not included as measures of engagement. These inclusion criteria resulted in final database of 23 studies, 25 independent samples, and a total sample size of 18,039.

Once a study passed these inclusion criteria, we coded relevant relationships according to the following coding rules. First, if a primary study reported relevant correlations at multiple time points, only time 1 estimates were included in the current analyses. Second, if a sample provided multiple measures of a single construct or multiple facet-level effect sizes for one relationship, a correlation based on a composite measure was estimated (Nunnally, 1978). The meta-analyses followed guidelines presented by Hunter and Schmidt (2004). All correlations were corrected for attenuation in the predictor and criterion. Finally, effect sizes were separated by type of engagement measure in order to investigate instrument as a moderator (only UWES engagement estimates were used in Figure 4.3). Results of the original meta-analyses and moderator analyses are presented in Table 4.1. The resulting meta-analytic correlation matrix was used to estimate Figure 4.3.

As shown in Figure 4.3, Panel A, the estimated latent correlation between measures of employee engagement and the A-factor of job attitudes was $\varphi = 0.77$ (harmonic mean $N = 4,341$; the correlation magnitude remains 0.77 regardless whether the A-factor is specified via parallel or congeneric indicators). In other words, both the conceptual definition and the empirical evidence tend to suggest that employee engagement greatly overlaps with the A-factor of job attitudes. This finding is consistent with the observation that the UWES is composed entirely of items taken from measures of job satisfaction, organizational commitment, job involvement, and job affect (Newman & Harrison, 2008). Thus, our results show

Panel A: Engagement correlation with *A*-factor = 0.77

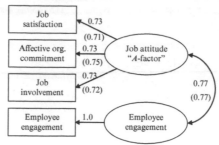

Note: Parallel indicator model estimates are presented first; congeneric indicator model estimates are in parentheses; RMSEA = 0.105 (0.180); NNFI= 0.96 (0.89); CFI = 0.96 (0.96); SRMR = 0.039 (0.037); harmonic mean *N* = 4,341.

Panel B: Engagement loading onto *A*-factor: parallel model

Note: Parallel indicator model estimates; RMSEA = 0.095; NNFI = 0.97; CFI = 0.96; SRMR = 0.041; harmonic mean *N* = 4,341.

Panel C: Attitude bifactor model

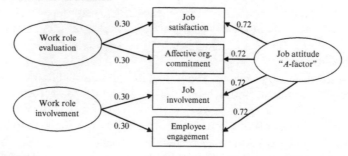

Note: Parallel indicator model estimates; RMSEA = 0.054; NNFI = 0.99; CFI = 0.99; SRMR = 0.023; harmonic mean *N* = 4,341.

Figure 4.3   Models of the relationships between employee engagement and job attitudes

that employee engagement as measured by the UWES is largely redundant with the *A*-factor.

Given the large correlation between employee engagement and the *A*-factor of job attitudes, one may wonder how employee engagement would fit conceptually into an overall job attitude measurement model. In this regard, we propose two possibilities: (a) engagement loads onto the *A*-factor (that is, satisfaction, commitment, involvement, and engagement fit a higher-order unidimensional model), or (b) engagement double-loads, once onto the *A*-factor and once onto a more specific group factor with job involvement (that is, satisfaction, commitment, involvement, and engagement fit a *bifactor* model; Yung et al., 1999). These two possibilities are depicted in Figure 4.3, Panels B and C. In Panel C (the bifactor model), job attitudes load onto both the *A*-factor and onto one of two, more-specific group factors, labeled 'work role evaluation' and 'work role involvement'. As seen in Figure 4.3, practical fit indices suggest that both possibilities (Panel B and Panel C) have some empirical merit (for example, CFI $\geq$ 0.96; NNFI $\geq$ 0.97; SRMR $\leq$ 0.041; Hu & Bentler, 1999). Also in both models, engagement exhibits a healthy loading onto the *A*-factor ($\lambda \geq 0.72$). Nonetheless, the bifactor model (Panel C) seems to fit the meta-analytic data slightly better than the one-factor model (Panel B) does. In other words, employee engagement loads onto both the *A*-factor and onto a group factor (that is, work role involvement) that it reflects mutually along with job involvement. The loading of engagement onto the *A*-factor is strong ($\lambda = 0.72$), while the loading onto the secondary group factor work role involvement is weak ($\lambda = 0.30$). To summarize, in all of the models estimated in Figure 4.3, employee engagement is a robust indicator of the *A*-factor.

Engagement versus job satisfaction and the issue of item difficulty/location
Another measurement issue in the study of employee engagement involves the contention that, "engagement connotes *activation*, whereas satisfaction connotes *satiation* (Erickson, 2005)" (italics added; quoted from Macey & Schneider, 2008, p. 8). That is, some proponents have offered the following conceptual distinction between job satisfaction and employee engagement: whereas *engagement* connotes passion and involvement, *job satisfaction* only connotes contentment and satiation, "similar to a cow on a hillside, chewing its cud" (Schneider, 2009). Macey and Schneider (2008, p. 7) have specifically noted the usage of the job satisfaction item, "Most days I feel enthusiastic about my work" (from the Overall Job Satisfaction scale; Brayfield & Rothe, 1951) – an item which clearly conveys engagement but appears on a job satisfaction scale – as an indication of confusion between the two concepts.

In an attempt to investigate the possible empirical distinction between engagement and job satisfaction, we conducted an item analysis to compare the measurement properties of the Brayfield–Rothe (1951) "enthusiastic" item with the measurement properties of an item from the same scale, which simply states, "I feel fairly well satisfied with my present job". Using a confirmatory factor analysis (CFA) on the item-level correlation matrix for nine items from the Brayfield–Rothe scale (reported in Babin and Boles, 1996, $N = 261$), we assessed the *metric equivalence* of the two items – do the "satisfied" and the "enthusiastic" items both exhibit similarly strong factor loadings on the latent attitude construct? Second, we assessed the *scalar equivalence* of the two items – does the "enthusiastic" item simply reflect a higher degree of positive evaluation than does the "satisfied" item? (that is, does the enthusiastic item have higher *item difficulty*? Hulin et al., 1983). Results of this analysis confirm a one-factor model of job satisfaction (CFI = 0.98; TLI (Tucker–Lewis index) = 0.98; RMSEA = 0.086; SRMR = 0.034), in which the factor loading for the "satisfied" item is 0.72, and the factor loading for the "enthusiastic" item is 0.73 (suggesting that an "enthusiastic" item measures the same construct, in basically the same way, as does the "satisfied" item). Item difficulty parameters also indicate the two items were virtually interchangeable, with the "satisfied" and "enthusiastic" items showing similar item intercepts of 3.34 and 3.73, respectively (suggesting that, if anything, the "satisfied" item would be more difficult/extreme than the "enthusiastic" item). In short, empirical evidence confirms a one-factor attitude model in which an "enthusiastic" item measures the same attitude construct, in the same way, as a "satisfied" item. A replication analysis based on another sample of $N > 500$ and using the complete 18-item Brayfield–Rothe scale yielded nearly identical results. Job enthusiasm and classic job satisfaction do *not* appear to be different constructs, in any empirical sense.

Discussion

In this chapter, we argued that researchers should be skeptical of the employee engagement construct because it is nearly redundant with a higher-order job attitude construct. Because of this redundancy with an attitude A-factor (parallel to the g-factor in cognitive ability: Spearman, 1904), employee engagement significantly, and often strongly, is related to a broad criterion construct that summarizes a number of organizational and scientifically relevant behaviors (Figure 4.2). Whether or not employee engagement reduces entropy in the space of the usual dependent variables in organizational research after other, more well-researched constructs such as job attitudes or job affect have been included in the predictive system, seems to be a matter of little concern to practitioners. In contrast, Seitz (2000) has argued that such entropy reduction in the total theoretical and empirical space involved is the *sine qua non* of useful constructs and models – a test which the employee engagement concept very likely would fail.

Nonetheless, the *A*-factor (and therefore employee engagement; see Figure 4.3) strongly predicts the broad behavioral criterion (Figure 4.2). The success of employee engagement in accounting for variance in a broad range of relevant organizational variables likely reflects its location at the broad-bandwidth end of the bandwidth/fidelity dilemma. This observation harkens the well-known phenomenon of broad-bandwidth measures that are composed of theoretically relevant but heterogeneous items having strong validity in terms of relations with behavioral measures, but often low reliability as assessed by internal consistency indices (see Cronbach and Gleser, 1957; Hulin and Humphreys, 1980; and Humphreys, 1985). The strong validity estimates for predictions of behavior ($r = 0.51$; Figure 4.2) reflect the phenomenon that broad behaviors are more likely to be influenced by broad, general individual traits than they are by narrow traits. Measures that are narrowly focused on single traits or constructs represent the fidelity end of the bandwidth/fidelity dilemma but do less well predicting broad behavioral constructs.

One question we raised in this chapter was the extent to which anything is gained by relabeling the A-factor as "employee engagement" – to what extent does the construct provide scientific information not already available in the construct of "overall job attitude"? In short, employee engagement likely predicts the work behavioral construct, but the *A*-factor already did that. Future discussions of employee engagement should note its redundancy with the *A*-factor. Doing so will ground the engagement construct in decades of informative empirical research on job satisfaction, organizational commitment, and job involvement.

Limitations and future directions

Our empirical analyses have focused on just one measure of engagement (UWES; Schaufeli & Bakker, 2003), albeit the most popular engagement measure. It is possible that other measures of employee engagement would produce different results; but this possibility must be empirically validated, not merely assumed. Given the suggestive results of the current chapter, we recommend that the following litmus test be applied for measures of employee engagement: anyone purporting to measure engagement as a unique or non-attitudinal construct should begin by first administering a brief measure of the "*A*-factor" (Brayfield & Rothe, 1951; Lodahl & Kejner, 1965; Meyer & Allen, 1997) and then estimate how strongly one's engagement instrument correlates with *A*. If the engagement–*A*-factor correlation exceeds 0.7, then the unique theoretical utility of the corresponding engagement concept is questionable. By the same token, results of the current study are supportive of using an engagement instrument such as the UWES as a brief, direct measure of the *A*-factor.

Aside from measurement research comparing the A-factor to a myriad of engagement instruments, future measurement research should also be undertaken on the criterion side of Harrison et al.'s (2006) attitude–engagement model (Figure 4.2). Such research might include developing a direct measure of *behavioral engagement*. Conceptually, it could also be useful for future research to consider whether counterproductive work behaviors (CWBs) – other than job withdrawal – can be incorporated into the behavioral engagement construct (see Dalal, 2005). Regardless how engagement is defined and measured in future research, it will help to have separate measures for attitudinal engagement and behavioral engagement. That is, researchers and practitioners should avoid the common tendency to include behavioral content on attitudinal engagement measures, so as not to commit the fallacy of confounding the attitudinal construct with its criterion (Newman & Harrison, 2008).

Beyond general constructs
Despite promising empirical results for a general attitude–general behavioral criterion model (see Figure 4.2 and Harrison et al., 2006), such general models do not capture the entire story of organizational behavior. For example, research on the Job Descriptive Index (Kinicki et al., 2002, p. 19) indicates that work-facet job satisfaction predicts turnover and turnover intentions uniquely, beyond the higher-order overall (facet composite) job satisfaction construct. That is, the presence of a strong correspondence between higher-order factors (Figure 4.2) does not negate the possibility of informative lower-order attitude–behavior relationships (for example, Getman et al., 1976; Hanisch & Hulin, 1991). The attitude–engagement model is not an attempt to close down avenues of investigation about lower-order attitude–behavior relationships – it rather represents a parsimonious and empirically well-supported explanation for individual-level relationships between work attitudes and behaviors. As a further caveat to the broad attitude–engagement model, we note that results based on meta-analytic averages (as used in the current chapter) may at times differ from results obtained in a single, particular setting (see Newman et al., 2007).

For approaching future research on multidimensional constructs, Edwards (2001) has proposed an enlightening analytical strategy for empirically addressing bandwidth/fidelity dilemmas, which we believe should be actively implemented in future work on this topic. That is, future work can simultaneously conceptualize attitudinal and behavioral constructs at both broad and narrow levels of specificity, and then estimate the corresponding connections between the two sets of constructs to ascertain the appropriate level of specificity for each attitude–behavior relationship. Until the sort of empirical work advocated by Edwards is conducted and results are found to suggest otherwise, we are left with Figure 4.2 (the attitude–engagement model) as the most parsimonious explanation for work attitude–behavior relationships. In light of this model, an extensive body of current data supports our conclusion that – for better or worse – employee engagement should be recognized as an indicator of the *A*-factor.

Note

*   The authors would like to thank Reeshad Dalal, David Harrison, and Ben Schneider for helpful comments on this chapter.

References

American Heritage® Dictionary of the English Language (2007), 4th edn, retrieved July 30, 2007, from Dictionary.com website: http://dictionary.reference.com/browse/engagement.

Babin, B.J. & Boles, J.S. (1996), "The effects of perceived co-worker involvement and supervisor support on service provider role stress, performance and job satisfaction", *Journal of Retailing*, **72**, 57–75.

Brayfield, A.H. & Rothe, H.F. (1951), "An index of job satisfaction", *Journal of Applied Psychology*, **35**, 307–11.

Brooke, P.P., Jr., Russell, D.W. & Price, J.L. (1988), "Discriminant validation of measures of job satisfaction, job involvement, and organizational commitment", *Journal of Applied Psychology*, **73**, 139–45.

Brown, S.P. (1996), "A meta-analysis and review of organizational research on job involvement", *Psychological Bulletin*, **120**, 235–55.

Campbell, D.T. & Fiske, D.W. (1959), "Convergent and discriminant validation by the multitrait-multimethod matrix", *Psychological Bulletin*, **56**, 81–105.

Cronbach, L.J. & Gleser, G.C. (1957), *Psychological Tests and Personnel Decisions*, Urbana, IL: University of Illinois Press.

Dalal, R.S. (2005), "A meta-analysis of the relationship between organizational citizenship behavior and counterproductive work behavior", *Journal of Applied Psychology*, **90**, 1241–55.

Dalal, R.S., Brummel, B.J., Wee, S. & Thomas, L.L. (2008), "Defining employee engagement for productive research and practice", *Industrial and Organizational Psychology*, **1**, 52–5.

Dalal, R.S., Lam, H., Weiss, H.M., Welch, E. & Hulin, C.L. (2009), "A within-person approach to work behavior and performance: concurrent and lagged citizenship-counterproductivity associations, and dynamic relationships with affect and overall job performance", *Academy of Management Journal*, **52**, 1051–66.

Edwards, J.R. (2001), "Multidimensional constructs in organizational behavior research: an integrative analytical framework", *Organizational Research Methods*, **4**, 144–92.

Erickson, T.J. (2005), "Testimony submitted before the U.S. Senate Committee on Health, Education, Labor and Pensions", May 26.

Fishbein, M. & Ajzen, I. (1974), "Attitudes towards objects as predictors of single and multiple behavioral criteria", *Psychological Review*, **81**, 59–74.

Fisher, C.D. (1980), "On the dubious wisdom of expecting job satisfaction to correlate with performance", *Academy of Management Review*, **5**, 607–12.

Fleeson, W. (2001), "Toward a structure- and process-integrated view of personality: traits as density distributions of states", *Journal of Personality and Social Psychology*, **80**, 1011–27.

Getman, J.P., Goldberg, S.B. and Herman, J.B. (1976), *Union Representation Elections: Law and reality*, New York: Russell Sage Foundation.

Hanisch, K.A. & Hulin, C.L. (1991), "General attitudes and organizational withdrawal: an evaluation of a causal model", *Journal of Vocational Behavior*, **39**, 110–28.

Hanisch, K.A., Hulin, C.L. & Roznowski, M. (1998), "The importance of individuals' repertoires of behaviors: the scientific appropriateness of studying multiple behaviors and general attitudes", *Journal of Organizational Behavior*, **19**, 463–80.

Harrison, D.A., Newman, D.A. & Roth, P.L. (2006), "How important are job attitudes? Meta-analytic comparisons of integrative behavioral outcomes and time sequences", *Academy of Management Journal*, **49**, 305–25.

Harter, J.K. & Schmidt, F.L. (2008), "Conceptual versus empirical distinctions among constructs: implications for discriminant validity", *Industrial and Organizational Psychology*, **1**, 36–9.

Hattrup, K., O'Connell, M.S. & Wingate, P.H. (1998), "Prediction of multidimensional criteria: distinguishing task and contextual performance", *Human Performance*, **11**, 305–20.

Hu, L.T. & Bentler, P.M. (1999), "Cutoff criteria for fit indexes in covariance structure analysis: conventional criteria versus new alternatives", *Structural Equation Modeling*, **6**, 1–55.

Hulin, C.L. (1982), "Some reflections on general performance dimensions and halo rating error", *Journal of Applied Psychology*, **67**, 165–70.

Hulin, C.L. (1991), "Adaptation, persistence, and commitment in organizations", in M.D. Dunnette & L.M. Hough (eds), *Handbook of Industrial and Organizational Psychology*, vol. 2, 2nd edn, Palo Alto, CA: Consulting Psychologists Press, pp. 445–505.

Hulin, C.L., Drasgow, F. & Parsons, C.K. (1983), *Item Response Theory: Applications to Psychological Measurement*, Homewood, IL: Dow Jones-Irwin.

Hulin, C.L. & Humphreys, L.G. (1980), "Foundations of test theory", in *Construct Validity in Psychological Measurement*, Proceeding of a colloquium on theory and application in education and employment, Princeton, NJ: US Office of Personnel Management and Educational Testing Service, pp. 5–10.

Humphreys, L.G. (1985), "General intelligence: an integration of factor, test, and simplex theory", in B.B. Wolman (ed.), *Handbook of Intelligence: Theories, Measurement, and Applications*, New York: Wiley, pp. 201–24.

Hunter, J.E. & Schmidt, F.L. (2004), *Methods of Meta-analysis: Correcting Error and Bias in Research Findings*, 2nd edn, Newbury Park, CA: Sage.

Ilies, R., Fulmer, I.S., Spitzmuller, M. & Johnson, M.D. (2009), "Personality and citizenship behavior: the mediating role of job satisfaction", *Journal of Applied Psychology*, **94**, 945–59.

Judge, T.A., Thoreson, C.J., Bono, J.E. & Patton, G.K. (2001), "The job satisfaction–job performance relationship: a qualitative and quantitative review", *Psychological Bulletin*, **127**, 376–407.

Kahn, W.A. (1990), "Psychological conditions of personal engagement and disengagement at work", *Academy of Management Journal*, **33**, 692–724.

Kanungo, R.N. (1982), "Measurement of job and work involvement", *Journal of Applied Psychology*, **67**, 341–9.

Kinicki, A., McKee-Ryan, F., Schriesheim, C. & Carson, K. (2002), "Assessing the construct validity of the Job Descriptive Index (JDI): a review and meta-analysis", *Journal of Applied Psychology*, **87**, 14–32.

Lodahl, T.M. & Kejner, M. (1965), "The definition and measurement of job involvement", *Journal of Applied Psychology*, **49**, 24–33.

Macey, W.H. & Schneider, B. (2008), "The meaning of employee engagement", *Industrial and Organizational Psychology*, **1**, 3–30.

March, J.G. & Simon, H.A. (1958), *Organizations*, 3rd edn, New York: Wiley.

Mathieu, J.E. & Farr, J.L. (1991), "Further evidence for the discriminant validity of measures of organizational commitment, job involvement, and job satisfaction", *Journal of Applied Psychology*, **76**, 127–33.

Meyer, J.P. & Allen, N.J. (1997), *Commitment in the Workplace: Theory, Research, and Application*, Thousand Oaks, CA: Sage.

Meyer, J.P., Stanley, D.J., Herscovitch, L. & Topolnytsky, L. (2002), "Affective, continuance, and normative commitment to the organization: a meta-analysis of antecedents, correlates, and consequences", *Journal of Vocational Behavior*, **61**, 20–52.

Miner, A.G., Glomb, T.M. & Hulin, C. (2005), "Experience sampling mood and its correlates at work", *Journal of Occupational and Organizational Psychology*, **78**, 171–93.

Newman, D.A. & Harrison, D.A. (2008), "Been there, bottled that: are state and behavioral work engagement new and useful construct 'wines'?", *Industrial and Organizational Psychology*, **1**, 31–5.

Newman, D.A., Jacobs, R.R. & Bartram, D. (2007), "Choosing the best method for local validity estimation: relative accuracy of meta-analysis vs. a local study vs. Bayes-analysis", *Journal of Applied Psychology*, **92**, 1394–413.

Nunnally, J.C. (1978), *Psychometric Theory*, New York: McGraw-Hill.

Organ, D.W. (1988), *Organizational Citizenship Behavior: The Good Soldier Syndrome*, Lexington, MA: Lexington Books.

Saks, A.M. (2008), "The meaning and bleeding of employee engagement: how muddy is the water?", *Industrial and Organizational Psychology*, **1**, 40–43.

Schaufeli, W.B. & Bakker, A.B. (2003), "Test manual for the Utrecht Work Engagement Scale", unpublished manuscript, Utrecht University, The Netherlands, Retrieved from www.schaufeli.com.

Schneider, B. (2009), "Engaging employee engagement: what it is, why it is important, and how to make it happen?", presented at the Spring 2009 University of Illinois Center for Human Resource Management Roundtable: Employee Engagement Driving Operational Excellence, Chicago, IL, March.

Seitz, S.T. (2000), "Virtual organization", in D.R. Ilgen & C.L. Hulin (eds), *Computational Modeling of Behavior Organizations: The Third Scientific Discipline*, Washington, DC: American Psychological Association, pp. 69–93.

Smith, P.C., Kendall, L.M. & Hulin, C.L. (1969), *The Measurement of Satisfaction in Work and Retirement: A Strategy for the Study of Attitudes*, Chicago, IL: Rand McNally.

Spearman, C. (1904), "'General intelligence', objectively determined and measured", *American Journal of Psychology*, **15**, 201–93.

Vance, R.J. (2006), *Employee Engagement and Commitment: A Guide to Understanding, Measuring, and Increasing Engagement in Your Organization*, Effective Practice Guidelines: Society for Human Resource Management, Alexandria, VA.

Viswesvaran, C. (1993), "Modeling job performance: Is there a general factor?", unpublished doctoral dissertation, University of Iowa.

Viswesvaran, C., Ones, D.S. & Schmidt, F.L. (1996), "Comparative analysis of the reliability of job performance ratings", *Journal of Applied Psychology*, **81**, 557–574.

Viswesvaran, C., Schmidt, F.L. & Ones, D.S. (2005), "Is there a general factor in ratings of job performance? A meta-analytic framework for disentangling substantive and error influences", *Journal of Applied Psychology*, **90**, 108–31.

Yung, Y.F., Thissen, D. & McLeod, L.D. (1999), "On the relationship between the higher-order factor model and the hierarchical factor model", *Psychometrika*, **64**, 113–28.

5 Toward an evidence-based model of engagement: what we can learn from motivation and commitment research

John P. Meyer, Marylène Gagné and
Natalya M. Parfyonova

Introduction

Like many of the concepts that are so important to us – love, trust, justice – employee engagement is relatively easy to recognize, but has proven very difficult to define. As elusive as its definition might be, however, engagement has become the new buzzword in organizations (Richman, 2006) and has been heavily marketed by human resources (HR) consulting firms as a strategy for competitive advantage (Macey & Schneider, 2008). This raises some interesting questions. Why is engagement so popular today? Where did it originate, and why? And, perhaps most importantly, what do we know about engagement and how can we leverage this knowledge to the benefit of organizations and their employees?

Macey and Schneider noted that interest in employee engagement is relatively recent and new, and originated in the business world rather than from academic research. Indeed, they argued that "[a]cademic researchers are now slowly joining the fray" (p. 3). We agree that the term has been popularized by HR consultants and that it has hit a cord with employers who are striving to do more with fewer resources in an increasingly competitive economic environment. However, we argue that academics know a great deal more about engagement than what we can learn from the relatively small body of recent engagement studies (for example, Schaufeli et al., 2002; May et al., 2004; Saks, 2006). Our objective is to show how our understanding of engagement is enhanced by research pertaining to long-standing theories of motivation (Deci & Ryan, 1985a; Ryan & Deci, 2000) and commitment (Meyer & Allen, 1991, 1997).

In what follows, we provide a brief discussion of the meaning of employee engagement. We then outline the key components of Deci and Ryan's (1985a) self-determination theory (SDT) of motivation and review relevant findings pertaining to its implications for work behavior and employee well-being. This is followed by a similar analysis of Meyer and Allen's (1991) three-component model (TCM) of commitment. Next, we illustrate how these theories combine to provide an overarching framework for understanding the nature, development, and consequences of employee engagement. We conclude by demonstrating how the large body of research generated by these theories can serve as a guide to organizations interested in fostering a higher level of engagement in their workforces.

The meaning of engagement

There is no universally accepted definition of engagement. HR consulting firms typically offer definitions that are compatible with the development strategies they are attempting to promote. Academic researchers are also influenced by their own disciplines and theoretical orientations. Despite the differences, however, there are commonalties that we can identify and use to generate a working definition for purposes of the present discussion. We focus here on definitions offered within the academic literature because they are more accessible and have been vetted in the peer-review process. Nevertheless, our intention is not to be exhaustive but rather to identify key characteristics of the construct that help to illustrate the relevance of the theories of motivation and commitment to be discussed below.

Perhaps the first definition of employee engagement was provided by Kahn (1990, p. 694) who described it "as the harnessing of organizational members' selves to their work roles; in engagement, people employ and express themselves physically, cognitively, and emotionally during role performances". In contrast, he noted that disengagement is "the uncoupling of selves from work roles; in disengagement, people withdraw and defend themselves physically, cognitively, and emotionally during role performances" (p. 694). What is particularly salient in this definition is the involvement of self in the work role.

Schaufeli et al. (2002, p. 74) defined engagement as "a positive, fulfilling, work-related state of mind that is characterized by vigor, dedication, and absorption". This definition is noteworthy because it served as the basis for what has arguably been the most widely used measure of engagement in academic research. More recently, Saks (2006) adopted the Kahn and Schaufeli et al. definitions but expanded the construct to include job and organizational engagement. Masson et al. (2008, p. 57) also acknowledged that while the focus of academic research is often on engagement with work and job roles, in applied settings there is also an interest in "engagement with the organization".

Macey and Schneider (2008) argued that engagement can be conceptualized as a trait, a state, or a behavioral tendency. From this perspective, Kahn's (1990) and Schaufeli et al.'s (2002) descriptions are best considered definitions of *state engagement*. Macey and Schneider's definition of *behavioral engagement* as "adaptive behavior intended to serve an organizational purpose, whether to defend and protect the status quo in response to actual or anticipated threats or to change and/or promote change in response to actual or anticipated events" (p. 18) focuses on the visible manifestations of employee engagement and helps to illustrate its importance for organizations. Their definition of *trait engagement* as "the [dispositional] tendency to experience work in positive, active, and energetic ways and to behave adaptively" (p. 21) suggests that, in addition to managing environmental influences, it might be possible to identify and select for characteristics that predispose employees to be engaged.

Considered together, these descriptions of the various facets and foci of engagement led us to offer the following working definition: engagement is experienced as enthusiasm and self-involvement with a task or collective (for example, organization), is fostered by a corresponding dispositional orientation and facilitating climate, and manifests itself in proactive value-directed behavior. With this definition in mind, we now turn to reviews of theory and research pertaining to work motivation and commitment to demonstrate the mechanisms underlying the development of engagement, the dispositions and situational factors that trigger these mechanisms, and the benefits that derive from high levels of engagement.

Self-determination theory of motivation

Although developed initially as a general model of motivation, SDT has been increasingly adapted as a framework for the investigation of work motivation (Gagné & Deci, 2005). The theory identifies two overarching forms of motivation. *Intrinsic motivation* refers to the involvement in an activity for its own sake, out of enjoyment and interest. *Extrinsic motivation* involves performance of an activity for instrumental reasons. Although extrinsic motivation is arguably predominant in a work context, it too can take different forms. According to SDT, extrinsic motivation can reflect a desire to gain rewards or avoid punishment (external regulation), boost one's ego or avoid feelings of guilt (introjection), attain a valued personal goal (identification), or express one's sense of self (integration). Identification and integration involve a high level of volition and, along with intrinsic motivation, are considered forms of *autonomous regulation*. External regulation and introjection involve more external influence and less authenticity, and are considered forms of *controlled regulation*.

The concept of autonomous regulation overlaps considerably with Macey and Schneider's (2008) conceptualization of "state engagement", and is also consistent with Kahn's (1990) notion that engagement entails self-involvement in the work role. In fact, SDT uses the concept of "internalization" (Ryan, 1995) to explain how the regulation of an activity by external sources (for example, rewards) can become internally regulated when a person comes to value of the activity for reaching personally meaningful goals. Moreover, the behavioral outcomes found to be associated with autonomous regulation (for example, persistence and creativity) correspond with what Macey and Schneider described as "behavioral engagement". The theory also identifies dispositional factors that might underlie "trait engagement", and elaborates on the situational factors that must be in place for individuals to feel autonomously regulated. What SDT contributes, beyond mere similarities with other frameworks, is an explanatory mechanism to understand the impact of dispositional and situational factors on state and behavioral engagement – the satisfaction of basic psychological needs.

According to SDT, the key to autonomous regulation is satisfaction of basic psychological needs for competence, autonomy, and relatedness. The need for *autonomy* is satisfied when, at the deepest levels of reflection, individuals believe that what they are doing is freely chosen and consistent with their core values. The need for *competence* is satisfied when people believe they have the capability and resources needed to accomplish their tasks and achieve their objectives. Finally, the need for *relatedness* is satisfied when they feel unconditionally valued and appreciated by others. There is considerable evidence demonstrating that the satisfaction of these basic needs is associated with greater autonomous regulation (for example, Deci et al., 2001; Baard et al., 2004) which, in turn, is associated with high levels of performance (for example, Baard et al., 2004), adaptation to change (Gagné et al., 2000) as well as employee well-being (for example, Deci et al., 2001; Richer et al., 2002).

Deci and Ryan (1985b) noted that some individuals are more predisposed than others to seek out situations where their needs are satisfied and they can behave in a way that is compatible with their core values. This dispositional autonomy orientation is measurable and can arguably be incorporated into the selection process. However, even among those who are predisposed to seek out engaging work, situational factors play a key role in engaging employees. Among the environmental conditions found to facilitate self-determination are task characteristics (Gagné et al., 1997), rewards and recognition (Deci et al., 1999; Gagné & Forest, 2008), and managerial styles (Deci et al., 1989; Baard et al., 2004). Managers play a particularly powerful role in creating an autonomy-supportive environment.

In sum, SDT addresses the mechanisms underlying employee engagement in their work activities and helps to make the connections between state engagement and its antecedents (that is, trait engagement and autonomy supportive work climate) and consequences (that is, behavioral engagement and employee well-being). We return to a more detailed discussion of implications for the management of activity engagement later. First, we provide an overview of theory and research pertaining to the TCM and its implications for understanding engagement in the organization itself.

The three-component model of commitment
The TCM was developed initially to integrate existing conceptualizations of commitment into a single multidimensional framework. Meyer and Allen (1991) noted that there were both similarities and differences in existing unidimensional conceptualizations. Common to all was the belief that commitment binds individuals to organizations thereby reducing the likelihood of turnover. The key differences were in the mindsets presumed to characterize the commitment. These mindsets reflected three distinguishable themes: affective attachment to the organization, perceived cost of leaving, and obligation to remain. Meyer and Allen argued that commitment can be accompanied by one or more of these mindsets and therefore incorporated all three into their model. To distinguish among the different forms of commitments, they labeled them "affective commitment", "continuance commitment", and "normative commitment", respectively.

The TCM parallels SDT in several respects, most notably in the notion of multiple mindsets. One of the more notable differences, however, is that the primary focus of the TCM has been on organizational engagement, whereas SDT focuses more on activity engagement. Therefore, we use the TCM as the basis for our discussion of organizational engagement. This is not without precedent. Macey and Schneider (2008) acknowledged that current conceptualizations of engagement share much in common with commitment, particularly affective commitment. Richman (2006) noted that many of the engagement models used by HR consulting firms were previously marketed as models of commitment.

The TCM has generated considerable research and, as a result, we have learned a great deal about the nature, development and consequences of commitment. Among other things, we know that employees are more likely to remain with their employer when they are committed, and that they attend more regularly, perform better, and exert more discretionary effort when their commitment reflects an affective attachment, a sense of obligation, or both, than when it is based on the perceived costs of leaving (Meyer et al., 2002). Meyer et al. (2004) noted that there are striking parallels between the commitment mindsets reflected in the TCM and the mindsets characterizing the different forms of motivational regulation in SDT. Employees with a strong affective commitment to the organization feel a greater sense of autonomous regulation as they perform their work activities than those who remain simply to avoid costs (for example, loss of pension benefits) – the latter experience more controlled regulation (Gagné et al., 2008).

Given the similarities in mindsets, Meyer and Maltin (2009) speculated that need satisfaction is implicated in the development of commitment as it is in motivational regulation – with satisfaction of the psychological needs being greater for affective commitment than it is for continuance commitment. An examination of the work conditions found to be most strongly associated with affective commitment in recent meta-analyses (for example, Meyer et al., 2002; Kristof-Brown et al., 2005) – namely, perceived organizational support (POS), value congruence, organizational justice, and transformational leadership – provides some substance to this speculation.

In sum, we have learned a great deal over the years about the nature, development, and consequences of organizational commitment. Whether it is considered identical or simply strongly related to employee engagement, we should not ignore the large body of research that exists as we contemplate the best strategies for engaging employees. Therefore, we turn now to the development of an integrative framework using SDT as the basis for our understanding of activity engagement, and the TCM as a basis for understanding organizational engagement. We describe this framework in the next section and then conclude with a discussion of its implications for management.

An evidence-based engagement framework
Our engagement framework is depicted in Figure 5.1. As mentioned above, we make a basic distinction between activity engagement (based on SDT) and organizational engagement (based on the TCM). Although space does not permit, it is important to note that there are likely to be other forms of engagement (for example, engagement in teams, projects, and change initiatives). These can be accommodated by recent efforts to extend the TCM to other commitment foci (Meyer & Herscovitch, 2001) as well as applications of SDT at different levels of abstraction (Vallerand, 1997).

For both the activity and organizational foci, we make basic distinctions between disengagement, full engagement, and contingent engagement. Employees who are disengaged will experience what is referred to in SDT as "amotivation" – the absence of intentional regulation or goal-directed activity. At the organization level, they have little commitment of any form and therefore can be expected to leave at their convenience. By contrast, fully engaged employees are autonomously regulated. This could

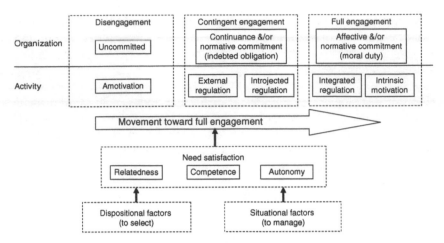

Figure 5.1   A model of employee engagement based on self-determination theory and the three-component model of commitment

take the form of intrinsic motivation where they find the performance of their duties enjoyable, or the form of identified or integrated regulation, when the work is not intrinsically interesting, but still meaningful. At the organizational level, fully engaged employees are likely to have a strong affective commitment, perhaps accompanied by strong normative commitment reflecting a sense of moral duty to remain and contribute to the success of the organization (Gellatly et al., 2006; Meyer & Parfyonova, in press).

We include a third level of engagement in our framework – contingent engagement – to acknowledge that many employees, perhaps a majority, fall somewhere between the two extremes. These employees recognize that performance of their tasks is a necessity and is linked to continued employment, compensation, and benefits. In SDT terminology, they experience a sense of controlled regulation – they do not enjoy their jobs or see them as particularly meaningful, but rather as a means to the attainment of desired outcomes largely controlled by others. At the organizational level, these employees are likely to experience high levels of continuance commitment, perhaps based on a lack of alternative employment opportunities or concerns over the potential loss of status, benefits, or other perks that depend on their continued membership in the organization. Employees who are contingently engaged are likely to stay and perform for the organization, but their efforts may be restricted to meeting minimum performance requirements. In the age where jobs were well defined and performance standards clearly articulated, the use of contingent rewards and sanctions could be quite effective. However, in today's competitive and ever-changing business environment where employees are expected to continually adapt to new conditions and to find innovative and creative ways to contribute to organizational success, contingent engagement may not be enough. Therefore, organizations must find ways to get employees more fully engaged.

In our engagement model, the key to moving employees along the continuum toward full engagement is the satisfaction of employees' basic psychological needs. This can be achieved in part by selecting employees who are predisposed to engagement, but will ultimately depend on the creation of a work climate that affords the opportunities for need satisfaction. Research pertaining to SDT and the TCM has identified many factors that can contribute to such a climate. Therefore, we turn now to a discussion of these factors and the practical implications of our engagement model.

Implications for management
According to SDT, some individuals are more predisposed to engagement than others. These individuals have a greater internal locus of control (that is, believe they can control their own destinies) and an autonomous causality orientation (that is, are more proactive in seeking out situations that allow them to fulfill their basic needs). There are various instruments that can be used to assess this predisposition, including measures of general causality orientation (Deci & Ryan, 1985b), proactive personality (Bateman & Crant, 1993), and core self-evaluation (Judge et al., 2003), but it is also possible to probe for these characteristics in structured interviews and situational judgment tests. Potential employees who are predisposed to engagement are likely to have a well-developed sense of personal values. Organizations can attract these individuals in the recruitment process by clearly articulating their own values and describing the opportunities they provide for employees to contribute to the fulfillment of these values. Organizations must of course live up to these expectations if they want to retain these high-potential employees. Therefore, a second key to creating an engaged workforce is to create a *climate for engagement.* (See Collins & Porras, 1996, for numerous examples of organizations that have succeeded in articulating, living up to, and reaping the benefits of a strong set of core values.)

Research pertaining to SDT and the TCM has identified many factors that can be leveraged to foster autonomous regulation and affective/ normative commitment to organizations. According to SDT, job design, management practices, and reward systems play an important role in satisfying employee needs and promoting autonomous regulation (Gagné & Deci, 2005). When jobs are designed to be more stimulating and meaningful, they are associated with high employee need satisfaction (Gagné et al., 1997). When managers act as transformational leaders, employees regulate their work goals more autonomously, and trust the organization more (Deci et al., 1989; Bono & Judge, 2003). Specific managerial behaviors have been found to be associated with employee engagement through the satisfaction of psychological needs (Parfyonova, 2009). Having choice on how to complete work tasks satisfies the need for autonomy. Setting expectations, explaining the purpose of work to employees, and providing performance feedback increases employee perceptions of competence which translates into higher levels of engagement and helping behaviors at work. Thus, managers should provide employees with direction for performance but let them decide themselves how to accomplish work tasks. Also, managers should create interaction opportunities and show personal concern for their needs, which will make employees feel more related to others at work (Vallerand, 2000).

When rewards and recognition are given to convey employee competence, and not to control employee behavior, they can increase autonomous motivation (Gagné & Forest, 2008). In other words, rewards that inform the employee about performance level are likely to increase autonomous motivation, while reward systems that require close behavior monitoring are likely to increase controlled motivation. Among the recommendations for setting a motivating reward system are that rewards be distributed equitably (Gagné et al., 2007) and that base pay be above the market average to enhance social comparisons and perceptions of justice (Kuvaas, 2006). Gagné and Forest (2008) also pointed out that group-based incentives and profit-sharing compensation systems are more likely to satisfy employee needs, in particular the need for relatedness, than individual incentives and commission-based systems. The latter tend to promote individualistic and competitive organizational culture, which induce controlled motivation.

As noted earlier, research pertaining to TCM has led to the identification of several workplace factors that are instrumental in the development of a strong affective and normative commitment to organizations (Meyer et al., 2002). Many of these factors are similar to those identified by the research on SDT. For instance, one of the strongest situational influences on employee affective and normative commitment is fair treatment of employees by their supervisor. It is recommended that managers treat employees with dignity and respect and provide them with sufficient information about decisions and processes in the organization.

Another workplace factor that bears on employee affective and normative commitment is transformational leadership (Bycio et al., 1995; Meyer et al., 2002). Employees become affectively attached to their organization and feel obligated to stay and contribute to it when leaders provide them with inspiring vision, intellectual stimulation, and individualized consideration. To build an engaged workforce, organizations are advised to train their managers on principles of interactional justice (that is, fair supervisory treatment) (Skarlicki & Latham, 1996) and transformational leadership (Barling et al., 1996).

Again, as is the case with autonomous motivation, a supportive and team-oriented organizational culture is likely to stimulate the development of affective and normative forms of employee commitment (Vandenberghe & Peiró, 1999). When employees perceive their organization as supportive, they are likely to reciprocate positive organizational treatment with a greater desire and obligation to stay in the organization and contribute to its success (Meyer et al., 2002).

This list of factors that can be leveraged to create a climate for engagement is by no means complete. Moreover, space does not permit us to elaborate on the specific strategies that organizations can use to take advantage of these factors. However, many of the major contributors to engagement that we reviewed here have received extensive research in their own right, and follow-up reviews of this research will provide a much broader range of strategies than we could provide here. Also, an essential component of our model is the satisfaction of the basic psychological needs identified in SDT. Organizations can evaluate any particular strategy or practice for its engagement potential by carefully considering whether and how it is likely to contribute to the satisfaction of employees' needs for relatedness, competence, and autonomy.

References

Baard, P.P., Deci, E.L. & Ryan, R.R. (2004), "Intrinsic need satisfaction: a motivational basis of performance and well-being in two work settings", *Journal of Applied Social Psychology*, **34**, 2045–68.

Barling, J., Weber, T. & Kelloway, K. (1996), "Effects of transformational leadership training on attendance and financial outcomes: a field experiment", *Journal of Applied Psychology*, **81**, 827–32.

Bateman, T.S. & Crant, J.M. (1993), "The proactive component of organizational behavior", *Journal of Organizational Behavior*, **14**, 103–18.

Bono, J.E. & Judge, T.A. (2003), "Self-concordance at work: toward understanding the motivational effects of transformational leaders", *Academy of Management Journal*, **46**, 554–71.

Bycio, P., Hackett, R.D. & Allen, J.S. (1995), "Further assessments of Bass's (1985) conceptualization of transactional and transformational leadership", *Journal of Applied Psychology*, **80**, 468–78.

Collins, J.C. & Porras, J.I. (1996), *Built to Last: Successful Habits of Visionary Companies*, New York: Harper Business.

Deci, E.L., Connell, J.P. & Ryan, R.M. (1989), "Self-determination theory in a work organization", *Journal of Applied Psychology*, **74**, 580–90.

Deci, E.L., Koestner, R. & Ryan, R.M (1999), "A meta-analytic review of experiments

6 Engagement as a motivational construct
Ilke Inceoglu and Steven Fleck

Introduction

A "motivated" workforce is clearly viewed as desirable in any organization, especially when it is facing more pressure to perform and increase organizational effectiveness. In this context, employee motivation and in particular work engagement have become popular concepts that are widely discussed and applied by human resources (HR) practitioners, consultancy firms and survey companies.

When practitioners and academics discuss work motivation, however, they tend to refer to different meanings of the term, ranging from being motivated by something (motivators), the actual feeling of being motivated (engagement), to the effort employees put into their work (motivated behavior). This confusion is heightened by the fact that the term "engagement" itself is often not properly defined (Macey & Schneider, 2008). As a result, practitioners are left to wonder about the difference between engagement and motivation and the value of measuring either or both in applied settings.

The objective of this chapter is to clarify the meanings of engagement and motivation and their relationships with each other by placing them in a motivational framework. Efforts to define engagement and delineate it from other constructs should prompt revisiting conceptualizations of motivation which are often ambiguous. Contemporary theoretical models and debates in motivational research (see, for example, Kanfer et al., 2008) offer approaches that help to clarify what we mean by motivation.

The engagement model proposed in the chapter by Fleck and Inceoglu (ch. 3, this volume) can be viewed as a motivational continuum, with stable, dispositional motivation at one pole and situational motivation at the other. Applying this continuum, conceptual and empirical relationships between engagement and stable, trait-like motivation are examined in this chapter. This helps to understand the nomological network of engagement within a motivational framework. The practical benefit of such a conceptual exercise is that it helps practitioners to decide on the construct that is more appropriate for a given context such as selection, staff development or employee surveys.

Engagement defined
Following approaches by Kahn (1990) and Schaufeli et al. (2006), engagement is defined as a psychological state that has a cognitive and an affective component (thinking and feeling). The cognitive and affective emphasis are captured here by the following two facets of engagement: *absorption* (being absorbed by one's work), which is more cognitive in nature, and *energy* (drawing energy from work, feeling energized), which has a stronger affective side. Engagement can also be defined in relation to a broader target, namely the organization (see Fleck & Inceoglu, ch. 3, this volume), but the focus in this chapter is on job engagement.

Defined as a state, absorption and energy can change across situations (Kahn, 1990), depending on work-context variables (for example, interesting work, having autonomy to organize one's work activities), occurrences outside work (for example, moving home) and a person's daily constitution (for example, feeling tired, being in a good mood). Feeling absorbed and energized is likely to lead to certain behaviors such as applying a lot of effort at work (in-role task effort) and going beyond the formal requirements of one's job (extra-role behaviors). These behaviors can be viewed as motivated behaviors, covering even more situational aspects of motivation on the conceptual continuum. Trait-like, dispositional motivation on the other hand – located at the other pole of the continuum – is expected to be enduring and to remain relatively stable across different situations.

A trait–state distinction in relation to engagement has been proposed by Macey and Schneider (2008) who explicitly defined state, trait and behavioral engagement as separate constructs. Trait engagement refers to personality constructs such as conscientiousness, proactive personality and trait positive affect, while state engagement includes feelings of energy, absorption, satisfaction, involvement, commitment and empowerment. Behavioral engagement is conceptualized as extra-role behavior, organizational citizenship behavior, personal initiative, role expansion and adaptive behaviors. As Vosburgh (2008, p. 73) succinctly put it, "state-trait engagement is powerful and explains it all. Perhaps the behavioral engagement is really the observable performance outcome that the combination of trait and state engagement creates". We concur with that view and expand on this idea by placing it into a motivational framework that is visualized as a motivational continuum (Figure 6.1).

Engagement as state motivation
Kahn observed: "in engagement, people employ and express themselves physically, cognitively, and emotionally during role performances" (1990, p. 694). Similarly, Schaufeli et al. defined work engagement as a "positive,

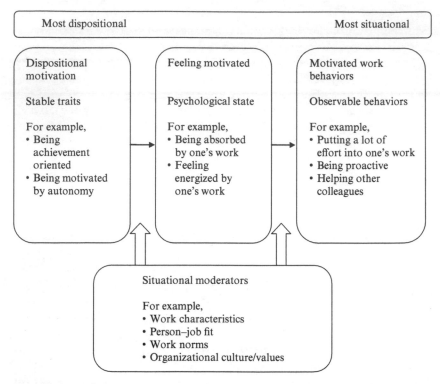

Figure 6.1   A motivational continuum model

fulfilling work-related state of mind that is characterized by vigor, dedication, and absorption" (2006, p. 702). Both definitions emphasize that engagement is a state that, as a consequence, should fluctuate over time, particularly in response to situational changes (for example, structural changes in the organization).

According to Schaufeli et al., however, engagement is not a momentary and very short-lived state, but "a more persistent and pervasive affective–cognitive state that is not focused on any particular object, event, individual, or behavior" (p. 702), which implies changeability but not erratic oscillation. To some extent the variability of engagement will depend on the specified timeframe within which it is measured: diary-type studies, for example, (using the Schaufeli et al. scale) show that engagement levels can change within a week (Sonnentag, 2003) and even within a day (Xanthopoulou et al., 2009). Measured within a longer period of time (explicitly worded in the instructions), engagement levels may reflect an accumulated series of states which form a baseline level of engagement, tapping into more trait-like aspects of engagement. On the motivational continuum such measures would be closer to dispositional motivation.

Common to both definitions is also the observation that engagement is a positive, activity-related state. This can be illustrated by comparing it to job satisfaction, a construct that is often used alongside engagement or even misleadingly labeled "engagement" in practical applications such as organizational surveys. Job engagement and job satisfaction can be placed in the well-established affective circumplex (Russell, 2003; Warr, 2007) which describes affect along the two axes of arousal and pleasure. Combining these two axes results in four main quadrants: activated positive affect (enthusiasm), activated negative affect (anxiety), low activation negative affect (depression) and low activation positive affect (contentment, satisfaction).

Although the affective side of engagement shares much variance with job satisfaction (for example, Newman & Harrison, 2008), both constructs can be placed in different quadrants of the affective circumplex. While engagement emphasizes the activated side of positive affect, job satisfaction refers to a more passive (low activated) positive affective state.

There are two implications of this. First, engagement may be more strongly associated with both in-role performance as well as more proactive, extra-role work behaviors, as has been indicated by existing research (for example, Rich et al., 2010). Job satisfaction, on the other hand, is likely to show some relationships with in-role performance (see Judge et al., 2001), but lower associations with proactive behaviors, as it more concerns contentment and implicitly keeping up the status quo. Second, each affective state would be expected to be differentially predicted by different antecedents.

In summary, we argue that work engagement is a positive cognitive–affective state that is activated (that is, involving higher arousal levels) and is likely to result in activated ("motivated") work behavior. On the motivational continuum we would therefore view engagement as state motivation. This is similar to the way Rich et al. (2010) view engagement by drawing on Kahn's (1990) perspective, that engagement is a motivational construct that leads to specific resource allocation. In other words, when individuals feel engaged at work, they are more likely to allocate personal resource to specific work activities.

Motivated work behavior

Moving towards the situational pole on the motivational continuum, we locate motivated work behavior. What makes these behaviors "motivated" is that they are active, positive and directed towards a desirable work outcome, be it the accomplishment of a work task or helping a colleague in need. They are relevant for work performance, leading to organizational effectiveness in an aggregated form.

Similar to the state of engagement, motivated work behaviors can change. Seo et al. (2004) suggested that feelings at work can affect three dimensions of behavioral outcomes at work: direction, intensity and persistence. Hence how we feel can influence how we behave and whether we allocate a lot of resource to a specific task. Changes in work behavior across situations may also be attributed to context variables (see Roe, 1999; Kanfer et al., 2008), such as work characteristics (for example, Warr, 2007) and organizational norms. For example, having good material resources required for completing a specific task and working in a high-performance culture are likely to enhance work behavior. On our motivational continuum, context variables are viewed as moderators (see Figure 6.1) that can influence relationships between dispositional motivation, state motivation and motivated work behaviors.

There are a range of behaviors that can be grouped under motivated work behaviors and two examples are in-role task effort (working hard, job dedication: Van Scotter & Motowidlo, 1996) and extra-role behavior (organizational citizenship behaviors: Organ, 1997; extra-role-behavior: Van Dyne et al., 1995). Measured over a longer timeframe these behaviors are also likely to reflect some more stable aspects of dispositional motivation (conscientiousness, achievement orientation).

Additional conceptualizations of work performance behaviors can also be classified as motivated work behaviors, including contextual performance (Borman & Motowidlo, 1997), prosocial organizational behavior (Brief & Motowidlo, 1986), proactive behaviors (Crant, 2000), creativity (see Parker & Ohly, 2008 for a discussion) and competencies (Bartram, 2005), defined as "sets of behaviors that are instrumental in the delivery of desired results or outcomes" (Bartram et al., 2002, p. 7). Griffin et al. (2007) proposed a model of work role performance that combines different individual work role behaviors (proficiency, adaptivity and proactivity), with three levels at which these behaviors are targeted (individual, team and organizational). Griffin et al. (2008) suggested using this model for structuring work role behaviors related to engagement (Griffin et al., 2007). The term "work performance" covers a wide array of definitions but our conceptualization of motivated work behaviors focuses on the process side of performance, whereby people try to achieve a given work goal (Roe, 1999).

To summarize, we place motivated work behaviors, which are active and directed towards a positive outcome such as behaviors valued by the organization, at the very situational side of the motivational continuum. These behaviors can be measured at a generic (for example, overall task performance, contextual work behaviors) or specific level (for example, specific competencies, domain-specific behaviors).

Dispositional motivation

At the other pole of the motivational continuum we locate stable traits such as motivation (see Figure 6.1). Similar to state motivation (engagement), dispositional motivation also involves an evaluative, cognitive–affective process. In contrast to state motivation, this process is more stable and can be attributed to stable schemata as proposed by Mischel and Shoda (1998).

There are many approaches to motivation in the literature and, using Kanfer et al.'s (2008) distinction between content, context and change, these approaches would fall under the content theme, which "provide the foundation for frequently studied individual difference determinants of motivation, such as needs, motives, traits, and values" (p. 9). Examples of such approaches include the "desire to learn and desire for personal mastery" (Kanfer & Ackerman, 2000), "ambitiousness" (Byrne et al., 2004), conceptualizations of perseverance (for example, Duckworth et al., 2007), achievement orientation and theories emphasizing human needs (for example, Murray, 1938; Maslow, 1954; Alderfer, 1972; McClelland, 1985).

Although different in their conceptualizations of specific content (for example, needs, motives, perseverance) all these approaches have in common that individuals have a range of stable motivators which can be specific, targeted (for example, being motivated by difficult goals in particular area) or broad (being achievement oriented). Dispositional, stable motivation can hence be viewed as encompassing broad or specific motivators which tend to be stable across situations. This would explain, for example, why some people always appear to be more achievement oriented than others, no matter what situation they are in.

Different conceptualizations of dispositional motivation have been linked to performance behaviors, which may be grouped under motivated work behaviors at the other end of the motivation continuum depicted in Figure 6.1. Motivated behavior (for example, working hard) in turn is likely to lead to certain performance outcomes (for example, successfully accomplishing a work task). In line with this, stable, trait-like motivation has been found to explain individual differences in performance (Duckworth et al., 2007). For example, Duckworth et al. reported that the perseverance aspect of motivation ("grit") predicted performance in an educational as well as a military context. Furthermore, Baum and Locke (2004) examined the effect of entrepreneurial traits, skill, and motivation on subsequent business growth. Goals, self-efficacy, and communicated vision had direct effects on business growth and these factors mediated the effects of passion, tenacity and new resource skill on subsequent growth. O'Reilly and Chatman (1994) found that in combination with ability, motivation predicted managerial job success measured by higher salaries, more promotions and more rapid pay increases. Moreover, managerial achievement motivation correlated positively with nurse job satisfaction and productivity, and patient satisfaction in healthcare in a study by McNeese-Smith (1999).

Relationships between dispositional motivation and motivated work behavior are, however, not always strong, although they incrementally explain variance in performance after controlling for cognitive ability and personality (Duckworth et al., 2007). For dispositional motivation to be translated into motivated behavior, the work environment has to be right (good "fit"), which will then give rise to motivated states (state motivation: engagement) that lead to motivated behavior.

Some propositions from the motivational continuum
Why should engagement be viewed within a motivational framework? It helps to understand the similarities and differences between engagement, dispositional trait-like motivation and motivated behavior. Using the motivational continuum we can explain what we mean by motivation and engagement, why dispositional motivation (that is, "highly motivated employees") may not always lead to performance (motivated work behavior) and what differentiates engagement from other constructs such as job satisfaction.

The motivational continuum enables us to make specific testable propositions about the relationships between different conceptualizations of motivation. To illustrate this, we make three specific propositions:

Proposition 1: As dispositional, trait-like motivation is more stable across different situations than engagement, we expect relationships between the two constructs to be moderately high.

Proposition 2: Both trait-like motivation and state motivation (engagement) have been shown to be related to motivated work behaviors. However, as engagement and motivated work behaviors are both more situation specific (more closely located on the continuum), we expect relationships with motivated work behaviors to be higher for engagement than for dispositional motivation.

Proposition 3: When controlling for dispositional motivation (that is, keeping people's dispositional motivation constant) in predicting performance, engagement will account for additional variance in motivated work behavior over and above dispositional motivation.

We collected data that enabled us to do some preliminary investigation of these propositions. As discussed earlier, motivated work behaviors can encompass a wide range of behaviors. Here we focus on two: *effort* (working hard) and *extra-role behavior* (going beyond the formal requirements of the job).

An empirical test of the propositions
The data are based on 307 working people from a wide range of industry sectors (for example, banking, education, financial services, health services) and business functions (for example, finance, information technology (IT), Accounting, Customer Services) who completed an online questionnaire which they accessed through a website for practicing tests for selection and development. The sample was composed as follows: 44 percent were women and the mean age (age bands were used) ranged from 30 to 34 years with 56.68 percent of participants being between 25 and 39 years old. Average tenure in current job was 4.03 years (SD = 5.40) and average tenure in organization 5.08 years (SD = 6.51).

Measures
To measure dispositional motivation we used the SHL Motivation Questionnaire (MQ; SHL, 1992, 2002). The MQ assesses individual differences in motivational strengths on 18 dimensions (eight items per dimension, 144 items in total). Respondents are asked to rate each statement as to how it would affect their motivation to work, for example, "having challenges to overcome" (achievement), or "being required to help other people" (affiliation). Reliabilities that are reported in the manual (SHL, 2002) range from 0.66 to 0.85 with a median of 0.75.

The two aspects of job engagement (absorption and energy) were each measured through 3-item scales which had alpha coefficients of 0.85 and 0.90, respectively. In addition, participants rated themselves on their effort (working hard, putting full effort into one's job: alpha = 0.92) and extra-role behavior (for example, helping co-workers, identifying new ways of improving work methods: alpha = 0.72). Effort and extra-role behavior were also measured through three items each (alpha = 0.92 and 0.72, respectively).

Results
Before analyzing the data, MQ and engagement scales were mapped in terms of content, following procedures by Warr (1999). Three subject matter experts rated the conceptual overlap between scale pairs of the motivation questionnaire and the two engagement facets based on item content using a 5-point continuum ranging from −2 to +2 (see ibid.). +2

indicated high positive conceptual overlap, −2 high negative conceptual overlap and 0 indicated that no conceptual overlap was evident. These mappings were carried out as it is not surprising to find moderate relationships for scale pairs that are very different in content.

As expected, moderate correlations were found for predicted MQ and engagement scale pairs with an average of 0.21 and a median of 0.27. When averaging correlations for different concordance levels, highly concordant scale pairs yielded higher correlations compared to low concordant pairs: +2: 0.25, +1: 0.19, 0 (absolute values): 0.09, −1 and −2: no predictions made. The highest correlation (r = 0.42) was observed for energy and the MQ scale immersion which is about being motivated by work that requires commitment beyond normal working hours.

Testing the second proposition, engagement and MQ scale pairs that were conceptually concordant (concordance of +1 and +2), were correlated with effort and extra-role behavior. All engagement and most MQ scales correlated positively and significantly with effort and extra-role behavior (see Table 6.1). As predicted, correlations were higher for the engagement scales (average: 0.51, maximum: 0.64) compared to the MQ scales (average 0.20, maximum: 0.39).

To test the third proposition, two separate linear hierarchical regression analyses were carried out with effort and extra-role behavior as the dependent variables. Conceptually concordant MQ scales were entered in step 1 and the engagement scales in step 2. In each of these regression analyses MQ scales significantly predicted effort as well as extra-role behavior and absorption and energy incrementally accounted for variance well above the MQ scales ($\Delta r^2 = 0.19$ and 0.26, respectively, $p < 0.001$). Multiple rs were 0.66 for effort ($r^2 = 0.43$, adjusted $r^2 = 0.41$) and 0.72 for extra-role behavior ($r^2 = 0.52$, adjusted $r^2 = 0.50$) indicating that a significant amount of the variance in effort and extra-role behavior could be explained by dispositional motivation and engagement.

Summary and conclusions
Engagement is often referred to in general terms as a "motivational construct". Here, we propose that the precise meaning of engagement as a motivational construct can be classified by locating it within a motivational framework. Conceptually, motivation can be visualized as a continuum, ranging from stable trait-like motivation (being motivated by something) to situation-specific state motivation (feeling engaged) and behavioral motivation (showing motivated work behaviors).

Applying this approach, we empirically tested three propositions which explored the relationships between trait-like motivation, engagement and motivated behavior and were confirmed by our study:

Table 6.1   Correlations between concordant MQ and engagement scales and effort and extra-role behavior (N = 307)

Dispositional motivation MQ scale (being motivated by. . .)	Effort	Extra-role behavior
Level of activity (working under pressure, coping with multiple demands)	0.333***	0.369***
Achievement (challenging targets, feeling that abilities are stretched)	0.307***	0.339***
Competition (working in competitive environment)	0.300***	0.277***
Fear of failure (fear of failing on a task, being exposed to criticism and negative judgments by others)	0.307***	0.254***
Power (exercising authority, taking responsibility)	0.188**	0.388***
Immersion (work which requires commitment way beyond "normal" working hours)	0.271***	0.285***
Personal growth (opportunities for further training and development and the acquisition of new skills)	0.144*	0.173**
Interest (variety, interesting tasks and stimulation)	0.020	0.191**
Autonomy (opportunities for further training and development and the acquisition of new skills)	0.037	0.162**
Progression (having good promotion prospects)	0.055	0.061

Engagement	Effort	Extra-role behavior
Absorption (being absorbed by one's work)	0.434***	0.505***
Energy (feeling energized by one's work)	0.589***	0.639***

Note: *** $p < 0.001$, ** $p < 0.01$, * $p < 0.05$.

1. Scales measuring dispositional motivation showed moderate relationships with the two engagement scales energy and absorption. Higher correlations were observed for scale pairs that were conceptually matched. This supports the assertion that dispositional motivation and engagement overlap, as both measure a form of motivation, but that they are also distinct, as engagement taps into state motivation which is more situation specific and likely to change over time and across different situations.
2. As predicted, correlations with motivated work behavior (effort and

extra-role behavior) were higher for engagement than dispositional, trait-like motivation. We suggested this to be the case as engagement and motivated work behaviors are more closely located on the motivational continuum, both being to some extent situation specific.
3. Both trait-like motivation and engagement were positively related to motivated work behavior. As hypothesized, engagement incrementally predicted effort and extra-role behavior over and above conceptually concordant dispositional motivation scales, indicating that both measure different aspects of motivation accounting for unique variance.

Although supporting our propositions, the results do not provide conclusive evidence. The empirical study was a first attempt to empirically test some of the conceptual propositions discussed and we are aware that it has several limitations. First, being entirely based on self-report data, results might be inflated by potential common source and common-method bias. External ratings of effort and extra-role behavior, for example, would be desirable here. Second, only two forms of motivated work behavior were measured while a whole range of other behaviors can be included. Third, this study relied on a set of specific instruments and one sample only, which makes generalization difficult. Nevertheless, the motivational continuum allows for specific propositions to be tested and initial results provide some preliminary support. There are also practical implications that can be drawn from the conceptual framework and the results.

Practical implications
A motivational framework that distinguishes between stable, dispositional motivation (being motivated by something), feeling motivated (engagement) and motivated behaviors (for example, effort and extra-role behaviors) helps to clarify the relationships between the engagement and motivation conceptually – and as an implication – to use them in a more targeted way in applied settings. A practical implication is that specific constructs can be selected for specific applications (for example, selection, staff development, employee survey) and measured more effectively (criterion specificity: for example, Brunswik, 1956; Ajzen & Fishbein, 1980). Emphasizing the usefulness of the engagement state/trait distinction, Vosburgh (2008, p. 73) draws the following practical conclusions: "To apply this, if I select for 'trait engagement', and then I create the conditions for quality performance (variety, autonomy, challenge, etc.) to produce "state engagement" the result will be performance leading to satisfaction. When we create this high-performance culture, the organization wins and the individual wins".

In combination, dispositional and state measures of motivation are likely to help explain more variation in performance than one measure alone supporting approaches that emphasize person–situation interaction (for example, Mischel & Shoda, 1995). In certain settings only the application of one measure might be feasible, such as deploying a dispositional motivation instrument for selection and assessment. To help understand employee performance in the life cycle better, however, state-specific measures of motivation can support employee development.

References

Ajzen, I. & Fishbein, M. (1980), *Understanding Attitudes and Predicting Social Behavior*, Englewood Cliffs, NJ: Prentice-Hall.

Alderfer, C. (1972), *Existence, Relatedness, and Growth*, New York: Free Press.

Bartram, D. (2005), "The Great 8 competencies: a criterion-centric approach to validation", *Journal of Applied Psychology*, **90**, 1185–203.

Bartram, D., Robertson, I.T. & Callinan, M. (2002), "Introduction: a framework for examining organizational effectiveness", in I.T. Robertson, M. Callinan & D. Bartram (eds), *Organizational Effectiveness: The Role of Psychology*, Chichester: John Wiley & Sons, pp. 1–10.

Baum, J.R. & Locke, E.A. (2004), "The relationship of entrepreneurial traits, skill, and motivation to subsequent venture growth", *Journal of Applied Psychology*, **89**(4), 587–98.

Borman, W.C. & Motowidlo, S.J. (1997), "Task performance and contextual performance: the meaning for personnel selection research", *Human Performance*, **10**, 99–109.

Brief, A.P. & Motowidlo, S.J. (1986), "Prosocial organizational behaviors", *Academy of Management Review*, **11**, 710–25.

Brunswik, E. (1956), *Perception and the Representative Design of Psychological Experiments*, Berkeley, CA: University of California Press.

Byrne, Z.S., Mueller-Hanson, R.A., Cardador, J.M., Thornton, G.C., Schuler, H., Frintup, A. & Fox, S. (2004), "Measuring achievement motivation: tests of equivalency for English, German, and Israeli versions of the achievement motivation inventory", *Personality and Individual Differences*, **37**, 203–17.

Crant, J.M. (2000), "Proactive behavior in organizations", *Journal of Management*, **26**, 435–62.

Duckworth, A.L., Peterson, C., Matthews, M.D. & Kelly, D.R. (2007), "Grit: perseverance and passion for long-term goals", *Journal of Personality and Social Psychology*, **92**, 1087–101.

Griffin, M.A., Neal., A. & Parker, S.K. (2007), "A new model of work role performance: positive behavior in uncertain and interdependent contexts", *Academy of Management Journal*, **50**, 327–47.

Griffin, M.A., Parker, S.K. & Neal, A. (2008), "Is behavioral engagement a distinct and useful construct?", *Industrial and Organizational Psychology*, **1**, 48–51.

Judge, T.A., Thoreson, C.J., Bono, J.E. & Patton, G.K. (2001), "The job satisfaction–job performance relationship: a qualitative and quantitative review", *Psychological Bulletin*, **127**, 376–407.

Kahn, W. (1990), "Psychological conditions of personal engagement and disengagement at work", *Academy of Management Journal*, **33**(4), 692–724.

Kanfer, R. & Ackerman, P.L. (2000), "Individual differences in work motivation: further explorations of a trait framework", *Applied Psychology: An International Review*, **49**, 470–82.

Kanfer, R., Chen, G. & Pritchard, R.D. (2008), "The three C's of work motivation: Content, Context, and Change", in R. Kanfer, G. Chen & R. Pritchard (eds), *Work Motivation: Past, Present, and Future*, New York: Psychology Press, pp. 1–16.

Macey, W.H. & Schneider, B. (2008), "The meaning of employee engagement", *Industrial and Organizational Psychology*, **1**, 3–30.

Maslow, A. (1954), *Motivation and Personality*, New York: Harper.

McClelland, D.C. (1985), *Human Motivation*, Glenview, IL: Scott, Foresman.

McNeese-Smith, D.K. (1999), "The relationship between managerial motivation, leadership, nurse outcomes and patient satisfaction", *Journal of Organizational Behavior*, **20**, 243–59.

Mischel, W. & Shoda, Y. (1995), "A cognitive–affective system theory of personality: reconceptualizing situations, dispositions, dynamics, and invariance in personality structure", *Psychological Review*, **102**, 246–68.

Mischel, W. & Shoda, Y. (1998), "Reconciling processing dynamics and personality dispositions", *Annual Review of Psychology*, **49**, 229–58.

Murray, H.A. (1938), *Explorations in Personality*, New York: Oxford University Press.

Newman, D.A. & Harrison, D.A. (2008), "Been there, bottled that: are state and behavioral work enagagement new and useful construct 'wines'?", *Industrial and Organizational Psychology*, **1**, 31–5.

O'Reilly, C. & Chatman, J. (1994), "Working harder and smarter: a longitudinal study of early career success", *Administrative Science Quarterly*, **39**, 603–27.

Organ, D.W. (1997), "Organizational citizenship behavior: it's construct clean-up time", *Human Performance*, **10**, 85–97.

Parker, S.K. & Ohly, S. (2008), "Designing motivating jobs: an expanded framework for linking work characteristics and motivation", in R. Kanfer, G. Chen & R.D. Pritchard (eds), *Work Motivation: Past, Present, and Future*, New York: Routledge, Taylor & Francis Group, pp. 233–84.

Rich, B.L., Lepine, J.A. & Crawford, E.R. (2010), "Job engagement: antecedents and effects on job performance", *Academy of Management Journal*, **53**.

Roe, R.A. (1999), "Work performance. a multiple regulation perspective", in G. Cooper & I.T. Robertson (eds), *International Review of Industrial and Organizational Psychology*, Vol. 14, Chichester: Wiley, pp. 231–335.

Russell, J.A. (2003), "Core affect and the psychological construction of emotion", *Psychological Review*, **110**, 145–72.

Schaufeli, W.B., Bakker, A. & Salanova, M. (2006), "The measurement of work engagement with a short questionnaire: a cross-national study", *Educational and Psychological Measurement*, **66**, 701–16.

Seo, M., Barrett, L.F. & Bartunek, J.M. (2004), "The role of affective experience in work motivation", *Academy of Management*, **29**, 423–39.

Sonnentag, S. (2003), "Recovery, work engagement, and proactive behavior: a new look at the interface between work and non-work", *Journal of Applied Psychology*, **88**, 518–28.

Van Dyne, L., Cummings, L.L. & McLean Parks, J. (1995), "Extra-role behaviors: in pursuit of construct and definitional clarity", in L.L. Cummings & B.M. Staw (eds), *Research in Organizational Behavior*, Greenwich, CT: JAI Press, pp. 215–85.

Van Scotter, J.R. & Motowidlo, S.J. (1996), "Interpersonal facilitation and job dedication as separate facets of contextual performance", *Journal of Applied Psychology*, **81**, 525–31.

Vosburgh, R.M. (2008), "State–trait returns! And one practitioner's request", *Industrial and Organizational Psychology*, **1**, 72–3.

Warr, P.B. (1999), "Logical and judgmental moderators of the criterion-related validity of personality scales", *Journal of Occupational and Organizational Psychology*, **72**, 187–204.

Warr, P.B. (2007), *Work, Happiness, and Unhappiness*, New York: Routledge.

Xanthopoulou, D., Bakker, A.B., Demerouti, E. & Schaufeli, W.B. (2009), "Work engagement and financial returns: a diary study on the role of job and personal resources", *Journal of Occupational and Organizational Psychology*, **82**(1), 183–200.

7 Measuring change: does engagement flourish, fade, or stay true?

Helena D. Cooper-Thomas, Nicola Leighton, Jessica Xu and Neal Knight-Turvey[*]

Introduction: how is employee engagement used?

Employee engagement has emerged as a useful, practical construct, with many organizations keen to measure and benchmark their employees' level of engagement. A variety of engagement measures exist, and these overlap in their core elements of "involvement, commitment, passion, enthusiasm, focused effort, and energy" (Macey & Schneider, 2008, p. 4). These measures help provide answers to a number of questions that employers, managers, and Human Resources have about whether employee engagement is flourishing or fading in their organizations. Questions include: (1) How engaged are my employees? (2) Are there specific areas that I should work on to increase engagement? (3) Are my employees showing changes in engagement over time? (4) Are there differences in employee engagement across departments in my organization? And (5) how does my organization compare with other organizations in this industry? Many consultancies and survey organizations have engagement measures which they use to provide answers to such questions. Typically, the same engagement measure is used with all clients, enabling the comparative analyses that provide answers to questions about changes and differences across groups and time (as in (3), (4), and (5) above). Analyses usually involve direct comparisons of the measures, for example, comparing the difference between the mean engagement scores of two departments using a *t*-test. This implicitly assumes that the underlying survey instrument is stable, yet this assumption of stability may be mistaken. In this chapter, we argue that researchers should explicitly test the stability of their engagement survey instrument so that analyses of change, and comparisons across groups, can be represented accurately. We provide a brief example (see Box 7.1, below) as an initial introduction to one procedure for assessing change.

What are the issues with engagement score comparisons?

There are three types of change that may be found in any multiple item composite measure that is compared across datasets. These are known as alpha, beta, and gamma (ABG) change (Golembiewski et al., 1976).

Table 7.1   JRA's engagement measure

Likert scale			
1	3	5	6
strongly disagree	neutral	strongly agree	do not know*

JRA EE1: I look for ways to do my job more effectively
JRA EE2: Overall, I'm satisfied with my job
JRA EE3: I take an active interest in what happens in this organisation
JRA EE4: I feel inspired to go the extra mile to help this organisation succeed
JRA EE5: I feel a sense of commitment to this organisation
JRA EE6: Overall, I would recommend this organisation as a great place to work

Note: * coded as missing.

Source: JRA (2009).

These types of change are particularly relevant to measures of engagement because many organizations are focused on improving their employees' engagement. Improvements are desirable because higher levels of engagement are associated with individual benefits, such as improved well-being and reduced turnover intention (Halberg & Schaufeli, 2006; Viljevac et al., 2010), and organizational benefits, including better employee performance, customer service, and profit (Harter et al., 2002; Salanova et al., 2005; Xanthopoulou et al., 2009). Hence, in comparing any engagement measure across two or more groups of data – whether those data are from the same or different people (as in examples 3, 4, and 5 above) – issues of ABG change should be considered.

Employers who undertake regular employee engagement surveys hope to see increases in scores over time. Assuming that the engagement measure is stable in other respects, this reflects true change, also called "alpha change" (Golembiewski et al., 1976). However, two other types of change may also occur. First, it is possible that respondents change their interpretation of the measurement scale, known as "beta change" (ibid.). For example, take the behavioral engagement item "I feel inspired to go the extra mile to help this organisation succeed" (JRA engagement survey, 2008; see Table 7.1 for the full measure) measured on a typical Likert scale from 1 "strongly disagree" through to 5 "strongly agree". At the first engagement measurement, respondents in an organization may feel that they are not exceptionally inspired, and may provide a rating of 3. However, engagement workshops may provide respondents with an opportunity to reconsider the ways in which they are positively influenced to behave more proactively. At the subsequent measurement, with no actual change in the degree to which they do their job more effectively, there has been a change in their accounting of this, and they may choose a rating of 4. Hence, the measurement points on the Likert scale have been recalibrated from one measurement time to the next, without any actual change in the underlying behavior. Under these circumstances, mean score change analyses may be meaningless (Millsap & Hartog, 1988).

A second issue is that scores may also be influenced by gamma change, which refers to a reconceptualization of the underlying construct (Golembiewski et al., 1976). In this case, an intervention (such as an engagement workshop) may influence how employees understand what engagement is. Using the same behavioral engagement item again, "I feel inspired to go the extra mile to help this organisation succeed", following an engagement intervention, respondents might have a broader understanding of organization success. Therefore, their responses will be relative to this reconceptualized criterion and, given that the criterion has changed, scale response changes are again meaningless (Millsap & Hartog, 1988).[1] In summary, changes in scores across datasets (for example, time, departments) may be due to "true change" (alpha), change in the calibration of the measurement scale (beta), or change in how respondents think about the underlying construct(s) (gamma). All these types of change may be the result of organizational efforts to improve levels of engagement (Golembiewski et al.); however, only alpha change represents a true shift in the level of a stable measure of engagement.

How can alpha, beta and gamma change be identified?
There are various methods for detecting ABG change (Millsap & Hartog, 1988; Vandenberg & Lance, 2000). Of these, confirmatory factor analysis offers the best combination of flexibility and accuracy, as it can be used to compare within groups across time, or across groups, and requires a minimum of only two comparisons (Riordan et al., 2001). In Box 7.1, we provide an illustration of the confirmatory factor analysis procedures using data from an engagement measure at two time points. Given the overlap of engagement measures (Macey & Schneider, 2008), assessing any one measure of employee engagement provides useful information about patterns of change. In this research, we take the predominant measure of employee engagement used by New Zealand companies, published by JRA.

Do beta and gamma changes affect alpha change: is it valid to compare across engagement surveys?
The results of our analyses suggest that engagement measures can show stability in their underlying measurement structures over time. This is good

---

BOX 7.1   AN EXAMPLE OF ABG CHANGE USING
JRA'S ENGAGEMENT MEASURE

JRA's employee engagement measure has six items, with two items each measuring behavioral, cognitive, and emotional engagement, respectively. This follows Kahn's (1990, 1992) conceptualization of engagement, which is the basis for a number of other commercial and academic engagement measures. The questions and scale are included in Table 7.1.

Some 2,820 participants, from 42 organizations in New Zealand and Australia, were matched from JRA's 2007 and 2008 databases. We decided to control for the potential confound of the onset of the Recession, which might have improved people's attitudes to work, for example promoting gratitude for being employed. Hence, we included only complete data that was collected before 27 September 2008, being the official start of the Recession in this region (Oliver, 2008). The demographics are based on those responding at 2007; percentages do not add up to 100 percent due to non-response. The sample comprised 40.5 percent males, and 46.6 percent females; 52.5 percent of whom held lower-level positions in their organizations, and 23.5 percent were in senior positions. Median age was 30–39 years.[2]

Analysis strategy
In brief, there are four stages for identifying whether and where change is present (Schmitt, 1982; Vandenberg & Self, 1993; Vandenberg & Lance, 2000).[3] The first, preliminary phase, examines the null hypothesis that the variance–covariance matrices are equal over time, which would indicate an absence of beta and gamma change. The second stage is to assess gamma change. This comprises an assessment of equivalent factor structures and equivalent factor covariances. Next, beta change is assessed, comparing the equivalence of factor variances, and then the equivalence of factor loadings. The fourth stage, alpha change, is to assess the equivalence of the model, comparing the results with means fixed to be equivalent versus allowing them to be freely estimated.

Each of the above stages requires additional constraints to be added to the model, resulting in a series of nested models. Each time constraints are added, the fit of the model to the data is compared to the previous model with one fewer set of constraints. If the model fit is significantly worsened by the additional constraints, then the presence of the corresponding type of change is inferred.

One question that arises with such nested models is whether, if you do find that the model fits significantly worse when a set of constraints is added, you stop testing further models. At the preliminary phase, the omnibus test is not always reliable, and we suggest that researchers continue with the analyses regardless of this preliminary result (Byrne, 2001; Steenkamp & Baumgartner, 1998). Following this, some authors suggest that analysis should cease if gamma or beta change is found, because the measurement is of a different construct or on a recalibrated scale (Millsap & Hartog, 1988). However, other authors suggest that if the factor loadings are equivalent, then this establishes measurement equivalence and other analyses can be conducted (Raju et al., 2002). An alternative is that partial measurement invariance is sufficient for means to be compared, with a minimum of two items having invariant factor loadings and intercepts (Steenkamp & Baumgartner, 1998). Further, fit indices may not agree on whether model fit is worsened. Overall, we suggest adopting the criteria of at least two items being invariant (loadings and intercepts; ibid.), and that all of the chosen fit indices must show worsened fit for the analysis to be stopped (Vandenberg & Self, 1993).

We present a sample of fit indices, noting that change in the comparative fit index (CFI) is particularly appropriate for assessing nested models (Cheung & Rensvold, 2002). We also report chi-squared (χ^2), chi-squared change ($\Delta\chi^2$), the Tucker–Lewis Index (TLI), and root mean square error of approximation (RMSEA). For these, a significant chi-squared change, when constraints are added, shows a worsening in model fit; CFI changes of 0.01 or greater indicate worsening model fit (Cheung & Rensvold, 2002); values of CFI and TLI at around 0.95 or greater, and RMSEA of around 0.06 or less show a good fit of the data to the model (Hu & Bentler, 1999).

Results

The data were screened and confirmed as suitable for confirmatory factor analysis.[4] Confirmatory factor analysis was conducted in Amos 7.0, with the results shown in Table 7.2.[5] With a unidimensional construct at two timepoints gamma change cannot be assessed. This applies to all unidimensional engagement measures which, we suggest, covers many of these. Following the baseline model, there are two analyses for beta change, and then a further two for alpha change. For beta change, the chi-squared change values are significant ($\Delta\chi^2 = 5.34$, $p < 0.05$ and $\Delta\chi^2 = 15.33$, $p < 0.01$, respectively). However, the other fit indices still show a good fit of the data to the model, with the CFI barely changing (CFI changes only 0.001 over the three models). Overall, these results suggest that factor variances and factor loadings are equivalent over time, hence an absence of beta change. In the bottom part of Table 7.2, the chi-squared change value is small but significant, showing reduced fit when means are fixed, but the other fit indices barely change, overall suggesting the absence of alpha change. Therefore, JRA's engagement measure is stable over time and, for the sample of approximately 2,000 respondents who could be matched across 2007 to 2008, their employee engagement showed no change.

Table 7.2   Tests for alpha, beta, and gamma change over time

Model	χ^2 (df)	$\Delta\chi^2$ (Δdf)	CFI	TLI	RMSEA
Baseline	619.46[‡] (18)		0.973	0.955	0.079
Equivalent factor variances	624.80[‡] (19)	5.34* (1)	0.973	0.957	0.077
Equivalent factor loadings	640.13[‡] (24)	15.33[†] (5)	0.972	0.965	0.069
Factor means[a] freely estimated	669.48[‡] (29)		0.971	0.970	0.064
Factor means constrained equivalent	673.45[‡] (30)	3.97* (1)	0.971	0.971	0.063

Note: $N = 2708$; * $p < 0.05$; [†] $p < 0.01$; [‡] $p < 0.001$. $\Delta\chi^2$ = change in chi-squared; Δdf = change in degrees of freedom; CFI = comparative fit index; TLI = Tucker–Lewis index; RMSEA = root means square error of approximation. [a] $M(2007) = 0.434$, SE = 0.002; $M(2008) = 0.438$, SE = 0.002.

news, especially given the overlap in engagement measures provided commercially (Macey & Schneider, 2008). But this does not let other engagement survey providers off the hook: each provider should be conducting ABG change analyses periodically. In this respect, we also note that beta and gamma change might be expected when organizations conduct certain types of interventions (Riordan et al., 2001). One example of deliberate beta change is training to improve rating scale accuracy, which is typically done to calibrate performance ratings across raters (ibid.). It is possible that an organization would implement training for staff to ensure similar understanding and use of a rating scale for engagement. In this case, beta change might be the explicit intention of training, and looked for in data analyses.

For gamma change, while Riordan et al. found no quantitative assessment of this in their review of intervention-based journal articles, they did find research on interventions relating to organizational change or restructuring. That is, shifting the way in which employees understood concepts relating to organizational change. This is relevant to engagement interventions, where leaders are often responsible for helping employees to have a common and accurate understanding of engagement (Welbourne, 2007; Xu & Cooper-Thomas, 2010).

So if beta and gamma changes are potentially anticipated and positive outcomes of engagement interventions, then how can we manage beta and gamma changes, and can we still say anything substantive about patterns of alpha change in employee engagement? Our answer is that ABG analyses should become part of the standard toolkit for engagement survey providers who supply comparative analyses. Hence, rather than viewing beta and gamma change as an error that gets in the way of viewing alpha change and needs managing, we should see them as useful in providing a deeper understanding of comparative analyses. We next discuss the practical implications of this approach.

Practical implications

Practical implications for survey providers
For survey providers, the integrity of their engagement measure is paramount. The potential for errors – that is, beta and gamma changes occurring solely due to poor survey construction – will be reduced if survey items are well designed. Good practices identified from research should be followed, such as using clear, positive wording, and avoiding double-barreled items (Schuman & Presser, 1981; Schreisheim & Eichenbach, 1995). We also note that terminology may become outdated over time, and hence items will need periodic assessment to ensure that they are still relevant (JRA, 2009). The statistical procedures of ABG change are one means for doing this, and can be done relatively easily with archival data. However, going forwards, simpler methods may allow early detection of potentially problematic items, such as item assessment in focus groups or other item piloting methods. We note here the potential clash between survey integrity

and amendments to survey items. Specifically, survey providers may be unwilling to amend survey items because of their historic use, and hence amassed data on those specific items necessary for benchmarking. Survey providers may be concerned about whether clients will still buy a survey if it has been amended. In our view, clients should be educated about the benefits and necessity of ongoing amendments to improve surveys (ibid.). It is here that ABG change procedures may be particularly useful; if beta or gamma changes are prevalent in archival survey data, then this is a clear indication that the survey needs amending. Furthermore, as part of a continuous program of survey improvement, ABG change can be used to justify amendments. For example, analyses may show greater equivalence of factor loadings for new items across datasets.

In addition to the necessity of maintaining the integrity of their engagement survey, survey providers often provide benchmarking analyses. Typically, clients want answers to questions such as how their engagement levels compare to industry peers, and whether their engagement results have improved since last year. These questions relate to alpha change, with clients assuming that analyses compare like with like. In these circumstances, beta and gamma changes are undesirable. Thus, engagement measures need to be stable with regard to conceptual (gamma) and measurement (beta) issues, yet sensitive to changes in engagement-related attitudes (alpha) (Vandenberg, 2002). We suggest that survey providers should assess for beta and gamma change, as well as alpha change, for those types of comparative analyses that clients are interested in.[6] This will ensure that only meaningful differences, that is, alpha change, will be presented as such.

While these two issues, of survey integrity and comparative analyses, require some costs to survey providers, there is also a business opportunity in ABG change. Specifically, many organizations undertake annual interventions to improve engagement scores. In these cases, it is possible that educational interventions may result in beta or gamma change (Riordan et al., 2001). Thus, client organizations may be offered a more accurate picture of what changes they have actually achieved through ABG analyses, in addition to more standard *t*-tests or analysis of variance procedures.

Practical implications for survey purchasers/client organizations
Those purchasing engagement surveys will benefit from being more informed about survey design and the types of change that are possible in comparative analyses. When purchasing such analyses from a survey provider, or putting out tenders, client organizations should ask about survey design procedures, updating of surveys, and ABG change analyses. The last are particularly relevant when a client anticipates purchasing

comparative analyses, or is interested to see the effects of interventions. In particular, employee engagement surveys and related interventions represent a large investment from client organizations. Requesting ABG analyses provides a clear picture of the returns on that investment. Further, from the client organization's perspective, the ability to carry out ABG change analyses shows how proficient a survey provider actually is, and indicates the ethicality of that provider, in that analyses of survey measures are accurately represented.

We also suggest that client organizations can reduce non-meaningful (error) beta and gamma change by taking responsibility for communicating engagement survey results in a meaningful way. Obtaining quality data in an engagement survey is dependent on accurate responding from a majority of employees. When employees are used to receiving summary reports on engagement surveys, believe that the data are credible, and see the results being used in meaningful ways for the business, then those employees are more likely to participate in the engagement survey in future years. So what we are saying is that the ongoing quality of engagement survey data, and hence analyses on that data, is dependent not only on the measurement expertise of the survey provider, but also on the client organization in doing something meaningful with the results.

Practical implications for survey participants
Survey participants are possibly the least invested in the engagement survey process. However, their motivated participation is essential to obtaining quality data (Weng & Cheng, 2000). It is important that they have the same frame of reference for responding to items, to reduce the potential for erroneous beta and gamma change. Hence, it is desirable for survey participants to read survey instructions, and give honest answers. Where items appear irrelevant or confusing, participants should be encouraged to feed back this information to the survey provider, to assist in the ongoing process of survey improvement. In this regard, we note that this feedback provides useful input to survey improvement, but that a survey cannot be tailored to suit one individual any more than a golf course can have specific trees pruned to accommodate a single player. Further, participants need to know that their input is valued, as otherwise survey data risks having representation primarily from those with the most positive views (Taris & Schreurs, 2007). This further underlines client organizations' responsibility for communicating and using engagement survey results.

Conclusion
In this chapter, we have introduced the ideas of ABG change, and emphasized the importance of investigating these to achieve a true picture of

difference or change. We have provided a brief illustration of how to conduct ABG analyses using a confirmatory factor analytic approach. We suggest that using an ABG change approach for comparative analyses has benefits for survey providers, client organizations, and survey participants. Ultimately, all parties benefit from knowing the true state of engagement, and whether it is flourishing, fading, or staying true.

Notes

*   Our thanks to Paul Barrett for his helpful comments.
1. These issues of alpha, beta, and gamma change are also known as "measurement equivalence or invariance" (ME/I; Vandenberg & Lance, 2000). Note that alpha is also referred to as "scalar invariance", beta as "metric invariance", and gamma as "configural invariance" (ibid., 2000).
2. Few organizations request full sociodemographic data. For example, ethnicity is often omitted, and therefore this was not included in the database.
3. Authors differ in the proposed number and sequence of tests for assessing measurement invariance (Vandenberg & Lance, 2000); we have chosen one approach as being relatively parsimonious and thus easier to implement.
4. Contact the first author for full details of preliminary data assessments.
5. Note that we have restricted the amount of information provided here on the fit indices with the aim of reducing the technical details for readers, but still keeping the essential information. Further details of fit indices can be obtained from the first author.
6. Note that such analyses are constrained by sample size, with 200 the lowest suggested sample size for confirmatory factor analyses (Hoelter, 1983; Loehlin, 1992).

References

Byrne, B.M. (2001), *Structural Equation Modelling with AMOS: Basic Concepts, Applications, and Programming*, Mahwah, NJ: Erlbaum.
Cheung, G.W. & Rensvold, R.B. (2002), "Evaluating goodness-of-fit indexes for testing measurement invariance", *Structural Equation Modeling*, 9(2), 233–55.
Golembiewski, R.T., Billingsley, K. & Yeager, S. (1976), "Measuring change and persistence in human affairs: types of change generated by OD designs", *Journal of Applied Behavioral Science*, 12, 133–57.
Halberg, U.E. & Schaufeli, W.B. (2006), "'Same same but different?' Can work engagement be discriminated from job involvement and organizational commitment?", *European Psychologist*, 11(2), 119–27.
Harter, J.K., Schmidt, F.L. & Hayes, T.L. (2002), "Business-unit level relationship between employee satisfaction, employee engagement, and business outcomes: a meta-analysis", *Journal of Applied Psychology*, 87, 268–79.
Hoelter, J.W. (1983), "The analysis of covariance structures: goodness-of-fit indices", *Sociological Methods and Research*, 11, 325–44.
Hu, L.-T. & Bentler, P.M. (1999), "Cutoff criteria for fit indexes in covariance structure analysis: conventional criteria versus new alternatives", *Structural Equation Modeling*, 6(1), 1–55.
JRA (2009), *Unlimited/JRA Best Places to Work Survey 2008: Changes from the 2007 Survey*, Auckland: JRA.
Kahn, W.A. (1990), "Psychological conditions of personal engagement and disengagement at work", *Academy of Management Journal*, 34(4), 692–724.
Kahn, W.A. (1992), "To be fully there: psychological presence at work", *Human Relations*, 45(4), 321–49.
Loehlin, J.C. (1992), *Latent Variable Models: An Introduction to Factor, Path, and Structural Analyses*, Hillsdale, NJ: Erlbaum.

Macey, W.H. & Schneider, B. (2008), "The meaning of employee engagement", *Industrial and Organizational Psychology*, **1**(1), 3–30.

Millsap, R.E. & Hartog, S.B. (1988), "Alpha, beta, and gamma change in evaluation research: a structural equation approach", *Journal of Applied Psychology*, **73**(3), 474–584.

Oliver, P. (2008), "Economy over the worst: Cullen", *The New Zealand Herald*, September 12, available from: http://www.nzherald.co.nz/nz/news/article.cfm?c_id=1&objectid= 10531795 (accessed February 22, 2009).

Raju, N.S., Laffitte, L.J. & Byrne, B.M. (2002), "Measurement equivalence: a comparison of methods based on confirmatory factor analysis and item response theory", *Journal of Applied Psychology*, **87**(3), 517–29.

Riordan, C.M., Richardson, H.A., Schaffer, B.S. & Vandenberg, R.J. (2001), "Alpha, beta, and gamma change. A review of past research with recommendations for new directions", in C.A. Schriesheim & L.L. Neider (eds), *Research in Management: Vol. 1. Equivalence in Measurement*, Greenwich, CT: Information Age, pp. 51–98.

Salanova, M., Agut, S. & Peiró, J.M. (2005), "Linking organizational resources and work engagement to employee performance and customer loyalty: the mediation of service climate", *Journal of Applied Psychology*, **90**, 1217–27.

Schmitt, N. (1982), "The use of analysis of covariance structures to assess beta and gamma change", *Multivariate Behavioral Research*, **17**, 343–58.

Schreisheim, C.A. & Eichenbach, R.J. (1995), "An exploratory and confirmatory factor-analytic investigation of item wording effects on the obtained factor structures of survey questionnaire measures", *Journal of Management*, **21**(6), 1177–93.

Schuman, H. & Presser, S. (1981), *Questions and Answers in Attitude Surveys: Experiments in Question Form, Wording, and Context*, New York: Academic Press.

Steenkamp, J.-B.E.M. & Baumgartner, H. (1998), "Assessing measurement invariance in cross-national consumer research", *Journal of Consumer Research*, **25**(1), 78–90.

Taris, T.W. & Schreurs, P.J.G. (2007), "How may nonresponse affect findings in organizational surveys? The tendency-to-the-positive effect", *International Journal of Stress Management*, **14**(3), 249–59.

Vandenberg, R.J. (2002), "Toward a further understanding of and improvement in measurement invariance methods and procedures", *Organizational Research Methods*, **5**(2), 139–58.

Vandenberg, R.J. & Lance, C.E. (2000), "A review and synthesis of the measurement invariance literature: suggestions, practices, and recommendations for organizational research", *Organizational Research Methods*, **3**(1), 4–70.

Vandenberg, R.J. & Self, R.M. (1993), "Assessing newcomers' changing commitments to the organizational during the first 6 months of work", *Journal of Applied Psychology*, **78**(4), 557–68.

Viljevac, A., Cooper-Thomas, H.D. & Saks, A.M. (2010), "An investigation into the validity of two measures of work engagement", manuscript submitted.

Welbourne, T.M. (2007), "Employee engagement: beyond fad and into the executive suite", *Leader to Leader*, **44**, 45–51.

Weng, L.-J. & Cheng, C.-P. (2000), "Effects of response order on Likert-type scales", *Educational and Psychological Measurement*, **60**, 908–24.

Xanthopoulou, D., Bakker, A.B., Demerouti, E. & Schaufeli, W.B. (2009), "Work engagement and financial returns: a diary study on the role of job and personal resources", *Journal of Occupational and Organizational Psychology*, **82**, 183–200.

Xu, J. & Cooper-Thomas, H.D. (2010), "How can leaders achieve high employee engagement?", manuscript submitted for publication.

8 "Engage me once again": is employee engagement for real, or is it "same lady – different dress"?

Lior M. Schohat and Eran Vigoda-Gadot

Introduction: evolution of the person–organization relationship

The implied understandings between employees and organizations, frequently referred to as "the (old) psychological contract", have changed drastically over the decades. It can be argued that, since the 1990s, there has been a mutual reduction of loyalty and a decrease in employee commitment to both work and organizations. This shift can be attributed to two major trends which reinforce and complement each other, making it difficult to determine what changed first. The first trend is the change in the employment paradigm of modern corporations. Organizations require greater flexibility in hiring and firing, and need their employee pool to expand or shrink according to their current needs and according to the rules of the market. Managing vested employees or those seeking one employer for life challenged the ability of human resources (HR) to constantly adjust the size of the workforce to the tune of strategic and operational needs (O'Reilly & Pfeffer, 2000; Ulrich & Brockbank, 2005; Boudreau & Ramstad, 2007).

The second trend is the change in the value system that contemporary employees exhibit. After many years of distinct preference for security and stable employment (which usually resulted in very long careers within a single company), employees gradually appreciated other psychological incomes over occupational stability. Nowadays, employees prefer to establish a different dialogue with the organizational systems in which they are living and working because of – among others – a move from institutional to self-reliance (Hall, 1986, 1996; London. & Stumpf, 1986) that upset the relationship between organizational and career commitments (Blau, 1985, 1988; Cohen, 2003).

Over the years, three major constructs were suggested as the "ultimate" description of the desired person–organization relationship which, while fostering individual loyalty and satisfaction, eventually contribute substantially to the firm's performance: organizational commitment (OC), job involvement (JI), and organizational citizenship behavior (OCB). More recently, employee engagement (EE) was mentioned as an optional redefinition for the individual–organization relationship. This chapter represents our attempt to evaluate EE's "added value" and assess its potential theoretical contribution over the other three well-established constructs.

Employee engagement: the birth of a concept

A thorough exploration of existing literature reveals a wealth of writing, mostly applied in nature. A simple search in Amazon online bookstore (October, 2009) yields a record 1,914 hits on the subject and yielded claims such as: "Employee engagement is the cornerstone of achieving a sustainable competitive advantage"; "there is clear and mounting evidence that employee engagement keenly correlates to individual, group, and corporate performance in areas such as retention, productivity, customer service, and loyalty"; or "engaged employees are more productive, engender greater customer satisfaction and loyalty, and help promote a company's brand". Given this enormous enthusiasm one can begin to wonder: what exactly is EE? How is it different from other existing concepts? Is it as simple and straightforward as it sounds?! What is the source of its enormous appeal?

According to Macey and Schneider (2008): "employee engagement is a desirable condition, has an organizational purpose, and connotes involvement, commitment, passion, enthusiasm, focused effort, and energy, so it has both attitudinal and behavioral components" (p. 4). The root of the EE concept lies in what has come to be known, in recent years, as "positive psychology" (Seligman & Csikszentmihalyi, 2000), namely the study of the characteristics of successful employees and managers and productive work groups (Harter et al., 2002).

In their exhaustive review of the literature, Macey and Schneider argued that most definitions of EE seem to have in common several constructs, already established in their own right. Chief among these are the constructs of: OC, JI, and OCB. Nonetheless, the literature is not very clear whether EE is a new concept/construct or whether it is simply a new concoction of existing and well-established constructs. Recently, the Society for Industrial and Organizational Psychology (SIOP, Division 14 of the American Psychological Association) launched a new journal titled *Industrial and Organizational Psychology: Perspectives on Science and Practice*. The very first focal article was the aforementioned Macey and Schneider piece. Among the dozen responses to that article very few writers were in favor of viewing EE as something new (as Macey & Schneider argue) and the majority considered it to be, at best, a re-alignment of old constructs.

Among the authors in favor of viewing EE as a new theoretical construct, some consider EE to be a continuum running between "actively engaged" and "actively disengaged". These authors wonder about the consequences of low as well as high levels of EE and whether high EE is always going to be favorable for individuals or the organization (Masson et al., 2008). Frese (2008) also claimed that EE is a new construct connoting active performance, and as a result requires a novel performance model that he saw as lacking in the literature.

A number of writers have argued against viewing EE as a new construct, claiming that it is an intuitive construct in the process of gaining legitimacy (Newman & Harrison, 2008); it might be theoretically distinct from other constructs, but it is not empirically distinct and therefore not superior to OC or job satisfaction (Harter & Schmidt, 2008); it lacks distinctive meaning (Saks, 2008); cannot be individually assessed (Pugh & Dietz, 2008); it is very difficult to measure or operationalize "extra-role" or "beyond expectations" performance (Griffin et al., 2008); it ignores intra-personal variability and mood swings during the day, hour or minute (Dalal et al., 2008); and ultimately EE lacks a comprehensive framework and should be included in the self-determination theory instead (Meyer & Gagné, 2008).

Past knowledge: commitment, involvement and citizenship

In order to look into the uniqueness of EE, if it exists, one needs first to draw the borders among competing concepts and to emphasize the contribution of EE beyond them. Let us try to summarize what present-day theory has to offer concerning OC, JI, and OCB.

Organizational commitment

OC has drawn massive interest from researchers as well as practitioners due to the belief that it is a more stable attitude and, therefore, a better predictor of work behavior than job satisfaction (Mottaz, 1986). The link between OC and organizational effectiveness was established by the pioneering work of Mowday et al. (1979, 1982). These authors defined organizational commitment as: "the relative strength of the individual's identification with and involvement in a particular organization . . . characterized by at least three related factors: (1) a strong belief in and acceptance of the organization's goals and values; (2) a willingness to exert considerable effort on behalf of the organization; and (3) a strong desire to maintain membership in the organization" (1979, p. 226).

In the past decades, since its original formulation, this perspective of OC remained largely unchallenged. However, over the years researchers have questioned the type of relationship between OC and organizational outcomes (for example, turnover, performance, and absenteeism). For example, Cohen (1991) conducted a meta-analysis of 41 studies relating career development and OC, and concluded that career stage moderates the relationship between OC and outcomes. He found that the relationship between commitment and turnover (actual and intended) is stronger in the early career stage than in the mid- and late-career stages. Similarly, Vandenberg and Lance (1992) established a causal relationship between OC and job satisfaction. Their results, based on a sample of 100 management information systems (MIS) professionals, lent support to the commitment-causes-satisfaction model.

Job involvement
JI has been defined as "psychological identification with a job" (Kanungo, 1982, p. 97) and was suggested as an important addition to understanding the nexus between individuals and the organization via the nature of the job. A job-involved person sees her or his job "as an important part of his self-concept" (Lawler & Hall, 1970, p. 311), and as defining "one's self-concept in a major way" (Kanungo, 1982, p. 82). JI is an attitude toward the work role and its context.

Conceptual definitions of JI have been of two basic types (see, for example, Lodahl & Kejner, 1965; Rabinowitz & Hall, 1977). One regards JI as reflecting the degree to which a person's sense of esteem is affected by job performance. The other views it as the centrality of work and the job context to the individual's self-image. There are also other views on the nature of the JI construct and little consensus on the most appropriate measure of this construct (Rabinowitz & Hall, 1977). Moreover, as is true of the conceptual definitions of many constructs, popular definitions of JI tend to confuse it with its antecedents (for example, work values) and consequences (for example, performance-based esteem changes), as they may be confused with EE as well. Researchers and theorists have equated JI, directly or indirectly, with such constructs as work centrality, employee morale, intrinsic motivation, job satisfaction, and the Protestant work ethic (ibid., 1977).

Organizational citizenship behavior
OCB was first mentioned in the early 1980s (Smith et al., 1983; Organ, 1988) and was suggested as the good soldier syndrome of extra-role behavior that is above formal requirements in the organization. The great Greek philosopher Aristotle was first to observe that (positive) citizenship is a behavior that contributes to the establishment, the security, and the continuous development of the community, while at the same time it is an expression of the individuals partaking in a purposeful collective enterprise (Elcock, 1976). Indeed, the initial formulations of good citizenship behavior in organizations expressed the ability and willingness of employees to contribute above and beyond the call of duty (for example, organizational

rules and procedures, job description, and so on). Based on an extensive review of earlier work, Robbins (2005) defined OCB as "voluntary individual behavior, that while it is not part of formal job requirements, is still promoting the effective functioning of the organization" (p. 28). He further suggested that successful organizations require employees that go beyond their formal job duties, and perform beyond expectations.

The benefits of having good organizational citizens are exhibited, for example, in: assisting other team members, volunteering and willingness to perform additional work (without being formally rewarded for these activities), abstaining from conflicts, and a non-simplistic interpretation of organizational rules and procedures. Other studies reveal that organizations possessing employees high on OCB are also more satisfied in the job, demonstrate higher organizational commitment and higher job involvement, and are more successful than others (Podaskoff et al., 2000; Bolino & Turnley, 2003).

Advanced conceptualizations of OCB place it within the realm of organizational performance. It can be argued that when we explore the reasons for organizational success, there is a distinct possibility that hardworking and devoted employees, doing their utmost above and beyond the call of duty, actually assist in increasing organizational effectiveness, efficiency and positive atmosphere – all of which produce jointly business and economic success. Since OCB involves a voluntary contribution to the organization – provided by participants independent of sanctions or economic inducements – such an accumulation, over time, contributes to organizational effectiveness (Vigoda-Gadot, 2006, 2007). Furthermore, OCB is not only a unique individual competency but rather a valuable source of social capital. It is perceived as the "lubrication" that facilitates organizational functioning, health, stability, and performance (Bolino et al., 2002). Good organizational citizens are responsible externally for the provision of better and more-qualitative customer service (Hui et al., 2001) and have a general positive impact at all levels of the organization.

The added value of EE: a comparative view
The adoption of new "game rules" (that is, new psychological contract) based on decreasing mutual commitment among employers and employees alike, is indeed compatible with the above-mentioned value shifts both among employees and organizations. We submit that the new commitment of people to organizations and of organizations to people is not lesser in its intensity, but rather shorter in its duration and more mobile or transferable across various organizational settings. In the new organizational context, a high degree of organizational commitment – a positive quality no doubt – may become more of a liability by making it more difficult for employees

to change their occupational setting and/or careers. Organizations may be less thrilled about having all of their personnel highly committed or highly involved since this might impact on their ability to manage downsizing and right-sizing processes in times of repeating economic crises and changing market conditions.

The new psychological contract ushers in a change to the totality of commitment between people and organizations. The new rules are based on multiple contacts (or multiple careers) – in accordance with the individual's multiple commitments (Cohen, 2003) – that are short term, in comparison to the old unitary long-term traditional psychological contract. As long as a specified occupational relationship lasts, the involved parties' mutual expectation is of total engagement. For this reason, organizational commitment that develops in one specific setting is going to create a major interference with the individual's ability to adjust to a new organizational system, as frequent career moves demand (Hall, 1996), while at the same time infringing on her/his career self-management capabilities. On the other hand and unlike OC or JI, OCB and EE are behavioral patterns that individuals can carry from one place to another, since they are not fixing the employee to a single given employment relationship, and therefore will be adaptive, positive and valued in any organizational setting.

Therefore, we propose to compare the four concepts on various dimensions along which the concepts differ. The dimensions are:

1. *Scope*   The range of job-related performance, specifically intra-role, extra-role or both.
2. *Source of behavior*   The source of the individual behavior either voluntary or as a result of a certain attitude or disposition.
3. *Personality type*   The value driver for the individual's behavior: respect of others or respect for authority.
4. *Basic orientation*   The individual's basic orientation toward life.
5. *Assistance target*   Which is likely to benefit from the individual's assistance: team, group, unit or the entire organization?
6. *Situational compatibility*   What are the situational requirements – inter-dependence or independence of units – facilitating or inhibiting individual behavior?
7. *Inter-organizational transferability*   Can an individual possessing this quality move freely between different organizations?
8. *Guiding discipline*   Academic domain that most frequently informed the writings on each quality.

Our efforts to summarize the fundamental characteristics of each of the four constructs are shown in Table 8.1. The table suggests that OC, JI, OCB

Table 8.1   Comparison of EE with OC, JI, and OCB

Dimension	OC	JI	OCB	EE
Scope	Intra-role	Intra-role	Extra-role	Intra- & extra-role
Source of behavior	Role identification/ internalization	Job identification	Voluntary, non-specific	Disposi-tional/ motivational
Personality type	Team player	Care and understanding	Respect toward people, authority and institutions	Optimistic/ proactive
Basic orientation	Social compliance/ collaborative	Normative compliance & participation	Normative compliance & participation	Initiative & enterprise
Assistance target	Unit/ organization	Unit/ organization	Personal/ team /work-group/unit	Organization
Situational compatibility	Unlimited	Job knowledge, skills, experience	Personal/ team interde-pendence	Unlimited
Inter-organizational transferability	Low	Medium	Medium	High
Guiding discipline	Industrial-organizational psychology	Industrial-organizational psychology	Management, political science	Social and behavioral science

and EE all share some variance as they are considered job- or work-related attitudes or behaviors that emphasize a positive interaction of individuals and the workplace. Nevertheless, EE emerges with some uniqueness compared with the others as a sort of an "omnibus" construct since: (i) its scope is larger than the other three, (ii) its source of behavior is related much more to work and organization, (iii) its personality type is high on "active coping", (iv) its basic orientation is non-submissive (therefore making its management more challenging), (v) its situational compatibility is unlim-ited, and (vi) it is high on inter-organizational transferability.

We consequently maintain that organizations should consider adding EE to the arsenal of theoretical concepts such as OC, OCB, and JI. EE may thus become a much more appropriate alternative to encourage highly committed and involved employees as well as fostering good organ-izational citizens. In contrast to OC or JI, OCB and EE are individual characteristics easily transferred from one organization to another since they reflect a principle attitude of individuals toward institutions. As a result, these are not likely to interfere with inter-organization moves, and will always allow the individual to express the same quality and intensity of involvement that organizations are so keen on having. EE on the other hand, seems unique compared with both OC and OCB being, at least in part, a dispositional characteristic rather than purely attitudinal (Macey & Schneider, 2008) and by being rooted in the general social and behavioral sciences rather than in a limited disciplinary section of industrial psychology or management.

Summary

There is no doubt in our minds that, presently, EE offers organizations a much more attractive profile of positive attitudes, life-related optimism and work-related enthusiasm combined with energetic intra-role proactivity. Studies should seriously discuss EE theoretically and test it empirically. It deserves scholarly attention for being a solid blend of commitment to the organization and its values, involvement in the specific job one exhibits, together with the positive citizenship assisting many in the organizational setting. Like OCB, EE is something that employees offer voluntarily in direct response to their organizational experience (for example, leadership, infrastructure, resources and so on) and therefore cannot be a simple part of the formal employment contract. However, unlike OCB, EE can be rooted in both formal and informal activities that involve commitment, care, respect, innovation, creativity, and other aspects of belonging. We feel that EE must be considered as a potentially new challenge for both theory and practice in management. Therefore, this theoretical observation should be challenged by empirical efforts to support (or reject) the thesis of EE's uniqueness. We may end up finding that EE consists of the best of what OC, JI, and OCB have to offer and therefore should be viewed as the most comprehensive description, to date, of the desired relationship between individuals and organizations. Although more studies, conceptual and empirical, are needed to support this idea, the effort must be made. Scientific knowledge creation pays homage to parsimony. EE may represent a breakthrough in social science's capability of describing the true individual–organization relationship, especially in modern times of complexity and fragility in markets and in organizational development.

References

Blau, G.J. (1985), "The measurement and prediction of career commitment", *Journal of Occupational Behavior*, **58**, 277–88.

Blau, G.J. (1988), "Further exploring the meaning and measurement of career commitment", *Journal of Vocational Behavior*, **32**, 284–97.

Bolino, M.C. & Turnley, W.H. (2003), "Going the extra mile: cultivating and managing employee citizenship behavior", *Academy of Management Executive*, August, 60–73.

Bolino, M.C., Turnley, W.H. & Bloodgood, J.M. (2002), "Citizenship behavior and the creation of social capital in organizations", *Academy of Management Review*, 27(4), 505–22.

Boudreau, J.W. & Ramstad, P.M. (2007), *Beyond HR: The New Science of Human Capital*, Boston, MA: Harvard Business School Press.

Cohen, A. (1991), "Career stage as a moderator of the relationships between organizational commitment and its outcomes: a meta-analysis", *Journal of Occupational Psychology*, 64, 253–68.

Cohen, A. (2003), *Multiple Commitments in the Workplace: An Integrative Approach*, Hillside, NJ: Lawrence Erlbaum.

Dalal, R.S., Brummel, B.J., Wee, S. & Thomas, L.L. (2008), "Defining employee engagement for productive research and practice", *Industrial and Organizational Psychology: Perspectives on Science and Practice*, 1, 52–5.

Elcock, H. (1976), *Political Behavior*, New York: Methuen.

Frese, M. (2008), "The word is out: we need an active performance concept for modern workplaces", *Industrial and Organizational Psychology: Perspectives on Science and Practice*, 1, 67–9.

Griffin, M.A., Parker, S.K. & Neal, A. (2008), "Is behavioral engagement a distinct and useful construct?", *Industrial and Organizational Psychology: Perspectives on Science and Practice*, 1, 48–51.

Hall, D.T. (ed.) (1986), *Career Development in Organizations*, London: Jossey-Bass.

Hall, D.T. (1996), *The Career Is Dead – Long Live the Career*, San-Francisco, CA: Jossey-Bass.

Harter, J.K. & Schmidt, F.L. (2008), "Conceptual versus empirical distinctions among constructs: implications for discriminant validity", *Industrial and Organizational Psychology: Perspectives on Science and Practice*, 1, 36–9.

Harter, J.K., Schmidt, F.L. & Hayes, T.L. (2002), "Business-unit-level relationship between employee satisfaction, employee engagement, and business outcomes: a meta-analysis", *Journal of Applied Psychology*, 87(2), 268–79.

Hui, C., Lam, S.S.K. & Schaubroeck, J. (2001), "Can good citizens lead the way in providing quality service? A field quasi experiment", *Academy of Management Journal*, 44(5), 988–95.

Kanungo, R.N. (1982), *Work Alienation: An Integrative Approach*, New York: Praeger.

Lawler, E.E. & Hall, D.T. (1970), "Relationship of job characteristics to job involvement, satisfaction, and intrinsic motivation", *Journal of Applied Psychology*, 54, 305–12.

Lodahl, T.M. & Kejner, M. (1965), "The definition and measurement of job involvement", *Journal of Applied Psychology*, 49, 24–33.

London, M. & Stumpf, S.A. (1986), "Individual and organizational career development in changing times", in Hall (ed.), pp. 21–49.

Macey, W.H. & Schneider, B. (2008), "The meaning of employee engagement", *Industrial and Organizational Psychology: Perspectives on Science and Practice*, 1, 3–30.

Masson, R.C., Royal, M.A., Agnew, T.G. & Fine, S. (2008), "Leveraging employee engagement: the practical implications", *Industrial and Organizational Psychology: Perspectives on Science and Practice*, 1, 56–9.

Meyer, J.P. & Gagné, M.N. (2008), "Employee engagement from a self-determination theory perspective", *Industrial and Organizational Psychology: Perspectives on Science and Practice*, 1, 60–62.

Mottaz, C.J. (1986), "An analysis of the relationship between education and organizational commitment in a variety of occupational groups", *Journal of Vocational Behavior*, 28, 214–28.

Mowday, R.T., Porter, L.W. & Steers, R.M. (1982), *Employer Organization Linkages: The Psychology of Commitment: Absenteeism and Turnover*, New York: Academic Press.

Mowday, R.T., Steers, R.M. & Porter, L.W. (1979), "The measurement of organizational commitment", *Journal of Vocational Behavior*, 14, 224–47.

Newman, D.A. & Harrison, D.A. (2008), "Been there, bottled that: are state and behavioral work engagement new and useful constructs 'Wines'?", *Industrial and Organizational Psychology: Perspectives on Science and Practice*, **1**, 31–5.

O'Reilly, C.A. III. & Pfeffer, J. (2000), *Hidden Value: How Great Companies Achieve Extraordinary Results with Ordinary People*, Boston, MA: Harvard Business School Press.

Organ, D.W. (1988), *Organizational Citizenship Behavior: The Good Soldier Syndrome*, Lexington, MA: Lexington Books.

Podaskoff, P.M., MacKenzie, S.B., Paine, J.B. & Bachrach, D.G. (2000), "Organizational citizenship behavior: a critical review of the theoretical and empirical literature and suggestions for future research", *Journal of Management*, **26**(3), 543–8.

Pugh, S.D. & Dietz, J. (2008), "Employee engagement at the organizational level of analysis", *Industrial and Organizational Psychology: Perspectives on Science and Practice*, **1**, 44–7.

Rabinowitz, S. & Hall, D.T. (1977), "Organizational research on job involvement", *Psychological Bulletin*, **84**, 265–88.

Robbins, S.P. (2005), *Organizational Behavior*, 11th edn, Upper Saddle River, NJ: Pearson Education.

Saks, A.M. (2008), "The meaning and bleeding of employee engagement: how muddy is the water?", *Industrial and Organizational Psychology: Perspectives on Science and Practice*, **1**, 40–43.

Seligman, M.E.P. & Csikszentmihalyi, M. (eds) (2000), "Special issue on happiness, excellence, and optimal human functioning", *American Psychologist*, **55**(1), 5–14.

Smith, C.A., Organ, D.W. & Near, J.P. (1983), "Organizational citizenship behavior: its nature and antecedents", *Journal of Applied Psychology*, **68**, 653–63.

Ulrich, D. & Brockbank, W. (2005), *The HR Value Proposition*, Boston, MA: Harvard Business School Press.

Vandenberg, R.J. & Lance, C.E. (1992), "Examining the causal order of job satisfaction and organizational commitment", *Journal of Management*, **18**(1), 153–67.

Vigoda-Gadot, E. (2006), "Compulsory citizenship behavior in organizations: theorizing some dark sides of the good soldier syndrome", *Journal for the Theory of Social Behavior*, **36**(1), 77–93.

Vigoda-Gadot, E. (2007), "Redrawing the boundaries of OCB? An empirical examination of compulsory extra-role behavior in the workplace", *Journal of Business and Psychology*, **21**(3), 377–405.

PART II

WHAT INFLUENCES EMPLOYEE ENGAGEMENT? KEY DRIVERS, MODELS AND ISSUES

9 Job demands and resources as antecedents of work engagement: a qualitative review and directions for future research

Saija Mauno, Ulla Kinnunen, Anne Mäkikangas and Taru Feldt

Introduction

What drives employees to work is a question which has prompted a lot of research since the early theories of human motivation were introduced in the 1950s. During the last two decades research on work motivation has expanded and many new constructs have been introduced. One of these is "work engagement" (WE), which refers to a positive, fulfilling work-related state of mind characterized by three related dimensions: vigor, dedication and absorption (Schaufeli et al., 2002; Schaufeli & Bakker, 2010).

Overall, energy and identification form the core content of WE; these two experiences are captured by the dimensions of vigor and dedication. "Vigor" refers to energy and mental resilience at work and the willingness to invest high effort in one's work. The motivational aspects of WE, comprising the facets of arousal, maintenance and direction of action (Katzell & Thompson, 1990), are best captured by vigor. "Dedication" is characterized by a sense of significance, enthusiasm, inspiration, pride and challenge in relation to one's work; this dimension has conceptual similarity with having a strong identification with one's work. "Absorption" refers to the feeling of being fully concentrated on one's work and finding detaching oneself from work difficult. This dimension resembles the concept of flow (Csikzentmihalyi, 1990).

The rapid proliferation of WE research has sparked interest in both its antecedents and outcomes. Consequently, the correlates of engagement have already been the topic of a few reviews (Christian & Slaughter, 2007; Simpson, 2008; Halbesleben, 2010). These reviews have focused on cross-sectional findings due to the lack of longitudinal studies on WE. However, longitudinal studies have now started to emerge. The main aim of this review is to summarize and evaluate the most recent longitudinal findings on WE.

In this chapter we examine the antecedents of WE according to longitudinal findings. Specifically, we apply the job demands–resources model (JD–R model; Demerouti et al., 2001; Bakker & Demerouti, 2007), which has been one of the key frameworks in WE research. We first introduce the basic principles of the JD–R model and summarize the cross-sectional findings on the antecedents of WE. We then review longitudinal findings, in particular the antecedents, in more detail, and in relation to the central hypotheses of the JD–R model. Finally, we offer suggestions for future research and consider the practical implications.

Job demands–resources model

The first assumption of the JD–R model is that regardless of type of job, psychosocial work characteristics can be categorized into two categories: job resources and job demands (Demerouti et al., 2001; Bakker & Demerouti, 2007). "Job demands" refer to those aspects of a job that require sustained physical and/or psychological effort and are therefore associated with certain physiological and/or psychological costs. While job demands are not necessarily negative, they may however turn into negative job stressors when meeting those demands requires major effort from an employee who feels already overburdened (Bakker & Demerouti, 2007).

"Job resources" refer to those aspects of a job that are functional in achieving work goals, may reduce job demands and the associated physiological and psychological costs, and stimulate personal growth, learning and development. Job resources may foster either extrinsic or intrinsic motivation at work. The former occurs because resources are necessary to cope with job demands and to achieve work goals. The latter relates to the view that by satisfying the basic psychological needs of autonomy, belongingness and competence, job resources are also intrinsically motivating for employees (Van den Broeck et al., 2008).

According to the second assumption of the JD–R model, two different underlying processes – the health impairment process and motivational process – play a role in the development of work strain and motivation (Bakker & Demerouti, 2007). In the *health impairment process*, chronic job demands exhaust employees' mental and physical resources and may therefore lead to the depletion of energy. In consequence, job demands are related to strain, including development of fatigue, burnout and health problems. In the *motivational process*, job resources are related to motivation, including work-related engagement and commitment.

The third assumption of the JD–R model is that lack of resources (for example, lack of job control and social support) is linked to fatigue and burnout at work. However, the original JD–R model does not hypothesize any relationship between job demands and WE, although it might be expected – according to other stress theories – that high job demands decrease WE. However, on the basis of the JD–R model, we expect a link to exist between job resources in particular and WE.

Antecedents of WE in cross-sectional studies

Cross-sectional studies have consistently found job resources to be the major determinants of WE. Job resources – especially job control and support – have also been the most frequently studied work characteristics. Table 9.1 summarizes the results of two recent meta-analyses on the antecedents of WE. Study 1 refers to the meta-analysis of Christian and Slaughter (2007) and Study 2 to that of Halbesleben (2010).

As Table 9.1 shows, several job resources have been found to associate positively with WE or its dimensions: job control, support at

Table 9.1   Summary table of the results of the meta-analyses on the antecedents of WE: estimated population correlations (Mρ)

Predictors	Overall score		Vigor		Dedication		Absorption	
	Study 1	Study 2	Study 1	Study 2	Study 1	Study 2	Study 1	Study 2
Job resources		0.35	0.29	0.30	0.34	0.34	0.25	0.25
Social support	–	0.37	0.28	0.25	0.32	0.27	0.20	0.25
Autonomy/ control	–	0.27	0.37	0.40	0.42	0.45	0.43	0.37
Feedback	–	–	0.40	0.41	0.45	0.46	–	–
Innovativeness	–	–	0.24	–	0.29	–	–	–
Org. climate	–	–	–	0.23	–	0.30	–	–
Personal resources								
Self-efficacy	–	0.59	0.76	0.50	0.73	0.47	0.71	0.31
Optimism	–	0.44	–	–	–	–	–	–
Job demands		−0.09	−0.07	−0.07	−0.04	−0.24	0.05	−0.07
Workload	–	0.19	−0.06	0.04	−0.05	0.05	–	–
Physical demands	–	–	−0.21	–	−0.26	–	–	–
Emotional demands	–	–	−0.04	–	0.05	–	–	–
Cognitive demands	–	–	0.26	–	0.34	–	–	–
W–F conflict	–	0.43	–	−0.22	–	–	–	–
F–W conflict	–	0.25	–	−0.19	–	–	–	–

Sources: Study 1: Christian and Slaughter (2007); Study 2: Halbesleben (2010).

work, feedback, innovativeness (Study 1) and positive organizational climate (Study 2). Of the personal resources, self-efficacy and optimism – self-efficacy has been investigated more often than optimism – show a strong positive link to WE or its dimensions. The strength of the relationship between self-efficacy and WE ($\rho = 0.71$–0.76 in Study 1), however, raises the issue of possible conceptual overlap between these constructs. In all, these cross-sectional findings are fully in line with the core assumptions of the JD–R model: job resources – and personal resources – are strong determinants of WE.

With respect to job demands, the original JD–R model posits that there is no relationship between job demands and WE. Table 9.1 does not fully support this initial hypothesis, as a strong relationship has been found between cognitive job demands and vigor and dedication (Study 1). However, the direction of this relationship is positive: the higher the job demands, the higher are vigor and dedication. Physical and emotional demands at work (Study 1) and workload (Study 1), in turn, show a modest negative relationship with vigor and dedication. However, workload (Study 2) has positively been associated with WE and with the dimensions of vigor and dedication. Thus, it seems that the relationship between job demands and WE has not been fully established, possibly because job demands are not necessarily negative job stressors (Bakker & Demerouti, 2007). For example, cognitive demands are typical in challenging and interesting jobs, and they might turn into negative stressors when excessive effort is required to meet them.

Table 9.1 also shows an interesting pattern of relationships concerning work-to-family (W–F) conflict and family-to-work (F–W) conflict (see Study 2). Both, however, have been studied more rarely as antecedents of WE. The pattern for the dimension of vigor is that both types of conflict are negatively related to vigor. This finding is consistent with the W–F conflict theories (for example, Frone, 2003), according to which low W–F conflict associates with positive outcomes. However, the pattern looks different when the overall score of WE is the criterion: the higher the amount of W–F conflict, the higher is WE. It might be that highly work-engaged persons have less interest in or time for non-work demands and activities, which is likely to trigger the experience of conflict between these two life domains. Other reasons might be more methodological (Halbesleben, 2010).

Furthermore, the associations between job demands, resources and WE may not only be direct, as hypothesized in the original JD–R model. In fact, the recently revised JD–R model (Bakker & Demerouti, 2007) proposes that *interaction* between job demands and job resources is important for the development of work motivation (including WE) and job strain. There is already some evidence to support this notion. For example, Hakanen et al. (2005) showed that variability in professional skills (resource) boosted WE when the qualitative workload (demand) was high. Thus, professional skills mitigated the negative effect of high qualitative workload on WE. Later, Bakker et al. (2007) found that job resources (for example, supervisor support, appreciation at work) diminished the negative relationship between pupils' misbehavior and teachers' WE. This preliminary evidence suggests that job resources might play an even more important role when job demands are high.

Antecedents of WE in longitudinal studies
As stated at the outset, longitudinal studies on WE have recently begun to appear. After mapping the literature in the PsycINFO database by using three keywords "work engagement", "job demands–resources model" and "job resources", we found ten studies which met our criteria, that is, (a) were longitudinal, (b) used the JD–R model as a framework, and (c) measured WE by the Utrecht Work Engagement Scale (UWES) or by its specific dimensions. These 10 studies are summarized in Table 9.2.

A cursory glance at the samples and designs of these 10 studies reveals some interesting features. First, all the studies have sampled European workers, probably because the UWES was developed in Europe (in the Netherlands) and thus widely used by European researchers. Second, all the studies (except for two diary studies: Xanthopolou et al., 2008, 2009a) have used a two-wave design with time lags between the measurements ranging from three weeks to three years, but no longer. Third, methodologically, many of these studies show high quality. For example, a full panel design has been used in six studies, signifying that the direction of causality (normal, reversed and reciprocal causality) between the selected predictors and WE has also been tested over time. Structural equation modeling (SEM) has been used in six studies, hierarchical regression analysis (including a baseline control of the dependent variable) in two, and multilevel modeling in the two diary studies. Fourth, three of the ten studies (Hakanen et al., 2008b; Lorente et al., 2008; Schaufeli et al., 2009) have tested both the motivational (WE) and the health impairment (job burnout) paths underlying the JD–R model. However, our review focuses only on the results for WE.

Longitudinal findings supporting traditional causality
A more detailed look into the longitudinal findings (see Table 9.2; "Main results") reveals many interesting results. First, the two most often studied job resources, namely job control/autonomy and support at work, predict an increase in WE over time. This was the case for control/autonomy in

Table 9.2 Summary table of longitudinal WE studies in relation to antecedents

Authors and publication year	Participants, design and statistical analyses	Work-related variables	Measurement of WE	Main results in relation to causality models
De Lange, De Witte & Notelaers (2008)	Belgian employees with heterogeneous backgrounds (n = 871, 53.5% women, mean age = 36.2 years) Two-wave full panel design with 16 months lag and comparison groups as follows: (1) "stayers" (no work changes); (2) "promotion makers" (promotion or better job with the same employer); and (3) "external movers" (new job with different employer) SEM	Job resources: Social support from colleagues Supervisor support Autonomy Departmental resources	Overall mean score	*Traditional causality* model supported: Autonomy at T1 predicted WE at T2 (among stayers) *Reverse causality* model supported: WE at T1 predicted social support from colleagues (among stayers and external movers), supervisory support (among stayers), and autonomy and departmental resources (among promotion makers) at T2

Hakanen, Perhoniemi & Toppinen-Tanner (2008a)	Finnish dentists ($n = 2,555$, 73.5% women, mean age $= 45.5$) Two-wave full panel design with 3-year lag SEM	Job resources: Overall latent factor including craftsmanship, pride in one's profession, and direct and long-term results Others: Personal initiative	Overall latent factor including the dimensions of vigor, dedication and absorption	Reciprocal causality model supported: Job resources and WE were related reciprocally and positively over time WE and personal initiative were related reciprocally and positively over time
Hakanen, Schaufeli & Ahola (2008b)	Finnish dentists ($n = 2,555$, 73.5% women, mean age $= 45.5$) Two-wave full panel design with 3-year lag SEM Health impairment path of the JD–R model was also tested (burnout as an outcome)	Job resources: Overall latent factor including craftsmanship, professional contacts, long-term and immediate results Job demands: Overall latent factor including workload, work contents stressfulness, and physical work environment	Overall latent factor including dimensions of vigor and dedication	Traditional causality model supported: Job resources at T1 positively predicted WE at T2 Job demands at T1 negatively predicted WE at T2

Table 9.2 (continued)

Authors and publication year	Participants, design and statistical analyses	Work-related variables	Measurement of WE	Main results in relation to causality models
		Others: Home resources and demands (for example family/ partner support, quantitative home demands)		
Llorens, Schaufeli, Bakker & Salanova (2007)	Spanish university students (*n* = 110, 85% women, mean age = 22.6 years) Two-wave full panel design with 3-week lag SEM	Task/job resources: Time control Method control	Overall mean score including vigor and dedication	*Traditional causality* model supported: Task resources at T1 predicted efficacy beliefs at T2, which in turn, predicted WE at T2 (lagged effect)
Lorente, Salanova, Martínez & Schaufeli (2008)	Spanish secondary school teachers (*n* = 274, 57% women, mean age = 40)	Job resources: Autonomy Support climate Job demands: Quantitative overload	Dimension-specific analysis for: Vigor Dedication	*Traditional causality* model supported Other causality models were not tested Role ambiguity at T1 negatively predicted the dimension of dedication at T2

Study	Design	Variables	Dimension	Results
	Two-wave panel design with 8-month lag Hierarchical multiple regression analysis (baseline of dependent variable was controlled for) Health impairment path of the JD–R model was also tested (burnout as an outcome)	Mental and emotional demands Role ambiguity Role conflict (each predictor analyzed separately) Others: Personal resources: Mental competence Emotional competence		Work overload positively predicted the dimension of dedication at T2
Mauno, Kinnunen & Ruokolainen (2007)	Finnish healthcare personnel ($n = 409$, 88% women, mean age = 46.4) Two-wave panel design with 2-year lag Hierarchical regression analysis (baseline of dependent variable was controlled for)	Job resources: Job control Organization-based self-esteem Management quality Job demands: Job insecurity Time demands at work Work-to-family conflict (each predictor analyzed separately)	Dimension-specific analysis for: Vigor Dedication Absorption	*Traditional causality* model supported: Other causality models were not tested Job control at T1 positively predicted dedication at T2 Job insecurity at T1 negatively predicted dedication at T2

Table 9.2 (continued)

Authors and publication year	Participants, design and statistical analyses	Work-related variables	Measurement of WE	Main results in relation to causality models
Schaufeli, Bakker & van Rhenen (2009)	Dutch telecom company managers and executives ($n = 201$, 89% men, mean age = 44.3) Two-wave full panel design with 1-year lag SEM Health impairment path of the JD–R model was also tested (burnout as an outcome)	Job resources: Overall latent factor including social support, autonomy, learning opportunities and performance feedback Job demands: Overall score of work overload, emotional demands and work–home interference Others: Sickness absence	Overall latent factor including the dimensions of vigor and dedication	*Reverse causality* model supported: WE at T1 predicted an increase in job resources (between T1 and T2) which, in turn, associated positively with WE at T2
Xanthopoulou, Bakker, Demerouti & Schaufeli (2009a)	Greek employees working for a fast-food company ($n = 42$, 71% men, mean age = 29 years)	Job resources at day level: Autonomy Supervisory coaching	Day-level WE as overall mean score of containing 3 dimensions	*Mediator model* was supported: Day-level job resources had an effect on day-level WE via personal resources (self-

Author(s)	Method	Measures	Results
	A diary study over 5 consecutive workdays Multilevel analysis	Team climate (each resource analyzed separately) Others: Day-level financial returns	efficacy, self-esteem and optimism as mediators) *Traditional causality* model supported: Day-level coaching had a direct positive effect on day-level WE, which in turn, predicted daily financial returns Previous day's coaching had a positive lagged effect on WE the next day (via next day's optimism), and on financial returns the next day
Xanthopoulou, Bakker, Demerouti & Schaufeli (2009b)	Employees working for an engineering and electronics company in the Netherlands (n = 163, 80% men, mean age 42 years) Two-wave full panel design with 18-month lag SEM	Job resources: Overall score of autonomy, social support, supervisory coaching, performance feedback, and opportunities for professional development Overall mean score containing 3 dimensions	*Reciprocal causality* model supported: Job resources and WE were related reciprocally over time

Table 9.2 (continued)

Authors and publication year	Participants, design and statistical analyses	Work-related variables	Measurement of WE	Main results in relation to causality models
Xanthopoulou, Bakker, Heuven, Demerouti & Schaufeli (2008)	Flight attendants working for a European airline (*n* = 44, 89% women, 25–44 years) A diary study over 3 consecutive destinations Multilevel analysis	Job resources : Day-level colleague support Others: Day-level work-related self-efficacy Job performance	Overall mean score of day-level WE containing 3 dimensions Overall mean score measured before the diary study (that is, WE as a trait-type experience)	*Traditional causality* model supported: Colleague support was associated with WE over time, which, in turn, was associated with higher self-efficacy beliefs *Mediator model* was also supported: Colleague support and self-efficacy were related to performance via WE (mediator)

five studies and for support in two diary studies. In addition, two longitudinal studies have also examined occupation-specific job resources as
antecedents of WE. Namely, Hakanen et al. (2008a, 2008b) found in two
separate studies, both based on the same sample of Finnish dentists, a
positive lagged relationship between craftsmanship (for example, the possibility to work with one's hands and be creative), professional contacts
(interacting with colleagues), and WE. These findings are fully consistent
with the basic assumptions of the JD–R model and support the traditional
causality assumption (that is, high job resources predict high WE over
time).

Second, these longitudinal studies show that job demands also matter.
All four studies in which job demands were examined indicated that
certain job demands had prospective associations with WE or with some
of its dimensions. As can be expected, the pattern was not as clear as that
found for job resources. For example, one study indicated that quantitative workload, work content stressfulness and a physically demanding
work environment decreased WE across time (Hakanen et al., 2008b).
Two other studies showed that the dimension of dedication was negatively
influenced by job insecurity (Mauno et al., 2007) and role ambiguity at
work (Lorente et al., 2008). Altogether, the longitudinal links from job
demands to WE turned out to be negative, supporting the traditional
causality assumption (that is, high job demands predict low WE over
time). However, consistent with the key premises of the JD–R model, job
demands have received less attention than job resources in these longitudinal WE studies.

Longitudinal findings supporting reversed or reciprocal causality
In the six longitudinal studies, based on a full panel design, different causal
models have been tested. Thus, the picture is not as simple as the findings
presented above might suggest. It seems that high WE might also predict
high job resources over time (reversed causality), or that high job resources
predict high WE and vice versa (reciprocal causality).

Reversed causality was supported in two of the six studies with a full
panel design. De Lange et al. (2008) showed that high WE predicted
positive employee evaluations of co-worker support, supervisory support,
autonomy, and departmental resources over time. In a more recent study,
Schaufeli et al. (2009) found that an increase in WE at Time 1 caused a
subsequent increase in job resources (for example, support, autonomy),
and in turn, WE at Time 2. Reciprocal causality was supported in two
studies. Hakanen et al. (2008b) and Xanthopoulou et al. (2009b) found
positive resource spiral between WE and job resources, that is, high job
resources at Time 1 predicted high WE at Time 2 and vice versa. The idea

of resources accumulating in spirals was presented by Hobfoll and Shirom (2001) in the conservation of resources theory. It is worth noticing that the direction of causal links between job demands and WE was tested in only one study (see Schaufeli et al., 2009), which failed to find evidence for reversed or reciprocal causality.

As with cross-sectional studies, longitudinal study designs have also improved over time. Besides testing different causality models, as described above, mediator paths have also received some attention in prospective studies. Personality factors have most frequently been considered as potential mediators in the relationship between job resources and WE. Two longitudinal studies showed that job resources were linked to WE via personal resources, for example, self-efficacy, and self-esteem (Llorens et al., 2007; Xanthopoulou et al., 2009a). Thus, job resources might boost WE because they initially improve one's personal resources, creating a resource spiral between these positive experiences (Hobfoll & Shirom, 2001). In another diary study, Xanthopoulou et al. (2008) showed that WE mediated the relationship between support at work and self-efficacy and job performance: first, resources improved WE, which, in turn, was related to high job performance.

It should be noted, however, that testing longitudinal mediator effects ideally requires at least three measurement points. In the light of this criterion with respect to the ten longitudinal studies reviewed here, it becomes obvious that this criterion is better fulfilled in diary studies (Xanthopoulou et al., 2008, 2009a) than in studies with only two measurement points. Naturally, questions about why and how a relationship occurs are also important in WE research.

Conclusions

Suggestions for future research
This review shows that although WE research has expanded during the last decade, there is also much room for new research, particularly, on the antecedents of WE. First, it seems that some important topical work characteristics – both from the demands and resources sides – have largely been neglected thus far. For example, job insecurity, work–family conflict and ethical stress at work merit more attention as up-to-date job demands. Among job resources, especially at the organizational level, for example, organizational justice and fair treatment of employees, and value congruence also seem worth mapping in relation to WE. Second, as we know quite a lot about general work characteristics – especially job resources – in relation to WE, it is perhaps time to focus more on occupation-specific work characteristics. This is the direction taken by, for example, Hakanen

et al. (2008a, 2008b) who found that craftsmanship played a central role for WE in dentists' work. Third, job demands deserve further attention as their role seems to be mixed – probably because job demands are not necessarily negative job stressors (Bakker & Demerouti, 2007).

A related point is that although it has been a natural starting point to search for the predictors of WE in the work domain, this has led to neglect of non-work-related antecedents. For example, different forms of support or perceived control in the non-work domain might be worth examining (Hakanen et al., 2008b). Also recovery research may contribute to WE research. As shown by Sonnentag et al. (2008), for highly engaged employees, psychological detachment from work is important in order to remain engaged in the long term. Thus constantly being "fully absorbed" at work may not be beneficial for long-term engagement, although firm empirical evidence for this view continues to be lacking. Therefore, we do not yet know whether high WE can deplete energy and lead eventually to burnout (Bakker et al., 2008). We still know little about the long-term consequences of WE.

Our review also reveals that study designs have improved over time. Pioneer studies tended to focus on the direct relationships, whereas the more recent studies have also focused on indirect (mediator, moderator) linkages. Nevertheless, some important potential mediators and moderators have been ignored. Although some personality or trait-like characteristics, for example self-efficacy (Xanthopoulou et al., 2008, 2009a), have received some attention, there are many others which deserve more attention. Among them are, for example, coping strategies and recovery experiences. In fact, there already exists evidence that this might be a promising avenue of research in the future. Kinnunen et al. (2010) showed that, of the recovery experiences, mastery experiences (that is, doing challenging things) during off-job time partially mediated the link from job resources to WE.

Finally, the longitudinal studies reviewed here have three notable limitations. First, most of them utilized only two waves (except for diary studies). We urgently need more multi-wave studies with different time lags in order to test the mediator relationships more reliably and to show whether high WE is beneficial in the long run. Also, the question of how WE develops over time is interesting, for example, do certain dimensions of WE (for example, vigor) give rise to other dimensions (for example, dedication)? As we know, burnout research has generated several developmental models (Schaufeli & Enzmann, 1998), while WE research totally lacks them. However, if WE is seen as an antipode of burnout (Maslach et al., 2001), process-oriented models of the development of WE should be developed.

Second, from a methodological point of view, all the longitudinal studies reviewed above used a variable-focused approach. Such an approach fails to account for the possible simultaneous occurrence of several distinct patterns of change in WE. This heterogeneity can be manifested in the identification of different groups of individuals who share similar patterns of relations among variables over time (Laursen & Hoff, 2006; Marsch et al., 2009). Thus, longitudinal WE research may also benefit from a person-oriented approach which seeks to identify different naturally occurring groups of employees with similar mean levels of change in WE (that is, developmental trajectories). Third, all the longitudinal studies we reviewed have examined European workers, which means that the findings might not be generalized to other cultures. Consequently, cross-cultural, preferably longitudinal, comparative research on WE is also needed.

Practical implications
WE is an essential, positive element of employee health and well-being and it is important for today's organizations, given the changes they currently face (Schaufeli & Salanova, 2007). Therefore, from both the employee and organizational viewpoints, the crucial question is how to increase employees' WE. In order to boost WE, the first step is to increase job resources, which are important in many respects: they are important in their own right because they stimulate personal growth and learning at work, but they are also needed to deal with job demands; moreover they spark gain spirals that increase WE. Which job resources, then, matter most? The answer depends partly on the job itself and partly on individual preferences; both of which should be scrutinized before implementing WE interventions. However, there are also resources which benefit all employees, such as job control, social support, and security. Yet, the type and quality of these three resources might be more context dependent: determined by job and organization type. The role of leaders in fostering WE has also been emphasized. Thus, it is important, for example, that team leaders provide positive feedback to employees, help employees set attainable goals, inform employees about important issues, and offer emotional support. Such leadership behaviors enhance both employees' and teams' WE (ibid.).

Another interesting question is whether WE is trainable (Bakker et al., 2008). This seems plausible by increasing efficacy beliefs (Schaufeli & Salanova, 2007). As already shown, self-efficacy and WE have a strong positive relationship, therefore the promotion of WE would benefit from boosting efficacy beliefs. Self-efficacy determines how much effort and persistence is mobilized for overcoming obstacles. Thus, employees should be provided with mastery experiences (that is, experiences of vocational success) as they are probably the most powerful tool for triggering efficacy beliefs. To our knowledge, no WE-enhancing intervention studies have yet been published. Finally, as said before, we do not know whether WE has a "dark side" in the long run (Bakker et al., 2008). Although the evidence thus far does not point to this, we encourage employees to detach from their jobs outside, working to ensure that they can also enjoy their work in the future (Sonnentag et al., 2008). Being engaged at work and disengaged off the job is probably beneficial for employee well-being, health and motivation in the long run.

References

* Study is included in the review (Table 9.2)

Bakker, A.B. & Demerouti, E. (2007), "The job demands–resources model: state of the art", *Journal of Managerial Psychology*, **22**, 309–28.

Bakker, A.B., Hakanen, J.J., Demerouti, E. & Xanthopoulou, D. (2007), "Job resources boost work engagement particularly when job demands are high", *Journal of Educational Psychology*, **99**, 274–84.

Bakker, A.B., Schaufeli, W., Leiter, M. & Taris, T. (2008), "Work engagement: an emerging concept in occupational health psychology", *Work & Stress*, **22**, 187–200.

Christian, M.S. & Slaughter, J.E. (2007), "Work engagement: a meta-analytic review and directions for research in an emerging area", Congress paper in 67th annual meeting of Academy of Management, Philadelphia, PA, August.

Csikzentmihalyi, M. (1990), *Flow: The Psychology of Optimal Experience*, New York: Harper & Row.

*De Lange, A.H., De Witte, H. & Notelaers, G. (2008), "Should I stay or should I go? Examining longitudinal relations among job resources and work engagement for stayers versus movers", *Work & Stress*, **22**, 201–23.

Demerouti, E., Bakker, A.B., Nachreiner, F. & Schaufeli, W.B. (2001), "The job demands–resources model of burnout", *Journal of Applied Psychology*, **86**, 499–512.

Frone, M. (2003), "Work–family balance", in J.C. Quick & L.E. Tetrick (eds), *Handbook of Occupational Health Psychology*, Washington, DC: APA, pp. 143–62.

Hakanen, J.J., Demerouti, E. & Bakker, A.B. (2005), "How dentists cope with their demands and stay engaged: the moderating role of job resources", *European Journal of Oral Science*, **113**, 479–87.

*Hakanen, J.J., Perhoniemi, R. & Toppinen-Tanner, S. (2008a), "Positive gain spirals at work: from job resources to work engagement, personal initiative and work unit innovativeness", *Journal of Vocational Behavior*, **73**, 78–91.

*Hakanen, J.J., Schaufeli, W.B. & Ahola, K. (2008b), "The job demands–resources model: a three-year cross-lagged study of burnout, depression, commitment, and work engagement", *Work & Stress*, **22**, 224–41.

Halbesleben, J.R.B. (2010), "A meta-analysis of work engagement: relationships with burnout, demands, resources and consequences", in A.B. Bakker & M.P. Leiter (eds), *Work Engagement: Recent Developments in Theory and Research*, New York: Psychology Press, pp. 102–17.

Hobfoll, S. & Shirom, A. (2001), "Stress and burnout in the workplace", in R. Golembiewski (ed.), *Handbook of Organizational Behavior*, Vol. 2, New York: Dekker, pp. 41–60.

Katzell, R.A. & Thompson, D.E. (1990), "Work motivation. Theory and practice", *American Psychologist*, **45**, 144–53.

Kinnunen, U., Feldt, T., Siltaloppi, M. & Sonnentag, S. (2010), "Job demands–resources model in the context of recovery: testing recovery experiences as mediators", manuscript submitted for publication.

Laursen, B. & Hoff, E. (2006), "Person-centered and variable-centered approaches to longitudinal data", *Merrill-Palmer Quarterly*, **52**, 390–419.

*Llorens, S., Schaufeli, W., Bakker, A.B. & Salanova, M. (2007), "Does a positive gain spiral of resources, efficacy beliefs and engagement exist?", *Computers in Human Behavior*, **23**, 825–41.

*Lorente, L.R., Salanova, M.S., Martínez, I.M. & Schaufeli, W.B. (2008), "Extension of the job-demands–resources model in the prediction of burnout and engagement among teachers over time", *Psicothema*, **20**, 354–60.

Marsh, H.W., Ludtke, O., Trautwein, U. & Morin, A.J.S. (2009), "Classical latent profile analysis of academic self-concept dimensions: synergy of person- and variable-centered approaches to theoretical models of self-concept", *Structural Equation Modeling*, **16**, 191–225.

Maslach, C., Schaufeli, W.B. & Leiter, M.P. (2001), "Job burnout", *Annual Review of Psychology*, **52**, 397–422.

*Mauno, S., Kinnunen, U. & Ruokolainen, M. (2007), "Job demands and resources as antecedents of work engagement: a longitudinal study", *Journal of Vocational Behavior*, **70**, 149–71.

Schaufeli, W.B. & Bakker, A.B. (2010), "Defining and measuring work engagement: bringing clarity to the concept", in A.B. Bakker & M.P. Leiter (eds), *Work Engagement: A Handbook of Essential Theory and Research*, New York: Psychology Press, pp. 10–24.

*Schaufeli, W.B., Bakker, A.B. & van Rhenen, W. (2009), "How changes in job demands and resources predict burnout, work engagement, and sickness absenteeism", *Journal of Organizational Behavior*, **30**, 893–917.

Schaufeli, W.B. & Enzmann, D. (1998), *The Burnout Companion to Study and Practice: A Critical Analysis*, Washington, DC: Taylor & Francis.

Schaufeli, W.B. & Salanova, M. (2007), "Work engagement: an emerging psychological concept and its implications for organizations", in S.W. Gilliland, D.D. Steiner & D.P. Skarlicki (eds), *Managing Social and Ethical Issues in Organizations*, Greenwich, CT: Information Age, pp. 135–77.

Schaufeli, W.B., Salanova, M., González-Romá, V. & Bakker, A.B. (2002), "The measurement of engagement and burnout: a two sample confirmatory factor analytic approach", *Journal of Happiness Studies*, **3**, 71–92.

Simpson, M. (2008), "Engagement at work: a review of the literature", *International Journal of Nursing Studies*, **46**, 1012–24.

Sonnentag, S., Mojza, E., Binnewies, C. & Scholl, A. (2008), "Being engaged at work and detached at home: a week-level study on work engagement, psychological detachment, and affect", *Work & Stress*, **22**, 257–76.

Van den Broeck, A., Vansteenkiste, M., De Witte, H. & Lens, W. (2008), "Explaining the relationships between job characteristics, burnout and engagement: the role of basic psychological need satisfaction", *Work & Stress*, **22**, 277–94.

*Xanthopoulou, D., Bakker, A.B., Demerouti, E. & Schaufeli, W.B. (2009a), "Work engagement and financial returns: a diary study on the role of job and personal resources", *Journal of Occupational and Organizational Psychology*, **82**, 183–200.

*Xanthopoulou, D., Bakker, A.B., Demerouti, E. & Schaufeli, W.B. (2009b), "Reciprocal relationships between job resources, personal resources, and work engagement", *Journal of Vocational Behavior*, **74**, 235–44.

*Xanthopoulou, D., Bakker, A.B., Heuven, E., Demerouti, E. & Schaufeli, W.B. (2008), "Working in the sky: a diary study on work engagement among flight attendants", *Journal of Occupational Health Psychology*, **13**, 345–56.

10 Using the demands–control–support model to understand manager/supervisor engagement

Gabriel M. De La Rosa and Steve M. Jex

Introduction

Kahn (1990) proposes engagement to be the "harnessing of organizational members' selves to their work roles" (p. 694). The critical component of this definition is the employee linking personal well-being to task performance. An engaged employee thinks about and feels various aspect of the job.

Other researchers interested in engagement have focused on the lack of certain psychological states (for example, exhaustion), and the presence of positive psychological states (for example, involvement) (Maslach & Leiter, 1997). An engaged employee exhibits positive energy, feels involved with the job, and feels that his/her contributions are productive (ibid.). Engaged employees have positive energy focused towards their work and a consistent commitment to the quality of their work (Maslach et al., 2001). The differentiator between an engaged and a non-engaged employee is the degree of personal investment an employee has in his or her task performance.

Engaging supervisors and managers

Decentralization of decision making and increasing responsibility of mid-level managers and first-line supervisors has created a pressing need for information that can be used to understand engagement in these employees.

Supervisory and managerial employees must disseminate information from upper levels of the organization while taking into consideration the needs of first-line employees. The specifics goals of these employees will vary by unit or function; the general goal of these employees is to organize first-line staff members to achieve organizational mandates. Communicating, organizing, rewarding, and being available to various stakeholders as needed make up some of the duties of these employees (US Bureau of Labor Statistics, 2008–09).

Typically, these employees are selected into mid-level management because of their performance in lower roles in the organization and willingness to exert additional effort. As such, new supervisors can usually benefit from training on how to lead people (Hogan & Kaiser, 2005). Given their perceived authority, these employees tend to expect reasonable freedom in how they accomplish their tasks (for example, scheduling, rewarding, and disciplining subordinates). These employees have important *demands*, expect a certain degree of *control* over their jobs, and require organizational *support*. As such, the job demands–control–support model (JDC(S)) is a well suited model for this sub-population.

The JDC(S) model
Karasek's (1979) job demand–control (JDC) model proposes that employees will suffer from strain if they experience high demands from their work role, and at the same time, have little control over how tasks are performed. Job demands refer to aspects of the job that constitute workload (Karasek, 1989).

Research looking at the moderating effect of control over demands is generally categorized under the rubric of the "buffer" hypothesis; control is hypothesized to attenuate the relationship between job demands and strain. Research looking at the additive effects of demands and control is generally categorized as "strain" hypothesis. The strain hypothesis predicts decreased employee well-being from low employee control or high job demands. In general, research on the strain and buffer hypotheses have shown that strain (for example, depression) will increase as job demands increase relative to decreased job control (Van der Doef & Maes, 1999).

The JDC(S) model expands the JDC model such that two JDC matrices are used to categorize jobs, one matrix for those jobs low in support and one matrix for those jobs high in support (Johnson & Hall, 1988). Employees working without support are hypothesized to develop strain at a higher rate than employees who receive positive support (ibid.).

Demands and engagement
Job demands are defined as an employee's perception of the pace of work and/or the excessive quantity of work to do. The excessive quantity of job demands often makes employees feel that they do not have enough time to finish all required tasks and is related to the development of personal strain (Spector & Jex, 1998).

One of the necessary conditions that must be met for an employee to experience engagement is a sufficient amount of work to do. When employees have no job demands, they will likely become bored because of this. Indeed, these situations correspond well to Karasek's (1979) passive and low-strain jobs. As job demand increases, employees have more to do. Increases in activity and time at work should facilitate employee engagement up to a point; beyond this threshold, demands will become taxing.

Addressing job demands requires mental and physical resources. While some level of job demands is necessary to facilitate employee engagement, employees have limited sources of personal energy. Because of the finite level of resources that employees have to apply to their jobs, at extremely high levels of job demands, employees will have fewer personal resources available to engage themselves in their work. The relationship between demands and engagement should be stronger at low levels of demand than at higher levels of demand.

Hypothesis 1: A positive and non-linear relationship will exist between demands and engagement such that the relationship between demands and engagement will be stronger at low levels of demand than at high levels of demand.

Control and engagement

Job control refers to the extent to which an employee is able to act in a proactive fashion to attain organizational goals (Herrenkohl et al., 1999) and is related to organizational commitment and organizational citizenship behavior (Menon, 2001). Perceptions of job control positively relate to psychological constructs hypothesized to influence employee engagement (Spence-Laschinger & Finegan, 2005). Kahn (1990, p. 708) proposed that being able to "employ one self without fear of negative consequences" is a critical dimension to enhance engagement.

Employees with decision-making power will come to feel a heightened sense of ownership over the results because they feel personally responsible for how things are accomplished. A supervisor who is allowed to use judgment to solve problems as they arise would feel a sense of ownership over the solutions. Lack of control would likely result in feelings of frustration and disengagement.

Hypothesis 2: After controlling for job demands, ratings of job control will be positively related to employee engagement.

Demands and control

The JDC(S) model speculates that positions of high control are optimal, and will lead to positive outcomes (Karasek, 1979). Positive outcomes (for example, intrinsic motivation, well-being) will result from situations of both high control and high demands (ibid.). Negative outcomes will result from high demands *and* low control (ibid.).

Those with lower job control will likely feel less responsible for the manner in which demands are met. As such, the potentially engaging consequence of increasing job demands is less likely among those with low levels of control. Higher engagement will likely be found in jobs with moderate demands and high control, while lower ratings of engagement will be related to low demands and low control.

Hypothesis 3: Job control will moderate the relationship between job demands and engagement such that the positive relationship between demands and engagement will be weakest at lower levels of control.

Demands, control, and support
Workplace support will provide employees with resources to cope with stressors (Karasek et al., 1982). Engagement at work is dependent on employees having personal resources; the provision of support should give employees additional resources to focus on their job.

Hypothesis 4: After controlling for demands and control, ratings of support will be positively related to engagement.

Method
The data for the current study come from 4,470 managers and supervisors (741 females; 3,614 males; 115 anonymous) working in North America, Latin America, Europe, and Asia. Employees were briefed and gave informed consent to voluntarily fill out the survey.

Measures
All measures were composed of items offered by a consulting organization. For all items, respondents indicate the extent to which they agree or disagree on a five-point scale. To measure engagement, a four-item measure was used. "My work gives me a feeling of personal accomplishment" is a representative sample item. To measure job demands, a four-item measure was used. "I find it difficult to keep up with the work that is expected of me" is a representative sample item. To measure job control, a four-item measure was used. "I am satisfied with my involvement in decisions that affect my work" is a representative sample item. To measure perceptions of organizational support, a four-item measure was used. "My Supervisor is available to me when I have questions or need help" is a representative sample item.

Analysis and results
Hierarchical regression analysis was used to test all hypotheses (Aiken & West, 1991). Curvilinear regression techniques were employed to test for a nonlinear relationship between demands and engagement.

Table 10.1   *Means, standard deviations, and reliability estimates for study variables*

Variable	Mean	SD	1	2	3	4	5
1. Gender	1.17	0.38					
2. Engagement	3.90	0.73	−0.01	(0.78)			
3. Demands	3.21	0.86	0.00	0.44**	(0.73)		
4. Control	3.71	0.79	−0.03	0.68**	0.40**	(0.78)	
5. Support	3.86	0.74	−0.04*	0.59**	0.36**	0.64**	(0.84)

Note: Values in parentheses are reliability estimates. $* p < 0.05$; $** p < 0.01$.

Table 10.2   *Results of hierarchical regression analyses for full sample*

	Variable	β	ΔR^2	ΔF
Step 1	Gender	−0.013	0.000	0.779
Step 2	Demands	0.439**	0.193	1036.678**
Step 3	Control	0.606**	0.310	2703.555**
Step 4	Support	0.226**	0.029	270.875**
Step 5	Demands^2	−0.044**	0.001	11.253**
Step 6	Demands × Control	−0.037*	0.001	5.999**

Note: $N = 4347$ after listwise deletion. Standardized coefficients reported.
$* p < 0.05$, $** p < 0.01$; coefficients reported reflect final step of the model. Quadratic and linear interactions reflect centered variables.

Means, standard deviations, and correlations are reported in Table 10.1. All measures show acceptable reliability coefficients (Cronbach, 1951). Gender was found to significantly relate only with support ($r = -0.04$, $p < 0.05$); females were likely to report lower levels of support. Demands, control, support, and engagement were all significantly and positively correlated with one another. This correlation matrix provides support for hypotheses 2 and 4 such that control and support are positively related to engagement.

Table 10.2 displays results for the regression analyses. Because past research has shown that gender may influence the experience of work and subsequent energy at work (Gyllensten & Palmer, 2005), gender was controlled. Study variables were entered in on separate steps to illustrate the additive effects of these variables on ratings of engagement.

Hypothesis 1 predicted a curvilinear relationship between demands and engagement. The linear term regressing engagement on demands was significant ($\beta = 0.44$, $p < 0.01$). Furthermore, in partial support of Hypothesis 1, the quadratic term was subsequently found to be significant ($\beta = -0.04$, p

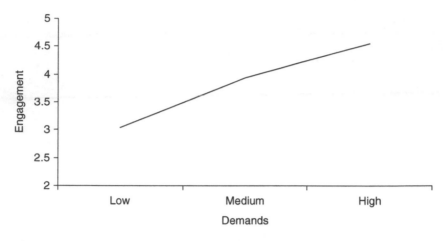

Figure 10.1   Relationship between demands and engagement

< 0.01) thereby suggesting a curvilinear relationship between demands and engagement. Figure 10.1 reveals that at low to moderate levels of engagement, the relationship between engagement and demands is positive; this positive relationship is slightly less strong at higher levels of demands.

Hypothesis 2 predicted an additive relationship of control after controlling for demands. This hypothesis received support, control was positively related to engagement ($\beta = 0.61$, $p < 0.01$).

Hypothesis 3 predicted the relationship between demands and engagement to be moderated by control. The demands X control interaction term was statistically significant ($\beta = -0.05$, $p < 0.04$). Figure 10.2 displays the relationships between demands, control, and engagement. Engagement is highest among employees reporting both high job demands and high job control.

The relationship between demands and engagement is positive across all levels of control; however this positive relationship is slightly stronger at high levels of control. Figure 10.2 illustrates the importance of considering both demands and control in understanding engagement.

Hypothesis 4 predicted a relationship between perceptions of support and ratings of engagement after taking demands and control into consideration. After entering control and demands, support was considered, this coefficient was statistically significant ($\beta = 0.23$, $p < 0.01$).

Discussion
The extent to which supervisors/managers are engaged depends, to some extent, on characteristics of the job such as job demands, job control, and

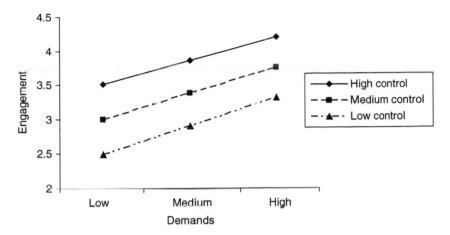

Figure 10.2   Relationship between demands, control, and engagement

support from organizational leadership. Organizations seeking to optimize employee engagement should consider JDC(S) theory. Results of the current study suggest the main effects proposed by the JDC(S) model are applicable when considering supervisors and managers working in various cultures.

Some researchers emphasize the importance of control and support in *moderating* the relationship between demands and employee outcomes (Johnson & Hall, 1988). Others emphasize the importance of considering *additive* relationships between demands, control, support and employee outcomes (Karasek, 1989). The current study and the majority of the JDC(S) literature report significant additive relationships (Van der Doef & Maes, 1999). This pattern of results suggests the robustness of strain-based hypotheses in contrast to buffer hypotheses.

The positive relationship between demands and engagement sheds light on the nature of employee engagement in managerial/supervisory employees. A manager or supervisor with little work to do will likely become bored at work; a bored employee is not an engaged employee. Not enough work may lead to feelings of job insecurity, which do not facilitate employee engagement. Past research on job satisfaction and turnover intent uncovered similar results (Beehr et al., 2001) – demands were negatively related to turnover intent and positively related to job satisfaction.

Managers or supervisors who perceive an adequate amount of work to be done will likely attribute more personal importance to their work and will feel that what they do is important; it is more likely that they will be engaged at work. When considering employee engagement, the importance of employees' perception that they "have enough to do" should not be underestimated. Traditionally, demands are conceptualized as negatively relating to desired outcomes. Results of the current study highlight the potential for job demands to be interpreted by employees as challenging; many employees will respond to challenges in a positive manner.

Given the positive relationship between job demands and employee engagement it is tempting to conclude that supervisory/managerial employees should be given extensive job demands to increase engagement. The current research does not entirely support this conclusion. While, Figure 10.1 suggests that a linear relationship could describe the relationship between demands and engagement, the significant negative quadratic term suggests that there may be limits to the quantity of demands that an employee can experience before becoming fatigued.

To maximize the engaging consequences of workload, one should consider research on job overload (Spector & Jex, 1998) and job characteristics (Hackman & Oldham, 1975), which suggest that the manner in which the work is perceived will impact on an employee's psychological response to job demands. For this reason, it is important for managerial employees to understand the importance of the work they do. Organizational efforts at recognizing efforts will likely result in increased levels of engagement. Public recognition of the value of hard work or long hours can create a positive culture that energizes those who choose to invest discretionary effort into their job role (within limits).

The additive relationship between job control and engagement highlights the importance of ensuring employees perceive that they are able to make decisions about how they perform their job duties. With regard to the interaction between demands and control, the coefficient associated with this interaction term was statistically significant. However, after charting the relationship between demands, control, and engagement it is apparent that the moderating role of control over demands is less important to consider than the main effect of control. Figure 10.2 clearly shows an overall difference in levels of engagement for low, high, and medium ratings of control across the observed range of job demands. What is less obvious is that differences in engagement between employees reporting low, medium, and high levels of control are minimized at low levels of demands.

Allowing employees to make job-relevant decisions can be beneficial. This will help employees to vest not only their labor but also their opinions and beliefs; thus employees will be more likely to engage themselves at work. In the case of the first-line supervisor or manager, knowledge of procedures, machinery, and the line employees is likely; their guidance on these matters will result in operational insight for the organization and a heightened sense of investment in their job role.

Without control over the task at hand, an employee may feel harnessed (that is, constrained) by the organization. An employee's perception of job control will shift focus from "harnessing of an employee's whole self to the work role" from an employee mentally attaching to the job to an employee being yoked by organizational constraints.

Providing supervisors and managers with the training, tools, and resources necessary to succeed in their job and to further develop their professional acumen will likely result in a more capable leadership pipeline for the organization and increase the levels of engagement among the employees who accept support from the organization.

Limitations

The current study was conducted using data collected from employees working for a multinational organization in numerous countries across the globe at one time point. The main limitation of using self-report data at one time point is that common method variance can influence observed results (Podsakoff & Organ, 1986). The current study is further limited by the inability to control for individual differences (for example, positive affectivity, negative affectivity, and locus of control) noted to influence the perception of demands, control, and support.

References

Aiken, L.S. & West, S.G. (1991), *Multiple Regression: Testing and Interpreting Interactions*, Newbury Park, CA: Sage.

Beehr, T.A., Glaser, K.M., Canali, K.G. & Wallwey, D.A. (2001), "Back to basics: re-examination of demand-control theory of occupational stress", *Work & Stress*, **15**, 115–30.

Cronbach, L.J. (1951), "Coefficient alpha and the internal structure of tests", *Psychometrika*, **6**, 297–334.

Gyllensten, K. & Palmer, S. (2005), "The role of gender in workplace stress: a critical literature review", *Health Education Journal*, **64**, 271–88.

Hackman, J.R. & Oldham, G.R. (1975), "Development of the Job Diagnostic Survey", *Journal of Applied Psychology*, **60**, 159–70.

Herrenkohl, R.C., Judson, G.T. & Heffner, J.A. (1999), "Defining and measuring employee empowerment", *Journal of Applied Behavioral Science*, **35**, 373–89.

Hogan, R. & Kaiser, R.B. (2005), "What we know about leadership", *Review of General Psychology*, **9**, 169–80.

Johnson, J.V. & Hall, E.M. (1988), "Job strain, workplace social support, and cardiovascular disease: a cross-sectional study of a random sample of the Swedish working population", *American Journal of Public Health*, **78**, 1336–42.

Kahn, W.A. (1990), "Psychological conditions of personal engagement and disengagement at work", *Academy of Management Journal*, **33**, 692–724.

Karasek, R.A. (1979), "Job demands, job decision latitude, and mental strain: implications for job redesign", *Administrative Science Quarterly*, **24**, 285–308.

Karasek, R. (1989), "Control in the workplace and its health-related aspects", in S.L. Sauter, J.J. Hurrell & C.L. Cooper (eds), *Job Control and Worker Health*, Chichester: Wiley, pp. 129–60.

Karasek, R.A., Triantis, K. & Chaudhry, S. (1982), "Co-worker and supervisor support as moderators of associations between task characteristics and mental strain", *Journal of Occupational Behavior*, **3**, 147–60.

Maslach, C. & Leiter, M.P. (1997), *The Truth About Burnout: How Organizations Cause Personal Stress and What to Do About It*, San Francisco, CA: Jossey-Bass.

Maslach, C., Schaufeli, W. & Leiter, M.P. (2001), "Job burnout", *Annual Review of Psychology*, **52**, 397–422.

Menon, S.T. (2001), "Employee empowerment: an integrated psychological approach", *Applied Psychology: An International Review*, **50**, 153–80.

Podsakoff, P.M. & Organ, D.W. (1986), "Self-reports in organizational research: problems and prospects", *Journal of Management*, **12**, 531–44.

Spector, P.E. & Jex, S.M. (1998), "Development of four self-report measures of job stressors and strain: Interpersonal Conflict at Work Scale, Organizational Constraints Scale, Quantitative Workload Inventory, and Physical Symptoms Inventory", *Journal of Occupational Health Psychology*, **3**, 356–67.

Spence-Laschinger, H.K. & Finegan, J.P.D. (2005), "Empowering nurses for work engagement and health in hospital settings", *Journal of Nursing Administration*, **35**, 439–49.

US Bureau of Labor Statistics (2008–09), US Department of Labor, *Occupational Outlook Handbook*, Washington, DC: US Government Printing Office.

Van der Doef, M. & Maes, S. (1999), "The job-demand–control–(support) model and psychological wellbeing: a review of 20 years of empirical research", *Work & Stress*, **13**, 87–114.

11 Engaging middle managers: activities and resources which enhance middle manager engagement

Karina Nielsen and Eusebio Rial González

Introduction

The importance of engaged employees has received widespread attention and the antecedents and consequences of engagement are well documented (Schaufeli & Salanova, 2008). Engagement has been defined as a positive, affective–motivational work-related state of fulfillment that is characterized by vigor, dedication and absorption (Schaufeli et al., 2002). In a review of the literature, Schaufeli and Salanova (2008) concluded that engaged employees were both more productive and reported higher levels of job satisfaction, commitment and fewer intentions to quit. There has, however, been less interest in middle managers, whose engagement can have wide-ranging consequences: unengaged middle managers may make faulty decisions or leave the organization and the costs may be far-reaching. Alternatively, the engaged middle manager may perform his/her job well and provide a positive example for other staff. In this chapter we review the literature on engagement in middle managers and draw from related research that may contribute to our understanding of the engaged middle manager. Furthermore, we shall also present some as yet unpublished data on the antecedents of engagement among leaders.

Why is engagement in middle managers important?

Engaged middle managers are particularly important for two reasons: first, because they play a decisive role in allowing the organization to achieve its objectives and maintain staff well-being and second, because engaged middle managers may to a larger extent be engaging.

Individuals high in engagement experience more positive emotions (Schaufeli & Van Rhenen, 2006). Research shows that happy people are more likely to seek out opportunities at work, they are more outgoing and helpful to others, and more confident and optimistic (Cropanzano & Wright, 2001). According to the broaden-and-build theory (Fredrickson, 2001) positive emotions broaden people's spontaneous thoughts, thus widening the array of thoughts and actions that come to mind. Joy also encourages individuals to be creative and increases the desire to explore and grow, and assimilate new information. Such attitudes to work are crucial for organizations to maintain their competitiveness and are particularly important in middle managers who need to take the lead.

Guth and Macmillan (1986) described middle managers as the organizations' central nervous system. They are responsible for receiving information and communicating this to their followers, they are responsible for facilitating communication between top management and shop-floor levels and integrating and implementing changes made by senior management in followers' daily work practices. Middle managers play a key role in setting a clear vision for what can be achieved through the implementation of senior management decisions (Parker & Williams, 2001). For example, Randall et al. (2005) found that the degree to which middle managers had communicated changes designed to improve role clarity and job enrichment determined changes in employee well-being.

Middle managers help to ensure that senior management decisions are implemented at a pace where employees' skills and adaptability are taken into consideration (Parker & Williams, 2001), thus supporting employees in their work and personal development (van Dierendonck et al., 2004; Nielsen et al., 2008). In a study of pastors who are leaders of their congregations, Little et al. (2007) found that engagement was negatively related to revenge behaviors; leaders who feel engaged in their jobs are less likely to exert revenge behaviors. This is particularly important among middle managers as the negative consequences of abusive leadership behaviors on followers' well-being have been documented (Yagil, 2006; Harvey et al., 2007; Wu & Hu, 2009).

As direct *drivers of change*, middle managers play a crucial role in implementing change decisions made at the top levels in the organization (Guth & Macmillan, 1986). Middle managers may resist implementing change for various reasons: (i) they may feel that they do not have the skills to successfully implement the strategy, (ii) they doubt the potential effectiveness of the change, or (iii) they may perceive a conflict between the goals of the strategy and their own personal goals (ibid.). As a result, they may not support the changes made and procrastinate in communicating and implementing decisions (passive resistance) or directly sabotage and build coalitions against the decisions made (active resistance). A qualitative study of highly engaged employees revealed that these were active agents; they showed initiative and were open to challenges at work, and were proactive at seeking new challenges (Schaufeli et al., 2001). Koyuncu et al. (2006) found that the values of engaged workers matched the values of the organizations.

Engaged middle managers may be more ready to act as leaders if they share the values of the organization: they are more likely to be appreciative of and welcome senior management decisions, and ready to role model these values. As a result, they may take a lead in implementing changes and buy in to changes and continually seek to improve working conditions and develop themselves and their employees. Being an active agent may be particularly important in times of change but also during "business as usual". Engaged workers take responsibility and try to solve problems when they face them. This may be an especially desired characteristic of middle managers as agents that monitor and act upon problems in the workplace. The adverse effects of managers escaping responsibility have been confirmed by research on *laissez-faire* leaders (managers who avoid making decisions, delay actions and ignore leader responsibilities) where links have been found to poor well-being (Skogstad et al., 2007).

The contagion effect (Westman, 2001) – the transfer of positive (or negative) experiences from one individual to another – has received increased research attention. The cross-over of the mood and emotions of middle managers to their followers has been examined. Sy et al. (2005) found that managers' moods influenced their followers' moods: when leaders were in a positive mood their staff also experienced more positive moods, and managers in positive moods exhibited more coordination and expended less effort. Support for the contagion effect was also found in a study by Glasø and Einarsen (2006) who found that during interactions, managers and employees shared emotions. When managers showed positive emotions, such as feeling respected, wanted and confident, so did employees. Glasø and Einarsen suggested that emotions displayed during interaction may function as a "thermometer"; followers perceive and interpret the own emotions as well as those of their superiors. This interpretation functions as a reality check as to how followers are doing – are managers satisfied with their behaviors and performance, and is the relationship between managers and employees a positive one?

The possible contagious effect of engagement from middle managers to their staff is indicated by research on the cross-over of engagement between husbands and wives (Bakker et al., 2005). Also, Bakker et al. (2006b) found that team members reported higher levels of engagement when their team colleagues also reported higher levels of engagement, also after controlling for individual-level job demands and job resources.

The contagion effect may be even more important in middle managers (Schaufeli & Salanova, 2008) as they function as role models and through their behavior can influence their employees' health in a number of ways. The engagement of middle managers is likely to have a cross-over effect as employees who perceive their manager to be making an extra effort and enjoying what he or she is doing are more likely to mimic these behaviors. In transformational leadership research the ability of middle managers to influence their followers' well-being is well established (Arnold et al.,

2007; Nielsen et al., 2008; Nielsen & Munir, 2009). The transformational leader formulates a clear vision, acts as a role model in exerting desired behaviors and encourages followers to take responsibility and seek novel ways of solving problems (Bass & Riggio, 2006). Moss (2009) found that middle managers influenced their employees' engagement through exerting transformational leadership behaviours. Bakker et al. (2006a) found in their study of school principals that engaged managers were more creative and exerted more transformational leadership behaviors, as rated by their followers – engaged leaders were found to be able to inspire, stimulate and coach their followers. Due to these potential benefits of engaged middle managers, it is important to know how organizations may promote engagement among middle managers.

The antecedents of middle managers' engagement: job demands–job resources
In recent years there has been an increasing interest in the factors that may influence how middle managers act towards their followers. Winsløw et al. (2009) found that the degree to which middle managers received support from their peers predicted the degree to which their employees experienced receiving support from their managers. In other words, the degree to which middle managers felt supported themselves was related to the support their followers experienced receiving from them. Reciprocity theory lends support to the fact that how middle managers perceive their working conditions and themselves may in fact influence how they behave towards their followers.

The antecedents of engagement in managers have been examined only sporadically. In a sample of women managers and professionals, Koyuncu et al. (2006) found that control, rewards and recognition, and value fit all predicted engagement. In an opportunity sample of managers in manufacturing, Schaufeli et al. (2008) examined the antecedents of engagement in managers – both middle managers and executives. They found that although engaged managers worked longer hours in highly demanding jobs, they experienced good mental health. Job resources such as social support and good social functioning predicted engagement among managers, as did high levels of job control (ibid.). Thus job resources were found to be related to engagement.

Also personal resources have been found to predict engagement in middle managers: Bakker et al. (2006a) reported that female school principals high in self-efficacy (an individual's belief about his or her abilities to mobilize cognitive resources and actions to execute a specific task within a given context; Bandura, 1997) and resilience were more engaged.

In a recent longitudinal study, Schaufeli et al. (2009) examined the positive gain spiral of engagement; that is, they examined how engagement may lead to increases in job resources which again predict engagement. They found that engagement did indeed lead to increases in job resources, as measured by autonomy, social support, performance feedback and opportunities to learn, which in turn predicted engagement at follow-up. Schaufeli et al. (ibid.) did, however, fail to find any relationships between engagement and job demands.

Antecedents of engagement in middle managers: new findings

Engagement in middle managers has to date been examined as a stable characteristic using questionnaire designs. However, the study of engagement as a transient state also carries value in that (i) it enables us to understand psychological variables at the time and level they are manifested, (ii) states can explain within-person differences, that is, why a person feels engaged at times and not at other times, and finally (iii) it can capture the day-to-day triggers of state engagement (Bakker et al., 2008; Xanthopoulou et al., 2009). There is therefore a need to explore the antecedents of state engagement as well as the more stable antecedents in order to gain a complete view of how engagement may be encouraged in middle managers. In the following we shall present unpublished data which help increase our understanding of the antecedents of engagement in middle managers both in terms of the tasks middle managers engage in but also the impact of their staff.

We examined the antecedents of middle manager engagement in two samples: Accountancy and elderly care ($N = 58$). Middle managers participated in an experience sampling method study and the followers completed a survey on their working conditions and health and well-being (Nielsen et al., 2008). The results of the analyses can be found in Figure 11.1.

Who influences whom? Employees as determinants of middle manager engagement

A reverse contagion effect may also take place: just as middle managers may influence their followers, followers may also influence their managers. A growing body of research has found that the well-being of followers influence the managers' behaviors (van Dierendonck et al., 2004; Nielsen et al., 2008). Also, employees' levels of engagement have been found to be related to middle managers' self-efficacy which in turn predicted middle managers' performance (Luthans & Peterson, 2002). It is likely that the degree to which employees are high in well-being also affects the engagement of middle managers. If employees are vigorous and full of energy they are more likely to be responsive to their leaders' actions, thus reinforcing their confidence in their own ability to lead, and therefore he or she may

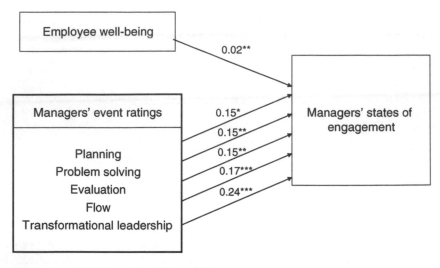

Note: * $p < 0.05$; ** $p < 0.01$; *** $p < 0.001$.

Figure 11.1   Antecedents of engagement states in middle managers

become more engaged as positive feedback from employees is received. People, including managers, have a tendency to avoid depressed people (Joiner & Coyne, 1999) and prefer to interact with people who are feeling more positive as it is more pleasant (Schaufeli et al., 1993). We found significant but small effects suggesting that followers who reported high levels of well-being had leaders who reported high levels of engagement. Engagement may therefore be best perceived as an ongoing co-creation between employees and their leaders.

Do transformational leaders transform themselves?
In a study of managers in five countries around the world, Konrad et al. (2001) found that middle managers enjoyed leading followers.

As mentioned previously, the study by Bakker et al. (2006a) suggested that engaged leaders are also transformational leaders – engaged leaders inspire and motivate their followers. At the core of transformational leadership is to encourage and facilitate growth in others – this is likely to have a growth effect on the agents of transformational leadership as well. When becoming transformational leaders, the role of the middle manager changes from being the one in charge to the one helping others to be in charge and making the necessary decisions (Bass & Riggio, 2006). The study by Konrad et al. (2001) indicates that the least enjoyable activities reported by managers involved controlling followers and the most enjoyable were related to actually *leading* followers. The analyses indicated that exerting transformational leadership behaviors did indeed predict states of engagement.

Activities predicting middle manager engagement

Identifying the activities that middle managers enjoy performing may help organizations to align their incentives and training, thus helping middle managers to focus their activities (ibid.). Engaging in *planning* may offer the middle manager the opportunity to be proactive. Planning also requires full concentration and the individual may experience enjoyment as he or she gets an overview of the work. *Problem solving* offers the opportunity for the middle managers to engage in a situation that is intrinsically motivating and makes full use of their skills as they appertain to the task at hand. *Evaluation* is also a cognitively challenging task which enables the middle manager to get feedback on his/her job and to reflect on his/her work and consider alternative ways of action. Evaluation requires the middle manager to actively collate the information from many sources, order it and the reward is immediate: feedback about his or her performance: thus it is likely to engage the middle manager. All of these activities were found to predict states of engagement.

The job resources model (see, for example, Bakker & Demerouti, 2008) suggests that a job that offers opportunities for growth and skills use is likely to promote engagement. Opportunities to learn have been found to be especially important in middle managers as they have a particularly strong need for learning and career advancement (Tharenou & Conroy, 1994). Thus flow conditions (situations where the individual feels challenged and able to use his or her skills) may also predict engagement states. This relationship has been found among students (Shernoff et al., 2003) and our analyses support this link in middle managers.

Implications for practice

This chapter emphasized the importance of engaged middle managers in engaging followers and ensuring their health and well-being. We reviewed the literature on what may engage middle managers at work and suggested some new ways in which this may be done. Below we discuss how the engaged middle manager may engage his/her followers. Transformational middle managers may promote engagement in followers in a number of ways but they may also themselves become more engaged.

Through intellectual stimulation and positive feedback, middle managers may build gain spirals and promote self-efficacy leading to engagement. Through encouraging novel ways of approaching challenges, middle managers may themselves also have the opportunity to grow and engage. Further, engagement may be promoted through the transformational leader formulating a clear vision and facilitating the development of specific goals and supporting the achievement of such goals. This process may also engage the middle manager him-herself: the route to success through the involvement of others requires an overview and the ability to network and encourage others to explore new perspectives. The study by Konrad et al. (2001) found that the most enjoyable activity reported by managers was innovating.

The transformational leader encourages the group as a whole to develop norms for good behavior and a collective responsibility for tasks including nurturing a shared goal. Through creating a clear vision the transformational leader may encourage positive reframing – which may also impact on the middle manager him-herself. Finally, transformational leaders may keep the job challenging through coaching and mentoring. This suggests that training transformational leaders may bring about engagement in followers – and in themselves – and may be a cost-effective way of increasing engagement. Research has confirmed that transformational leadership behaviors may be learned: studies by Barling et al. (1996) and Parry and Sinha (2005) found that employees reported their managers to exert more transformational leadership behaviors after training, with the result that employees were then found to be more engaged and exerting greater effort.

Middle managers may also promote engagement through the expression of positive emotions; however, this is likely to happen through a positive gain spiral: engaged managers promote employees high in well-being which again increases the middle manager's engagement – thus a double contagion effect may be at play. Further, if middle managers are engaged they may "contaminate", their followers, due to their envisioning position and function as role models, and the contagion effect may be particularly powerful. Also, by creating a social climate in which engagement is encouraged, middle managers may promote engaged followers. In today's ever-changing globalized environment, a middle manager who is engaged and open to change is vital. Research on resilience and engagement suggests that those managers who find it easier to adapt to new situations (resilient managers) are higher in engagement (Bakker et al., 2006a; Bakker & Demerouti, 2008) and therefore may be more willing to accept and implement changes. Recent research has found that middle managers do indeed play an important role in ensuring employee well-being and job satisfaction during organizational change (Nielsen & Randall, 2009).

References

Arnold, K.A., Turner, N., Barling, J., Kelloway, E.K. & Mckee, M.C. (2007), "Transformational leadership and psychological well-being: the mediating role of meaningful work", *Journal of Occupational Health Psychology*, **12**, 193–203.

Bakker, A.B. & Demerouti, E. (2008), "Towards a model of work engagement", *Career Development International*, **13**, 209–23.

Bakker, A.B., Demerouti, E. & Schaufeli, W.B. (2005), "The cross-over of burnout and work engagement among working couples", *Human Relations*, **58**, 661–89.

Bakker, A.B., Gierveld, J.H. & Van Rijswijk, K. (2006a), "Succesfactoren bij vrouwelijeki schooleiders in het primair oderwijs: een onderzok naar burnout, bevlogenheid en prestaties" (Success factor among female school principals in primary teaching: A study on burnout, work engagement, and performance), Right Management Consultants, Diemen.

Bakker, A.B., Schaufeli, W.B., Leiter, M.P. & Taris, T.W. (2008), "Work engagement: an emerging concept in occupational health psychology", *Work & Stress*, **22**, 187–200.

Bakker, A.B., van Emmerik, H. & Euwema, M.C. (2006b), "Crossover of burnout and engagement in work teams", *Work & Occupations*, **33**, 464–89.

Bandura, A. (1997), *Self-efficacy: The Exercise of Control*, New York: Freeman.

Barling, J., Weber, T. & Kelloway, K. (1996), "Effects of transformational leadership training on attitudinal and financial outcomes: a field experiment", *Journal of Applied Psychology*, **81**, 827–32.

Bass, B.M. & Riggio, R.E. (2006), *Transformational Leadership*, 2nd edn, Mahwah, NJ: Lawrence Erlbaum.

Cropanzano, R. & Wright, T.A. (2001), "When a 'happy' worker is really a 'productive' worker", *Career Development International*, **53**, 182–99.

Fredrickson, B.L. (2001), "The role of positive emotions in positive psychology: the broaden-and-build theory of positive emotions", *American Psychologist*, **56**, 218–26.

Glasø, L. & Einarsen, S. (2006), "Experienced affects in leader–subordinate relationships", *Scandinavian Journal of Management*, **22**, 49–73.

Guth, W.D. & Macmillan, I.C. (1986), "Strategy implementation versus middle manager self-interest", *Strategic Management Journal*, **7**, 313–27.

Harvey, P., Stoner, J., Hochwarter, W. & Kacmar, C. (2007), "Coping with abusive supervision: the neutralizing effects of ingratiation and positive affect on negative employee outcomes", *Leadership Quarterly*, **18**, 264–80.

Joiner, T. & Coyne, J.C. (1999), *The Interactional Nature of Depression: Advances in Interpersonal Approaches*, Washington, DC: American Psychological Association.

Konrad, A.M., Kashlak, R., Yoshioka, I., Waryszak, R. & Toren, N. (2001), "What do managers like to do?", *Group and Organization Management*, **26**, 401–33.

Koyuncu, M., Burke, R.J. & Fiksenbaum, L. (2006), "Work engagement among women managers and professionals in a Turkish bank: potential antecedents and consequences", *Equal Opportunities International*, **25**, 299–310.

Little, L.M., Simmons, B.L. & Nelson, D.L. (2007), "Health among leaders: positive and negative affect, engagement and burnout, forgiveness and revenge", *Journal of Management Studies*, **44**, 243–60.

Luthans, F. & Peterson, S.J. (2002), "Employee engagement and manager self-efficacy: implications for managerial effectiveness and development", *Journal of Management Development*, **21**, 376–87.

Moss, S. (2009), "Cultivating the regulatory focus of followers to amplify their sensitivity to transformational leadership", *Journal of Leadership and Organization Studies*, **15**, 241–59.

Nielsen, K. & Munir, F. (2009), "How do transformational leaders influence followers' affective well-being? Exploring the mediating role of self-efficacy", *Work & Stress*, **23** (4), 313–29.

Nielsen, K. & Randall, R. (2009), "Managers' active support when implementing teams: the impact on employee well-being", *Applied Psychology: Health & Well-being*, **1**, 374–90.

Nielsen, K., Randall, R., Yarker, J. & Brenner S.-O. (2008), "The effects of transformational leadership on followers' perceived work characteristics and psychological well-being: a longitudinal study", *Work & Stress*, **22**, 16–32.

Parker, S. & Williams, H. (2001), *Effective Teamworking: Reducing the Psychosocial Risks*, Norwich: HSE Books.

Parry, K.W. & Sinha, P.N. (2005), "Researching the trainability of transformational organisational leadership", *Human Resource Development International*, **8**, 165–83.

Randall, R., Griffiths, A. & Cox, T. (2005), "Evaluating organizational stress-management interventions using adapted study designs", *European Journal of Work and Organizational Psychology*, **14**, 23–41.

Schaufeli, W.B., Bakker, A.B. & Van Rhenen, W. (2009), "How changes in job demands and resources predict burnout, work engagement, and sickness absenteeism", *Journal of Organizational Behavior*, **30**, 893–917.

Schaufeli, W.B., Maslach, C. & Marek, T. (1993), *Professional Burnout: Recent Developments in Theory and Research*, Washington, DC: Taylor & Francis.

Schaufeli, W.B. & Salanova, M. (2008), "Enhancing work engagement through the management of human resources", in K. Näswall, J. Hellgren & M. Sverke (2008), *The Individual in the Changing Working Life*, Cambridge: Cambridge University Press, pp. 380–402.

Schaufeli, W.B., Salanova, M., González-Romá, V. & Bakker, A. (2002), "The measurement of engagement and burnout: a two-sample confirmatory factor analytic approach", *Journal of Happiness Studies*, **3**, 71–92.

Schaufeli, W.B., Taris, T.W., Le Blanc, P., Peeters, M., Bakker, A.B. & de Jonge, J. (2001), "Maakt arbeid gezond? Op zoek naar de bevlogen werknemer" (Does work make you happy? In search of the engaged worker), *De Psycholoog*, **36**, 422–8.

Schaufeli, W.B., Taris, T.W. & Van Rhenen, W. (2008), "Workaholism, burnout, and work engagement: three of a kind or three different kinds of employee well-being?", *Applied Psychology: An International Review*, **57**, 173–203.

Schaufeli, W.B. & Van Rhenen, W. (2006), "Over de rol van positieve and negatieve emoties bij het welbevinden managers: enn studie de Job-related Affective Well-being Scale (JAWS)" (About the role of positive and negative emotions in managers' well-being: a study using the Job-related Affective Well-being Scale (JAWS)), *Gedrag & Organisatie*, **19**, 223–44.

Shernoff, D.J., Csikszentmihalyi, M., Schneider, B. & Shernoff, E.S. (2003), "Student engagement in high school classrooms from the perspective of flow theory", *School Psychology Quarterly*, **18**, 158–76.

Skogstad, A., Einarsen, S., Torsheim, T., Aasland, M.S. & Hetland, H. (2007), "The destructiveness of laissez-faire leadership behavior", *Journal of Occupational Health Psychology*, **12**, 80–92.

Sy, T., Cote, S. & Saavedra, R. (2005), "The contagious leader: impact of the leader's mood on the mood of group members, group affective tone, and group processes", *Journal of Applied Psychology*, **90**, 295–305.

Tharenou, P. & Conroy, D. (1994), "Men and women managers' advancement: personal or situational determinants", *Journal of Applied Psychology: An International Review*, **43**, 5–31.

Van Dierendonck, D., Haynes, C., Borril, C. & Stride, C. (2004), "Leadership behavior and subordinate well-being", *Journal of Occupational Health Psychology*, **9**, 165–75.

Westman, M. (2001), "Stress and strain cross-over", *Human Relations*, **54**, 717–51.

Winsløw, J.H., Nielsen, K. & Borg, V. (2009), "Generating support from supervisors to their subordinates in organizations under external pressure: a multilevel multi-source study of support and reciprocation in the Danish elder care", *Journal of Advanced Nursing*, **65** (12), 2649–57.

Wu, T.Y. & Hu, C. (2009), "Abusive supervision and employee emotional exhaustion: dispositional antecedents and boundaries", *Group and Organization Management*, **34**, 143–69.

Xanthopoulou, D., Bakker, A.B., Demerouti, E. & Schaufeli, W.B. (2009), "Work engagement and financial returns: a diary study on the role of job and personal resources", *Journal of Vocational Behavior*, **82**, 183–20.

Yagil, D. (2006), "The relationship of abusive and supportive workplace supervision to employee burnout and upward influence tactics", *Journal of Emotional Abuse*, **6**, 49–65.

12 Leadership and engagement: a brief review of the literature, a proposed model, and practical implications
Jesse Segers, Peggy De Prins and Sonja Brouwers

Introduction
The claim that leaders can influence the engagement level of their staff is for most employees stating the obvious. The academic literature has not, however, paid attention to this assumption and has hardly addressed the question of how leaders influence the engagement level of their followers. The purpose of this chapter is to address this question by reviewing the few studies available in this area, proposing some avenues for future research, and by offering some implications for leadership development that follow from the preliminary research.

Positive leadership and state engagement
Engagement has been described in many different ways in the literature (Macey & Schneider, 2008), but refers in this chapter to "a persistent, positive, affective-motivational *state* of fulfilment in employees that is characterized by vigor, dedication, and absorption" (Maslach et al., 2001, p. 417, italics added). This form of engagement is empirically distinct from organizational commitment and job involvement, but shares at the same time the positive attachment to work (Hallberg & Schaufeli, 2006).

Given that state engagement belongs to the positive organizational behavior movement (Bakker & Schaufeli, 2008), it is not surprising that some studies have researched its link with positive forms of leadership (that is, transformational leadership, empowering leadership, and the coaching style of leadership).

Leaders influence other states of their followers that influence state engagement
Segers et al. (2009a) revealed in a cross-sectional Belgian study (n = 2,868) that perceived transformational leadership indirectly and positively influenced employee vigor, dedication, and absorption (see Figure 12.1). The opposite was observed for perceived directive leadership.

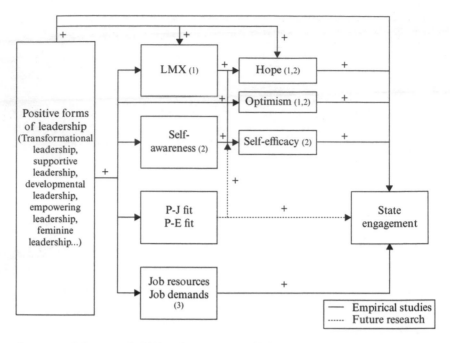

Sources: (1) Segers et al. (2009a); (2) Segers et al. (2009b); (3) Tuckey et al. (2009).

Figure 12.1   Leadership and engagement

Directive leadership and transformational leadership were measured with the Managerial Style Questionnaire (MSQ: McBer & Company, 1993). Transformational leadership was operationalized as a combination of visionary, coaching, affiliative, and participative leadership style, while directive leadership was operationalized in terms of task-oriented behavior, with a strong focus on targets, close supervision, and control of subordinate actions (Euwema et al., 2007).

More specifically, individuals who perceived their leader to have a transformational style of leadership characterized their relationship with him/her as being high in mutual respect, reciprocal trust and career-oriented obligation (compare "leader–member exchange" (LMX), Graen & Uhl-Bien, 1995). This positive high-quality relation in turn made the followers feel more engaged, probably because of feeling supported by their leader in their capabilities, and trusting him/her not to punish them if they engage themselves behaviorally at work (for example, the process of job creep: extra-role behaviors become viewed as in-role obligations by the leader) (Macey & Schneider, 2008).

In addition, the perception of working for a transformational leader, and the subsequent high-quality relationship, increased employee levels of hope and optimism. Hopeful employees are more motivated to attain goals ("willpower"), and to find ways to reach the set goals, even if the initial paths towards their goals are blocked ("waypower") (Snyder et al., 1991). Optimistic employees make more positive attributions about succeeding now and in the future, as they have an explanatory style that attributes negative events to external, temporary and situation-specific factors, while attributing positive events to internal, stable and pervasive causes (Seligman, 1998). This higher state of optimism, and especially the higher state of hope, was found to be associated with increased levels of engagement of the employees in our study. Interesting to note is that at the same time this mechanism led employees to feel generally happier in life as well.

Perceived directive leadership on the other hand, led to a decline in hope, optimism, and a lower quality of the relationship between the leader and the follower (as perceived by the follower), and hence to lower state engagement and subjective happiness.

In a second analysis of their cross-sectional study, Segers et al. (2009b) looked at one specific aspect of transformational leadership, namely individualized consideration (see Figure 12.1). Rafferty and Griffin (2006) demonstrated that this dimension consists of two further dimensions: supportive and development leadership. Supportive leadership entails providing emotional support, which involves sympathy, evidence of liking, caring and listening; as well as informational, instrumental and appraisal support to followers (House, 1981; Rafferty & Griffin, 2006), while developmental leadership involves career counseling, careful observation of staff, recording followers' progress and encouraging them to attend technical courses (Bass, 1985; Rafferty & Griffin, 2006). Stated differently, individualized consideration can be considered as the coaching style of leadership (Graham et al., 1993).

The results indicated that leaders who demonstrated individualized consideration increased, both directly and indirectly, the vigor, dedication, and absorption of their followers at work, and their global subjective feeling of happiness in life. Beyond the expected effects of increased hope and optimism, this leadership style also increased the self-awareness of followers and their belief that they are able to successfully execute specific tasks (compare "self-efficacy", Stajkovic & Luthans, 1998). Self-efficacy was a positive predictor of state engagement, while self-awareness was not. Higher levels of self-awareness, were however, associated with higher levels of hope, optimism and self-efficacy. It needs to be noted that both studies have limitations in that they did not take into account the influence of work characteristics and were cross-sectional in nature.

The leader creates an environment that influences state engagement
Apart from influencing different states that have a positive effect on engagement, it seems that leaders can also create an environment that increases the state engagement of their followers directly. Tuckey et al. (2009) demonstrated in a multilevel study that Australian fire brigade captains ($n = 84$) with an empowering leadership style increased the vigor, dedication, and absorption of their voluntary workforce ($n = 540$) (see Figure 12.1). An empowering leadership style is characterized by coaching behaviors, leading by example, showing concern/interacting with their team members, participative decision making, and explaining to followers the goals, decisions, rules, and so on. The fire brigade captains increased engagement by optimizing the working conditions in terms of job demands and job resources. This type of leadership style, which resembles the idealized influence and individual consideration dimension of transformational leadership, had an especially positive effect on state engagement in "active work" contexts. In other words, they created more cognitive demands (for example, job complexity) but at the same time offered more cognitive resources (for example, job control) and strengthened the effect of this environment on the state engagement of their followers. In addition, this empowering leadership style directly influenced the state engagement of volunteer fire fighters. A limitation of this study was, however, that it did not take into account other individual states of the followers.

Future research: the leader influences person–environment fit and person–job fit
Taking the above results together, it seems that positive forms of leadership such as supportive, developmental, empowering and transformational leadership, have a direct and indirect influence on state engagement by influencing other states such as hope, optimism, and self-efficacy which in turn increases employee feelings of vigor, dedication, and absorption. The last is partially achieved by creating high-quality relationships with followers and by increasing their self-awareness. In addition, "positive" leaders create and strengthen the positive effect of active work contexts on state engagement.

Building upon the notion of active work contexts, Inceoglu and Warr (2009) demonstrated that many job features (including workload, challenge, high standards, and so on) of the vitamin model proposed by Warr (2007) predicted job engagement. Moreover, in many cases the difference between wanted and actual job features significantly explained incremental variance in state engagement. Given that participative leadership correlates positively with person–job fit (Mulki et al., 2006), some of the positive effects of these positive leadership styles on state engagement might be explained by the idea that those leaders increase the person–job fit of their employees. Moreover, Li (2006) demonstrated in a Chinese study that perceived feminine leadership behavior, which again resembles the individual consideration, but also the idealized influence dimension of transformational leadership (being a good listener, showing empathy, sharing information with others, as well as participative decision making, fostering mutual trust and respect among organizational members, and teambuilding) increases person–organization value fit. The latter increased employees' motivation and commitment, which are constructs that share some overlap with state engagement (Macey & Schneider, 2008). Hence, positive styles of leadership might also increase the state engagement of followers by increasing their person–environment fit. Both types of fit in turn might make employees feel more optimistic or comfortable in executing specific tasks successfully, or they might find more ways to reach goals they have set themselves (see Figure 12.1). In sum, it seems that future research might usefully explore the role of person–job and person–environment fit in relation to engagement.

Implications for managers

Although more research is needed in order to come to definitive conclusions (for example, longitudinal and cross-cultural designs), the current research indicates that leaders with a positive style of leadership can influence the engagement level of their staff. Hence, the question for managers becomes: how to develop engaging leadership?

The following proposed modules for a workshop draw from field experiments that have demonstrated how to develop transformational leadership (for example, Bass & Avolio, 1992; Barling et al., 1996; Kelloway et al., 2000). The modules also draw from research that has demonstrated how to develop hope, optimism, and self-efficacy in a work context (Luthans et al., 2006, 2008) and research that investigated how leaders can create quality relationships with all members in their team (Graen et al., 1982, 1986; Scandura & Graen, 1984).

Important to note is that one of the things that most of these training efforts have in common is that they start top-down, and try to blend these with ongoing organizational efforts. They stress, for example, the importance of only investing in changes that can be integrated into the daily routine of the participants. The latter is partially done to overcome the cynical idea that a new training initiative is just the "new flavor of the month" and, more importantly, not only to develop leaders (individual), but also to develop leadership (individual + organization).

Basic leadership workshop to increase employee engagement
In a first module, participants are asked to describe the behaviors of the best and worst leaders they have experienced. Next, with the help of a workshop facilitator, these characteristics are placed within the framework of the "positive forms" of leadership (see Figure 12.1), transactional and *laissez-faire* leadership. In the second module, participants are introduced to the theories and research findings of the different constructs and the three different styles of leadership.

The third module has a double purpose: first, applying the conceptual constructs, and second, to increase the participants' engagement to become a more engaging leader. Hence, participants are asked to work through seven basic steps that were offered as part of the theory to increase engagement with followers. For the purpose of this chapter, we indicated in brackets the construct to which each step relates:

1. Identify personal goals, and how these relate to your personal values, that are specific and difficult but attainable (Locke & Latham, 1990) in relation to your own development towards becoming an engaging leader in this organization (hope).
2. Make these goals as concrete and action-oriented as possible. Ask for help of the facilitator in case you are stuck and let him/her review them when ready (hope).
3. Break the goals into sub-goals (hope, optimism, self-efficacy).
4. Work together with a colleague to come up with as many ways as possible to reach the desired goals (hope, optimism, self-efficacy).
5. Working together with a colleague, create for each goal a list of paths on the basis of the various means necessary to achieve those goals. Next, eliminate any paths that are unrealistic in your organization after careful deliberation (hope, optimism, self-efficacy).
6. Think of potential obstacles you might encounter in trying to reach the envisaged goals, and how best to avoid them. If any of the perceived hurdles are deemed to be insurmountable, think of aspects you can control and reflect on the actual impact of not being able to attain the goal (optimism, resiliency).
7. Finally, describe positive outcomes if you were a more engaging leader in this organization (optimism).

In the fourth module, the participants view a video of managers with a "positive" and a "negative" leadership style. Then, they are asked to create a video themselves where they demonstrate the different styles. The different videos are then viewed in the group, and feedback by the other participants and the workshop facilitator is provided, based upon the theory (modeling and positive feedback increases self-efficacy). Next, they receive feedback based on a "positive leadership" questionnaire (for example, the Multifactor Leadership Questionnaire (MLQ), Bass & Avolio, 1990; the Empowering Leadership Questionnaire (ELQ), Arnold et al., 2000) they completed prior to the workshop on their personal leadership style.

In the next three modules attention is focused on learning some concrete skills: active listening, learning how to delegate (and investigating the reluctance to do so) in order to develop subordinates, improving the quality of the relationship between the leader and the member, diagnosing own strengths and weaknesses and those of followers, learning how to provide constructive and positive feedback, and helping employees to go through the seven engaging steps described above. Each skill is taught through real case studies in the organization and various interactive exercises. In order to improve the LMX, for example, participants participate in role-play, in which they have to find out about the concerns and job expectations of the employees, the managers, and their working relationship using active listening skills. The managers have to refrain from imposing their usual frame of reference on the issues raised. Next they have to share some of their own job expectations about the manager's job, the members' job and their working relationship. In order to provide constructive and positive feedback, peer ratings on the different aspects of positive leadership are collected for each member from the rest of the team, and they work in small teams on providing and working with the summarized outcome.

In the final module, the preliminary self-development plan of the third module is revised in light of the feedback received from their peers, hereby following again the seven engaging steps. At the end of this module, the participants are encouraged to imagine, with the aid of some techniques facilitated by the trainer, such as visualization techniques, what it would feel like if they were able to achieve their personal challenges and valuable goals in the organization, as this helps to increase their self-efficacy. Before they leave the workshop, permission from each participant is received to collect data anonymously from their followers on how engaging they are as leaders in the coming three months. This will be done with the help of questionnaires that measure the different constructs in Figure 12.1, as well as from their manager, who will rate them in terms of their leadership style.

Interval period
During the interval period, participants are encouraged to have a meeting with their manager to discuss their personal development, and to have LMX meetings with their followers (which they exercised in role-plays). They also receive key readings. Data on how engaging they are as a leader

is collected from their followers and the manager. The participants are also asked to come up with a real organizational problem that they are facing or have faced in those three months, and receive a template for writing it up, as the real organizational problems will be discussed in the follow-up workshop.

Follow-up workshop to increase employee engagement
The first module of the follow-up workshop starts off with discussing in small groups the improvement the participants feel they have made on their personal development plan. A summary is presented in a plenary session as structured in the model in Figure 12.1. Hereafter, detailed feedback is provided to each participant based upon the data collected from their followers and managers. The results are then incorporated into their personal development plan.

With the new personal challenges in mind, the participants start working in the third module on the real organizational problems they prepared. Nobody works, however, on his/her own problem; participants swap problems and work on someone else's. When the exercise is completed, the person responsible for the problem reviews the proposed solution and examines its feasibility.

Conclusion
The proposed workshop structure is obviously only one way to develop more engaging leaders. Counseling/coaching, for example has been shown to be as effective as workshops in developing transformational leaders. However, the combination of both is no more effective than either approach alone (Kelloway and Barling, 2000). Nevertheless, developing engaging leadership is more complex as it depends on the interaction with the organizational environment (Fiedler, 1996). Creating workshops as described above that blend in specific training with ongoing organizational efforts are therefore just a start to developing engaging leadership in organizations.

In sum, it is clear that more research is required that explores the links between leadership and state engagement, but it is our hope that the current chapter can serve as a first step towards creating more engaging leadership in organizations and, hence happier and more productive employees.

References
Arnold, J.A., Arad, S., Rhoades, J.A. & Drasgow, F. (2000), "The Empowering Leadership Questionnaire: the construction and validation of a new scale for measuring leader behaviors", *Journal of Organizational Behavior*, **21**, 249–69.

Bakker, A.B. & Schaufeli, W.B. (2008), "Positive organizational behavior: engaged employees in flourishing organizations", *Journal of Organizational Behavior*, 29, 147–54.

Barling, J., Weber, T. & Kelloway, E.K. (1996), "Effects of transformational leadership training on attitudinal and financial outcomes: a field experiment", *Journal of Applied Psychology*, 81, 827–32.

Bass, B.M. (1985), *Leadership and Performance Beyond Expectations*, New York: Free Press.

Bass, B.M. & Avolio, B.J. (1990), *Manual for the Multifactor Leadership Questionnaire*, Palo Alto, CA: Consulting Psychologists Press.

Bass, B.M. & Avolio, B.J. (1992), "Developing transformational leadership: 1992 and beyond", *Journal of European Industrial Training*, 14(5), 21–7.

Euwema, M., Wendt, H. & Van Emmerik, H. (2007), "Leadership styles and group organizational citizenship behavior", *Journal of Organizational Behavior*, 28, 1035–57.

Fiedler, P.E. (1996), "Research on leadership selection and training: one view of the future", *Administrative Science Quarterly*, 41, 241–50.

Graen, G.B., Novak, M. & Sommerkamp, P. (1982), "The effects of leader–member exchange and job design on productivity and satisfaction: testing a dual attachment model", *Organizational Behavior and Human Performance*, 30, 109–31.

Graen, G.B., Scandura, T.A. & Graen, M.R. (1986), "A field experimental test of the moderating effects of growth need strength on productivity", *Journal of Applied Psychology*, 71, 484–91.

Graen, G.B. & Uhl-Bien, M. (1995), "Relationship-based approach to leadership: development of leader–member exchange (LMX) theory of leadership over 25 years: applying a multi-level multi-domain perspective", *Leadership Quarterly*, 6, 219–47.

Graham, S., Wedman, J.F. & Garvin-Kester, B. (1993), "Manager coaching skills: development and application", *Performance Improvement Quarterly*, 6(1), 2–13.

Hallberg, U.E. & Schaufeli, W.B. (2006), "'Same same' but different? Can work engagement be discriminated from job involvement and organizational commitment?", *European Psychologist*, 11(2), 119–27.

House, J.S. (1981), *Work Stress and Social Support*, Reading, MA: Addison-Wesley.

Inceoglu, I. & Warr, P. (2009), "Person-oriented aspects of job design: predicting engagement from person–job fit", paper presented at An International Symposium on Disentangling Engagement at the 2009 Society for Industrial and Organizational Psychology conference, New Orleans, April.

Kelloway, E.K. & Barling, J. (2000), "What we have learned about developing transformational leaders", *Leadership and Organization Development Journal*, 21, 355–62.

Kelloway, E.K., Barling, J. & Helleur, J. (2000), "Enhancing transformational leadership: the roles of training and feedback", *Leadership and Organizational Development Journal*, 21(3), 145–9.

Li, J. (2006), "The interactions between person-organisation fit and leadership styles in Asian firms, an empirical testing", *International Journal of Human Resource Management*, 17, 1689–706.

Locke, E.A. & Latham, G.P. (1990), *A Theory of Goal Setting and Task Performance*, Englewood Cliffs, NJ: Prentice-Hall.

Luthans, F., Avey, J.B., Avolio, B.J., Norman, S.M. & Combs, G.M. (2006), "Psychological capital development: toward a micro-intervention", *Journal of Organizational Behavior*, 27, 387–93.

Luthans, F., Avey, J.B. & Patera, J.L. (2008), "Experimental analysis of a web-based training intervention to develop positive psychological capital", *Academy of Management Learning and Education*, 7(2), 209–21.

Macey, W.H. & Schneider, B. (2008), "The meaning of employee engagement", *Industrial and Organizational Psychology*, 1, 3–30.

Maslach, C., Schaufeli, W.B. & Leiter, M.P. (2001), "Job burnout", *Annual Review of Psychology*, 52, 397–422.

McBer & Company (1993), *The Managerial Style Questionnaire*, Boston, MA: McBer & Co.

Mulki, J.P., Jaramillo, F. & Locander, W.B. (2006), "Emotional exhaustion and organizational deviance: can the right job and a leader's style make a difference?", *Journal of Business Research*, **59**, 1222–30.

Rafferty, A.E. & Griffin, M.A. (2006), "Refining individualized consideration: distinguishing developmental leadership and supportive leadership", *Journal of Occupational and Organizational Psychology*, **79**, 37–61.

Scandura, T. & Graen, G.B. (1984), "Moderating effects of initial leader–member exchanges status on the effects of a leadership intervention", *Journal of Applied Psychology*, **69**, 428–36.

Segers, J., De Prins, P., Brouwers, S. & Vloeberghs, D. (2009a), "How perceived leadership engages employees and makes them happy: the role of the quality of the leader–member relationship, hope and optimism", paper presented at An International Symposium on Disentangling Engagement at the 2009 Society for Industrial and Organizational Psychology conference, New Orleans, April.

Segers, J., De Prins, P., Brouwers, S. & Vloeberghs, D. (2009b), "The leader as coach: understanding the way towards engaged and happy employees", paper presented at An International Symposium on Disentangling Engagement at the 2009 European Congress of Work and Organizational Psychology, Santiago De Compostella, May.

Seligman, M. (1998), *Learned Optimism*, New York: Pocket Books.

Snyder, C.R., Irving L. & Anderson, J. (1991), "Hope and health: measuring the will and the ways", in Snyder & D.R. Forsyth (eds), *Handbook of Social and Clinical Psychology*, Elmsford, NY: Pergamon, pp. 285–305.

Stajkovic, A.D. & Luthans, F. (1998), "Social cognitive theory and self-efficacy: going beyond traditional motivational and behavioural approaches", *Organizational Dynamics*, **26**, 62–74.

Tuckey, M.R., Dollard, M.F., Klemasz, B. & Bakker, A.B. (2009), "Leader behavior and follower engagement: a multilevel study", paper presented at The Secrets of Employee Engagement Symposium at the 2009 European Congress of Work and Organizational Psychology, Santiago de Compostella, May.

Warr, P.B. (2007), *Work, Happiness, and Unhappiness*, Mahwah, NJ: Erlbaum.

13 The role of employee trust in understanding employee engagement

Benjamin Schneider, William H. Macey, Karen M. Barbera and Scott A. Young

Introduction

We base this chapter on the now demonstrated relationship between employee engagement and performance at the individual (Bakker et al., 2004), unit (Harter et al., 2002), and organizational (Schneider et al., 2009a) levels of analysis (see Bakker et al., 2008 for a review). Here, our focus is on trust as a specific and critical antecedent of engagement. While other situational job resources (for example, autonomy, supervisory coaching, performance feedback) and personal resources (for example, optimism, self-efficacy, self-esteem) have been shown to predict engagement (Bakker et al., 2008), we believe these fail to capture the psychological experiences employees have that most significantly impact their engagement.

We present a conceptual model where the level of trust employees experience at work is a psychological antecedent of employee engagement, which we hypothesize results in them feeling safe to feel and be engaged. As Kahn (1990, p. 708) put it in his pathbreaking explication of engagement: "Psychological safety [is] feeling able to show and employ one's self without fear of negative consequences to self-image, status, or career. People [in the research effort] feel safe in situations in which they trusted that they would not suffer from their personal engagement".

In brief, we present a mediated model after Kahn (1990), shown schematically in Figure 13.1, in which employees' experiences of fair work conditions, among other factors, lead them to trust their co-workers, supervisors and the system such that they feel safe enough to both feel engaged and act in engaged ways. That is, while other factors in the work environment can lead people to feel engaged (for example, an exciting work project, a compelling company mission), our model indicates that these result in engagement behavior under the conditions of trust. In what follows we discuss the various elements of the model shown in Figure 13.1 and conclude with some practical implications of the issues raised for management.

On this last point it is important to note that our discussion of the model shown in the figure will focus on employee engagement at the unit or

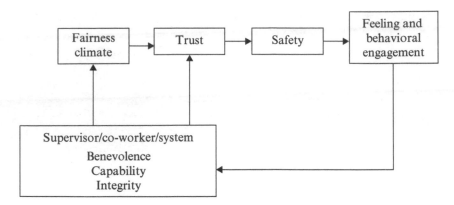

Figure 13.1   Antecedents and consequences of experienced trust in work organizations

organizational level of analysis, not the individual level. From a practical standpoint, what is of most interest to companies is employee engagement in the aggregate, not the engagement of individual employees one at a time. By implication and extension, our focus is on the trust that employees in the aggregate have in their co-workers, their supervisors, and the system as a whole rather than the way each employee individually experiences trust in each of these.

Trust
Our model for understanding employee engagement is presented in detail in Macey et al. (2009). Our model proposes that engagement has both psychological (feelings) and behavioral components to it. Feelings define engagement for the individual, and engagement behavior operationalizes engagement in the aggregate for people (for example, the work group, the organization). In Macey et al. (2009) feeling engaged has the following psychology: feelings of urgency, of being focused, of intensity, and enthusiasm. These are quite similar to the meaning of engagement in other research as well (see Schaufeli et al., 2006). Behavioral engagement in Macey et al. is the overt operationalization of engagement: being persistent, being proactive, expanding one's roles as needed, and adapting readily to necessary change. There is little comparable work on behavioral engagement except that work on personal initiative (Frese, 2008) and organizational citizenship behavior (OCB; Organ et al., 2006) would be similar in connotation. But what are the antecedents to feeling and being engaged?

As the core construct in Figure 13.1, trust is the issue we first present in some detail. We conceptualize trust as the core mediating variable in understanding employee engagement based on the logic and thinking about trust of Kahn (1990) and Schoorman and his colleagues (Mayer et al., 1995; Schoorman et al., 2007). As they stated (Schoorman et al., 2007, p. 348): "The basis of our [1995] model [of trust] was to understand how parties process information about others thereby deciding how much risk to take with those others". Thus, in our framework, feeling and being engaged is a risk that employees take, and they take that risk to the extent that they feel psychologically safe (Kahn, 1990). Further, psychological safety is a direct function of the degree to which they trust the people and the system in which they work. In short, if management wants to reap the benefits of having an engaged workforce, management needs to attend to all of the features that promote and sustain trust, and conversely, avoid those actions that erode trust. In addition, they need to recognize that trust is a two-way street. Employees not only must have trust in others and the system to feel safe, but also need to feel that they are trusted by management. This latter point will not be a focus of the present chapter but we state it to be sure to recognize that trust has its maximum effect when it is truly bi-directional.

People know they trust others when: (a) they are willing to reciprocate the care and consideration they receive from others (Konovsky & Pugh, 1994) and (b) when they feel that the others with whom they interact have integrity, capability, and benevolence (Mayer et al., 1995; Dirks, 2006; Kim et al., 2009) and thus will not behave opportunistically (Madhock, 2006). Thus, trust in others is most clearly revealed by people when they willingly cooperate with others (Konovsky & Pugh, 1994; McAllister, 1995; Lewicki et al., 2006) and when they behave in free and open ways with others rather than in restrained ways, indicating that they are trying to cover their backs (Dirks, 2006). Thus, feeling free to behave this way and actually doing so extends the vague concept of "cooperate" to our definitions of engagement feelings and behavior. We hypothesize that this happens when trust exists because people feel safe to feel and be engaged. Management wants engagement because such behavior is an important foundation for organizational effectiveness (Schneider et al., 2009a).

We have mentioned that employees who feel engaged and display engagement behavior are taking some risk in doing so, and there are a couple of reasons why we believe this to be the case. First, engagement involves an investment of one's energy in pursuit of organizational goals. Employees may be reluctant to invest their full energy if they do not trust that some personal and/or organizational benefit will follow, and that no negative consequence will result. With regard to engagement behavior, one example of risk-taking is raising a concern or identifying a potential flaw in a strategy proposed by management. An employee who fears that expressing his or her point of view may lead to the perception that he or she is a complainer, an obstacle, or a cynic, is unlikely to voice the opinion. The cost is greatest when the energy invested is on something of significant personal meaning – something of particular self-interest to the employee. When the focus is innovation, what may be at risk is the ownership of the idea and the rewards and recognition that should come to the contributor. In a service environment what may be at risk is the pain of emotional labor. Even in more ordinary circumstances, it may be the pain of lost credibility or reputation. Hofmann et al. (2009) demonstrated that nurses are less likely to seek advice from experts in the absence of trust, a result supporting what O'Toole and Bennis (2009) have suggested, namely that there is potential for catastrophic consequences when employees possessing critical knowledge fail to bring that knowledge forward due to a lack of trust.

Conversely, employees will speak up with little or no hesitation when they trust that others will attribute their expression of concern to an interest in the success of a project and the well-being of the organization. The same is true of other engagement behaviors such as proposing a new idea, or volunteering to work on a new project, or in other ways taking a personal risk.

We have deliberately turned the discussion of trust from one of feeling safe to one of risk management with the attendant emphasis on investment losses precisely because it clarifies the role of trust as an enabling condition for engagement. That is, it is useful to think of engagement as an expression of willingness to make an investment of something personally valuable (time, energy, reputation, credibility) under conditions of risk. Thus, trust matters little when no risk is perceived because there is nothing to be lost. But, it is also obvious that a significant investment of effort or time is unlikely to be as trivial – particularly when personal reputation or credibility is at stake. So, in situations of risk such as these, we predict that people who do not have trust will be less likely to seek out and/or offer support precisely in those situations where that support or information sharing is most critical, or seek out those they trust who may possess less relevant expertise (Hofmann et al, 2009). If trust governs behavior even in less critical situations, how much more significant is its impact on behavior in situations more compelling to action? Thus, our reference to risk management clarifies why so much thinking and discussion around the topic of engagement focus on the notion of discretionary effort – energy applied in the most ordinary of contexts.

In our conceptualization of trust, and in the examples noted above, there are at least three targets of trust that must be considered to understand engagement as a workforce issue: leaders/supervisors, co-workers, and the company as a whole. While the research literature has certainly focused on the leader as the target (Dirks, 2006), it is clear to us that one may trust one's supervisor but not one's co-workers or the organization as a whole. In fact, we propose as shown in Figure 13.1 that trust in these three targets cumulates to drive the feelings of safety that are the precursor of the engagement that follows. Of the three parties in whom trust may be placed, co-workers are likely in the best position to report on the presence or absence of engagement within a work group. In the framework of risk management, it is interesting to ask the question of where employees would find themselves at greater risk, one where there is a lack of trust between employee and supervisor, or one where there is distrust among peers within the team. It seems relevant that some relationships might matter more than others. The paradox is that research on co-worker trust is difficult if not impossible to find in the trust literature, although the work of Edmondson (1999) on psychological safety in work teams is relevant, as is the literature on communication in work teams (Bennis et al., 2008). From an everyday management perspective, the implication is that employees are unlikely to feel safe and be engaged when they lack trust in their co-workers; thus, supervisors must be sensitive not only to the trust they personally earn but also to the trust that their direct reports have for each other.

At one time it was assumed that trust developed slowly over time based on numerous opportunities for interaction, but recent research suggests that this is not always true (Kim et al., 2009). Research shows that people vary in their dispositions to trust and the rapidity with which people evaluate the trustworthiness of others and the subsequent attributions they make about them regarding their trustworthiness (Elangoven et al., 2007). Research also suggests that early in a new relationship, trust can be established relatively quickly by others demonstrating behaviors that reflect trust (more on this later) because there is little to no competing information that questions others' intentions or discounts their trustworthiness. Of course, this suggests that for newcomers early instances of behavior that might yield distrust also have quick and perhaps damaging effects, especially for those with a predisposition to distrust. This fact suggests that the on-boarding experiences newcomers have play a crucial role in the extent to which they will develop the trust necessary for the cooperative behavior that follows it. And this point may be particularly salient for virtual work in which early experiences may be even more critical in the absence of face-to-face interaction opportunities (Fineman, 2006).

Just as trust can seem to emerge in very short periods of exposure to others, it can also be easily violated with subsequent decreases in cooperative behavior. And the violations of trust, interestingly, need not be directly observed for distrust to occur. In fact, one can lose trust without actually even being a party to whatever violation leads to this distrust. In fact, studies show that people are sometimes willing to accept unsubstantiated rumors about others (Bell & Loftus, 1989), and research also reveals that observations of others having trust violated can be a potent instigator of distrust (Kim et al., 2004). These findings suggest the importance of not only dyadic trust but also the trust behaviors displayed throughout a work group and organization because these also have an impact on the trust that people will develop. To summarize then, trust is a function not only of personal experiences but also of the observations people make of what happens to others.

We adopt the concept of the psychological contract (Rousseau, 1995) as a vehicle for understanding the psychology of trust and distrust within organizations, because employees have such contracts with each of the potential targets of trust in the workplace: their supervisors, their co-workers, and the organization as a whole. In Rousseau's conceptualization, all three parties implicitly have, and explicitly make, contracts with employees through everyday interaction, their behaviors towards others as well as trustees themselves, and the administrative policies and procedures that occur. In short, to the extent that employees feel that the promises made implicitly or explicitly in these contracts are met, employees will trust the targets. Research reveals though that management does not have good data about what employees' implicit contracts actually are, making it easy to unknowingly violate them. In addition, psychological contracts evolve throughout an employee's life span, so what may fulfill a contract at one point in time may be seen as a violation at a later point. It could prove useful for companies to do some research on their employees' implicit contracts so that they have some data to use as a basis for taking actions that would enhance trust. One avenue for doing so is within an exit survey program. Note that it is important to determine not only what contracts employees feel were not fulfilled but also the source of the contract (for example, information on the company's career page and/or supervisor comments during the recruitment interview).

Violations of contracts lead to distrust, and these violations can occur in many ways. For example, supervisors can say one thing and do another, co-workers can fail to provide support, and systems can fail in many ways: a change in healthcare benefits or failure to provide the training and resources needed to achieve job goals (ibid., p. 114). The challenge from a psychological contract point of view, of course, is that employees may not reveal to the target that they perceive a contract violation. The challenge then is to continuously monitor cooperative behaviors on the part of employees and use such data as indicators of possible mistrust due to unspoken contract violations.

Such evidence is the first step in trust repair. As it is clear that trust in someone else (and the system) emerges both relatively quickly as well as over time, trust repair must focus on the same elements as those that were involved in building that trust in the first place. As Kim et al. (2009, p. 404) put it: "[T]he trust repair process ultimately involves the interaction of both the trustor and the trustee as they attempt to resolve discrepancies in their beliefs".

This sounds easy but it has many difficulties, the greatest hurdle to overcome being that it is far more difficult to overcome distrust than it is to create trust in the first place. This is so because trust is something that people voluntarily give to others, and the psychological act of giving is central to the ways people view themselves. To give psychologically and have this abused creates dissonance for the trustor; viewing the other person as untrustworthy is the way to resolve this dissonance.

Research suggests that when the trustee directly addresses the violation (when he or she becomes aware of it) by acknowledging and apologizing for it, there is potential for effectively repairing the trust. In contrast, perhaps the worst thing to do is to deny culpability (Bottom et al., 2002). Supervisors – and perhaps even employees who must interact with co-workers – must obviously be carefully and experientially trained to do trust repair because they will have to do it. Covey (the author of *The 7 Habits of Highly Effective People* in which he also discussed trust) and Merrill (2009) see trust and trust repair as an essential issue in understanding organizational effectiveness.

In summary, trust concerns the degree to which people feel safe around others (co-workers, supervisors) and in their organization as a whole in that they feel that: (a) these others will not act opportunistically in ways that might harm them and (b) investing their energy toward organizational goals will yield positive consequences. In response to trusting, people are engaged in cooperating with the others they trust, and we believe this happens because they feel safe. Trust – and distrust – can happen quite quickly, especially for newcomers who enter organizations with implicit contracts for how they will be treated and how they will in turn behave. In addition, trust and distrust can happen as a result of behavior directed at the trustor or by behavior observed by the trustor happening to others.

Antecedents of trust: focus on fairness
As is obvious from the discussion of what trust is and how it is earned/lost, separating the antecedents and consequences from the discussion of trust itself is quite arbitrary. Thus, we have already noted that trust in others may be conceptualized as a function of their benevolence, capabilities,

and integrity, as demonstrated through their behavior (Mayer et al., 1995; Dirks, 2006). In addition, we noted that one may conceptualize the relationship between people and the organizations in which they work as having met or failing to meet their psychological contracts, with a failure here potentially leading to distrust. In our way of thinking, the extent to which people's psychological contracts are met, including the extent to which others are experienced as benevolent, capable and acting with integrity, all reveal to people the degree to which they are being fairly treated. We propose that people put their trust in others and the organization in exchange for such fair treatment.

As Li and Cropanzano (2009) noted in their extensive review of the justice climate literature, justice (fairness) has been studied in the organizational sciences as an individual construct, but recently this has changed with the introduction of the concept of justice climate. Justice climate is defined as a group-level cognition that the work group as a whole is treated fairly (Naumann & Bennett, 2002). Li and Cropanzano (2009) noted that two major foci of justice climate have been studied, the manner in which people are treated by agents outside of their work unit, and the manner in which people within a work unit treat each other.

Trust in others is a prediction that those others will not behave in an opportunistic fashion. We propose that this prediction is based on the fairness climate people experience. This proposal suggests that the key psychological base from which people predict they can trust others is that they themselves have been treated fairly by them in the past and, further, that they have observed others also being fairly treated – that they work in a climate of justice or fairness. A half-century ago McGregor (1960) proposed that the key issue for manager–subordinate relationships in organizations was the extent to which what he called a "managerial climate" existed between them. For McGregor, this managerial climate was based on fair treatment – and that fair treatment was the key to creating a managerial climate in which employees had confidence in (trust in) their superior(s). McGregor (p. 135) put the issue this way:

> The research studies of the superior–subordinate relationship have pointed to a number of variables in the behavior and attitude of the superior which correlate both with high productivity and with morale of subordinates. Many of these have to do with the subordinate's expectations that he will receive a fair break in attempting to achieve his own goals.

Numerous studies of the relationship between leaders and their subordinates since McGregor's early observations have supported this basic point (Dirks & Ferrin, 2002; Lau & Liden, 2008). And the basic point is that experiencing fair treatment yields the prediction that the manager will act in ways that are not opportunistic but will promote opportunities for subordinates to achieve their own goals; in short that they can be trusted. We propose that this same model applies to the link between fairness and trust in co-workers and the system as a whole. This means that it is not sufficient for only the boss to treat employees in the work group fairly, but co-workers and the system must do so also if trust is to be the outcome.

It is important to note that the literature on fairness climate has focused on supervisory treatment and treatment by the larger system, but not on co-workers. For example, in Aquino et al. (2006), the items focus on organizational procedures associated with performance appraisal, promotions, and termination – a system view. In contrast, other measures focus on both how procedurally fair the supervisor is *and* how fair the organization is (for example, Liao & Rupp, 2005), with still others actually confounding the two foci (Mossholder et al., 1998). None of the measures conveniently presented in Li and Cropanzano (2009) asks about treatment by co-workers, an oversight that needs to be corrected in future research. Of course, from a practical standpoint, it is critical for supervisors to manage not only their own fairness behavior, but that the employees they supervise treat each other fairly as well. We need not review the basic literature on justice or on justice climate (see instead ibid.) except to make the point that research reveals that justice climate as a group-level phenomenon is related in turn to employee turnover and customer satisfaction (Simons & Roberson, 2003) and OCB (Chen et al., 2005). Our proposal in keeping with Figure 13.1 is that these relationships with these outcomes are mediated by trust; fairness leads to trust and it is trust that produces engagement through people feeling safe to take the risks associated with feeling and being engaged.

In summary, being in environments that are psychologically perceived to be fair leads to trust of the individuals (supervisors, co-workers) and system to whom such fairness is attributed (Cropanzano et al., 2007). Feeling fairly treated is a function of supervisory, co-worker, and system attributes (benevolence, capability, integrity) but perhaps more importantly, the fact that they happen in procedurally fair ways. We again invoke psychological contracts to make the point that people come to organizations with the idea that they will be treated fairly, and it is important for organizations to know what the key issues are for people to meet their end of the contract. It is also important for organizations to recognize that standards of fairness (and unfairness) may change over time due to broader societal and/or economic changes (Cropanzano & Prehar, 2002).

Safety

We repeat our earlier quote on trust from Schoorman et al. (2007, p. 348): "The basis of our [1995] model [of trust] was to understand how parties process information about others thereby deciding how much risk to take with those others". In our model, this is the key psychological issue for people: how safe do they feel to take the risk of being and feeling engaged? To drive home that point we repeat also Kahn's (1990, p. 708) conceptualization of the connection between trust and safety: "Psychological safety [is] feeling able to show and employ one's self without fear of negative consequences to self-image, status, or career. People [in the research effort] feel safe in situations in which they trusted that they would not suffer from their personal engagement".

The psychology of safety, trust, and fairness have not been considered much in recent conceptualizations of employee engagement and to our knowledge are absent from measures used in engagement research. Thus, the focus in such research has been on leadership behaviors and job design and not the psychology of the experiences that might yield engagement. We obviously see these experiences and specifically the experience of psychological safety as the key determinant of people taking risks to feel and be engaged.

The importance of feeling safe enough to feel and behave engaged is heightened in times of stress in organizations where people can feel threatened (for example, economic downturn, proposed merger). How leaders behave in defining moments such as these is how the organizational culture is established, reinforced, and changed. Defining moments – times of criticality and stress – are the foundation on which employees base their personal opinions about how the organization and its leaders will act, what values they truly possess and live by, and the degree to which they can be trusted. As we documented in Macey et al. (2009), organizations can demonstrate to their employees in these kinds of circumstances that their implicit and explicit promises are and were true; this in turn will increase the level of safety that people feel and experience – and then their levels of engagement.

On workforce engagement
It may seem strange to some readers that we speak of the *psychology* of engagement (and, earlier, the psychology of trust, fairness, and safety) but we have written this chapter with the workforce, not individuals, as our focus. We implicitly and now explicitly argue that the psychology of individuals in teams, groups, and indeed in entire organizations is shared, making such psychology as important as any other attribute of the organization (Schneider et al., in press). In our own research (Schneider et al., 2009a), we have shown that feelings of engagement aggregate to the level of the firm and that such aggregated feelings relate significantly with customer satisfaction, profits, and market value. There is other research

that reveals similar results. For example, Bartel and Saavedra (2000) and Barsade (2002) show how affect and mood become collectively relevant phenomena in groups. This is also true in the climate literature where research seems to always reveal more between- than within-group agreement regardless of whether the unit of analysis is groups, units within organizations, or organizations as a whole (Schneider et al., in press).

This sharing of moods, affect, and perceptions likely occurs as a result of the natural interaction people have with each other in which they share their moods, affect and perceptions such that there comes to be a shared reality. But this is not a false reality or some socially constructed reality unrelated to fact (Young & Parker, 1999). Evidence for this statement emerges in research that has linked, for example, service climate to customer satisfaction (Schneider et al., 2009b) and safety climate to accidents (Zohar, 2000).

As we noted early in the chapter, our opinion is that management is most interested in psychological constructs when those are shown to be related to performance at the work group or organizational level, rather than individual performance, because they can then take action that will have greater returns. The bad news in what we have presented is that management must attend to many issues if they are to observe engagement in their employees: they must attend to fairness and trust issues for themselves, their teams, and the organization as a whole to create the psychology of safety that will yield the workforce engagement they seek.

On the feedback loop
Figure 13.1 shows a feedback loop from engagement feelings and behavior to the ways in which supervisors, co-workers, and the system treat people. Thus we see our model as a virtuous cycle in which positive organizational behaviors yield engagement feelings and behavior, which in turn produce positive organizational behaviors. The management implications of such a virtuous cycle are important because the cycle says management can intervene at any point in the model and produce effects that will translate into other linked issues in the model. The challenge to management is that there is no "silver bullet" to produce that elusive engagement!

Summary with practical implications
Our chapter presumes that employee engagement has positive consequences for organizational performance and the presumption is supported by the research literature (Bakker et al., 2008). We further presumed that generic issues of leadership and job challenge had also been shown in the literature to be related to employee engagement (ibid.). We felt, however, that the psychology underlying engagement – the psychological

experiences of workers – had not been explored as extensively, though these psychological issues were the key issues with which Kahn (1990) had begun the current interest in engagement. In some sense, our view is that we rushed to show that engagement was important and did not spend as much time on the antecedents of engagement.

Figure 13.1 summarizes our position on the importance of trust as a central issue in employee engagement. The figure indicates that trust emerges in situations where people describe fair treatment by supervisors, peers, and the system in which they work. We propose that fairness leads to trust and trust in turn yields improved likelihood that people will take risks to be engaged. They will do this because they feel safe – do not fear retribution – and implicitly or explicitly assume that they will be recognized and reinforced for being innovative, proactive, and in other ways taking risks.

While Figure 13.1 proposed a straightforward model of the development of trust and the ways in which trust yields the risk-taking necessary for engagement, the model fails to explicate the issues to which management must attend if engagement is the outcome desired. Suggestions for these management actions were presented throughout the chapter but it is important to summarize them here. We do so by revisiting the sequence of the topics as we presented them.

Trust must be built and it can happen or fail to happen very quickly in organizations, especially for newcomers. This suggests that great care must be given to the on-boarding/socialization experiences of newcomers to organizations because they arrive with implicit expectations – they have a psychological contract (Rousseau, 1995) – to be fairly treated and to be trusting. What is critical about this point is that people learn to trust based on not only what happens or fails to happen to them but also the observations they have of what happens to others. This means that management must carefully attend to not only what happens to people but what happens around them, too. The clear implication is that the work group must be continuously monitored for the behaviors displayed in it if trust is to: (a) be developed and (b) be sustained.

And the behaviors of central interest to us *vis-à-vis* trust concerned fairness behaviors. Li and Cropanzano (2009) comprehensively clarified the issue of fairness climate in organizations and the behaviors that make for fairness – equitable outcomes for people, procedurally consistent treatment with options to question the procedures and outcomes, and interpersonally fair support. We learned from the trust literature that there are three foci for trust – peers, supervisors, and the system as a whole – and these same foci apply to the issue of fair treatment as well. We noted that supervisors/leaders and somewhat the system as a whole had been foci of attention in understanding trust but that the issue of co-workers has not been explored much in either the trust or the fairness literatures. From a practical vantage point we suspect that the same oversight is true – supervisors/leaders are potentially sensitized to trust and fairness issues but typical employees and their co-workers are not. Our framework indicates that this is a potentially severe oversight because it is likely in today's world of team work that it is the relationship between peers *vis-à-vis* trust that is central to employee engagement. Role-play exercises in addition to overt early experiences revealing fairness to establish trust as well as training on how to repair trust should be central components of both informal and formal (training) experiences both for newcomers and for incumbent employees. In addition, we propose that issues of fairness and the building of trust be included in the appraisal not only of supervisors/leaders but of shop-floor employees and their relationships with their peers too. It should also be a factor in performance management/appraisal and promotion decisions as well.

The creation and maintenance of a climate of fairness and the trust engendered by it yields feelings of psychological safety that result in engagement. Our model suggests that people working in an environment where they can feel safe leads them to invest discretionary effort in taking risks to be proactive and innovative and to work with a sense of urgency and enthusiasm without fear of negative repercussions.

Our framework in Figure 13.1 further showed that engagement itself feeds back into people being fairly treated – in a sense they have earned that – and the cycle is a self-reinforcing one yielding superior organizational performance and competitiveness.

Building and maintaining trust in organizations is not simple; it requires attention to many simultaneous issues by management, but the payoffs may be very impressive indeed.

References

Aquino, K., Tripp, T.M. & Bies, R.J. (2006), "Getting even or moving on? Power, procedural justice, and types of offense as predictors of revenge, forgiveness, reconciliation, and avoidance in organizations", *Journal of Applied Psychology*, **91**, 653–68.

Bakker, A.B., Demerouti, E. & Verbeke, W. (2004), "Using the job demands–resources model to predict burnout and performance", *Human Resource Management*, **43**, 83–104.

Bakker, A.B., Schaufeli, W.B., Leiter, M.P. & Taris, T.W. (2008), "Work engagement: an emerging concept in occupational health psychology", *Work & Stress*, **22**, 187–200.

Barsade, S. (2002), "The ripple effects: emotional contagion and its influence on group behavior", *Administrative Science Quarterly*, **47**, 644–75.

Bartel, C. & Saavedra, R. (2000), "The collective construction of work group moods", *Administrative Science Quarterly*, **45**, 197–231.

Bell, B.E. & Loftus, E.F. (1989), "Trivial persuasion in the courtroom: the power of (a few) minor details", *Journal of Personality and Social Psychology*, **56**, 669–79.

Bennis, W., Goleman, D., O'Toole, J. & Ward Biederman, P. (2008), *Transparency: How Leaders Create a Culture of Candor*, San Francisco, CA: Jossey-Bass.

Bottom, W.P., Gibson, K., Daniels, S. & Murningham, J.K. (2002), "When talk is not cheap: substantive penance and expressions of intent in rebuilding cooperation", *Organization Science*, **13**, 497–513.

Chen, X.P., Lam, S.S.K., Naumann, S.E. & Schaubroeck, J. (2005), "Group citizenship behavior: conceptualization and preliminary tests of its antecedents and consequences", *Group and Organization Review*, **1**, 273–300.

Covey, S.M. & Merrill, R.R. (2009), *The Speed of Trust: The One Thing that Changes Everything*, New York: Simon & Schuster.

Cropanzano, R., Bowen, D.E. & Gilliland, S.W. (2007), "The management of organizational justice", *Academy of Management Perspectives*, **21**, 34–48.

Cropanzano, R. & Prehar, C.A. (2002), "Emerging justice concerns in an era of changing psychological contracts", in R. Cropanzano, (ed.), *Justice in the Workplace: From Theory to Practice*, Vol. 2, Mahwah, NJ: Lawrence Erlbaum, pp. 245–69.

Dirks, K.T. (2006), "Three fundamental questions regarding trust in leaders", in R. Bachmann & A. Zaheer (eds), *Handbook of Trust Research*, Cheltenham, UK and Northampton, MA, USA: Edward Elgar, pp. 15–28.

Dirks, K.T. & Ferrin, D.L. (2002), "Trust in leadership: meta-analytic findings and implications for research and practice", *Journal of Applied Psychology*, **87**, 611–28.

Edmondson, A. (1999), "Psychological safety and learning behavior in work teams", *Administrative Science Quarterly*, **44**, 350–83.

Elangoven, A.R., Auer-Rizzi, W. & Szabo, E. (2007), "Why don't I trust you? An attributional approach to erosion of trust", *Journal of Managerial Psychology*, **22**, 4–24.

Fineman, S. (2006), "Emotion and organizing", in S.E. Clegg, C. Hardy, T.B. Lawrence & W.R. Nord (eds), *The Sage Handbook of Organizational Studies*, 2nd edn, Thousand Oaks, CA: Sage, pp. 675–700.

Frese, M. (2008), "Commentary on Macey and Schneider: the meaning of employee engagement", *Industrial and Organizational Psychology: An Exchange of Perspectives on Science and Practice*, **1**, 67–9.

Harter, J.K., Schmidt, F.L. & Hayes, T.L. (2002), "Business-unit-level relationship between employee satisfaction, employee engagement, and business outcomes: a meta-analysis", *Journal of Applied Psychology*, **87**, 268–79.

Hofmann, D.A., Lei, Z. & Grant A.M. (2009), "Seeking help in the shadow of doubt: the sensemaking processes underlying how nurses decide whom to ask for advice", *Journal of Applied Psychology*, **94**, 1261–74.

Kahn, W.A. (1990), "Psychological conditions of personal engagement and disengagement at work", *Academy of Management Journal*, **33**, 692–724.

Kim, P.H., Dirks, K.T. & Cooper, C.D. (2009), "The repair of trust: a dynamic bilateral perspective and multilevel conceptualization", *Academy of Management Review*, **94**, 401–23.

Kim, P.H., Ferrin, D.L., Cooper, C.D. & Dirks, K.T. (2004), "Removing the shadow of suspicion: the effects of apology versus denial for repairing ability- versus integrity-based trust violations", *Journal of Applied Psychology*, **89**, 104–18.

Konovsky, M. & Pugh, D. (1994), "Citizenship behavior and social exchange", *Academy of Management Journal*, **37**, 656–69.

Lau, D.C. & Liden, R.C. (2008), "Antecedents of coworker trust: leaders' blessings", *Journal of Applied Psychology*, **93**, 1130–38.

Lewicki, R.J., Tomlinson, E.C. & Gillespie, N. (2006), "Models of interpersonal trust development: theoretical approaches, empirical evidence, and future directions", *Journal of Management*, **32**, 992–1021.

Li, A. & Cropanzano, R. (2009), "Fairness at the group level: justice climate and intraunit justice climate", *Journal of Management*, **35**, 564–99.

Liao, A. & Rupp, D.E. (2005), "The impact of justice climate and justice orientation on work outcomes: a cross-level multifoci framework", *Journal of Applied Psychology*, **90**, 242–56.

Macey, W.H., Schneider, B., Barbera, K.M. & Young, S.A. (2009), *Employee Engagement: Tools for Analysis, Practice, and Competitive Advantage*, Malden, MA: Wiley–Blackwell.

Madhock, A. (2006), "Opportunism, trust, and knowledge: the management of firm value and the value of firm management", in R. Bachmann & A. Zaheer (eds), *Handbook of Trust Research*, Cheltenham, UK and Northampton, MA, USA: Edward Elgar, pp. 107–23.

Mayer, R.C., Davis, J.H. & Schoorman, F.D. (1995), "An integrative model of organizational trust", *Academy of Management Review*, **20**, 709–34.

McAllister, D.J. (1995), "Affect- and cognition-based trust as foundations for interpersonal cooperation in organizations", *Academy of Management Journal*, **38**, 25–59.

McGregor, D.M. (1960), *The Human Side of Enterprise*, New York: McGraw-Hill.

Mossholder, K.W., Bennett, N. & Martin, C.L. (1998), "A multilevel analysis of procedural justice context", *Journal of Organizational Behavior*, **19**, 131–41.

Naumann, S.E. & Bennett, N. (2002), "A case for procedural justice climate: development and test of a multi-level model", *Academy of Management Journal*, **43**, 881–9.

O'Toole, J. & Bennis, W. (2009), "What's needed next: a culture of candor", *Harvard Business Review*, **87**, 54–61.

Organ, D.W., Podsakoff, P.M. & MacKenzie, S.B. (2006), *Organizational Citizenship Behavior: Its Nature, Antecedents, and Consequences*, Thousand Oaks, CA: Sage.

Rousseau, D.M. (1995), *Psychological Contracts in Organizations*, Thousand Oaks, CA: Sage.

Schaufeli, W.B., Bakker, A.B. & Salanova, M. (2006), "The measurement of work engagement with a short questionnaire: a cross-national study", *Educational and Psychological Measurement*, **66**, 701–16.

Schneider, B., Ehrhart, M.G. & Macey, W.H. (in press), "Perspectives on organizational climate and culture", in S. Zedeck (ed.), *Handbook of Industrial and Organizational Psychology*, Washington, DC: APA.

Schneider, B., Macey, W.H., Barbera, K.M. & Martin, N. (2009a), "Driving customer satisfaction and financial success through employee engagement", *People and Strategy*, **32**, 22–7.

Schneider, B., Macey, W.H., Lee, W. & Young, S.A. (2009b), "Organizational service climate drivers of the American Customer Satisfaction Index (ACSI) and financial and market value performance", *Journal of Service Research*, **32**, 3–14.

Schoorman, F.D., Mayer, R.C. & Davis, J.H. (2007), "An integrative model of organizational trust: past, present, and future", *Academy of Management Review*, **32**, 344–54.

Simons, T. & Roberson, Q. (2003), "Why managers should care about fairness: the effects of aggregate justice perceptions on organizational outcomes", *Journal of Applied Psychology*, **88**, 432–43.

Young, S.A. & Parker, C.P. (1999), "Predicting collective climates: assessing the role of shared work values, needs, employee interaction and work group membership", *Journal of Organizational Behavior*, **20**, 1189–218.

Zohar, D. (2000), "A group level model of safety climate: testing the effect of group climate on micro-accidents in manufacturing jobs", *Journal of Applied Psychology*, **85**, 587–96.

14 Organizational conditions fostering employee engagement: the role of "voice"
Constant D. Beugré

Introduction

Employee engagement refers to a positive, fulfilling, work-related state of mind that is characterized by vigor, dedication, and absorption and represents a more permanent and pervasive state of being that characterizes an individual rather than a momentary and specific state (Schaufeli et al., 2002). Macey and Schneider (2008) identified three types of engagement: (i) trait engagement, (ii) state engagement, and (iii) behavioral engagement. Trait engagement can be regarded as an inclination to experience the world from a particular vantage point, whereas psychological state engagement is conceptualized as feelings of energy and absorption in one's work. Behavioral engagement is defined in terms of discretionary effort or a specific form of in-role behavior.

Although trait engagement is a personal disposition and therefore, beyond the purview of outside factors, managers and organizations can create conditions that foster state and behavioral engagement. One such organizational factor is "voice", construed as verbal behavior that is improvement oriented and directed towards a specific target that holds power inside the organization (Detert & Burris, 2007). Voice may promote the perception that the employee is concerned about the welfare of the organization and its members. It may also entail risk to the extent that it can be considered as a difficult and costly action (Rusbult et al., 1988). Speaking up can feel risky because it involves pointing out a need for improvement in a program or policy to those who may have devised, be responsible for, or feel personally attached to the status quo (Detert & Burris, 2007). Although voice may be a facilitator of positive behavior in organizations, the literature has not explored its impact on employee engagement.

Assessing the effect of voice on employee engagement is important for both research and management practice. From the research perspective, voice could contribute to the emerging literature on employee engagement by adding to the organizational conditions that facilitate engagement at work. From the practical standpoint, a voice perspective could help managers create working environments that facilitate employee engagement to the extent that having engaged employees could be a key to competitive advantage (Macey & Schneider, 2008). The chapter is organized as follows. First, I briefly review the extant literature on employee voice. Next, I analyze the impact of voice on employee engagement. I conclude the chapter with a discussion on the research and practical implications of a "voice perspective" of employee engagement.

Understanding employee voice

Exploring the nature of employee voice

Hirschman (1970) was the first to introduce the concept of voice in his seminal book *Exit, Voice, and Loyalty*. He defined voice as any attempt at all to change an objectionable state of affairs, not only by petitioning management or higher authorities, but also through protests including the mobilization of public opinion (p. 30). According to Rusbult et al. (1988), voice describes "actively and constructively trying to improve conditions through discussing problems with a supervisor or co-workers, taking action to solve problems, suggesting solutions, seeking help from an outside agency like a union or whistle-blowing" (p. 601). Voice underscores both employees' discontent with the organization and the hope that things will get better in the future.

In the organizational justice literature, voice often refers to the extent to which people have the opportunity to provide input into the decision-making process (Folger, 1977). This literature argues that employees favor voice situations compared to no-voice situations. Two models, the "instrumental" approach and the "non-instrumental" approach help explain people's preference for voice conditions as opposed to no-voice conditions. The instrumental explanation of voice draws from Thibaut and Walker's (1975) model of process control, which contends that people prefer to have voice because it helps them control the outcomes derived from the process. Voice affects people's attitudes toward a decision because they feel that they have had a chance to indirectly influence the decision (Korsgaard & Roberson, 1995).

The non-instrumental explanation of voice, however, draws from the value-expressive model, according to which the opportunity to voice one's opinions is a desired end in itself (Lind & Tyler, 1988; Korsgaard & Roberson, 1995). Katz (1960), who first suggested the idea of a value-expressive function, argued that under some circumstances, people might find the opportunity to express themselves rewarding in and of itself. Following this line of reasoning, the group-value model also views voice as an indication of one's standing within a group or organization (Lind & Tyler, 1988; Tyler & Lind, 1992). The model argues that the voice effect stems from the implication that those accorded an opportunity to present information are valued fully fledged members of the group enacting the procedure (Lind et al., 1990).

Exploring the voice effect
Lind and Tyler (1988) and Tyler and Lind (1992) noted that voice increases perceptions of fairness because participants feel that they are being treated with politeness, dignity, and respect appropriate for full group membership. Similarly, Kotter (1996), Axelrod (2001) and Luecke (2003) argued that voice empowers people to act, thereby contributing to successful organizational change:

> The cornerstone of any democratic process is voice – the power to be heard and to influence outcomes. Maximizing voice means widening the circle of involvement to encompass those likely to be affected by the change process, including those who might be opposed or think differently. When people really believe that their voice counts, a critical mass for change spontaneously emerges. (Axelrod, 2001, p. 1)

Research on the consequences of voice has focused on the relationship between voice and employee perceptions of fairness, specifically, procedural justice (Thibaut & Walker, 1975; Folger, 1977; Bies & Shapiro, 1988; Brockner et al., 2001). Folger (1977) found that participants considered procedures offering the opportunity to voice one's opinion as more fair than those that did not provide such an opportunity. In light of these findings, Van den Bos and Van Prooijen (2001) argued that voice is one of the key determinants that lead people to judge a particular procedure as fair or unfair. According to Folger et al. (1979), voice may be desirable for at least two reasons. First, voice may be preferable to mute procedures because the latter are based on incomplete information. Second, being given voice in the decision-making process is considered to be a fairer procedure than being given no voice.

Other studies have reported the existence of mediators or moderators, such as expectations of voice, appropriateness of voice, the importance of the decision for the individual, and voice as meeting cultural norms. When employees expect voice, having voice would positively affect perceptions of justice (Daly & Geyer, 1994). However, when employees do not expect voice, having voice would not have any significant effect on perceptions of justice. Van den Bos et al. (1996) also found that participants who expected no voice, yet received voice, perceived the process as less fair and performed at lower levels than participants who neither expected nor received voice. "The value associated with different levels of voice may depend on the participants' expectations. Voice that exceeds expectations may be perceived as a gain and voice that falls below expectations may be seen as a loss" (Price et al., 2001, p. 101). Reactions to voice may also depend on existing organizational traditions and societal norms. Brockner et al. (2001) found that the more that cultural norms legitimize voice, the more likely are people to respond unfavorably to relatively low levels of voice. Thus, it is not the lack of voice that people object to; rather, it is when the lack of voice violates cultural norms that people respond unfavorably.

The importance of a decision also mediated the relationship between voice and perceptions of procedural justice. Van den Bos and Spruijt (2002) found that when people are faced with decisions that are relatively unimportant to them, they are not strongly affected by variations of voice. Thus, what makes voice relevant is the extent to which the decision is important for the individual. The positive effects of voice can depend on the extent to which voice-based participation is solicited or not (Folger & Cropanzano, 1998). Voice appropriateness was also considered as a variable mediating the voice–procedural justice relationship. Van den Bos and Spruijt (2002) found that voice led to procedural justice when participation to the decision was appropriate. However, when participation to the decision was not appropriate, no effect or even a reverse effect was observed. A missing link in studying the voice effect is whether voice could influence other outcome variables, such as performance or employee engagement. In the following lines, I propose a conceptual model that explores the impact of voice on employee engagement.

A voice perspective of employee engagement
The model depicted in Figure 14.1 suggests a positive relationship between voice and state engagement, which then influences behavioral engagement. State engagement can be conceived as an attitude. As such, it implies having a positive predisposition toward one's organization, which can be translated into behavioral engagement. As an attitude, state engagement cannot be observed; it can only be inferred from an employee's actual behavior, such as behavioral engagement. State engagement is an antecedent of behavioral engagement, which represents a form of pro-organizational behavior involving persistence, adaptability, and taking initiatives.

In general, employees who are offered opportunities to voice their opinions are likely to be engaged. This is consistent with Hirschman and others' conceptualization of voice as a means to improve an existing state of affairs. The presence of voice can lead to employee engagement, which in turn can result in behaviors that are likely to improve the organization. For example, the presence of voice can help employees express

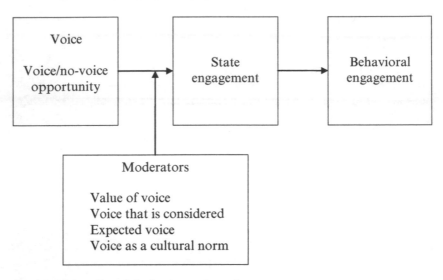

Figure 14.1   A model of voice and employee engagement

their discontent with current situations prevailing in their organization. Expressing their discontent can lead managers to take corrective actions to improve the organization. In such a situation, the presence of voice would have contributed to a positive outcome.

Although the model advocates the positive impact of voice on employee engagement, it also acknowledges the existence of four boundary conditions that could intercede to mitigate the voice–engagement relationship and help delineate the conditions under which voice leads to engagement. These boundary conditions include: (i) the value of voice, (ii) the extent to which voice is considered by decision makers, (iii) the extent to which voice is expected, and (iv) voice as corresponding to cultural values. Employees may attach specific values to these conditions. Those who consider voice as important would be engaged when they are given the opportunity to voice their opinions. However, employees who attach less value to voice would not be positively affected by the opportunity to voice their opinions.

The second moderating variable is the extent to which voice is considered, or attended to, in the decision-making process. I contend here that when voice is considered, it would positively affect the relationship between voice and engagement. However, when voice is ignored it would negatively influence the voice–engagement relationship. Voice that is ignored can be more damaging for an organization than the lack of voice. The "deaf-ear" syndrome may discourage voice and even lead to employee disengagement. By voicing their opinions, employees expect to see organizational conditions changed. However, if voice is ignored, it may lead to cynicism or outright rebellion. If the solicitation of voice is perceived to be disingenuous, then the exercise of voice can result in frustration (Price et al., 2001).

The third moderating variable is expected voice – defined as the extent to which employees expect to have voice in the decision-making process. When employees expect to have voice, the presence of voice can positively moderate the voice–engagement relationship. However, when employees do not expect voice, providing it may not have a strong positive effect on the voice–engagement relationship. Finally, the model considers cultural norms as a potential moderator. Some cultures may be sensitive to voice. In such cultures, the provision of voice could have a positive effect on the voice–engagement relationship. However, in cultures where employees are not sensitive to voice, the provision of voice would not have a significant effect on the voice–engagement relationship. A voice perspective of employee engagement has implications for both research and practice.

Discussion and implications

Implications for research
Several research avenues could be explored when assessing the impact of voice on engagement. Researchers could investigate whether employees who have the opportunity to voice their opinions are more likely to be engaged compared to those who do not have such an opportunity. In addressing this question, researchers could compare voice situations to no-voice situations. Since most organizations offer some forms of voice opportunity, researchers could consider voice as a continuum rather than a dichotomous variable. Some organizations may offer more voice opportunities than others. Thus, the extent to which organizations offering more voice opportunities have employees who are more engaged than those that offer few voice opportunities warrants empirical investigation.

The model identified four boundary conditions that could moderate the voice–engagement relationship. Researchers could investigate whether employees who value voice tend to be more engaged when given the opportunity to voice their opinions compared to those who value voice less. Similarly, they could also assess the extent to which the effects of voice that is considered, and voice expectation, act as moderators of the voice–engagement relationship. For example, are employees who expect and receive voice more likely to be more engaged than those who receive voice but did not expect it? Finally, researchers could also assess the moderating impact of culture on the voice–engagement relationship. Knowledge gleaned from such research could provide guidelines for managers to use voice as a mechanism to foster employee engagement.

Implications for practice
Engaged employees would be more likely to display organizational citizenship behaviors, be more productive, and indicate low turnover and absence rates than non-engaged employees. They would also be more likely to facilitate change in organizations. Although unionization has declined over the past twenty years, the increasing number of knowledge workers calls for more voice opportunities. Knowledge workers are more demanding and willing to have a say in their work activities and decisions. The lack of voice in organizations can exact a high psychological price on individuals, generating feelings of humiliation, pernicious anger, resentment, and the like which, if unexpressed contaminate every interaction, shut down creativity, and undermine productivity (Perlow & Williams, 2003). In his book, *Good to Great*, Collins (2001) argued that organizations should create climates that provide employees the opportunity to speak up. Thus, organizations should strive to provide voice mechanisms to their employees. Doing so is not only good business but it also addresses an essential ethical issue – the importance of voice in human societies. It is my hope that this chapter will spark further theorizing and empirical investigations on the impact of voice on employee engagement.

References

Axelrod, R. (2001), "Democratic approaches to change make a big difference in turbulent times", *Harvard Management Update*, November.

Bies, R.J. & Shapiro, D.L. (1988), "Voice and justification: their influence on procedural fairness judgments", *Academy of Management Journal*, **31**, 676–85.

Brockner, J., Ackerman, G., Greenberg, J., Gelfand, M.J., Francesco, A.M., Chen, Z.X., Leung, K., Bierbrauer, G., Gomez, C., Kirman, B.L. & Shapiro, D. (2001), "Culture and procedural justice: the influence of power distance on reactions to voice", *Journal of Experimental Social Psychology*, **37**, 300–315.

Collins, J. (2001), *Good to Great: Why Some Companies Make the Leap and Others Don't*, New York: HarperBusiness.

Daly, J.P. & Geyer, P.D. (1994), "The role of fairness in implementing large-scale change: employee evaluations of process and outcome in seven facility relocations", *Journal of Organizational Behavior*, **15**, 623–38.

Detert, J. & Burris, E. (2007), "Leadership behavior and employee voice: is the door really open?", *Academy of Management Journal*, **50**, 869–84.

Folger, R. (1977), "Distributive and procedural justice: combined impact of voice and improvement on experienced inequity", *Journal of Personality and Social Psychology*, **35**, 108–19.

Folger, R. & Cropanzano, R. (1998), *Organizational Justice and Human Resource Management*, Beverly Hills, CA: Sage.

Folger, R., Rosenfield, D., Grove, J. & Corkran, L. (1979), "Effects of voice and peer opinions on responses to inequity", *Journal of Personality and Social Psychology*, **37**, 2253–61.

Hirschman, O.A. (1970), *Exit, Voice and Loyalty*, Cambridge, MA: Harvard University Press.

Katz, D. (1960), "The functional approach to the study of attitudes", *Public Opinion Quarterly*, **24**, 163–204.

Korsgaard, M.A. & Roberson, L. (1995), "Procedural justice in performance evaluation: the role of instrumental and non-instrumental voice in performance appraisal discussions", *Journal of Management*, **21**, 657–69.

Kotter, P.J. (1996), *Leading Change*, Boston, MA. Harvard Business School Press.

Lind, E.A., Kanfer, R. & Early, P. (1990), "Voice, control, and procedural justice: instrumental and noninstrumental concerns in fairness judgments", *Journal of Personality and Social Psychology*, **59**, 952–9.

Lind, E.A. & Tyler, T.R. (1988), *The Social Psychology of Procedural Justice*, New York: Plenum Press.

Luecke, R. (2003), *Managing Change and Transition*, Boston, MA: Harvard Business School Press.

Macey, W.H. & Schneider, B. (2008), "The meaning of employee engagement", *Industrial and Organizational Psychology*, **1**, 3–30.

Perlow, L. & Williams, S. (2003), "Is silence killing your company?", *Harvard Business Review*, **81**(5), 52–8.

Price, K.H., Hall, T.W., Van den Bos, K., Hunton, J.E., Lovett, S. & Tippett, M.J. (2001), "Features of the value function for voice and their consistency across participants from four countries: Great Britain, Mexico, the Netherlands, and the United States", *Organizational Behavior and Human Decision Processes*, **84**, 95–121.

Rusbult, C.E., Farrell, D., Rogers, G. & Mainous III, G.A. (1988), "Impact of exchange variables on exit, voice, loyalty, and neglect: an integrative model of responses declining job satisfaction", *Academy of Management Journal*, **31**, 599–627.

Schaufeli, W.B., Salanova, M., González-Romá, V. & Bakker, A.B. (2002), "The measurement of engagement and burnout: a two sample confirmatory factor analytical approach", *Journal of Happiness Studies*, **3**, 71–92.

Thibaut, J.W. & Walker, L. (1975), *Procedural Justice: A Psychological Analysis*, Hillsdale, NJ: Lawrence Erlbaum.

Tyler, T.R. & Lind, E.A. (1992), "A relational model of authority in groups", in M. Zanna (ed.), *Advances in Experimental Social Psychology*, Vol. 25, New York: Lexington Books, pp. 115–91.

Van den Bos, K. & Spruijt, N. (2002), "Appropriateness of decisions as a moderator of the psychology of voice", *European Journal of Social Psychology*, **32**, 57–72.

Van den Bos, K. & Van Prooijen, J.W. (2001), "Referent cognitions theory: the role of closeness of reference points in the psychology of voice", *Journal of Personality and Social Psychology*, **81**, 616–26.

Van den Bos, K., Vermunt, R. & Wilke, H.A.M. (1996), "The consistency rule and the voice effect: the influence of expectations on procedural fairness judgments and performance", *European Journal of Social Psychology*, **26**, 411–28.

15 Key driver analyses: current trends, problems, and alternative approaches

Charles A. Scherbaum, Dan J. Putka,
Loren J. Naidoo and David Youssefnia

Introduction

Managers and organizational leaders are interested in understanding the factors in their organizations that can produce high levels of employee engagement (Macey et al., 2009). At the core of their interest are two questions:

1. What are the most important organizational factors in predicting engagement?
2. Where should the organization focus its resources and take action to improve engagement?

Answers to the first question can be informed by theory and prior research regarding determinants of employee engagement (for example, ibid.), an empirical analysis of engagement data from an organization, and the nuances of the organization. Answers to the second question also draw on this information, but also reflect practical considerations (for example, feasibility of various actions for improving engagement). Although non-empirical factors are important to consider, this chapter focuses on empirical approaches for addressing these questions.

The term "key driver analysis" refers to a set of statistical approaches to identifying important predictors of employee engagement. These analyses provide leaders an empirical basis for making decisions and taking action on the most important factors for influencing employee engagement. Unfortunately, the statistical techniques commonly used for key driver analyses can be problematic. The common approaches (a) use key driver selection strategies that have been heavily criticized in the scientific literature, (b) often ignore the multiply determined nature of employee engagement, (c) cannot rank key drivers on their relative importance for predicting engagement, and (d) fail to capitalize on modern analytical approaches. Taken together, the common approaches may result in inaccurate conclusions regarding key drivers of engagement and misdirected organizational actions aimed at improving engagement.

This chapter provides a brief overview of the current approaches to key driver analyses, identifies the problems with these approaches, and describes modern analytical approaches to identifying the key drivers. In all cases, we focus on linear models with continuous outcomes. With regard to modern analytical approaches, we discuss (a) relative importance analyses (Budescu, 1993; Johnson, 2000), and (b) model-averaging approaches (Hoeting et al., 1999; Burnham & Anderson, 2002; Hastie et al., 2009). We provide an overview of the benefits of these approaches relative to current key driver analyses, as well as an empirical example of the advantages they offer. Lastly, recommendations for best practices are provided.

Current approaches to key driver analysis

Practitioners working with employee engagement data often must answer what appears to be a simple question: "among a set of potential drivers which are most important for predicting employee engagement?". However, this question can be very complex to address empirically because it includes two distinct parts. First, among a set of drivers, which are critical to include in a model of engagement? Second, which of the drivers included in the model are the most important for predicting engagement?

To facilitate our review of current approaches to key driver analysis, we have classified them into three broad categories: (a) bivariate approaches, (b) full-model approaches, and (c) model-selection approaches. As we discuss, none of these approaches on their own, or in combination, provides satisfactory answers to the questions posed above.

Bivariate approaches

In the most common approaches to key driver analysis, the bivariate relation between a potential driver and employee engagement is computed. The focus of these approaches is simply identifying the single drivers that are most strongly related to engagement (that is, the *key drivers*). These relations are estimated using bivariate correlations or univariate regression analyses (that is, a separate model is fitted for each driver). The magnitude of the driver's correlation with engagement or its standardized regression coefficient indexes the strength of the relationship.

These approaches are intuitive and simple, but provide limited insights. First, engagement is determined by multiple drivers simultaneously. Bivariate approaches ignore the often substantial correlations (for example, $r > 0.60$) between the drivers impacting engagement. These intercorrelations lead to problems interpreting the relative importance of key drivers. For example, if satisfaction with leadership and perceived organizational support (POS) emerged as key drivers based on the bivariate approach described above, yet respondents' satisfaction with leadership was primarily determined by their perceptions of organizational support, then the relative importance of satisfaction for predicting engagement would *actually* be close to nil. Its strong relation with engagement would be spurious, due primarily to its relation with POS. This is a critical insight that bivariate approaches would fail to reveal.

Regression coefficients estimated under the bivariate approach are no help in this regard. The value of a driver's regression coefficient is conditional on the other drivers in a model. Because bivariate approaches fit a separate model for each driver, regression coefficients from bivariate models shed no light on how much predictive value a given driver would offer if other potential drivers of engagement were considered. Again, this might skew judgments regarding the importance of a driver.

Full-model approaches
In contrast to bivariate approaches, full-model approaches simultaneously include all available drivers (for example, survey items or dimensions) in a model to predict employee engagement. Regression coefficients from such models serve as indicators of the strength of the relationship between each driver and engagement. Drivers with the largest coefficients are subsequently identified as the key drivers. Instead of reporting regression coefficients for each driver, investigators sometimes report (a) partial and semipartial correlations of each driver with engagement (controlling for other variables in the predictive model), (b) path coefficients for each driver, or (c) coefficients from a structural equation model linking potential drivers to engagement. Regardless of the exact nature of the coefficients reported, all of them are conditional on all other drivers in the model and might change substantially if one or more drivers are removed from the model. Full-model approaches place a premium on (a) maximizing the amount of variance explained in engagement (that is, achieving the highest model R^2 possible), and (b) avoiding the omission of variables that might predict engagement. Omitting key variables from regression models can result in biased regression coefficients estimated for drivers in one's model (James, 1980). Unfortunately, there are drawbacks of this "include everything" approach.

First, many of the drivers in the model may have little value for predicting engagement. Including such drivers in the model can lead to (unnecessary) instability in the resulting predictions. This instability will be exacerbated when there are strong relations between drivers in the model (that is, multicollinearity) which is usually the case with drivers from a common engagement survey. Thus, there is an unfortunate tradeoff when using regression models for key driver analyses. As the number of drivers in a model increases, the predictive accuracy of the model *in one's sample* tends to increase (that is, R^2 will increase), but the generalizability of these predictions decreases (that is, the ability to consistently predict engagement across different samples). Though it might be tempting to view the full model as "best" (that is, it will have a higher R^2 than all models based on any subset of the full set of drivers), and use it as the basis for judging the relative importance of potential key drivers of engagement, that desire should be balanced against the need to produce a model of engagement that is not specific to the data from that particular point in time.

A second drawback of full-model approaches is that they can produce extremely unstable estimates for the regression coefficients associated with each driver. The stability of such regression coefficients is critical in key driver analyses because they are often interpreted as indicators of the importance of each driver. As with the first drawback, the instability in coefficients results from multicollinearity among drivers. When multicollinearity is present, including all possible drivers in a model of engagement is unnecessary, and can detract from finding statistically significant drivers. To illustrate, consider our previous example involving satisfaction and POS. Including satisfaction with leadership in a model for predicting engagement that already included POS would be unnecessary (with regard to the model's overall predictiveness) and lead to less stable regression coefficients for POS and satisfaction (that is, the coefficients would have higher standard errors), thus increasing the likelihood that they would *not* be deemed significant drivers of engagement.

A third drawback of full-model approaches is that the resulting regression coefficients can rarely, legitimately be interpreted as indices of the relative importance of each driver in the model. This observation has been made repeatedly in the literature on the relative importance of drivers in the context of regression models (see Budescu, 1993). When correlations are present among drivers of engagement and those drivers are included in a predictive model of engagement, the regression coefficients do not reflect the relative contribution of a given driver to the variance that the model explains in engagement (that is, the model R^2). As we note later in this chapter, approaches have emerged for judging the relative importance of drivers in the face of multicollinearity.

Model-selection approaches

In light of the drawbacks of full-model approaches, a common strategy for performing key driver analyses has been to use statistical techniques to identify a reduced set of drivers for inclusion in a predictive model of engagement. Those adopting such approaches realize that not all of the possible drivers may be needed to effectively predict engagement. These approaches essentially attempt to find a subset of drivers that maximizes the percent of variance explained in engagement with the fewest number of drivers.

Perhaps the most common model-selection techniques used are those that are fully automated by standard statistical software (for example, SPSS), and enter or remove drivers from a model in either a particular sequence (forward or backward variable selection) or a combination of sequences (for example, stepwise variable selection) based purely on statistical criteria (for example, p-values associated with regression coefficients included or excluded from the model) (Thompson, 1995). The end result of such fully automated model-selection techniques is a single "best" model. Some techniques may be partially automated, such as those in which standard statistical software produce a variety of models to consider (for example, all possible subsets of drivers) and then require the investigator to select a "best" model on some criterion of model fit (for example, R^2, Akaike's information criterion). Other techniques might not be automated at all, and could involve specifying and comparing models based on existing theory, research, or knowledge of the organization.[1] Once the "best" is identified via one of these methods, regression coefficients for drivers comprising the reduced model are often used to determine their relative importance.

On the surface, the automated model-selection techniques appear ideal for key driver analyses. Drivers are selected based on an objective set of statistical rules. However, the objectivity of the driver-selection process is a mirage. Even fully automated model-selection techniques require subjectively specified rules for including or excluding drivers from a model (for example, what p-value does each driver need to remain in the model?). Such choices are often arbitrary (for example, based on the defaults of the statistical software) and hard to defend. As Harrell (2001) outlines, automated model-selection techniques have numerous drawbacks including:

- upwardly biased R^2 values;
- downwardly biased standard errors for regression coefficients, thus increasing the chances of concluding that a driver is significant, when in reality, it is not;
- upwardly biased regression coefficients further exacerbating the likelihood of falsely concluding that significant driver effects exist; and
- inclusion of key drivers in the final model becomes more arbitrary as multicollinearity increases.

Additionally, all model selection techniques focus on identifying a single "best" model for predicting engagement. A fundamental problem with this focus stems from the notion of "model uncertainty" (Chatfield, 1995). That is, for any given *set* of drivers, there can be several combinations (subsets) of drivers that predict engagement almost as well as the single "best" model that emerges from the model-selection techniques. Thus, labeling any such model as "best", and its set of drivers, *the* key drivers of engagement, may be arbitrary. Furthermore, model uncertainty increases as correlations among the set of drivers being considered increase. Given that key driver analyses are often based on highly correlated drivers, substantial levels of model uncertainty will likely be present (Burnham & Anderson, 2002).

Model uncertainty can be particularly problematic from the perspective of acting on the results of a model of engagement identified through a variable selection technique. For example, say that an organization used one of the model-selection techniques and finds that the "best" model comprises three key drivers (out of a starting set of 10) and has a model R^2 of 0.50 (that is, it accounts for half of the variance in engagement). Unfortunately, the organization finds that each of the key drivers in the model is very difficult to act on. Now say another subset of three drivers (out of the starting set of 10) could be used to create a model of engagement that has an R^2 of 0.49 (that is, it performs nearly as well as the "best" model). In this case though, the organization finds that each of the key drivers is easy to act on. Had the organization *solely* relied on the "best model" based on the model-selection approach, they would have overlooked a set of key drivers upon which they could have acted on to easily impact employee engagement.

Modern approaches to key driver analysis
In this chapter, we consider two modern developments for identifying and ranking key drivers with regard to importance for predicting employee engagement. Both approaches address some of the limitations of commonly used approaches and provide additional insights into the variables that are the most important drivers of engagement.

Relative-importance analyses
The first modern approach, relative-importance analyses, can be used to supplement to the full-model and model-selection approaches. These analyses estimate the percentage of the model's R^2 that is accounted for by each driver relative to other drivers in the model (Budescu, 1993; Johnson & LeBreton, 2004; LeBreton et al., 2007). The drivers can then be rank ordered by their individual contributions to the total variance explained. A key benefit of these analyses is that they can be explained in very simple terms to organizational decision makers. For example, for

a given predictive model, one can make statements such as 50 percent of the model's ability to predict engagement stems from X, 35 percent stems from Y, and only 15 percent stems from all other drivers considered.

To date, these analyses have not achieved widespread use among survey professionals (Lundby & Johnson, 2006; LeBreton et al., 2007). However, they are extremely useful with the employee engagement survey items and dimensions where the drivers are highly correlated (that is, multicollinearity). Unlike the regression coefficients based on the full-model and model-selection approaches, even in the presence of multicollinearity, relative-importance analyses can index the relative-importance of drivers in a model. As a result of relative-importance analyses' effective handling of multicollinearity, one may come to different conclusions regarding the relative importance of drivers when comparing regression coefficients and relative weights (LeBreton et al., 2004a).

There are several different analytical approaches to conducting relative-importance analyses. The two most currently favored approaches are dominance analysis (Budescu, 1993) and relative-weights analysis (Johnson, 2000). These two approaches provide essentially the same results (LeBreton et al., 2004b). The primary difference is that relative-weights analysis is easier to implement with five or more drivers in the model (Johnson & LeBreton, 2004). As this is typically the case in key driver analyses of employee engagement, we focus on Johnson's (2000) relative-weights analysis (RWA).

The mathematical basis of the RWA is complicated and a detailed presentation is beyond this chapter's scope. The basic logic, however, is to create a new set of transformed variables that are maximally related to the original drivers, but the new variables are unrelated to one another. The RWA then uses the values of these transformed variables to estimate the unique contribution of each variable and then rescales the new variables back into the original drivers. The variance contributed by each driver to explaining variance in engagement can be clearly identified.

Although relative-importance analyses help overcome a key limitation of the full-model and model-selection approaches by providing a viable metric for judging the relative importance of drivers, they still share the other limitations. Relative-importance analyses do not (a) help identify the best model of engagement from a full set of potential drivers, (b) resolve the biases that stem from the use of automated model-selection methods, or (c) address model uncertainty.

Another caution with relative-importance analyses is that the rank order and percentage of explained variance contributed by each driver depends on which other drivers are entered in the model. Like regression coefficients, the relative importance can change as drivers are entered or removed from the model. The quality of the driver-selection process impacts on which drivers will be identified as the most important. Additionally, statistical significance tests for these analyses are a developing area (Tonidandel et al., 2007). Currently, there is little guidance on determining if the weights differ, either from one another or from zero. This is a potential problem because there can be cases where a regression coefficient is not statistically significant, but the driver is ranked as one of the most important drivers.

Model-averaging approaches

An alternative approach to the typical model selection-parameter estimation sequence is to avoid the first step altogether, and derive parameter estimates (that is, regression coefficients, relative-importance weights) that do not choose any single model as best, but rather capitalize on information that *all of the models considered* have to offer. Past literature (for example, Anderson, 2008; Hastie et al., 2009) has described a straightforward approach to model averaging that involves:

1. Fitting models for all possible subsets of available drivers.
2. Estimating the probability that each of the models considered is the best model using a simple formula that uses the fit statistics for each model as input.
3. Taking a weighted sum of the regression coefficients for each driver across all models (weights reflect the model probabilities calculated above) and letting the coefficients for a given driver equal zero in those models in which it does not appear.

The "model-averaged" regression coefficients created using this process account for the uncertainty in the model-selection process, and if applied to the original data will produce predicted values that equal the weighted average of predicted values based on all models considered. In other words, rather than basing regression coefficient estimates *and* predictions on a single model fraught with uncertainty, the analyst capitalizes on the information offered by each model.

This process offers other benefits as well. First, it clarifies the degree of uncertainty in the model-selection process. To the extent the probability value for the most probable model diverges from 1.0, the more uncertainty there is in the process (that is, the more likely there are several models that provide approximately the same level of best prediction). Second, the resulting regression coefficient for any given driver is "shrunken" proportional to the probability that the models in which the driver appears *do not* include the best model. This appears to be a more effective way to deal with "borderline" drivers that might be included or excluded from a model based on arbitrary criteria used by automated model-selection techniques (Harrell, 2001; Anderson, 2008). Third, this process offers intuitive indices of driver *criticality* (Azen et al., 2001). By summing the model probabilities for those models that include a given driver, one effectively estimates the probability that the models in which the driver appears include the best model. Such metrics are very easy for organizational decision makers to understand. Lastly, it is possible to generate the relative-importance of each driver to the average model composite by regressing the predicted values from the average model on the full set of drivers and performing a relative-importance analysis. Such an analysis could provide a measure of the relative importance of each potential driver of engagement that reflects the uncertainty in the modeling process.

Empirical comparison of different key driver analyses

To demonstrate the bivariate, full-model, model-selection, and modern approaches (and the differences one can obtain), we applied these techniques to data from an employee engagement survey collected at a large private sector company. The database consisted of responses to items on 13 survey dimension (for example, top leadership, organizational vision) from 1,500 employees.[2] To give one a sense for multicollinearity, the range of correlations among the 13 dimensions was 0.16 to 0.70 ($M = 0.46$).

For the bivariate approach, we calculated the correlation between each driver and engagement, and then ranked drivers based on the magnitude of the correlations. For the full-model approach, we regressed engagement on all 13 drivers simultaneously, and then ranked drivers based on the magnitude of their standardized regression coefficients. For the model-selection approach, we used stepwise variable selection (per the default method in SPSS) to identify a reduced set of key drivers, and then ranked the drivers based on the magnitude of their standardized regression coefficients. For the relative-weights approach, we estimated the relative weights for each of the 13 drivers in the full model and ranked the drivers based on those weights. Finally, we examined two variants of the model-averaging approach. We first followed the model-averaging approach outlined above, and ranked drivers in terms of the probability that they would be part of the best model for predicting engagement. Next, using the model-averaged predicted values for employee engagement as a criterion, we estimated relative weights for the full set of 13 drivers, and ranked the drivers based on those weights.

Before interpreting the results for Table 15.1, there are a few important points to make regarding the overall modeling results that will help put the findings in context. First, both the full and stepwise models' R^2 was

Table 15.1 Rank order of key drivers of employee engagement by analytical approach

Rank	Bivariate	Stepwise	Full model	RWA	Model averaging (P₁)	Model averaging (RW)
1	Organization's vision (0.72*)	Organization's vision (0.37*)	Organization's vision (0.37*)	Employee development (17.8%)	(tie) Employee development & organization's vision (1.0)	Employee development (18.1%)
2	Employee development (0.65*)	Employee development (0.27*)	Employee development (0.27*)	Organization's vision (17.6%)	—	Organization's vision (17.9%)
3	Focus on innovation (0.59*)	Internal communications (0.08*)	Internal communications (0.073*)	Top leadership (7.9%)	Internal communications (0.996)	Top leadership (7.9%)
4	Top leadership (0.57*)	Top leadership (0.071*)	Top leadership (0.072*)	Focus on collaboration (7.4%)	Organizational culture (0.954)	Focus on collaboration (7.1%)
5	Focus on collaboration (0.55*)	Organizational culture (0.067*)	Organizational culture (0.059*)	Focus on innovation (7.2%)	Top leadership (0.927)	Internal communications (6.934%)
6	Competitive rewards (0.53*)	Managerial support (0.049*)	Nature of the work (−0.055*)	Managerial support (7.0%)	Global orientation (0.844)	Focus on innovation (6.932%)
7	Nature of the work (0.527*)	Global orientation (0.048*)	Managerial support (0.05*)	Organizational culture (6.8%)	Managerial support (0.800)	Organizational culture (6.92%)

Table 15.1 (continued)

Rank	Bivariate	Stepwise	Full model	RWA	Model averaging (P)	Model averaging (RW)
8	Managerial support (0.52*)	–	Global orientation (0.04*)	Internal communications (6.8%)	Nature of the work (0.665)	Managerial support (6.8%)
9	Internal communications (0.51*)	–	Competitive rewards (0.035)	Competitive rewards (6.4%)	Work–life balance (0.553)	Competitive rewards (6.0%)
10	Organizational culture (0.50*)	–	Focus on innovation (0.0324)	Nature of the work (5.4%)	Focus on collaboration (0.528)	Nature of the work (5.8%)
11	Resources and processes (0.48*)	–	Focus on collaboration (0.0319)	Resources and processes (4.6%)	Competitive rewards (0.491)	Resources and processes (5.0%)
12	Work–life balance (0.3041*)	–	Resources and processes (−0.031)	Global orientation (2.7%)	Focus on innovation (0.481)	Global orientation (2.6%)
13	Global orientation (0.3036*)	–	Work–life balance (0.025)	Work–life balance (2.5%)	Resources and processes (0.404)	Work–life balance (2.2%)

Note: Statistics for each approach are noted in parentheses. Statistics for the bivariate approach reflect zero-order correlations between each driver and engagement (starred correlations were statistically significant, $p < 0.05$, two-tailed). Statistics for the stepwise and full-model approaches reflect standardized regression coefficients (starred coefficients were statistically significant, $p < 0.05$, two-tailed). Statistics for the relative weights analysis (RWA) reflect the percentage of the full model R^2 accounted for by each driver. Statistics for the model-averaging (P) approach reflect the probability that the given driver is part of the best model. Statistics for the model-averaging (RW) approach reflect the percentage of variance each driver accounts for in the model-averaged predicted level of employee engagement.

0.60. However, only seven drivers were part of the final stepwise model. These results suggest that there was a great deal of redundancy among the drivers in the full model, as a model with only seven drivers produced the same R^2 as the full model. Nevertheless, the model-averaging approach revealed that the model identified through stepwise was far from the only best model. Specifically, it revealed that 816 of the 8,191 models that could potentially be formed from the set of 13 drivers (reflecting all possible combinations of the 13 key drivers) had an R^2 of 0.60 (28 of these models had only six drivers). Furthermore, 1,996 of the 8,191 models had R^2 of 0.59 or above (three of these models had only three drivers). These latter results not only demonstrate the arbitrariness (uncertainty) of labeling any single model as best, but also illustrate that with only three drivers we could achieve a model that was nearly as predictive of engagement as the full model based on 13 drivers or the stepwise model based on seven drivers.

As noted above, there were three models with only three drivers identified via the model-averaging approach that produced R^2 of 0.59. Each of these models included employee development and organizational vision as drivers. This is noteworthy because these two drivers consistently emerged as the most important key drivers based on all approaches examined (see Table 15.1). A model with only these two drivers had an R^2 of 0.58. Though all approaches shown in the table successfully identified the top two drivers, there were differences (across approaches) in the rank ordering of drivers beyond that. For example, the third most important driver of the bivariate approach was a focus on innovation. The stepwise, full-model, and model-averaging approach probabilities identified internal communications as the third most important driver. The relative-weights approach and the model-averaging approach coupled with relative weights identified top leadership as the third most important driver. Overall the results, in Table 15.1 illustrate the importance of using multiple approaches to help identify and rank order the key drivers of employee engagement, as different approaches can lead to different answers. Based on the limitations of the bivariate, full-model, and model-selection techniques described earlier, when reconciling results across approaches, we would place more confidence in the results of the modern approaches, in particular the model-averaging approaches, given their ability to provide insight into uncertainty in the modeling process itself.

Conclusions and recommendations for best practice
In this chapter, we have highlighted some of the current approaches to key driver analysis, the problems with these approaches, and modern

alternatives that overcome many of these problems. We have demonstrated how the approach taken to key driver analysis can impact which drivers are identified as the most important. Although we have demonstrated these techniques in the context of key driver analyses, they can easily be applied to other questions that regard the prediction of employee or customer attitudes and behaviors.

In terms of our recommendations for best practice in key driver analysis, we want to reinforce a key point made earlier. When attempting to identify the key drivers of engagement and deciding where to focus efforts to improve engagement, empirical analyses such as those reviewed above provide only part of the answer. Other factors such as theory and prior research regarding determinants of employee engagement, the nuances of the organization, and practical considerations (for example, feasibility of various efforts for improving engagement) should be considered. Although these other factors were not our focus, they become very important when empirical data are not available to support the approaches discussed here.

Given the qualification noted above, as well as the variation in the results presented earlier, we recommend that future key driver analyses rely on multiple methods to examine key drivers of engagement, but that the modern approaches should be given emphasis. If one is confident in the best model for his or her situation, relative-weights analysis can provide a clear indicator of the relative importance of each driver in the model. If one is less confident in which drivers comprise the best model (that is, there is a good deal of model uncertainty), model averaging approaches can be quite helpful. As noted earlier, in a typical key driver analysis, model uncertainty is high as a result of considering many highly correlated drivers. Couple this typical situation with the idiosyncrasies of the organization that make more theory-driven approaches difficult, and model-averaging approaches may prove to be particularly useful in most cases. As we have noted, one should be wary of simply using a model with all drivers or selecting a single best model based on arbitrary statistical criteria that masquerade as "objective" unless the data, theory, and local conditions all suggest that it is warranted.

In addition to the statistical advantages of the modern approaches, there are practical benefits as well. As illustrated earlier, relative-weights analysis and model-averaging approaches produce statistics that are expressed in a metric that is easy for organizational decision makers to understand. Furthermore, model-averaging approaches can facilitate the integration of statistical results with practical concerns. Recall that model-averaging approaches can produce fit statistics for all possible models based on a set of drivers. From these results it is easy to see if there are several models that perform equally as well. Such results can allow organizations to see how much predictive power may be lost (or not lost) by adopting a reduced model that may be far more feasible to act upon relative to fuller models. Combining practical concerns with rigorous statistical analyses is likely to lead to the identification of key drivers that can and will be acted on by an organization.

In closing, we want to offer a caution for future users and consumers of key driver analyses. Although modern approaches offer several advantages over traditional approaches to key driver analyses, the quality of results they produce is necessarily limited by the quality of data put into them. All of the approaches discussed in this chapter, if based on poorly conceived engagement surveys, have the potential to mislead organizational decision makers. Thus, future practice should first ensure that measures included in the key driver analyses (both drivers, and the engagement criterion itself) are of sufficient quality. Second, even with high-quality measures, the analyses above may lead to unwarranted conclusions if one does not gather enough data. The stability of results produced by all of the approaches discussed here are contingent on having enough data, both in terms of the power to detect statistically significant relationships as well as accurately estimate the coefficients of interest (for example, Kelley & Maxwell, 2003). Thus, future practice should ensure that it gathers sufficient data to support the key driver analyses to be conducted. Third, even with high-quality measures, and sufficient data, the results may be skewed or lack generalizability without proper screening of the data for outliers and checking of model assumptions (Berry, 1993). All of the approaches discussed here come with assumptions that should, and can be easily checked (Fox, 1991). In sum, we would strongly recommend that when leveraging the approaches discussed here, future efforts to identify key drivers remember the fundamental data analysis issues that come with these approaches.

Notes

1. Though this last approach may be viewed as ideal from a scientific perspective, often in the context of key driver analyses, there is insufficient theory and research, and many potential drivers that are idiosyncratic to the organization. Thus, there is often some degree of "exploration" required or else potentially salient drivers of engagement in the organization might be missed. For this reason, we focus our subsequent critique on the automated model-selection methods described above.
2. To de-identify the data, we have replaced the original dimension names with alternative names typically included in employee engagement surveys.

References

Anderson, D.R. (2008), *Model Based Inference in the Life Sciences: A Primer on Evidence*, New York: Springer Science + Business Media.

Azen, R., Budescu, D.V. & Reiser, B. (2001), "Criticality of predictors in multiple regression", *British Journal of Mathematical and Statistical Psychology*, **54**, 201–25.

Berry, W.D. (1993), *Understanding Regression Assumptions*, Newbury Park, CA: Sage.

Budescu, D.V. (1993), "Dominance analysis: a new approach to the problem of relative importance of predictors in multiple regression", *Psychological Bulletin*, **114**, 542–51.

Burnham, K.P. & Anderson, D.R. (2002), *Model Selection and Multimodel Inference: A Practical Information-Theoretic Approach*, 2nd edn, New York: Springer Science + Business Media.

Chatfield, C. (1995), "Model uncertainty, data mining, and statistical inference", *Journal of the Royal Statistical Society A*, **158**, 419–66.

Fox, J. (1991), *Regression Diagnostics*, Newbury Park, CA: Sage.

Harrell, Jr., F.E. (2001), *Regression Modeling Strategies: With Applications to Linear Models, Logistic Regression, and Survival Analysis*, New York: Springer Science + Business Media.

Hastie, T., Tibshirani, R. & Friedman, J. (2009), *The Elements of Statistical Learning: Data Mining, Inference, and Prediction*, New York: Springer Science + Business Media.

Hoeting, J.A., Madigan, D., Raferty, A.E. & Volinksy, C.T. (1999), "Bayesian model averaging: a tutorial", *Statistical Science*, **14**, 382–417.

James, L.R. (1980), "The unmeasured variables problem in path analysis", *Journal of Applied Psychology*, **65**, 415–21.

Johnson, J.W. (2000), "A heuristic method for estimating the relative weight of predictor variables in multiple regression", *Multivariate Behavioral Research*, **35**, 1–19.

Johnson, J.W. & LeBreton, J.M. (2004), "History and use of relative importance indices in organizational research", *Organizational Research Methods*, **7**, 238–57.

Kelley, K. & Maxwell, S.E. (2003), "Sample size for multiple regression: obtaining regression coefficients that are accurate, not simply significant", *Psychological Methods*, **8**, 305–21.

LeBreton, J.M., Binning, J.F., Adorno, A.J. & Melcher, K.M. (2004a), "Importance of personality and job-specific affect for predicting job attitudes and withdrawal behavior", *Organizational Research Methods*, **7**, 300–325.

LeBreton, J.M., Hargis, M.B., Griepentrog, B., Oswald, F.L. & Ployhart, R.E. (2007), "A multidimensional approach for evaluating variables in organizational research and practice", *Personnel Psychology*, **60**, 475–98.

LeBreton, J.M., Ployhart, R.E. & Ladd, R.T. (2004b), "A Monte Carlo comparison of relative importance methodologies", *Organizational Research Methods*, **7**, 258–82.

Lundby, K. & Johnson, J. (2006), "Relative weights of predictors", in A. Kraut (ed.), *Getting Action from Organizational Surveys*, San Francisco, CA: Jossey-Bass, pp. 326–51.

Macey, W., Schneider, B., Barbera, K. & Young, S. (2009), *Employee Engagement: Tools for Analysis, Practice, and Competitive Advantage*, Malden, MA: Wiley-Blackwell.

Thompson, B. (1995), "Stepwise regression and stepwise discriminant analysis need not apply here: a guidelines editorial", *Educational and Psychological Measurement*, **55**, 525–34.

Tonidandel, S., LeBreton, J. & Johnson, J. (2007), "Determining the statistical significance of relative weights", paper presented at the annual conference of the Society for Industrial and Organizational Psychology, New York, April.

16 The personal side of engagement: the influence of personality factors
Cristina de Mello e Souza Wildermuth

Introduction

> If we are truly interested in a personal connection to work, shouldn't we
> measure the person instead?
> (Ed Gubman, 2004)

We must bring the *person* to the engagement debate. This was the gist of the argument made by business consultant Ed Gubman (2004) in "From engagement to passion for work: the search for the missing person". Gubman argued that current discussions on engagement involve two components: *where* the person works and *what* the person does. Additionally, organizations should start focusing on *who* the person is.

William Kahn's (1990) landmark study on engagement did not have a direct focus on the person. Instead, Kahn sought to understand the powerful psychological conditions that could "survive the gamut of individual differences" (p. 695). Kahn identified three such conditions: meaningfulness (the perceived "worth" of engaging at work), safety (how safe it is to be oneself at work), and availability of resources, both emotional and physical, to perform one's duties.

Kahn did, however, acknowledge that individual differences might influence the kinds of roles employees find engaging or disengaging as well as personal experiences of meaningfulness, safety, and availability of resources. Additionally, Schaufeli and Bakker (2003) described engagement as a relatively "persistent and pervasive affective–cognitive state" (p. 4). Such a longer-term conceptualization of engagement seems to suggest at least some level of connection between engagement and the makeup of the individual – the potential impact of the *person* on engagement.

This chapter addresses the personal side of engagement. Specifically, the relationship between engagement and the five-factor model of personality (FFM) is explored. The chapter includes (a) an introduction to the FFM; (b) a review of Macey and Schneider's (2008) tridimensional model of engagement including trait, state, and behavioral components; (c) a summary of recent research studies on personality and engagement; and

(d) a discussion of existing findings, including practical implications, an integrated model of engagement, and topics for future research.

The five factor model of personality

During the last decade, the FFM of personality has gained considerable support among researchers. The origins of the model are deeply embedded in the history of personality testing and are generally linked to the pioneering work of Gordon Allport on personality and linguistics. While the exact names attributed to each FFM trait may vary, most researchers (McCrae & Costa, 1997; Mount et al., 1998; Howard & Howard, 2001a; Judge et al., 2002) have agreed on the following five traits: neuroticism (also referred to as need for stability and emotional stability), extraversion, openness to experiences (also called originality and intellect), agreeableness (also called accommodation) and conscientiousness (also called consolidation).

Neuroticism has to do with the individual's general tolerance for stress. Individuals who are high in neuroticism are more reactive than average and often report less satisfaction with life. Conversely, those who are low in neuroticism tend to present more composed, resilient, and adaptable behaviors (Howard & Howard, 1995).

Extraversion represents a person's general sociability and tolerance for sensory stimulation (Howard & Howard, 2001a). Extraverts tend to be ambitious, assertive, adventuresome and gregarious (Walsh & Eggerth, 2005). Introverts, on the other hand, may be more reserved and comfortable with solitude (Howard & Howard, 1995).

Openness to experiences refers to an individual's general range of interests, comfort with change, and fascination with innovation. Individuals who score high in this trait tend to be original and take an interest in a wide range of topics and theories. Those who score low, on the other hand, tend to present a more conservative worldview (Howard & Howard, 2001a).

Agreeableness relates to service orientation, harmony seeking, and the propensity to defer to others. Individuals who are high in agreeableness are known to be more courteous, good natured, cooperative, and caring. Individuals who are low in agreeableness tend to focus on their own needs and be more competitive (ibid.).

Finally, *conscientiousness* (ibid.) relates to methodicalness and discipline. Individuals who are high in conscientiousness tend to be careful, thorough, organized, and focused (Walsh & Eggerth, 2005). On the other hand, those low in conscientiousness may be more spontaneous and "free flowing" (Howard & Howard, 2001a).

Three characteristics of the five factors are noteworthy. First, the factors are thought to be quasi-normally distributed (McCrae, 2006). In other words, the distribution of any given trait approximately follows a normal curve, where most people score somewhere in the middle between two extremes. Second, there seems to be a strong biological/genetic basis for the five factors (McCrae et al., 2000). Finally, the five factors are believed to be *stable*. A person's personality is not expected to change significantly during adult years. Indeed, even though some variation is to be expected, personality traits could provide a "core of consistency" (Matthews et al., 2003, p. 3) that influences the way one responds to *most* situations one encounters.

In particular, this last characteristic of FFM traits – stability – may impact on our ability to connect personality and engagement. Logically, personality traits are more likely to relate to either a reasonably stable engagement or to the tendency to experience engagement more frequently. If, on the other hand, engagement varies constantly according to the "momentary ebbs and flows" (Kahn, 1990, p. 693) of self-in-role, a strong relationship between engagement and personality is unlikely. A possible solution to this dilemma is reviewed next.

Macey and Schneider's tridimensional model of engagement
While Kahn (1990) suggested that individuals frequently "calibrate" their levels of engagement at work (thus engaging or disengaging according to their perceptions of meaningfulness, safety, and availability of resources) other researchers (Schaufeli & Bakker, 2003) positioned engagement as a longer-term *state of mind*. Indeed, Schaufeli and Bakker argued that "rather than a momentary and specific state, engagement refers to a more persistent and pervasive affective–cognitive state that is not focused on any particular object, event, individual, or behavior" (pp. 4–5).

Recently, Macey and Schneider (2008) proposed a tridimensional model of engagement that might reconcile Kahn's (1990) "momentary" and Schaufeli and Bakker's (2003) "persistent" portrayals of engagement. Macey and Schneider's model included three engagement components: behaviors, state, and traits.

First, engaged individuals demonstrate certain visible *behaviors*. These behaviors surpass the "typical" expectations for a professional role. For instance, a teacher might spend extra time tutoring students and a customer service agent may help a customer solve a personal problem.

Second, these engaged behaviors may result from a "state" of engagement. The person who goes "above and beyond" at work may do so because of general and longer-term feelings of energy, enthusiasm, and pride. Macey and Schneider proposed that the "state" of engagement is a complex combination of constructs such as job satisfaction, organizational commitment, job involvement, and empowerment.

Third, certain individuals could have a "disposition" or "tendency" towards feelings of engagement. This tendency increases the likelihood of a longer-term state of engagement in these individuals. Macey and Schneider connected the tendency to engage to the following engagement traits: conscientiousness, proactivity, positive affect, and an "autotelic personality" (Csikszentmihalyi & Nakamura, 2002). Conscientiousness, an FFM trait, was defined previously in this chapter. Following are possible connections between the other listed traits and the FFM.

Proactivity means a "general tendency to create or influence the work environment" (Macey & Schneider, 2008, p. 20). Proactive individuals take initiative and persevere until they are able to improve their environment (Bateman & Crant, 1993). Major et al.'s (2006) study on the proactive personality found significant correlations between proactivity and four of the FFM traits. Proactivity correlated positively with conscientiousness, extraversion, and openness to experience, and correlated negatively with neuroticism.

Positive affect (PA) is the "degree to which an individual feels enthusiastic, active, and alert" (Rich, 2006, p. 15). PA has been connected to pleasant experiences and interpersonal satisfaction. Watson and Clark (1992) found that PA correlated positively with conscientiousness, extraversion, openness to experience, and agreeableness, and negatively with neuroticism.

Finally, the "autotelic personality" combines higher than average levels of curiosity, interest in life, and perseverance (Csikszentmihalyi & Nakamura, 2002). *Curiosity* has been found to be positively related to openness to experience and conscientiousness and *perseverance* positively related to conscientiousness and negatively related to neuroticism (Johnson & Ostendorf, 1993).

Logically, connections between personality and engagement lie primarily in "trait" engagement. After all, a psychological state – while relatively durable – is still time-bound (Macey & Schneider, 2008). A trait, on the other hand, is expected to endure across situations. The findings of three studies investigating personality and engagement are reviewed in the following section.

Personality and engagement: a research review and leadership implications

Three studies recently connected engagement and personality: Langelaan et al.'s (2004) study on personality, temperament, burnout, and engagement; Rich's (2006) validation study for the development of a new job engagement scale; and my own study (Wildermuth, 2008) contrasting engagement and the FFM.

Langelaan et al. (2004) conducted the first study in Holland. The sample included 572 Dutch employees from various organizations and professional backgrounds (111 blue-collar workers, 338 managers from a telecom organization, and 123 participants at a seminar on "positive thinking"). Participants completed the Utrecht Work Engagement Scale (UWES) (Schaufeli & Bakker, 2003) to assess engagement and McCrae and Costa's (1997) NEO inventory to test the FFM. The researchers examined two engagement components: vigor and dedication. Vigor encompasses energy, resilience, and perseverance. Items measuring vigor included "When I get up in the morning, I feel like going to work" and "I can continue working for very long periods of time" (Schaufeli & Bakker, 2003, p. 5). Dedication encompasses a sense of pride and enthusiasm. Items measuring dedication included "I find the work that I do full of meaning and purpose" and "my job inspires me" (p. 5). Likewise, the researchers measured two FFM traits: neuroticism and extraversion.

The results revealed significant relationships between engagement (characterized by high vigor and high dedication) and the two analyzed personality traits. First, vigor correlated negatively with neuroticism ($r = -0.48$) and positively with extraversion ($r = 0.44$). Second, dedication correlated negatively with neuroticism ($r = -0.40$) and positively with extraversion ($r = 0.37$). The researchers were able to accurately classify 84.4 percent of the sample as engaged (high vigor and high dedication) or non-engaged (low vigor and low dedication) according to scores in extraversion and neuroticism.

Rich (2006) conducted the second study as part of his dissertation at the University of Florida. Rich's study involved 245 Northern-California fire fighters. The researcher's primary objective was to develop and validate a new job engagement scale measuring Kahn's (1990) physical, emotional, and cognitive engagement components. Rich's results supported a positive correlation between conscientiousness and engagement ($r = 0.59$). The researcher concluded that "certain types of individuals are more likely to become engaged in their work role than others" (p. 126) and recommended that organizations "assess an applicant's self evaluations as well as conscientiousness in order to select individuals who have a general proclivity for job engagement" (p. 130).

Finally, I recently investigated relationships between engagement and FFM traits (Wildermuth, 2008). My sample included 292 non-managerial professional and paraprofessional employees from three social service agencies in the Midwest of the United States. Two of the agencies provided various health and social services to individuals with developmental challenges. The third agency was a faith-based organization. Respondents received a survey combining a shortened version of the WorkPlace Big Five Profile™ (Howard & Howard, 2001b) and Rich's (2006) Job Engagement

Survey. The WorkPlace Big Five Profile™ is an FFM instrument designed for applications in the workplace. The short version of the instrument – which I used – includes 48 items. All five FFM traits were measured.

The results supported significant correlations between three FFM traits and engagement: neuroticism, extraversion, and conscientiousness. The correlations, however, were low (neuroticism, $r = -0.19$; extraversion, $r = 0.30$; conscientiousness, $r = 0.16$).

The study data analysis also included a multiple regression and a series of two-way ANOVAS (analyses of variance). The multiple regression analysis revealed an overall predictive model of engagement including extraversion and conscientiousness. These two traits, combined, affected 9 percent of the variability in engagement. Results from the ANOVAS supported interactions between two personality traits and job rank: extraversion and agreeableness. Paraprofessionals were more engaged when their extraversion scores were high and their agreeableness was low. Professionals were more engaged when their extraversion was high and their agreeableness was medium. Effect sizes, however, were low for both extraversion and agreeableness ($\eta^2 = 0.04$).

To summarize, research results so far support a low to modest relationship between FFM traits and engagement. The following section discusses these findings, suggests practical implications, offers a model of engagement, and recommends topics for further research.

Personality, engagement and implications for leaders

The results from the reviewed engagement studies (Langelaan et al., 2004; Rich, 2006; Wildermuth, 2008) supported significant negative relationships between neuroticism and engagement and significant positive relationships between extraversion/conscientiousness and engagement. The following subsections discuss the possible impact of each personality trait on engagement and implications for leaders.

Extraversion and engagement

Extraversion had a low or modest correlation to engagement in two of the studies described (Langelaan et al., 2004; Wildermuth, 2008). The following are possible explanations. First, extraverted individuals are naturally energetic, enthusiastic, and action oriented (Howard & Howard, 2001a). These characteristics logically tie to physical and emotional components of engagement. After all, physical engagement relates to energy and emotional engagement relates to enthusiasm (Schaufeli & Bakker, 2003). For instance, two of the items of the UWES are "at work, I feel bursting with energy" and "I am enthusiastic about my job" (p. 5).

Second, extraverts' sociability and relationship-building abilities could positively impact on all three psychological conditions of engagement: meaningfulness, safety, and the availability of resources (Kahn, 1990). By definition, extraverts are more comfortable with social interactions *in general*. Extraverted workers might thus invite and receive feedback that is more positive and supportive from colleagues and clients. The highly social world of work, therefore, could simply be more comfortable for extraverts.

What may be most important for leaders is not the simple realization that the naturally enthusiastic and energetic extraverts may be, predictably, more enthusiastic and energetic at work. Rather, leaders may need to understand why and how extraversion impacts on engagement and use such understanding to engage *introverts*. For instance, leaders may provide educational opportunities for all employees on personality differences, encourage networking in ways that are more comfortable for employees who are less sociable and gregarious (via smaller or quieter opportunities for networking, small-group meetings, and mentoring partnerships), and promote a culture of support and recognition for *all* employees. Additionally, leaders may pay special attention to the importance of team and relationship-building activities. While extraverts may forge relationships on their own, introverts may need "special nudging" or help.

Neuroticism and engagement

Neuroticism correlated negatively with engagement in two of the studies (Langelaan et al., 2004; Wildermuth, 2008). A possible explanation could lie in the feelings of self-consciousness and worry (Howard & Howard, 2001c) found in individuals high in neuroticism. Indeed, Langelaan et al. suggested that "employees high in *N* perceive their work environment as more threatening" (p. 529). Such perception could reduce a person's feelings of safety and drain his or her emotional resources.

Two types of leadership interventions might benefit the engagement of high neuroticism employees. First, leaders could alleviate these employees' feelings of self-consciousness and anxiety by increasing their own levels of tact (especially during performance-appraisal processes and feedback sessions). Intensifying positive feedback and enhancing recognition processes might be helpful. Second, employees higher in neuroticism may have less tolerance for stress. Leaders should pay special attention to times of high turmoil, change, or instability in the workplace. Additionally, leaders should promote a safe work environment and take action to prevent workplace harassment and bullying.

Conscientiousness and engagement

Conscientiousness correlated significantly with engagement in two of the studies (Rich, 2006; Wildermuth, 2008). Research shows that highly conscientious individuals tend to be more focused and goal oriented and find it easier to succeed (Judge et al., 1999). Individuals high in conscientiousness will find it easier to plan their workdays, follow up on agreed-upon actions, focus on objectives and persist in the face of obstacles (Johnson & Ostendorf, 1993). Highly conscientious employees might also be more successful in changing their environment to fit their needs.

Low conscientiousness, however, may generate greater ease in multi-tasking (Howard & Howard, 2001b). Thus, individuals lower in conscientiousness might find it more comfortable to work in occupations requiring constant switches between activities. Leaders must understand this natural tendency and strive to distribute job responsibilities and requirements accordingly.

Agreeableness, openness to experiences, and engagement
Only one of the three studies described (Wildermuth, 2008) investigated relationships between *all five* traits and engagement. This study did not identify significant correlations between engagement and openness to experience or agreeableness. Further, a multiple regression revealed only two traits composing an overall predictive model of engagement: extraversion and conscientiousness. It was somewhat surprising that neither agreeableness nor openness to experience were associated with engagement. I expected that high agreeable individuals might better be able to mobilize social supports and resources to engage more directly in their job roles and organizational context. I also expected openness to experience to correlate significantly with engagement because various authors (Kahn, 1990; Macey & Schneider, 2008) have connected engagement and innovation. For instance, Kahn argued that those who are disengaged "act as custodians rather than innovators" (p. 702) for the role they occupy. Macey and Schneider suggested that engaged employees do not simply work *more* – they work *differently*, "initiating or fostering change" (p. 18). Both innovation and comfort with change are connected to openness to experience (Howard & Howard, 2001b). It is noteworthy, however, that I found a significant (albeit small) interaction between agreeableness and job type influencing engagement (for further details on such interaction, see Wildermuth, 2008). Overall, despite the absence of main effects, further research to examine the potential influence of agreeableness and openness on engagement using a broader range of occupational samples and job roles is warranted.

The following section connects personality, Kahn's (1990) psychological conditions of engagement, additional antecedents of engagement, and Macey and Schneider's (2008) tridimensional engagement model.

An integrated model: personality, engagement and context

Even though current evidence supports significant relationships between certain personality traits and engagement, these relationships were not very strong. Four possible explanations emerge. First, various situational antecedents – consisting of organizational and job-related characteristics – could *also* support or hinder engagement. Examples include job variety and wholeness (Hackman et al., 1975); organizational support (Saks, 2006); the availability of rewards and recognition (Koyuncu et al., 2006); and the authenticity of the leader (Avolio et al., 2004).

Second, personality could impact on individual perceptions of meaningfulness, safety, and availability within a given situation. For instance, the same situation may be perceived by a calm individual as safe and by a nervous individual as unsafe.

Third, personality may influence a person's decision to engage or disengage. For instance, someone who is calm, resilient, energetic and action oriented may choose to engage *in spite of* a perception of lack of meaningfulness or safety.

Fourth, personality traits could help individuals *change* a situation. For instance, someone who is action and goal oriented (high in conscientiousness and extraversion) could interact with an environment and make it more engaging. This view is consistent with Macey and Schneider's (2008) inclusion of "proactivity" among engagement traits.

Thus, a complex interaction of personality and several other environmental and job antecedents could impact on employees' state of engagement and subsequent engaged behaviors. Figure 16.1 offers an integrated model of engagement connecting the situation experienced by the employee (including organizational and job characteristics) personality traits, Kahn's (1990) psychological conditions of engagement (meaningfulness, safety, and availability), and Macey and Schneider's (2008) state of engagement and engagement behaviors.

Future directions

Further research is needed to analyze relationships between engagement and personality across situations and professional fields. In particular, research is needed to (a) investigate connections between personality traits and Kahn's (1990) psychological antecedents of engagement; (b) refine and test the integrated model of engagement offered; and (c) explore connections between openness to experience, agreeableness, and engagement. In particular, qualitative studies investigating the *processes* through which personality impacts on engagement might be valuable.

While future studies may refine the exact way in which personality traits influence employee engagement, there seems to be some support

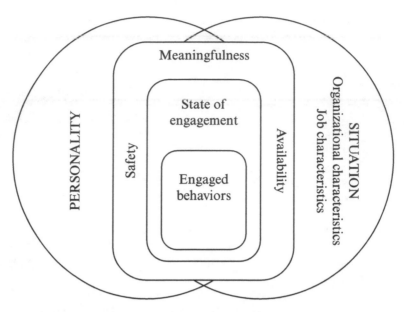

Figure 16.1   An integrated model of engagement

for the notion that personality matters. Specifically, employees who are extraverted, calm, and focused may have an "edge" in the search for engagement.

This "edge," however, is slight. The relationships identified so far between personality and engagement still leave plenty of room for uncertainty. It may be premature, therefore, to start "selecting for passion" (Gubman, 2004, p. 44). For practical purposes, leaders need to understand that individuals of various personalities may still be engaged or disengaged.

The benefit of the personality–engagement research, however, may not lie in identifying those who are "born to be engaged" for selection purposes. Instead, personality–engagement research may help leaders promote an environment where *all* employees are free to express their true identity and find strong meaning, regardless of their personality traits.

References

Avolio, B.J., Gardner, W.L., Walumbwa, F.O., Luthans, F. & May, D.R. (2004), "Unlocking the mask: a look at the process by which authentic leaders impact follower attitudes and behaviors", *Leadership Quarterly*, **15**(6), 801–23.
Bateman, T. & Crant, J.M. (1993), "The proactive component of organizational behavior: a measure and correlates", *Journal of Organizational Behavior*, **14**(2), 103–18.
Csikszentmihalyi, M. & Nakamura, J. (2002), "The concept of flow", in C.R. Snyder & S.J.

Lopez (eds), *The Handbook of Positive Psychology*, New York: Oxford University Press, pp. 89–105.

Gubman, E. (2004), "From engagement to passion for work: the search for the missing person", *Human Resource Planning*, **27**, 42–6.

Hackman, J.R., Oldham, G., Janson, R. & Purdy, K. (1975), "A new strategy for job enrichment", *California Management Review*, **17**(4), 57–71.

Howard, P.J. & Howard, J.M. (1995), "Buddy, can you paradigm?", *Training & Development*, **49**(9), 28–34.

Howard, P.J. & Howard, J.M. (2001a), *The Owner's Manual for Personality at Work*, Austin, TX: Bard Press.

Howard, P.J. & Howard, J.M. (2001b), *The Workplace Big Five Profile*, Charlotte, NC: Centacs.

Howard, P.J. & Howard, J.M. (2001c), *The Workplace Big Five Professional Manual*, Austin, TX: Bard Press.

Johnson, J.A. & Ostendorf, F. (1993), "Clarification of the five-factor model with the abridged Big Five dimensional circumplex", *Journal of Personality and Social Psychology*, **65**(3), 563–76.

Judge, T.A., Heller, D. & Mount, M.K. (2002), "Five-factor model of personality and job satisfaction: a meta-analysis", *Journal of Applied Psychology*, **87**(3), 530–41.

Judge, T., Higgins, C., Thoresen, C. & Barrick, M. (1999), "The Big Five personality traits, general mental ability, and career success across the life span", *Personnel Psychology*, **52**, 621–52.

Kahn, W.A. (1990), "Psychological conditions of personal engagement and disengagement at work", *Academy of Management Journal*, **33**, 692–724.

Koyuncu, M., Burke, R. & Fiksenbaum, L. (2006), "Work engagement among women managers and professionals in a Turkish bank: potential antecedents and consequences", *Equal Opportunities International*, **25**(4), 299–310.

Langelaan, S., Bakker, A.B., Van Doornen, L.J. & Schaufeli, W.B. (2004), "Burnout and work engagement: do individual differences make a difference?", *Personality and Individual Differences*, **40**, 521–32.

Macey, W.H. & Schneider, B. (2008), "The meaning of employee engagement", *Industrial and Organizational Psychology*, **1**(1), 3–30.

Major, D.A., Turner, J.E. & Fletcher, T.D. (2006), "Linking proative personality and the Big Five to motivation to learn and development activity", *Journal of Applied Psychology*, **91**(4), 927–35.

Matthews, G., Deary, I. & Whiteman, M.C. (2003), *Personality Traits*, New York: Cambridge University Press.

McCrae, R.R. (2006), "Psychopathology from the perspective of the five factor model", in S. Strack (ed.), *Differentiating Normal and Abnormal Personality*, New York: Springer, pp. 53–64.

McCrae, R.R. & Costa, P.T. (1997), "Personality trait structure as a human universal", *American Psychologist*, **52**(5), 509–16.

McCrae, R.R., Costa, P.T., Ostendorf, F., Angleitner, A., Hrebickova, M. & Avia, M.D. (2000), "Nature over nurture: temperament, personality, and life span development", *Journal of Personality and Social Psychology*, **78**(1), 173–86.

Mount, M.K., Barrick, M.R., & Stewart, G.L. (1998), "Five-factor model of personality and performance in jobs involving interpersonal interactions", *Human Performance*, **11**(2/3), 145–65.

Rich, B. (2006), "Job engagement: construct validation and relationships with job satisfaction, job involvement, and intrinsic motivation", unpublished doctoral dissertation, University of Florida, Tallahassee, FL.

Saks, A.M. (2006), "Antecedents and consequences of employee engagement", *Journal of Management Psychology*, **21**, 600–619.

Schaufeli, W.B. & Bakker, A.B. (2003), *Utrecht Work Engagement Scale*, Utrecht: Utrecht University.

Walsh, B. & Eggerth, D.E. (2005), "Vocational psychology and personality: the relationship of the five-factor model to job performance and job satisfaction", in B. Walsh & M.L. Savickas (eds), *Handbook of Vocational Psychology*, 3rd edn, Mahwah, NJ: Lawrence Erlbaum, pp. 267–96.

Watson, D. & Clark, A. (1992), "On traits and temperament: general and specific factors of emotional experience and their relation to the five-factor model", *Journal of Personality*, **60**(2), 441–76.

Wildermuth, C. (2008), "Engaged to serve: the relationship between employee engagement and the personality of human services professionals and paraprofessionals", unpublished doctoral dissertation, Bowling Green State University, Bowling Green, OH.

17 Analyzing the contribution of emotional intelligence and core self-evaluations as personal resources to employee engagement

M. Auxiliadora Durán, Natalio Extremera and Lourdes Rey

Introduction

The advocated purpose of positive psychology is "to begin to catalyze a change in the focus of psychology from pre-occupation only with repairing the worst things in life to also building positive qualities" (Seligman & Csikzentmihalyi, 2000, p. 5). As a result, positive organizational psychology is concerned with the application of psychology to improve the quality of working life and to promote employees' health, safety and well-being. In this context, the emerging construct of employee engagement (EE) may be a key factor in the development of organizations' human capital and to offer organizations a competitive advantage (Bakker & Schaufeli, 2008). This is because engaged workers are able and willing "to go the extra mile", will be active agents committed to high-level performance, will take initiative at work, generate their own positive feedback, look for job challenges, and will respond adequately and quickly to changes (Bakker & Schaufeli, 2008; Schaufeli & Salanova, 2007, 2008).

Employee engagement: definition, antecedents and consequences

Although different approaches to EE have been identified, the most fruitful perspective defines engagement independently from both job resources and organizational outcomes. EE is most widely defined as a positive, fulfilling, work-related state of mind characterized by vigor, dedication, and absorption (Schaufeli et al., 2002). Engaged employees will thus show high levels of energy, feel enthusiastic about their work, and will often be fully engrossed in their work. This affective–motivational, persistent and pervasive state of work-related well-being is not focused on any particular object, event, individual or behavior.

Empirical research has consistently shown positive associations between EE and job resources, such as social support, performance feedback, job autonomy, coaching, job control, training facilities, task variety and opportunities for professional development (Schaufeli & Bakker, 2004; Bakker & Schaufeli, 2008), especially in high job demands situations (Halbesleben, 2010). Thus, the more job resources are available, the more likely it is that employees feel engaged.

By building engagement, positive synergies emerge between employees and organizations, with optimal outcomes for both. Adaptive outcomes for engaged employees could include: (a) positive job-related attitudes and a strong identification with one's work (job satisfaction and organizational commitment); (b) good mental and psychosomatic health, including positive emotions and lower risk of burnout; (c) good performance (in-role and extra-role); (d) increased intrinsic motivation, personal initiative or proactive behavior; and (e) the acquisition of job and personal resources, particularly self-efficacy. For organizations, high levels of EE might result in adaptive outcomes such as retention of talented employees, a positive corporative image and business-unit performance, financial returns or service quality (that is, Xanthopoulou et al., 2007, 2009; Schaufeli & Salanova, 2008).

Personal resources as a relevant factor in the JD–R model
In general studies on the job demand–resources (JD–R) model have focused more on job resources neglecting to some extent the role of *personal resources* (with research interest on self-efficacy being somewhat of an exception), which might be important determinants of employees' adaptation to work environments (Judge et al., 1997). Nevertheless, a relatively new line of research has focused on state-like personal resources as predictors of EE. In this context, personal resources are described as positive self-evaluations that are linked to resiliency and refer to individuals' sense of their ability to control and impact upon their environment effectively (Hobfoll et al., 2003). Diverse scholars have argued that self-evaluations are the most essential antecedents of employee well-being, which may well determine the perception of the work environment. Along this line, empirical research has also shown that positive self-evaluations predict various aspects of work-related well-being, such as goal-setting, motivation, performance, job and life satisfaction (Judge et al., 2004). At present, personal resources such as self-efficacy, organization-based self-esteem, optimism, resilience, or an active coping style, have been recognized as crucial for individuals' psychological and work-related well-being, and associated with EE (Xanthopoulou et al., 2007, 2009). Indeed, such personal resources seem to help engaged workers to control their work environment successfully (Luthans et al., 2008). Further, this involvement of the self appears as a prerequisite for the experience of engagement.

Xanthopoulou et al. (2007, 2009) have contributed to the theoretical development of the JD–R model by proposing that personal resources play a significant role in this model since, and along with job demands and resources, they contribute to and explain unique variance in exhaustion and EE. In general, personal resources may be promoted by a meaningful, manageable and comprehensive environment and they might also determine how individuals perceive or interpret the environment and react to it. EE is related to both job and personal resources over time. The availability of job resources may enhance the employees' feelings about being more able to deal with work goals. Likewise, employees who feel self-efficacious, valuable and optimistic may create a resourceful work environment. Furthermore, engaged employees tend to easily recognize, activate or create resources that facilitate goal attainment.

Core self-evaluations and emotional intelligence as personal resources
This chapter focuses on two relatively new, and promising, constructs within the individual domain, and their relationships with EE: the concepts of core self-evaluations (CSE) and emotional intelligence (EI).

CSE is viewed as a bottom-line appraisal of one's self-worth. This broad, latent personality trait is indicated by self-esteem, generalized self-efficacy, locus of control, and (low) neuroticism (high emotional stability). CSE reflects beliefs in one's capabilities (to control one's life) and competence (to perform, cope, persevere, and succeed) and a general sense that life will turn out well for oneself (Judge et al., 2004).

As core self-evaluations define how an individual sees her- or himself, they also affect how a person perceives and assesses situations. CSE has emerged as a valid predictor of both affective and objective work outcomes. For example, the relationship between CSE and job satisfaction has been confirmed in a wide range of studies (Bono & Judge, 2003). In addition, CSE has been linked to life satisfaction (Judge et al., 1998), and happiness in both individualistic and collectivistic cultures (Piccolo et al., 2005), and job performance (Judge & Bono, 2001). In recent studies, CSE was also shown to have a strong negative main effect on perceived job stress (Brunborg, 2008), a negative association with burnout (Best et al., 2005), and a direct positive association with affective organizational commitment (Stumpp et al., 2009).

As a whole, the empirical research suggests that positive attitudinal and behavioral outcomes are produced by both encouraging environmental conditions combined with the 'right' employee temperament – such as high CSE. Moreover, individuals with high levels of CSE report lower levels of stress and conflict, including work–family conflict, are more successful in their careers, cope more effectively with setbacks, show more constructive reactions to feedback, better capitalize on advantages and opportunities, and have higher earnings (Judge, 2009).

In addition to CSE, EI has emerged as a popular and growing area of social research, having caught the imagination of the general public and the scientific community (Zeidner et al., 2004). Following Mayer and Salovey's (1997) theoretical approach, EI is defined as a set of interrelated skills concerning the ability to perceive accurately, appraise and express emotion, the ability to access and/or generate feelings when they facilitate thought, and the ability to regulate emotions to promote emotional and intellectual growth.

Several studies have demonstrated that EI is related to a number of aspects of positive well-being or psychological adjustment (Mayer et al., 2008) and to be predictive of coping behaviors, well-being and health (Heck & Oudsten, 2008). EI has also been proposed as an important predictor of key organizational outcomes such as job satisfaction (Van Rooy & Viswesvaran, 2004; Daus & Ashkanasy, 2005). However, the empirical research has yielded mixed findings, with weak to modest relationships between trait EI and job satisfaction being reported (for example, Lopes et al., 2006; Kafetsios & Loumakou, 2007). Similarly, empirical studies have shown that emotionally intelligent employees are more prone to appraise potentially stressful events positively, and to cope better with potential harmful effects of stress (Gerits et al., 2004).

The mediating role of individual differences in the EI–job satisfaction relationship has been tested by Kafetsios and Zampetakis (2008). Their results indicated that positive and negative affect at work largely mediate the influence of EI on job satisfaction. EI thus appears as an important personality-level predictor of work affectivity and job satisfaction. More specifically, the EI facets of "use of emotion" and "emotion regulation" were the two EI dimensions most predictive of positive and negative affect at work. Additionally, the direct effect of EI on trait affect was stronger for positive affect, thus predisposing people to cognitions, feelings and actions that promote the building of personal and social resources in the context of their work.

While only a few studies have simultaneously analyzed the influence of both CSE and EI on outcomes, it appears that measures of EI can contribute something unique. In a recent study, Kluemper (2008) found that with Big-Five dimensions and IQ controlled, trait EI predicted coping, stress, and life satisfaction. When CSE and social desirability were added as control variables in the model, although the incremental validity coefficients were reduced, trait EI still accounted for significant incremental variance in the criteria.

In this chapter we extend the existing research on CSE and EI and aim to determine how these constructs influence employee engagement (EE) and personal accomplishment (PA). Zeidner et al. (2004) recommended that researchers assess the incremental variance explained by EI with regard to conventional criteria and assess whether EI remains predictive after IQ and personality factors have been statistically controlled. As relatively new constructs, EI and CSE must be analyzed in order to test if they provide independently additional variance to the prediction of personal and work-related well-being. Considering that the effect of CSE may overlap in some way with that tapped by EI, and that both CSE and EI have been found to be significantly associated with well-being, it would be important to determine the extent to which the influences of CSE on EE can be distinguished from the influences of EI on this well-being indicator. In this sense, as new constructs, EI and CSE must demonstrate both discriminant and incremental validity. We report results from a study conducted using a Spanish employee sample. We examine the incremental validity of EI above and beyond CSE as predictor of EE and PA.

Examining the potential predictive of CSE and EI on EE and PA

The main objective of the study was to test the potential influence of EI and CSE on EE (vigor, dedication, absorption), and PA. Also we predicted that EI, as a new and distinct theoretical construct, would exert significant influence on EE and PA even when the effect of CSE, a broader personality dimension, was statistically controlled.

Data were collected from a multi-professional sample (N = 413; 43.7 percent male, 56.3 percent female; mean age: 32.04 (SD 9.68). In order to test our hypotheses, a series of hierarchical regression analysis was conducted. The measures and their alpha coefficients obtained are included in Table 17.1.

The data showed that all three EE dimensions were differentially predicted by the use of emotions to facilitate performance, CSE, and emotional regulation. Specifically, the final model showed that use of emotion and CSE were the most significant predictors of vigor and dedication. For absorption only emotional regulation had a statistically significant effect. With respect to personal accomplishment, CSE and others' emotional appraisal were statistically significant, with CSE showing the stronger influence. Hierarchical regression analyses are shown in Table 17.2.

Discussion and practical implications

As a whole, the results corroborate the predictive validity of personal resources on employee engagement, and by extension the relevance of building individual well-being in the organizational context. The studies lend support to both the literature on individual resources that underlines

Table 17.1   Instruments and alpha values

Instruments	
● Core Self-evaluations Scale, CSES (Judge et al., 2003)	0.82
● Wong and Law Emotional Intelligence Scale, WLEIS (Wong & Law, 2002)	
Self-emotion appraisal	0.74
Others' emotion appraisal	0.74
Use of emotion	0.78
Regulation of emotion	0.84
● Utrecht Work Engagement Scale, UWES (Salanova et al., 2000)	
Vigor	0.83
Dedication	0.92
Absorption	0.87
● Personal Accomplishment subscale: Maslach Burnout Inventory, MBI (Maslach & Jackson, 1986). Spanish version Seisdedos, 1997	0.66

the role of personality and emotions as predictors of work engagement and the incremental validity of relatively new constructs such us EI with respect to a broader personality dimension such as CSE. Results support the idea of CSE as a relevant criterion variable for vigor, dedication and personal accomplishment. Moreover in three final regression models EI dimensions demonstrated their incremental validity over and beyond CSE. That is, employees skilled at making use of their emotions by directing them towards constructive activities and personal performance are likely to experience high levels of energy and feel more enthusiastic about their work. Also, employees skilled at regulating their emotions, which will enable a more rapid recovery from psychological distress, might be more engrossed in their daily tasks. Finally, people sensitive to the feelings and emotions of others, that is, skilled at perceiving and understanding the emotions of those people around them, might achieve higher feelings of personal accomplishment.

Based on our results, organizational training program developers should consider essential dimensions of CSE, such as self-esteem or generalized self-efficacy, as well as EI skills, for increasing work engagement and thus to contribute to better employee personal well-being. Although in the workplace context many factors are out of individual control, it seems that the development of training programs which help employees to understand their own emotions and repair their moods together with the necessary organizational changes which promote higher dedication

Table 17.2   Hierarchical regression analyses

	R^2	β	ΔR^2
Vigor	13.1%		
Step 1			0.078**
Core self-evaluations		0.279**	
Step 2			0.053**
Core self-evaluations		0.155**	
Use of emotion		0.216**	
Dedication	11.7%		
Step 1			0.068**
Core self-evaluations		0.261**	
Step 2			0.049**
Core self-evaluations		0.162**	
Use of emotion		0.252**	
Absorption	3.9%		
Step 1			0.015*
Core self-evaluations		0.122*	
Step 2			0.024**
Regulation of emotion		0.142*	
Personal accomplishment	16.4%		
Step 1			0.103**
Core self-evaluations		0.321**	
Step 2			0.061**
Core self-evaluations		0.262**	
Others' emotion appraisal		0.186**	

*Note: * $p < 0.05$; ** $p < 0.01$.*

(absorption) and vigor feelings are complementary and useful interventions to increase employee psychological well-being.

As Xanthopoulou et al. (2009) stated, organizations must consider that job and personal resources lead to engaged employees, who seem able to mobilize additional resources. Human resources policies should focus on creating resourceful work environments and on training programs that enhance employees' positive self-beliefs. Organizations should avoid overwhelming job demands and pay attention to the fact that empowerment of employees' personal resources may also be profitable. Personal resources such as CSE and EI seem useful tools to promote EE, and their improvement might become an important issue in the organizational agenda. Different interventions in areas such as personnel selection, support, leadership, distribution of stressful assignments, and so on, could also be of benefit. Future research might also examine the level to which interventions to develop perceptions of control, self-image, and improved positive moods leads to implementing more effective coping strategies. Moreover, future longitudinal research would further increase our understanding of how employees maintain and improve positive affective–cognitive states at work.

References

Bakker, A.B. & Schaufeli, W.B. (2008), "Positive organizational behavior: engaged employees in flourishing organizations", *Journal of Organizational Behavior*, **29**, 147–54.

Best, R.G., Stapleton, L.M. & Downey, R.G. (2005), "Core self-evaluations and job burnout: the test of alternative models", *Journal of Occupational Health Psychology*, **10**, 441–51.

Bono, J.E. & Judge, T.A. (2003), "Core self-evaluations: a review of the trait and its role in job satisfaction and job performance", *European Journal of Personality*, **17**, 5–18.

Brunborg, G.S. (2008), "Core self-evaluations. A predictor variable for job stress", *European Psychologist*, **13**(2), 96–102.

Daus, C.S. & Ashkanasy, N.M. (2005), "The case for the ability-based model of emotional intelligence in organizational behaviour", *Journal of Organizational Behavior*, **26**, 453–66.

Gerits, L., Derksen, J. & Verbruggen, A. (2004), "Emotional intelligence and adaptive success of nurses caring for people with mental retardation and severe behavior problems", *Mental Retardation*, **42**(2), 106–21.

Halbesleben, J.R.B. (2010), "A meta-analysis of work engagement: relationships with burnout, demands, resources and consequences", in A.B. Bakker & M.P. Leiter (eds), *Work Engagement: The Handbook of Essential Theory and Research*, New York: Psychology Press, pp. 102–17.

Heck, G.L. van & Oudsten, B.L. den (2008), "Emotional intelligence: relationship to stress, health, and well-being", in A. Vingerhoets, I. Nyklicek & J. Denollet (eds), *Emotion Regulation: Conceptual and Clinical Issues*, New York: Springer, pp. 97–121.

Hobfoll, S.E., Johnson, R.J., Ennis, N. & Jackson, A.P. (2003), "Resource loss, resource gain, and emotional outcomes among inner city women", *Journal of Personality and Social Psychology*, **84**, 632–43.

Judge, T.A. (2009), "Core self-evaluations and work success", *Current Directions in Psychological Science*, **18**(1), 58–62.

Judge, T.A. & Bono, J.E. (2001), "Relationship of core self-evaluations traits – self-esteem, generalized self-efficacy, locus of control, and emotional stability – with job satisfaction and job performance: a meta-analysis", *Journal of Applied Psychology*, **86**, 80–92.

Judge, T.A., Erez, A., Bono, J.E. & Thoresen, C.J. (2003), "The Core Self-Evaluations Scale (CSES): development of a measure", *Personnel Psychology*, **56**, 303–31.

Judge, T.A., Locke, E.A. & Durham, C.C. (1997), "The dispositional causes of job satisfaction: a core evaluations approach", *Research in Organizational Behavior*, **19**, 151–88.

Judge, T.A., Locke, E.A., Durham, C.C. & Kluger, A.N. (1998), "Dispositional effects on job and life satisfaction: the role of core evaluations", *Journal of Applied Psychology*, **83**, 17–34.

Judge, T.A., Van Vianen, A.E.M. & De Pater, I. (2004), "Emotional stability, core self-evaluations, and job outcomes: a review of the evidence and an agenda for future research", *Human Performance*, **17**, 325–46.

Kafetsios, K. & Loumakou, M. (2007), "A comparative evaluation of the effects of trait emotional intelligence and emotion regulation on affect at work and job satisfaction", *International Journal of Work Organization and Emotion*, **2**(1), 71–87.

Kafetsios, K. & Zampetakis, L.A. (2008), "Emotional intelligence and job satisfaction: testing the mediatory role of positive and negative affect at work", *Personality and Individual Differences*, **44**, 712–22.

Kluemper, D.H. (2008), "Trait emotional intelligence: the impact of core-self evaluations and social desirability", *Personality and Individual Differences*, **44**, 1402–12.

Lopes, P.N., Grewal, D., Kadis, J., Gall, M. & Salovey, P. (2006), "Evidence that emotional intelligence is related to job performance and affect and attitudes at work", *Psicothema*, **18**(1), 132–8.
Luthans, F., Norman, S.M., Avolio, B.J., & Avey, J.B. (2008), "The mediating role of psychological capital in the supportive organizational climate–employee performance relationship", *Journal of Organizational Behavior*, **29**, 219–38.
Maslach, C. & Jackson, S.E. (1986), *Maslach Burnout Inventory Manual*, Palo Alto, CA: Consulting Psychologists Press (Spanish version, Seisdedos, N. (1997) TEA Ediciones).
Mayer, J., Roberts R. & Barsade, S.G. (2008), "Human abilities: emotional intelligence", *Annual Review of Psychology*, **59**, 507–36.
Mayer, J.D. & Salovey, P. (1997), "What is emotional intelligence?", in P. Salovey & D. Sluyter (eds), *Emotional Development and Emotional Intelligence: Implications for Educators*, New York: Basic Books, pp. 3–31.
Piccolo, R.E., Judge, T.A., Takahashi, K., Watanabe, N. & Locke, E.A. (2005), "Core self-evaluations in Japan: relative effects on job satisfaction, life satisfaction and happiness", *Journal of Organizational Behavior*, **26**, 965–84.
Salanova, M., Schaufeli, W.B., Llorens, S., Peiró, J.M. & Grau, R. (2000), "Desde el burnout al engagement: ¿una nueva perspectiva?", (From burnout to engagement: a new perspective?), *Revista de Psicología del Trabajo y las Organizaciones*, **16**(2), 117–34.
Schaufeli, W.B. & Bakker, A.B. (2004), "Job demands, job resources, and their relationship with burnout and engagement: a multi-sample study", *Journal of Organizational Behavior*, **25**, 293–315.
Schaufeli, W.B. & Salanova, M. (2007), "Work engagement: an emerging psychological concept and its implications for organizations", in S.W. Gilliand, D.D. Steiner & D.P. Skarlicki (eds), *Research in Social issues in Management. Vol. 5: Managing Social and Ethical Issues in Organizations*, Grenwich, CT: Information Age Publishers, pp. 135–77.
Schaufeli, W.B. & Salanova, M. (2008), "Enhancing work engagement through the management of human resources", in K. Näswall, M. Sverke & J. Hellgren (eds), *The Individual in the Changing Working Life*, Cambridge: Cambridge University Press, pp. 380–404.
Schaufeli, W.B., Salanova, M., González-Romá, V. & Bakker, A.B. (2002), "The measurement of engagement: a confirmative analytic approach", *Journal of Happiness Studies*, **3**, 71–92.
Seligman, M.E.P. & Csikszentmihalyi, M. (2000), "Positive psychology: an introduction", *American Psychologist*, **55**, 5–14.
Stumpp, T., Hülsheger, U.R., Muck, P.M. & Maier, G.W. (2009), "Expanding the link between core self-evaluations and affective job attitudes", *European Journal of Work and Organizational Psychology*, **18**(2), 148–66.
Van Rooy, D.L. & Viswesvaran, C. (2004), "Emotional intelligence: a meta-analytic investigation of predictive validity and nomological net", *Journal of Vocational Behavior*, **65**(1), 71–95.
Wong, C.S. & Law, K.S. (2002), "The effects of leader and follower emotional intelligence on performance and attitude: an exploratory study", *The Leadership Quarterly*, **13**, 243–74.
Xanthopoulou, D., Bakker, A.B., Demerouti, E. & Schaufeli, W.B. (2007), "The role of personal resources in the job demands–resources model", *International Journal of Stress Management*, **14**(2), 121–41.
Xanthopoulou, D., Bakker, A.B., Demerouti, E. & Schaufeli, W.B. (2009), "Reciprocal relationships between job resources, personal resources, and work engagement", *Journal of Vocational Behavior*, **74**, 235–44.
Zeidner, M., Matthews, G. & Roberts, R.D. (2004), "Emotional intelligence in the workplace: a critical review", *Applied Psychology: An International Review*, **53**(3), 371–99.

18 Mindsets and employee engagement: theoretical linkages and practical interventions
Peter A. Heslin

Introduction

Engaged employees work with dedication, vigor, and absorption (Schaufeli et al., 2006). They exhibit persistent motivation, emotional connections to their work and other people, as well as the vigilance associated with flow (Kahn, 1990). Various factors are known to cultivate employee engagement. These include fair and trustworthy leaders who show employees how their work makes a positive difference (Avolio et al., 2004), jobs designed to provide optimal levels of autonomy, challenge, and feedback (Saks, 2006), restorative non-work recovery (Sonnentag, 2003), freedom from sexual harassment (Cogin & Fish, 2009), and a work environment in which employees are consulted, appreciated, and have a best friend (Harter, 2008). Regardless of the work context, why are some employees still inclined to be more engaged than others?

We propose that employees' engagement also depends upon their mindset about the extent to which their abilities are malleable[1] (Dweck, 2006). We begin by outlining the nature of mindset. Next we discuss how employees' mindsets affect whether they approach their work with energy, enthusiasm, and immersion (that is, engagement), or with the ambivalence, anxiety, and risk avoidance that are hallmarks of disengagement (Kahn, 1990). Then we review how mindset can influence managerial behaviors. We conclude by discussing how organizations, managers, and employees can foster the mindsets likely to either facilitate or undermine employee engagement.

Mindsets

Mindsets embody the assumptions people hold about the plasticity of their abilities. A *fixed mindset* reflects the implicit belief that human attributes are essentially stable entities, as revealed by agreement with statements such as "You have a certain amount of ability and really can't do much to change it". A *growth mindset* reflects the alternative assumption that abilities are pliable and thus amenable to being cultivated, as signified by agreement with statements including "You can always greatly develop your abilities".[2] A fixed mindset is embodied in the popular view of IQ as largely constant across a person's life, while a growth mindset inclines people to focus more on how IQ can be developed through targeted developmental efforts (Dweck, 1999, 2006).

Some noteworthy characteristics of mindsets are as follows. First, although mindset is a continuum, most individuals tend to gravitate towards holding either a fixed or a growth mindset. Second, each mindset occurs with roughly equal frequency within most populations. Third, neither mindset is predicted by a person's ability level, personality, education, or cognitive complexity. Fourth, people can simultaneously hold differing mindsets, such as a growth mindset about their computing ability and a fixed mindset about their public-speaking ability (Dweck, 1999, 2006). Finally, Dweck et al. (1995, p. 279) conceptualized mindsets as "relatively stable but malleable personal qualities, rather than as fixed dispositions". Although chronic mindsets are fairly stable over at least three years (Robins & Pals, 2002), research (for example, Aronson et al., 2002; Heslin et al., 2005) has supported Dweck's (1999) notion that mindsets can be cultivated by compelling or continuing messages. This potential of mindsets to be changed by an intervention parallels the well-established ontology of other moderately stable though potentially malleable individual differences including need for achievement (McClelland & Winter, 1969), hope (Snyder et al., 2006), and optimism (Seligman, 1998). We now consider how mindsets cue the types of thoughts, feelings, and motivation associated with engagement.

Employees' mindset and engagement
Mindset can influence employees' engagement in several ways; specifically, via their zeal for development, view of effort, psychological presence, and interpretation of setbacks.

Zeal for development
When people have a growth mindset, they construe their abilities as able to be cultivated through targeted practice and other developmental initiatives (for example, coaching, reading, or taking a class). A fixed mindset leads to perceiving novel or challenging tasks as a test of inherent abilities. The risk that such "tests" might diagnose unalterable ability deficiencies can cause those with a fixed mindset to disengage and avoid challenges from which they may learn.

Based on English proficiency scores, Hong et al. (1999) identified students entering the University of Hong Kong (where English proficiency is a necessity) who could benefit from remedial English classes. After the students' mindsets were assessed, they were asked about their willingness to undertake a remedial English class. Among the students with low English proficiency, those with a growth mindset were much more interested in taking such a course than were the students with a fixed mindset. Rather than reveal a deficiency and remedy it, the students with a fixed mindset preferred to put their academic career at risk. This illustrates that a fixed mindset can lead people to avoid rather than engage in useful developmental opportunities.

View of effort

Is sweat and toil an indispensible ingredient for effective learning and performance, or an indicator of lacking talent? How people respond to this question depends upon their mindset. Those with a fixed mindset believe that having ability is a largely sufficient condition for learning – that if you have ability, you should not need to expend considerable effort. A related idea is that having to work hard indicates that you are obviously not gifted in a particular area. It is thus not surprising that students with a fixed mindset report that one of their main goals in school is to exert as little effort as possible (Blackwell et al., 2007).

People who hold a growth mindset generally view high effort as essential to developing virtually any ability. They attribute their disappointing performances to inadequate *effort* and/or *strategies*, followed by intensified effort and striving hard to discover ways to perform more effectively. A fixed mindset is associated with attributing disappointing performance to low *ability*, exerting less effort going forward, trying to avoid the area in which they performed poorly, and even considering deception (for example, cheating) as a means to inflate future performance ratings (ibid.). Such cynicism about the utility of effort could clearly undermine the wholehearted investment of oneself that characterizes engagement.

Psychological presence

Another hallmark of engagement is psychological presence (Kahn, 1990). Attentiveness, a key facet of psychological presence, can facilitate interpersonal relationships, as well as learning and performance on dynamic tasks. Inadequate vigilance can jeopardize safety and potentially lead to deadly accidents (Saks, 2008). Mindset plays an important role in receptiveness to evolving realities, as shown by data collected at the behavioral (Heslin et al., 2005), attentional (Plaks et al., 2001) and neurological levels (Mangels et al., 2006).

Mangels et al. tracked college students' event-related brain potentials as they worked on a difficult general knowledge task. Shortly after participants had typed each answer, they were given ability-related feedback about whether their answer had been right or wrong, followed soon afterwards by learning-relevant feedback about the correct answer. The waveforms associated with error detection and correction revealed that participants with a fixed mindset had significantly less neural activity in the region of the brain associated with processing the corrective feedback, compared to those with a growth mindset. A fixed mindset also undermined learning from the corrective feedback, as revealed by inferior subsequent retest performance relative to that exhibited by those with a growth mindset. These results reveal how a growth mindset facilitates the alertness to new information that helps people to flourish.

Interpretation of setbacks
Feedback indicating that one's performance has fallen short of expectations is to be expected in modern workplaces. The meaning ascribed to failures and setbacks, such as whether they are seen as threatening cherished abilities and identities, determines how well people recover, learn, and persist. People with a growth mindset tend to view setbacks as an inevitable part of the learning process and thus a useful indicator of which strategies work and which do not. A growth mindset stimulates the self-improvement focus of studying the strategies of better performers and choosing challenging tasks on which learning (and also risking failure) is more likely (Nussbaum & Dweck, 2008). People with a growth mindset thus respond to setbacks by staying engaged via continued task focus, vigorous effort, and systematic strategy development (Tabernero & Wood, 1999; Blackwell et al., 2007).

From the perspective of a fixed mindset, failure provides people with diagnostic information about how little ability they possess – and will likely ever possess – often leading to self-defeating cognitions, affect, and behaviors. These include wanting to study what worse performers did and opting to do unchallenging, uninformative tasks in order to make themselves feel better (Nussbaum & Dweck, 2008). Other dysfunctional manifestations of a fixed mindset are withdrawal of effort, willingness to lie about a poor score, worrying, and not seeking feedback (Heslin & VandeWalle, 2005).

In summary, a growth mindset generally increases – and a fixed mindset undermines – employees' zeal for development, belief in the utility of effort, attentiveness to corrective information, and likelihood of construing "failures" as challenging and energizing, rather than undermining and debilitating.

Mindset and managerial style
Managers' mindsets affect how they treat their subordinates. Specifically, a growth mindset predicts a manager's vigilance to both improvements *and* decline in employee performance (Heslin et al., 2005). Managers

who do not recognize improvements are demoralizing and thereby erode employee engagement. Recognition of decreasing performance is imperative for taking needed remedial action.

When performance improvements are required, holding the fixed mindset assumption that human attributes are innate and essentially unalterable makes managers disinclined to invest effort in coaching their employees (Heslin et al., 2006). Related research shows that a growth mindset positively predicts managers' perceived fairness in dealing with their employees (Heslin & VandeWalle, in press, 2010) – a critical factor for enticing employees to identify with their work and passionately invest themselves in performing it.

Practical implications: cultivating a growth mindset

If fixed mindsets are so toxic to engagement, why are they still prevalent within contemporary organizations? Possible sources of fixed and growth mindsets are as follows.

Organizational signals

An organizational culture that glorifies inherent "genius" (for example, Enron) over heroic efforts to improve (for example, Southwest Airlines) – via cultural artifacts such as newsletters, speeches by top management, selection and promotion criteria, and award ceremonies – can elicit thoughts, feelings and behaviors indicative of a fixed mindset (Murphy & Dweck, 2010). Similarly, a strong focus on recruiting external talent with the "right stuff" to the relative neglect of cultivating current personnel, might convey and foster a fixed mindset within both current and potential employees. Finally, a "rank-and-yank" appraisal system, requiring that the bottom 10–15 percent of employees be identified and fired, could also propagate the fixed mindset view that the abilities of those ranked the lowest cannot be developed.

The alternative growth mindset conviction that employees' abilities can be stimulated to grow might be conveyed through a range of developmentally oriented organizational programs. Examples include comprehensive on-boarding, mentoring, special assignments, multisource feedback, sponsored continuing education, and study-leave programs. Publicizing inspiring profiles of real-life career journeys within the organization – focusing not only on those whose careers have led them to the upper echelons – could also serve as a powerful indicator that employee growth is possible.

Managerial actions

Managers often have a powerful influence on their employees' thoughts, feelings, and behavior. Telling people they did well because they are "smart", rather than because they "worked hard", can create a fixed mindset focused on not jeopardizing the treasured self-impression of being smart. Subsequent engagement and performance is diminished (Mueller & Dweck, 1998). This finding highlights the potential peril to employees' growth mindset of well-intentioned managers labeling their subordinates using ostensibly positive terms such as "star performer", "superstar", or "A-player".

There are, however, viable alternative means of providing positively reinforcing feedback that fosters rather than erodes employees' growth mindsets. The common theme within each is praising the *process* employees undertook to attain a good outcome (for example, a sale or positive client evaluation), as opposed to their *traits* that enabled them to do it. Examples include underscoring to employees what they achieved when they set challenging goals, worked hard, persisted in the face of setbacks, and systematically strived to identify ways to improve. As long as such feedback is sufficiently grounded in reality to be credible, this approach to describing what employees have *done* to perform well – rather than who or what they *are* – has clear potential to foster growth mindsets.

Experienced managers (and parents) are familiar with having disengaged and demoralized employees (and children) who exhibit few positive behaviors or results to reinforce. Even in such situations, there are options available that can help convert a fixed mindset into a more growth mindset.[3] These include:

- *Highlighting brain potential*   Share with employees that neuropsychological research is establishing that whenever we focus our minds and learn something, new connections are established in our brains. Thus, the brain and its abilities are capable of growing like a muscle throughout life, whenever they are exercised properly. This message can be usefully supplemented with anecdotes of how familiar people – ultimately including yourself – have substantially developed certain abilities, sometimes beginning later in life.
- *Counter-attitudinal reflection*   Have employees identify an area (for example, using a complex web-based application, playing golf, speaking a second language) where they had initially struggled but now perform well and with relative ease. Encourage them to explain in detail the steps they took along their developmental path (for example, setting goals, taking risks, getting lessons, practicing hard, seeking feedback). Then ask the employee why a similar process might not work in an area where they doubt that their ability can be developed.
- *Counter-attitudinal advocacy*   Have employees identify someone they care about (for example, a parent, child or protégé) who is

struggling to believe that their ability can be cultivated. Have them write an encouraging 2–3-page letter to this person in which they outline, in their own words, the reasons and evidence that abilities can be developed, including meaningful personal anecdotes such as those generated during the prior counter-attitudinal reflection exercise.

- *Inducing cognitive dissonance*   Have employees identify an instance when they observed somebody learn to do something that they earnestly thought this person could *never* do. Then invite them to ponder what could have been the implications of their doubting this person's capabilities. Leading people to reflect upon how their fixed mindset may have constrained others from realizing their potential is a compelling way to foster a growth mindset.

Self-development

Employees interested in cultivating a growth mindset within themselves are encouraged to work through the four techniques just outlined. When doing so, it is worth keeping in mind that public commitments and social learning can powerfully mold personal convictions (Aronson, 1999). Thus, to get the most out of these growth mindset exercises, it is recommended that you complete them in pairs or a small group, before reading aloud and discussing your encouraging message and responses to the cognitive dissonance questions.

Conclusion

A growth mindset is no magic bullet for cultivating employee engagement. As with any human experience, engagement is the culmination of a vast array of factors such as those identified in the opening paragraph and throughout this handbook. Nonetheless, it is hoped that this chapter conveys the potential role of mindset in understanding and increasing employee engagement.

Notes

1. Prior to Dweck (2006), the mindset concept was known as "implicit theories of ability" (see Dweck, 1999).
2. For full mindset measurement scales and information about their reliability and construct validity, see Dweck et al., (1995), Levy et al., (1998), as well as the appendix of Dweck (1999).
3. That can last for at least six weeks when the following techniques are applied together (Heslin et al., 2005).

References

Aronson, E. (1999), "The power of self-persuasion", *American Psychologist*, **54**, 873–90.
Aronson, J., Fried, C.B. & Good, C. (2002), "Reducing the effects of stereotype threat on

African American students by shaping theories of intelligence", *Journal of Experimental Social Psychology*, **38**, 113–25.

Avolio, B., Gardner, W., Walumbwa, F., Luthans, F. & May, D. (2004), "Unlocking the mask: a look at the process by which authentic leaders impact follower attitudes and behaviors", *Leadership Quarterly*, **15**, 801–23.

Blackwell, L., Trzesniewski, K. & Dweck, C. (2007), "Implicit theories of intelligence predict achievement across an adolescent transition: a longitudinal study and an intervention", *Child Development*, **78**, 246–63.

Cogin, J. & Fish, A. (2009), "An empirical investigation of sexual harassment and work engagement: surprising differences between men and women", *Journal of Management and Organization*, **15**, 47–61.

Dweck, C.S. (1999), *Self-theories: Their Role in Motivation, Personality, and Development*, Philadelphia, PA: Psychology Press.

Dweck, C.S. (2006), *Mindset: The New Psychology of Success*, New York: Random House.

Dweck, C.S., Chiu, C. & Hong, Y.Y. (1995), "Implicit theories and their role in judgments and reactions: a word from two perspectives", *Psychological Inquiry*, **6**, 267–85.

Harter, J. (2008), "Employee engagement: how great managing drives performance", *Positive Psychology: Exploring the Best in People, Vol 4: Pursuing Human Flourishing*, Westport, CT: Praeger, pp. 99–110.

Heslin, P.A., Latham, G.P. & VandeWalle, D. (2005), "The effect of implicit person theory on performance appraisals", *Journal of Applied Psychology*, **90**, 842–56.

Heslin, P.A. & VandeWalle, D. (2005), "Self-regulation derailed: implicit person theories and feedback-seeking", paper presented at the annual meeting of the Society for Industrial and Organizational Psychology, Los Angeles, CA, April.

Heslin, P.A. & VandeWalle, D. (in press, 2010), "Performance appraisal procedural justice: the role of managers' implicit person theory", *Journal of Management*.

Heslin, P.A. VandeWalle, D. & Latham, G.P. (2006), "Keen to help? Managers' IPTs and their subsequent employee coaching", *Personnel Psychology*, **59**, 871–902.

Hong, Y.Y., Chiu, C.Y., Dweck, C.S., Lin, D.M.S. & Wan, W. (1999), "Implicit theories, attributions, and coping: a meaning system approach", *Journal of Personality and Social Psychology*, **77**, 588–99.

Kahn, W.A. (1990), "Psychological conditions of personal engagement and disengagement at work", *Academy of Management Journal*, **33**, 692–724.

Levy, S.R., Stroessner, S.J. & Dweck, C.S. (1998), "Stereotype formation and endorsement: the role of implicit theories", *Journal of Personality and Social Psychology*, **74**, 1421–36.

Mangels, J.A., Butterfield, B., Lamb, J., Good, C. & Dweck, C.S. (2006), "Why do beliefs about intelligence influence learning success? A social cognitive neuroscience model", *Social Cognitive and Affective Neuroscience*, **1**, 75–86.

McClelland, D.C. & Winter, D.G. (1969), *Motivating Economic Development*, New York: Free Press.

Mueller, C. & Dweck, C. (1998), "Praise for intelligence can undermine children's motivation and performance", *Journal of Personality and Social Psychology*, **75**, 33–53.

Murphy, M.C. & Dweck, C.S. (2010), "A culture of genius: how an organization's lay theory shapes people's cognition, affect and behavior", *Personality and Social Psychology Bulletin*, **36**, 283–96.

Nussbaum, A.D. & Dweck, C.S. (2008), "Defensiveness versus remediation: self-theories and modes of self-esteem maintenance", *Personality and Social Psychology Bulletin*, **34**, 599–612.

Plaks, J., Dweck, C., Stroessner, S. & Sherman, J. (2001), "Person theories and attention allocation: preferences for stereotypic versus counterstereotypic information", *Journal of Personality and Social Psychology*, **80**, 876–93.

Robins, R.W. & Pals, J. (2002), "Implicit self-theories of ability in the academic domain: a test of Dweck's model", *Self and Identity*, **1**, 313–36.

Saks, A. (2006), "Antecedents and consequences of employee engagement", *Journal of Managerial Psychology*, **21**, 600–619.

Saks, A. (2008), "The meaning and bleeding of employee engagement: how muddy is the water?", *Industrial and Organizational Psychology: Perspectives on Science and Practice*, **1**, 40–43.

Schaufeli, W., Bakker, A. & Salanova, M. (2006), "The measurement of work engagement with a short questionnaire: a cross-national study", *Educational and Psychological Measurement*, **66**, 701–16.

Seligman, M.E.P. (1998), *Learned Optimism*, New York: A.A. Knopf.

Snyder, C.R., Rand, K.L. & Ritschel, L.A. (2006), "Hope over time", in L.J. Sanna & E.C. Chang (eds), *Judgments Over Time: The Interplay of Thoughts, Feelings, and Behaviors*, New York: Oxford University Press, pp. 110–19.

Sonnentag, S. (2003), "Recovery, work engagement, and proactive behavior: a new look at the interface between nonwork and work", *Journal of Applied Psychology*, **88**, 518–28.

Tabernero, C. & Wood, R.E. (1999), "Implicit theories versus the social construal of ability in self-regulation and performance on a complex task", *Organizational Behavior and Human Decision Processes*, **78**, 104–27.

PART III

THE DYNAMICS AND REGULATION OF EMPLOYEE ENGAGEMENT: FLUCTUATIONS, CYCLES, AFFECT AND FLOW

19 Engagement and "job crafting": engaged employees create their own great place to work
Arnold B. Bakker

Introduction
Each year, the Great Place to Work Institute produces a list with the best companies to work for, representing workplaces in 40 countries around the world. The selection of companies is based upon employee and management surveys regarding the relationships employees have with management, colleagues, and with their own jobs. Companies that take good care of their employees receive the highest rankings.

The question how companies can design great places to work has stimulated organizational psychology research for several decades. This has resulted in job design theories that can explain employee motivation and retention. The central assumption in these theories is that job characteristics with motivational potential (for example, job resources like autonomy, feedback, task identity) will lead to meaningful work and high productivity (Hackman & Oldham, 1980; Fried & Ferris, 1987). Research has indeed shown that job resources are important facilitators of employee engagement, particularly under conditions of high job demands (Bakker & Demerouti, 2008), and that engagement, in turn, has a positive impact on job performance (Bakker, 2009).

However, engaged employees are by no means passive actors in their work organizations. Instead, I shall argue that they are proactive job crafters who mobilize their own job challenges and job resources. Thus, this chapter proposes a proactive perspective of employee engagement in which engaged employees craft their own jobs to sustain their own engagement. Proactive perspectives "capture the growing importance of employees taking initiative to anticipate and create changes in how work is performed" (Grant & Parker, 2009, p. 317).

Work engagement
Work engagement is defined as "a positive, fulfilling, work-related state of mind that is characterized by vigor, dedication, and absorption" (Schaufeli et al., 2002, p. 74; Schaufeli & Bakker, 2010). In essence, work engagement captures how workers experience their work: as stimulating and energetic

and something to which they really want to devote time and effort (the *vigor* component); as a significant and meaningful pursuit (*dedication*); and as engrossing and something on which they are fully concentrated (*absorption*; Bakker et al., 2008). Qualitative research has revealed that engaged employees are highly energetic, self-efficacious individuals who exercise influence over events that affect their lives (Schaufeli et al., 2001). Because of their positive attitude and activity level, engaged employees create their own positive feedback, in terms of appreciation, recognition, and success. Many interviewees indicated that their enthusiasm and energy also appears outside work, for example in physical exercise, creative hobbies, and volunteer work. Engaged employees are no supermen – they do feel tired after a long day of hard work. However, they describe their tiredness as a rather pleasant state because it is associated with positive accomplishments. Finally, engaged employees are not addicted to their work. They enjoy other things outside work. Unlike workaholics, engaged employees do not work hard because of a strong and irresistible inner drive, but because for them working is fun (Schaufeli et al., 2006b).

The most often used instrument to measure engagement is the Utrecht Work Engagement Scale (UWES; Schaufeli et al., 2002; Schaufeli & Bakker, 2003, 2010) that includes a subscale for each of the three engagement dimensions: vigor, dedication and absorption. The UWES has been validated in several countries in Europe, but also in North America, Africa, Asia, and Australia (Bakker, 2009). Confirmatory factor analyses have repeatedly shown that the fit of the hypothesized three-factor structure to the data is superior to that of alternative factor models. In addition, the internal consistencies of the three subscales are sufficient in each study. Schaufeli et al. (2006a) developed a short nine-item version of the UWES, and provided evidence for its cross-national validity. They showed that the three engagement dimensions are moderately strong related.

Drivers of engagement

Job resources

Previous studies have consistently shown that job resources are positively associated with work engagement (Bakker & Demerouti, 2007; Bakker & Leiter, 2010). "Job resources" refer to those physical, social, or organizational aspects of the job that may: (a) reduce job demands and the associated physiological and psychological costs; (b) be functional in achieving work goals; or (c) stimulate personal growth, learning, and development (Schaufeli & Bakker, 2004; Bakker & Demerouti, 2007).

Job resources are assumed to play either an intrinsic motivational role because they foster employees' growth, learning and development, or an extrinsic motivational role because they are instrumental in achieving work goals. In the former case, job resources fulfill basic human needs, such as the needs for autonomy, relatedness and competence (Ryan & Frederick, 1997; Van den Broeck et al., 2008). For instance, proper feedback fosters learning, thereby increasing job competence, whereas decision latitude and social support satisfy the need for autonomy and the need to belong, respectively.

Job resources may also play an *extrinsic* motivational role, because resourceful work environments foster the willingness to dedicate one's efforts and abilities to the work task (Meijman & Mulder, 1998). In such environments it is likely that the task will be completed successfully and that the work goal will be attained. For instance, performance feedback and a supportive supervisor increase the likelihood of being successful in achieving one's work goals. In either case, be it through the satisfaction of basic needs or through the achievement of work goals, the outcome is positive and engagement is likely to occur (Schaufeli & Bakker, 2004).

Consistent with these notions about the motivational role of job resources, several studies have shown a positive relationship between job resources and work engagement (for a meta-analysis, see Halbesleben, 2010). For example, in their study among Dutch dentists, Gorter et al. (2008) found that higher scores on idealism, pride, aesthetics, and patient care coincided with higher scores on work engagement. Koyuncu et al. (2006) examined potential antecedents and consequences of work engagement in a sample of women managers and professionals employed by a large Turkish bank. Results showed that worklife experiences, particularly control, rewards and recognition and value fit, were significant predictors of all engagement dimensions. Further, in their study among managers and executives of a Dutch telecom company, Schaufeli et al. (2009) found that *changes* in job resources were predictive of work engagement over a period of one year. Specifically, results showed that increases in social support, autonomy, opportunities to learn and to develop, and performance feedback were positive predictors of time 2 (T2) work engagement after controlling for baseline engagement.

Active jobs

According to the job demands–resources model (Bakker & Demerouti, 2007), job resources become more salient and gain their motivational potential when employees are confronted with high job demands. Such conditions represent so-called "active jobs" (Karasek, 1979), in which employees become motivated to actively learn and develop their skills. Hakanen et al. (2005) tested this interaction hypothesis in a sample of Finnish dentists employed in the public sector. It was hypothesized that job resources (for example, variability in the required professional skills, peer contacts) are most predictive of work engagement under conditions of high job demands (for example, workload, unfavorable physical environment). The results largely confirmed the hypothesis by showing, for example, that variability in professional skills boosted work engagement when qualitative workload was high.

Bakker et al. (2007) reported conceptually similar findings. In their study among Finnish teachers working in elementary, secondary, and vocational schools, they found that job resources particularly influence work engagement when teachers are confronted with high levels of pupil misconduct. In particular, supervisor support, innovativeness, appreciation, and organizational climate were important job resources for teachers that turned demanding interactions with students into a challenge.

Finally, Tuckey et al. (2009) expanded these findings in their study among Australian volunteer fire fighters. Using a multilevel framework, they examined the role of empowering leadership by fire brigade captains in facilitating the motivational processes that underpin work engagement in volunteer fire fighters. Anonymous mail surveys were completed by 540 volunteer fire fighters from 68 fire brigades and, separately, by 68 brigade captains. In addition to directly inspiring engagement, empowering leadership had the effect of optimizing working conditions for engagement in two ways: (i) via increased levels of cognitive demands and cognitive resources in a partially mediated pathway; and (ii) by strengthening the positive effect of "active" working conditions, in which job demands and resources are both high. These findings shed light on one process through which leaders can empower workers and enhance work engagement: via their influence on and interaction with the work environment.

Personal resources as psychological capital

Psychological capital (PsyCap) has been defined as

> an individual's positive psychological state of development characterized by:
> (1) having confidence (self-efficacy) to take on and put in the necessary effort to succeed at challenging tasks; (2) making a positive attribution (optimism) about succeeding now and in the future; (3) persevering toward goals, and when necessary, redirecting paths to goals (hope) in order to succeed; and (4) when beset by problems and adversity, sustaining and bouncing back and even beyond (resilience) to attain success. (Luthans et al., 2007, p. 3)

Sweetman and Luthans (2010) have outlined why PsyCap should be related to work engagement. Employees high in PsyCap are characterized by their tenacity and persistence, driven by their belief in future success. Additionally, they continue to provide hope for goal achievement, even in the face of new challenges, and expect good things to happen to them.

In their study among highly skilled Dutch technicians, Xanthopoulou et al. (2007) examined the role of a slightly different operationalization of PsyCap (self-efficacy, self-esteem, and optimism – these elements are called "personal resources") in predicting work engagement. Results showed that engaged employees are highly self-efficacious; they believe that they are able to meet the demands they face in a broad array of contexts. In addition, engaged workers have the tendency to believe that they will generally experience good outcomes in life (optimistic), and can satisfy their needs by participating in roles within the organization (organizational-based self-esteem).

These findings were replicated and expanded in a two-year follow-up study (Xanthopoulou et al., 2009a). The findings indicated that self-efficacy, organizational-based self-esteem, and optimism make a unique contribution to explaining variance in work engagement over time, over and above the impact of job resources and previous levels of engagement. In short, engaged workers have psychological capital that helps them to control and impact upon their work environment successfully (see also Luthans et al., 2008).

Engagement and behavioral outcomes

There are at least four reasons why engaged workers perform better than non-engaged workers (Bakker, 2009). First, engaged employees often experience positive emotions, including happiness, joy, and enthusiasm. These positive emotions seem to broaden people's thought–action repertoire, implying that they constantly work on their personal resources (Fredrickson, 2001). Second, engaged workers experience better health. This means that they can focus and dedicate all their energy resources and skills to their work. Third, as will be illustrated later in more detail, engaged employees create their own job and personal resources (PsyCap). Finally, engaged workers transfer their engagement to others in their immediate environment (Bakker & Demerouti, 2009a; Bakker & Xanthopoulou, 2009). Since in most organizations performance is the result of collaborative effort, the engagement of one person may transfer to others and indirectly improve team performance.

Job performance

The number of studies showing a positive relationship between employee engagement and job performance is increasing (Demerouti & Cropanzano, 2010). For example, Bakker et al. (2004) showed that engaged Dutch employees received higher ratings from their colleagues on in-role and extra-role performance, indicating that engaged employees perform well and are willing to go the extra mile. In addition, Halbesleben and Wheeler

(2008) in their study among American employees, their supervisors, and their closest co-workers from a wide variety of industries and occupations showed that work engagement made a unique contribution (after controlling for job embeddedness) to explaining variance in job performance.

Salanova et al. (2005) conducted an interesting study among personnel working in Spanish restaurants and hotels. Contact employees ($N = 342$) from 58 hotel front desks and 56 restaurants provided information about organizational resources, engagement, and service climate. Furthermore, customers ($N = 1,140$) from these units provided information on employee performance and customer loyalty. Structural equation modeling analyses were consistent with a full mediation model in which organizational resources and work engagement predicted service climate, which in turn predicted employee performance and then customer loyalty.

Bakker and Demerouti (2009a) examined the crossover of work engagement in a study among 175 Dutch couples working in different occupational sectors. The results of moderated structural equation modeling analyses showed that the crossover of work engagement from wives to their husbands was strongest when men were high (versus low) in perspective taking (the spontaneous tendency of a person to adopt the psychological perspective of other people). In addition, work engagement was positively related to colleague ratings of performance.

As a final example, in their recent study among Greek employees working in a fast-food restaurant, Xanthopoulou et al. (2009b) expanded this research, and made a compelling case of the predictive value of work engagement for performance, on a daily basis. Participants were asked to fill in a survey and a diary booklet for five consecutive days. Consistent with hypotheses, results showed that employees were more engaged on days that were characterized by many job resources. Daily job resources, like supervisor coaching and team atmosphere, contributed to employees' PsyCap (day levels of optimism, self-efficacy, and self-esteem), which, in turn, explained daily engagement. Importantly, this study clearly showed that engaged employees performed better on a daily basis. Employees with higher levels of daily engagement produced higher objective daily financial returns.

Other positive behaviors
Recent studies show that it is not only job performance in which engaged employees differ from others and excel. Engaged employees show a variety of behaviors that may be good for themselves and the organization at large. For example, in an unpublished study among a heterogeneous group of Dutch employees, Bakker and Demerouti (2009b) showed that engagement is positively related to active learning behavior. Employees who scored high on vigor, dedication, and absorption also scored high on

supervisor ratings of active learning. Engaged workers were more likely to learn new things through their work activities, and to search for task-related challenges. They were also more likely to ask their colleagues for feedback about their performance.

In a longitudinal study among Finnish dentists, Hakanen et al. (2008) found a positive link between engagement on the one hand, and personal initiative and innovation on the other. They found that engaged dentists were more likely to do more than they are asked to do, and tried to be actively involved in organizational matters. In addition, engaged dentists constantly made improvements in their work and gathered feedback and ideas for improvements from clients.

Consistent with these findings, Schaufeli et al. (2006b) in their survey among Dutch employees from a wide range of occupations, reported a positive relationship between engagement on the one hand, and organizational citizenship behavior and innovativeness on the other. Engaged employees were more willing than workaholics to attend functions not required by the organization, but which help in its overall image. Additionally, the higher employees' levels of engagement, the more they were inclined to invent new solutions for problems at work.

Furthermore, Sonnentag (2003) conducted a diary study to examine the relationship between *recovery* during leisure time and work engagement, and to test the impact of daily engagement on proactive behavior. German employees completed a questionnaire and a daily survey over a period of five consecutive workdays. Multilevel analyses showed that day-level recovery was positively related to day-level work engagement. Daily engagement was, in turn, positively related to day-level proactive behavior (personal initiative and pursuit of learning) during the workday.

Finally, a recent study among almost 750 young Finnish managers (Hyvönen et al., 2009) showed that engaged managers were most eager to develop themselves in the job and increase their occupational knowledge. They were also most likely to have positive attitudes towards modernization and increased productivity. They tried to get their teams to function better towards achieving jointly agreed goals, and endorsed the strongest drive to strive. Taken together, these findings imply that engaged employees are not passive actors in work environments, but instead actively change their work environment if needed.

Engaged employees are active job crafters

Conservation of resources
According to Hobfoll (2002) the accumulation of resources is a pivotal drive that initiates and maintains people's behavior. The basic tenet of his

conservation of resources (COR) theory is that people are motivated to obtain, retain, foster and protect resources, defined as "those entities that either are centrally valued in their own right, or act as means to obtain centrally valued ends" (ibid., p. 307). A first assumption in COR theory is that people have to invest their resources in order to deal with stressful conditions and protect themselves from negative outcomes. For instance, employees may use social support from their colleagues in the form of hands-on assistance in order to deal with temporary work overload. Consequently, COR theory predicts that those with greater resources (for example, more-supportive colleagues) are less vulnerable to stress, whereas those with fewer resources (for example, less-supportive colleagues) are more vulnerable to stress.

A second assumption is that people must invest resources in order to protect against future resource loss, recover their resources, and gain new resources. Moreover, individuals not only strive to protect their current resources, but also to *accumulate* them. For instance, employees learn new skills and competencies in order to increase their employability and reduce the risk of being laid off. COR theory predicts that those who possess more resources are also more capable of resource gain. In other words, initial resource gain begets future gain, thus constituting so-called "gain spirals" (Salanova et al., 2010). For example, increased employability not only reduces the risk of unemployment but also augments the possibility of landing in a better job that offers additional opportunities for learning and development, which enhance engagement at work. Hence, gaining resources increases the resource pool, which makes it more likely that additional resources will be subsequently acquired.

According to COR theory, this accumulation and linking of resources creates "resource caravans". That is, resources tend not to exist in isolation, but rather they aggregate such that, for instance, employees working in a resourceful work environment (that is, have task discretion, or receive high-quality coaching) are likely to reinforce their beliefs in their capabilities and resilience, to feel valued, and be optimistic about meeting their goals. COR theory predicts that in the long run such resource caravans result in positive personal outcomes such as better coping, adaptation, and engagement. Recently, scholars have started to test this idea of resource caravans and cycles of employee engagement.

Cycles of engagement

In recent studies, researchers in the domain of work engagement have started to test the hypothesis that resources are reciprocally related to engagement. Do job resources positively affect work engagement, which, in turn, positively affects job resources? Is there evidence for the existence of "resources caravans" or gain processes? I shall discuss longitudinal and diary studies that are suggestive of gain spirals.

First, in their three-year panel study among 2,555 Finnish dentists, Hakanen et al. (2008) examined how job resources and work engagement may start a gain spiral. Drawing on COR theory, a reciprocal process was predicted: (i) job resources lead to work engagement and work engagement leads to personal initiative (PI), which, in turn, has a positive impact on work-unit innovativeness, and (ii) work-unit innovativeness leads to PI, which has a positive impact on work engagement, which finally predicts future job resources. The results generally confirmed these hypotheses. Positive and reciprocal cross-lagged associations were found between job resources and work engagement and between work engagement and PI. In addition, PI had a positive impact on work-unit innovativeness over time. This suggests that job resources fueled engagement and initiative, but also that engagement and personal initiative led to more resources over time.

Second, Xanthopoulou et al. (2009a) examined the role of personal resources (that is, self-efficacy, self-esteem, and optimism) and job resources (that is, job autonomy, supervisory coaching, performance feedback, and opportunities for professional development) in explaining work engagement. They carried out a two-wave longitudinal study among technical specialists with a two-year time interval. It was hypothesized that job and personal resources, and work engagement are reciprocal over time. Results showed that not only resources and work engagement but also job and personal resources were mutually related. These findings support the assumption of COR theory that various types of resources and well-being evolve into a cycle that determines employees' successful adaptation to their work environments. Since all causal and reversed-causal effects were equally strong, the findings suggest that neither resources nor engagement may be considered as the most important initiator of this cyclical process.

Third, Schaufeli et al. (2009) in their study among Dutch managers of a telecom company hypothesized that work engagement would have a positive impact on changes in job resources over a one-year time period. The results showed that changes in job resources predicted engagement, and that engagement was predictive of increases in social support, autonomy, opportunities for development, and performance feedback. Finally, in their study among starting teachers, Bakker and Bal (2010) found that weekly changes in work-related resources (autonomy, supervisory coaching, performance feedback, and opportunities for development) predicted week-levels of engagement. In addition, they found a reversed causal effect: engaged teachers were best able to mobilize their own job resources.

Taken together, these results show that employee engagement and behavior can have a positive effect on the available resources. Engaged employees seem to create or mobilize their own personal and job resources – they engage in job crafting (Wrzesniewski & Dutton, 2001). In this way, engaged employees seem to sustain and manage their own vigor and dedication (Bakker & Bal, 2010; Salanova et al., 2010). This dynamic, reciprocal relationship between resources and engagement as described by COR theory is compatible with and partly supports the notion of gain cycles.

Active job crafters

Employees may actively change the design of their jobs by choosing tasks, negotiating different job content, and assigning meaning to their tasks or jobs (Parker & Ohly, 2008). This process of employees shaping their jobs has been referred to as "job crafting" (Wrzesniewski & Dutton, 2001). It is defined as the physical and cognitive changes individuals make in their task or relational boundaries. Physical changes refer to changes in the form, scope or number of job tasks, whereas cognitive changes refer to changing how one sees the job. Changing relational boundaries means that individuals have discretion over whom they interact with while doing the job. As a consequence of job crafting, employees may be able to increase their person–job fit. According to Wrzesniewski and Dutton, job crafting focuses on the processes by which employees change elements of their jobs and relationships with others to revise the meaning of the work and the social environment at work. Thus, job crafting is about *changing* the job in order to experience enhanced meaning of it.

However, before employees can start crafting their job, they must perceive that they have the opportunity to make changes. This refers to the sense of autonomy employees have in what they do in their job and how they do it. For example, when employees perform tasks that are interdependent, there is not much room for changing how and when to perform the tasks and relational boundaries. Also, support from supervisors seems very important in perceiving opportunities to craft. A supervisor who understands the employee may offer the employee autonomy and thereby encourages self-initiation (Baard et al., 2004).

Tims and Bakker (in press) adopt the view that employees are active in changing their job tasks and relational boundaries. However, they argue that not every employee may have room for changing the job. Wrzesniewski et al. (1997) suggested that employees who view their work as a calling (that is, focus on enjoyment or fulfillment) are more likely to engage in job crafting, because work is more central in their lives. Consistent with this view, Tims et al. (in press) showed in three independent samples of Dutch employees that engagement has a positive relationship with job crafting. Engaged employees were most likely to increase their job resources, for example, ask for feedback from their supervisor and mobilize their social network. Additionally, engaged employees were most likely to increase their own job demands in order to create a challenging work environment. For example, they proactively volunteer to be involved in a project if possible. Additionally, if it is quiet at work they see this as an opportunity to start new projects.

Overall model of work engagement
The evidence regarding the antecedents and consequences of work engagement can be organized in an overall model of work engagement. This model is based on the job demands–resources (JD–R) model (Demerouti et al., 2001; Bakker & Demerouti, 2007). The first assumption is that job resources such as social support from colleagues and supervisors, performance feedback, skill variety, and autonomy, start a motivational process that leads to work engagement, and consequently to higher performance. The second assumption is that job resources become more salient and gain their motivational potential when employees are confronted with high job demands (for example, workload, and emotional and mental demands). Further, the model is based on the work of Xanthopoulou et al. (2007, 2009a, 2009b), who expanded the JD–R model and showed that job and personal resources are mutually related, and that personal resources can be independent predictors of work engagement. Thus employees who score high on optimism, self-efficacy, resilience and self-esteem are well able to mobilize their job resources, and generally are more engaged in their work.

The JD–R model of work engagement is graphically depicted in Figure 19.1. As can be seen, I assume that job resources and personal resources independently or combined predict work engagement. Further, job and personal resources particularly have a positive impact on engagement when job demands are high. Work engagement, in turn, has a positive impact on job performance. Finally, employees who are engaged and perform well are able to create their own resources, which then foster engagement again over time. They are active job crafters who change their job demands and resources if necessary.

Future research
Most previous studies on work engagement used a between-person design and cannot explain why even highly engaged employees may have an off-day and sometimes show below-average or poor performance. Researchers have therefore begun to examine *daily changes* in work engagement. An important advantage of diary research is that it relies less on retrospective recall than regular surveys, since the questions

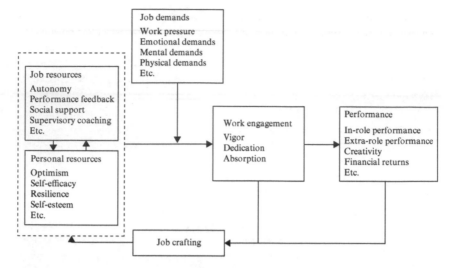

Source: Based on Bakker & Demerouti (2007, 2008).

Figure 19.1   The work engagement model

relate to individuals' perceptions and feelings on a specific day. In addition, when daily changes in work engagement are temporarily separated from daily changes in outcomes such as performance and job crafting, state work engagement could be causally related to such outcomes. Diary research may also reveal what the day-to-day triggers are of state engagement.

Sonnentag et al. (2010) suggest intensifying conceptual development on day-specific (or even momentary) work engagement in order to arrive at a better understanding of how day-specific engagement corresponds to enduring engagement in experienced quality and configuration. In addition, they argue that it is an open question whether the scales used to assess enduring work engagement (see Schaufeli & Bakker, 2003, 2010) are valid for the measurement of state work engagement. Clearly, the time anchors on the UWES and the Maslach Burnout Inventory–General Survey (MBI–GS) (for example, "a few times a month") do not fit with a daily reporting schedule. The appropriateness of item wording to capture the day-to-day variations in energy and dedication remains an open question. Expanding existing measures with new items or alternative response formats would help to refine critical instruments.

Additionally, it would be interesting to examine gain cycles of job resources and engagement at the day or week level. According to the work engagement model presented in this chapter, active job crafting would be an important mediator of the relationship between state engagement and (job and personal) resources. Engaged employees are expected to actively change their job demands and resources in order to stay engaged in their work.

Practical implications

Organizations have become increasingly interested in how to develop engagement in employees. The model of work engagement proposed in this chapter holds straightforward and valuable implications for practice. It suggests that job and personal resources play an important role in engagement. Redesigning jobs in order to promote engagement boils down to increasing job resources. Developing social support, and changing work procedures to enhance feedback and autonomy may create a structural basis for work engagement. Also, job rotation and changing jobs might result in higher engagement levels because they challenge employees, increase their motivation, and stimulate learning and professional development.

Furthermore, since engagement seems to be contagious and may spread across members of work teams (Bakker et al., 2006), leaders have a special role in fostering work engagement among their followers. It is to be expected that considerate leadership, and more particularly transformational leadership, is successful in accomplishing this. Indeed, research suggests that transformational leaders are key social resources for the development of employee engagement (Tims et al., in press; Tuckey et al., 2009). Finally, training programs in organizations that aim at increasing work engagement could focus on building personal resources or psychological capital (for example, efficacy beliefs, optimism, hope, and resiliency).

Conclusion

The overview in this chapter supports the contention that focusing on work engagement offers organizations a competitive advantage. Moreover, engaged employees create their own great place to work. They are active job crafters looking for possibilities to optimize their work environment. This takes the form of increasing job resources, or changing job demands so that work becomes more challenging. By proactively changing their work environment, engaged employees can sustain their own work engagement. This has positive consequences for employees and for organizations at large, since engagement leads to creativity, active learning, and optimal performance. I hope that the work engagement model stimulates future research on engagement and will be an important resource for scientists and practitioners alike.

References

Baard, P.B., Deci, E.L. & Ryan, R.M. (2004), "Intrinsic need satisfaction: a motivational basis of performance and well-being in two work settings", *Journal of Applied Social Psychology*, **34**, 2045–68.

Bakker, A.B. (2009), "Building engagement in the workplace", in R.J. Burke & C.L. Cooper (eds), *The Peak Performing Organization*, Oxford: Routledge, pp. 50–72.

Bakker, A.B. & Bal, P.M. (2010), "Weekly work engagement and performance: a study among starting teachers", *Journal of Occupational and Organizational Psychology*, **83**, 189–206.

Bakker, A.B. & Demerouti, E. (2007), "The job demands–resources model: state of the art", *Journal of Managerial Psychology*, **22**, 309–28.

Bakker, A.B. & Demerouti, E. (2008), "Towards a model of work engagement", *Career Development International*, **13**, 209–23.

Bakker, A.B. & Demerouti, E. (2009a), "The crossover of work engagement between working couples: a closer look at the role of empathy", *Journal of Managerial Psychology*, **24**, 220–36.

Bakker, A.B. & Demerouti, E. (2009b), "Work engagement and performance: the role of conscientiousness", manuscript in preparation.

Bakker, A.B., Demerouti, E. & Verbeke, W. (2004), "Using the job demands–resources model to predict burnout and performance", *Human Resource Management*, **43**, 83–104.

Bakker, A.B., Hakanen, J.J., Demerouti, E. & Xanthopoulou, D. (2007), "Job resources boost work engagement, particularly when job demands are high", *Journal of Educational Psychology*, **99**, 274–84.

Bakker, A.B. & Leiter, M.P. (eds) (2010), *Work Engagement: A Handbook of Essential Theory and Research*, New York: Psychology Press.

Bakker, A.B., Schaufeli, W.B., Leiter, M.P. & Taris, T.W. (2008), "Work engagement: an emerging concept in occupational health psychology", *Work & Stress*, **22**, 187–200.

Bakker, A.B., Van Emmerik, H. & Euwema, M.C. (2006), "Crossover of burnout and engagement in work teams", *Work & Occupations*, **33**, 464–89.

Bakker, A.B. & Xanthopoulou, D. (2009), "The crossover of daily work engagement: test of an actor–partner interdependence model", *Journal of Applied Psychology*, **94**, 1562–71.

Demerouti, E., Bakker, A.B., Nachreiner, F. & Schaufeli, W.B. (2001), "The job demands–resources model of burnout", *Journal of Applied Psychology*, **86**, 499–512.

Demerouti, E. & Cropanzano, R. (2010), "From thought to action: employee work engagement and job performance", in Bakker & Leiter (eds), pp. 147–63.

Fredrickson, B.L. (2001), "The role of positive emotions in positive psychology. The broaden-and-build theory of positive emotions", *American Psychologist*, **56**(3), 218–26.

Fried, Y. & Ferris, G.R. (1987), "The validity of the job characteristics model: a review and meta-analysis", *Personnel Psychology*, **40**, 287–322.

Gorter, R.C., Te Brake, J.H.M., Hoogstraten J. & Eijkman M.A.J. (2008), "Positive engagement and job resources in dental practice", *Community Dentistry and Oral Epidemiology*, **36**, 47–54.

Grant, A.M. & Parker, S.K. (2009), "Redesigning work design theories: the rise of relational and proactive perspectives", *Academy of Management Annals*, **3**, 317–75.

Hackman, J.R. & Oldham, G.R. (1980), *Work Redesign*, Reading, MA: Addison-Wesley.

Hakanen, J.J., Bakker, A.B. & Demerouti, E. (2005), "How dentists cope with their job demands and stay engaged: the moderating role of job resources", *European Journal of Oral Sciences*, **113**, 479–87.

Hakanen, J.J., Perhoniemi, L. & Toppinen-Tanner, S. (2008), "Positive gain spirals at work: from job resources to work engagement, personal initiative and work-unit innovativeness", *Journal of Vocational Behavior*, **73**, 78–91.

Halbesleben, J.R.B. (2010), "A meta-analysis of work engagement: relationships with burnout, demands, resources and consequences", in Bakker & Leiter (eds), pp. 102–17.

Halbesleben, J.R.B. & Wheeler, A.R. (2008), "The relative roles of engagement and embeddedness in predicting job performance and intention to leave", *Work & Stress*, **22**, 242–56.

Hobfoll, S.E. (2002), "Social and psychological resources and adaptation", *Review of General Psychology*, **6**, 307–24.

Hyvönen, K., Feldt, T., Salmela-Aro, K., Kinnunen, U. & Mäkikangas, A. (2009), "Young managers' drive to thrive: a personal work goal approach to burnout and work engagement", *Journal of Vocational Behavior*, **75**, 183–96.

Karasek, R.A. (1979), "Job demands, job decision latitude, and mental strain: implications for job redesign", *Administrative Science Quarterly*, **24**, 285–308.

Koyuncu, M., Burke, R.J. & Fiksenbaum, L. (2006), "Work engagement among women managers and professionals in a Turkish bank: potential antecedents and consequences", *Equal Opportunities International*, **25**, 299–310.

Luthans, F., Norman, S.M., Avolio, B.J. & Avey, J.B. (2008), "The mediating role of psychological capital in the supportive organizational climate–employee performance relationship", *Journal of Organizational Behavior*, **29**, 219–38.

Luthans, F., Youssef, C.M. & Avolio, B.J. (2007), *Psychological Capital: Developing the Human Competitive Edge*, Oxford: Oxford University Press.

Meijman, T.F. & Mulder, G. (1998), "Psychological aspects of workload", in P.J.D. Drenth & H. Thierry (eds), *Handbook of Work and Organizational Psychology*, Hove: Psychology Press, pp. 5–33.

Parker, S.K. & Ohly, S. (2008), "Designing motivating jobs: an expanded framework for linking work characteristics and motivation", in R. Kanfer, G. Chen & R. Pritchard (eds), *Work Motivation: Past, Present, and Future*, New York: LEA/Psychology Press, pp. 233–84.

Ryan, R.M. & Frederick, C.M. (1997), "On energy, personality, and health: subjective vitality as a dynamic reflection of well-being", *Journal of Personality*, **65**, 529–65.

Salanova, M., Agut, S. & Peiró, J.M. (2005), "Linking organizational resources and work engagement to employee performance and customer loyalty: the mediation of service climate", *Journal of Applied Psychology*, **90**, 1217–27.

Salanova, M., Schaufeli, W.B., Xanthopoulou, D. & Bakker, A.B. (2010), "The gain spiral of resources and work engagement: sustaining a positive work life", in Bakker & Leiter (eds), pp. 118–31.

Schaufeli, W.B. & Bakker, A.B. (2003), *UWES – Utrecht Work Engagement Scale: Test Manual*, Utrecht University, Department of Psychology (http://www.schaufeli.com).

Schaufeli, W.B. & Bakker, A.B. (2004), "Job demands, job resources and their relationship with burnout and engagement: a multi-sample study", *Journal of Organizational Behavior*, **25**, 293–315.

Schaufeli, W.B. & Bakker, A.B. (2010), "Defining and measuring work engagement: bringing clarity to the concept", in Bakker & Leiter (eds), pp. 10–24.

Schaufeli, W.B., Bakker, A.B. & Salanova, M. (2006a), "The measurement of work engagement with a brief questionnaire: a cross-national study", *Educational and Psychological Measurement*, **66**, 701–16.

Schaufeli, W.B., Bakker, A.B. & Van Rhenen, W. (2009), "How changes in job demands and resources predict burnout, work engagement, and sickness absenteeism", *Journal of Organizational Behavior*, **30**, 893–917.

Schaufeli, W.B., Salanova, M., González-Romá, V. & Bakker, A.B. (2002), "The measurement of engagement and burnout: a two sample confirmatory factor analytic approach", *Journal of Happiness Studies*, **3**, 71–92.

Schaufeli, W.B., Taris, T.W. & Bakker, A.B. (2006b), "Dr. Jekyll or Mr. Hyde: on the differences between work engagement and workaholism", in R.J. Burke (ed.), *Research Companion to Working Time and Work Addiction*, Cheltenham UK and Northampton, MA, USA: Edward Elgar, pp. 193–217.

Schaufeli, W.B., Taris, T.W., Le Blanc, P., Peeters, M., Bakker, A.B. & De Jonge, J. (2001), "Maakt arbeid gezond? Op zoek naar de bevlogen werknemer" (Does work make one happy? In search of the engaged worker), *De Psycholoog*, **36**, 422–28.

Sonnentag, S. (2003), "Recovery, work engagement, and proactive behavior: a new look at the interface between non-work and work", *Journal of Applied Psychology*, **88**, 518–28.

Sonnentag, S., Dormann, C. & Demerouti, E. (2010), "Not all days are created equal: the concept of state work engagement", in Bakker & Leiter (eds), pp. 25–38.

Sweetman, D. & Luthans, F. (2010), "The power of positive psychology: psychological capital and work engagement", in Bakker & Leiter (eds), pp. 54–68.

Tims, M. & Bakker, A.B. (in press), "Job crafting: towards a new model of individual job redesign", *South African Journal of Industrial Psychology*.

Tims, M., Bakker, A.B. & Derks, D. (2009), "The development of the job crafting scale", Internal report, Erasmus University, Rotterdam.

Tims, M., Bakker, A.B. & Xanthopoulou, D. (in press), "Do transformational leaders enhance their followers' work engagement?", *Leadership Quarterly*.

Tuckey, M.R., Bakker, A.B. & Dollard, M.F. (2009), "Empowering leadership and work engagement: A multilevel study", manuscript submitted for publication.

Van den Broeck, A., Vansteenkiste, M., De Witte, H. & Lens, W. (2008), "Explaining the relationships between job characteristics, burnout and engagement: the role of basic psychological need satisfaction", *Work & Stress*, 22, 277–94.

Wrzesniewski, A. & Dutton, J.E. (2001), "Crafting a job: revisioning employees as active crafters of their work", *Academy of Management Review*, 26, 179–201.

Wrzesniewski, A., McCauley, C., Rozin, P. & Schwartz, B. (1997), "Jobs, careers, and callings: people's reactions to their work", *Journal of Research in Personality*, 31, 21–33.

Xanthopoulou, D., Bakker, A.B., Demerouti, E. & Schaufeli, W.B. (2007), "The role of personal resources in the job demands–resources model", *International Journal of Stress Management*, 14, 121–41.

Xanthopoulou, D., Bakker, A.B., Demerouti, E. & Schaufeli, W.B. (2009a), "Reciprocal relationships between job resources, personal resources, and work engagement", *Journal of Vocational Behavior*, 74, 235–44.

Xanthopoulou, D., Bakker, A.B., Demerouti, E. & Schaufeli, W.B. (2009b), "Work engagement and financial returns: a diary study on the role of job and personal resources", *Journal of Occupational and Organizational Psychology*, 82, 183–200.

20 Affective states and affect regulation as antecedents of dynamic work engagement

Carmen Binnewies and Bettina Fetzer

Introduction

Both affect and work engagement are concepts that have gained increasing attention in organizational research within the last years (Elfenbein, 2007; Macey & Schneider, 2008). This increasing interest is probably due to the importance of affect and work engagement for organizational behavior (compare Brief & Weiss, 2002; Bakker & Demerouti, 2008). In this chapter, we shall discuss the role of affective states as predictors of employees' work engagement. In addition, we shall present theoretical and empirical work on how employees can self-regulate (improve) their affect by applying certain strategies and consequences for work engagement as a dynamic concept.

In our chapter, we refer to the work of Schaufeli et al. (2002) who defined work engagement as "a positive, fulfilling work-related state of mind that is characterized by vigor, dedication, and absorption" (p. 76).

> Vigor is characterized by high levels of energy and mental resilience while working. Dedication refers to being strongly involved in one's work and experiencing a sense of significance, enthusiasm, and challenge. Absorption is characterized by being fully concentrated and happily engrossed in one's work, whereby time passes quickly and one has difficulties with detaching oneself from work. (Bakker & Demerouti, 2008, pp. 209–10)

Affective states and work engagement

In general, affect can be described as a phenomenological state of feeling (Watson, 2000), usually captured in terms of emotional adjectives, such as sad, happy, and enthusiastic. Affective states refer to what an individual is feeling at any given moment in time, whereas affective traits (for example, affectivity) represent dispositions to experience certain affective states over time.

Although affective states and work engagement show a partial conceptual overlap (Macey & Schneider, 2008) – particularly when considering the energetic vigor dimension of work engagement – they can be discriminated. First, vigor is only one specific affect dimension, whereas affective states comprise a plethora of different states that can be arranged on a circumplex model along the dimensions of pleasantness and energy (see Russell, 1980). Second, work engagement is seen as a psychological state directly attributed to work characteristics whereas affective states are also influenced by non-work experiences, such as one's family life or recovery (Rothbard, 2001; Sonnentag et al., 2008). Third, work engagement involves not only an affective component but also a motivational and behavioral component (Bakker & Demerouti, 2008; Macey & Schneider, 2008). In sum, we argue that work engagement and affective states are different constructs and that affective states belong to the antecedents of work engagement.

As affective states are rather transient experiences that show certain dynamics over time they also relate to dynamic changes in outcomes (compare Beal et al., 2005). Therefore, when examining affective states as antecedents of work engagement, we refer to predictors of *dynamic work engagement* (that is, changes in work engagement over time) – also referred to as "state work engagement" (Sonnentag et al., 2010).

Two theoretical approaches are of particular importance to understand the relationship between affective states and work engagement: the broaden-and-build theory of positive emotions (Fredrickson, 2001) and the conservation of resources (COR) model of Hobfoll (1989). According to Fredrickson's broaden-and-build theory, positive emotions and affective states broaden people's thought and action repertoires and thus increase their personal resources (for example, physical, psychological, and social resources). For example, research on positive affect and cognitive processing showed that increased positive affect is associated with higher dopamine levels, which are in turn related to improved processing of different cognitive sets and to a better integrated memory (Isen et al., 1987; Ashby et al., 1999). In other words, positive affective states have the potential to positively influence people's minds and actions by increasing personal resources.

Resources also play a core role in Hobfoll's COR model. They are defined as "objects, personal characteristics, conditions, or energies that are valued by the individual or that serve as a means for attainment of these objects, personal characteristics, conditions, or energies" (1989, p. 516). According to the COR model, people strive to gain and protect their resources. If people's resources are depleted, they experience stress. Having a large amount of resources available and being able to allocate these resources to the task at hand is the key for peaks in dynamic resources (Beal et al., 2005). In other words, a person performs better on days when he or she has more resources available. Research on work engagement has shown that personal resources are predictors of work engagement (Xanthopoulou et al., 2007, 2009). As positive affective states increase people's resources, they should be associated with increased dynamic performance and work engagement.

Only a few studies have examined affective states as predictors of dynamic work engagement. Sonnentag (2003) showed in a sample of public administration workers that on days when a person feels more recovered in the morning, that is, an affective state reflecting high energy and built-up resources, he or she experiences more work engagement during the day. Similarly, Debus et al. (2009) found that the day-level state of being recovered is positively related to daily flow experienced at work – a concept closely related to work engagement (Bakker, 2008). Results of another diary study (Schulz, 2008) revealed that daily negative affect negatively and daily positive affect positively related to daily work engagement in a mixed sample of office workers. In addition, Xanthopoulou et al.'s (2009) diary study showed a positive relation between daily state optimism (that is, the daily tendency to believe that one will experience good outcomes) and daily work engagement.

Taken together, theoretical models and empirical evidence suggest that positive affective states are antecedents of dynamic work engagement. In the next section, we shall discuss how employees can deliberately influence their affect in a positive way and consequently foster work engagement by applying affect regulation strategies at work.

Affect regulation and work engagement

According to Parkinson and Totterdell (1999), affect regulation "includes any process directed at modifying or maintaining moods or emotions whose operation depends on monitoring of affective information" (p. 278). Affect regulation is a specific form of self-regulation (Baumeister et al., 2000) aiming at fostering one's positive affective states and coping with one's negative affective states.

Larsen (2000) provided a control theoretical framework for affect regulation: according to his model, people compare their current affect towards a desired state of affect. If there is a discrepancy between current and desired affect, a person engages in affect regulation mechanisms. In most situations people strive "to feel good, to create and maintain generally pleasant or positive subjective states" (ibid., p. 131). Although there are situations at work when an employee may aim at reducing positive affect – for example, when a doctor has to execute a painful procedure (see Molinsky & Margolis, 2005 for their work on necessary evils) – in this chapter, we focus on *upward affect regulation*, which means affect regulation that aims at experiencing positive affective states.

As people engage in all kinds of different strategies, research on affect regulation aimed at providing a taxonomy of affect regulation strategies (Thayer et al., 1994; Parkinson & Totterdell, 1999; Larsen, 2000). The two most basic differentiations for classifying affect-regulation strategies are (a) cognitive versus behavioral strategies, and (b) engagement versus disengagement strategies (Parkinson & Totterdell, 1999; Larsen, 2000). Cognitive strategies encompass mental or thinking strategies (for example, reinterpreting the situation, thinking of something pleasant) to improve one's affect whereas behavioral strategies encompass doing something to feel better (for example, taking a walk, talking to a friend). The differentiation between engagement versus diversion strategies refers to whether a person addresses the situation at hand or the related affect (engagement strategies) versus avoids the situation or affect, and aims at ignoring and redirecting cognition or action away from the current concern (Parkinson & Totterdell, 1999). Engaging in relaxing activities and energetic activities (for example, sports) are examples of behavioral diversion strategies. Thinking of something pleasant (for example, of one's family) is an example of cognitive diversion strategies. Reinterpreting and rationalizing the situation refer to cognitive engagement strategies, while venting and seeking social support refer to behavioral engagement strategies.

Prior research on affect regulation in private life showed that people self-regulate (improve) their affect by applying certain strategies (Thayer et al., 1994; Parkinson & Totterdell, 1999). In a diary study with trainee teachers, Totterdell and Parkinson (1999) found that reappraisal, rationalization (cognitive engagement strategies), seeking social support (behavioral engagement strategy), cognitive distraction (cognitive diversion strategy), relaxing activities and active/energetic activities (behavioral diversion strategies) were related to improved affect (for example, greater cheerfulness and more energy). Two strategies – venting and cognitive avoidance – were not related to affect improvement; venting was even associated with impaired affect. Although Totterdell and Parkinson's study captured trainee teachers' affect regulation both in their private life and at work, it is not clear what employees (can) do at work to promote both their work-related affect and well-being.

We addressed the topic of affect regulation in the workplace in our own research. First, Schulz (2008) conducted a diary study examining some of the strategies in the work context that proved to be effective in prior studies in the non-work context. Over the course of five working days, 140 employees from different occupations (for example, managers, salespersons) responded to twice daily surveys: (a) after the lunch break and (b) after finishing the working day. After the lunch break, participants were asked how much they engaged in different affect-regulation strategies at work during the morning and during their lunch break; after finishing the working day, they indicated their daily positive and negative affect and work engagement experienced during the day. Results showed that pleasant cognitive distraction (for example, thinking of one's family), reappraisal and seeking social support were positively related to work engagement during the day. Pleasant cognitive distraction was also positively related to daily positive affect, and positive affect mediated the relationship between pleasant cognitive distraction and daily work engagement. In other words, employees who engage more in pleasant cognitive distraction at work during the morning and during their lunch break experience more work engagement during the day because they experience more daily positive affect. In addition, employees who engage more in reappraisal and seek more social support, experience more work engagement during the day. However, these effects were not mediated via affective states. Contrary to expectations, seeking social support, was even related to higher daily negative affect. As the study allows no conclusions about causality, one possible explanation is that people seek more social support on days when they experience higher negative affect.

Second, Binnewies and Fetzer (2009; Fetzer, 2009) conducted a longitudinal study (two-week time lag) with employees from various occupations (for example, playschool teachers, managers) to investigate the role of affect regulation in the work context. Fetzer (2009) showed that engaging in relaxing activities at work (for example, listening to music, drinking a coffee during a break) was positively associated with work engagement. In addition, this relationship was stronger for people who experience a high level of time pressure at work. Seeking social support was not directly associated with work engagement. But seeking social support was related to higher work engagement, when people identified seeking social support as an effective strategy to regulate their own affect.

As prior research on affect regulation in the work context was based on affect-regulation strategies identified in the non-work context, Binnewies and Fetzer (2009) interviewed employees about the strategies they use at work to deliberately foster their affective states and well-being. Building a general taxonomy, the authors found that employees apply a range of engagement (for example, seeking social support, reappraisal, venting) and diversion affect-regulation strategies at work (for example, relaxing activities, active/energetic activities, cognitive distraction). Moreover, they identified a third category they termed "supporting strategies". Supporting affect-regulation strategies refer to strategies that aim at establishing a supporting working environment. Examples are an active management of one's work and break schedule (for example, doing a favored work task after finishing an unfavored work task, taking a long lunch break), actively promoting a positive (team) climate (for example, organizing a regular breakfast with co-workers in the office) and designing one's workplace (for example, putting personal pictures or plants in the office). Results showed that people who engage more in supporting affect-regulation strategies at work experience a higher work engagement (ibid.).

Practical implications
As we argued and summarized, research showing that positive affective states and affect regulation are related to increased work engagement, increasing employees' positive affective states and affect regulation should promote employees' work engagement. One way to improve affective states at work is workplace redesign. Designing a workplace in such a way that it provides greater job control, significance, feedback, identity and task variety should foster employees' positive affective states at work (Saavedra & Kwun, 2000). In addition, we assume that job control is an important factor determining to what degree employees can engage in affect-regulation strategies at work. Obviously, employees can arrange their work schedule in a way that benefits their affect only if they have control over work tasks' timing and sequencing. Increasing employees' job resources should have a double positive effect on work engagement, because it should both directly and indirectly (via affective states) promote employees' work engagement (Bakker & Demerouti, 2008; Schulz, 2008).

In addition, research on recovery during off-job time showed that recovery experiences, such as switching off from work during off-job time and relaxation, are positively related to employees' positive affective states (Sonnentag et al., 2008). Therefore, promoting recovery during off-job time is another way to promote employees' work engagement (Sonnentag, 2003).

In sum, we conclude by pointing out that investigating positive affective states and affect regulation fit into a positive psychology perspective. This line of research showed that it is fruitful to investigate positive conditions or processes that contribute to work engagement in particular, and to the flourishing and optimal functioning of individuals in general (Luthans & Youssef, 2007; Bakker & Demerouti, 2008).

References
Ashby, F.G., Isen, A.M. & Turken, A.U. (1999), "A neuropsychological theory of positive affect and its influence on cognition", *Psychological Review*, **106**, 529–50.
Bakker, A.B. (2008), "The work-related flow inventory: construction and initial validation of the WOLF", *Journal of Vocational Behavior*, **72**, 400–414.
Bakker, A.B. & Demerouti, E. (2008), "Towards a model of work engagement", *Career Development International*, **13**, 209–23.
Baumeister, R.F., Muraven, M. & Tice, D.M. (2000), "Ego depletion: a resource model of volition, self-regulation, and controlled processing", *Social Cognition*, **18**, 130–50.
Beal, D.J., Weiss, H.M., Barros, E. & MacDermid, S.M. (2005), "An episodic process model of affective influences on performance", *Journal of Applied Psychology*, **90**, 1054–68.

Binnewies, C. & Fetzer, B. (2009), "How can employees self-regulate their affect and well-being at work? A classification of work-related affect regulation strategies", presentation at the 14th European Congress on Work and Organizational Psychology, Santiago de Compostela, Spain, 14 May.

Brief, A.P. & Weiss, H.M. (2002), "Organizational behavior: affect in the workplace", *Annual Review of Psychology*, **53**, 279–307.

Debus, M.E., Sonnentag, S. & Deutsch, W. (2009), "Immersing in work: a day-level study on flow at work", manuscript submitted for publication.

Elfenbein, H.A. (2007), "Emotion in organizations", Ch. 7 in J.P. Walsh & A.P. Brief (eds), *The Academy of Management Annals*, Vol. 1, New York: Taylor & Francis Group/Lawrence Erlbaum, pp. 315–86.

Fetzer, B. (2009), "Affektregulationsstrategien bei der Arbeit: Zusammenhänge mit Persönlichkeit, Burnout und Arbeitsengagement" (Affect regulation strategies at work: relations with personality, burnout and work engagement), University of Konstanz, Konstanz.

Fredrickson, B.L. (2001), "The role of positive emotions in positive psychology: the broaden-and-build theory of positive emotions", *American Psychologist*, **56**, 218–26.

Hobfoll, S.E. (1989), "Conservation of resources: a new attempt at conceptualizing stress", *American Psychologist*, **44**, 513–24.

Isen, A.M., Daubman, K.A. & Nowicki, G.P. (1987), "Positive affect facilitates creative problem solving", *Journal of Personality and Social Psychology*, **52**, 1122–31.

Larsen, R.J. (2000), "Toward a science of mood regulation", *Psychological Inquiry*, **11**, 129–41.

Luthans, F. & Youssef, C.M. (2007), "Emerging positive organizational behavior", *Journal of Management*, **33**, 321–49.

Macey, W.H. & Schneider, B. (2008), "The meaning of employee engagement", *Industrial and Organizational Psychology: Perspectives on Science and Practice*, **1**, 3–30.

Molinsky, A. & Margolis, J. (2005), "Necessary evils and interpersonal sensitivity in organizations", *Academy of Management Review*, **30**, 245–68.

Parkinson, B. & Totterdell, P. (1999), "Classifying affect-regulation strategies", *Cognition & Emotion*, **13**, 277–303.

Rothbard, N.P. (2001), "Enriching or depleting? The dynamics of engagement in work and family roles", *Administrative Science Quarterly*, **46**, 655–84.

Russell, J.A. (1980), "A circumplex model of affect", *Journal of Personality and Social Psychology*, **39**, 1161–78.

Saavedra, R. & Kwun, S.K. (2000), "Affective states in job characteristic theory", *Journal of Organizational Behavior*, **21**, 131–46.

Schaufeli, W.B., Salanova, M., González-Romá, V. & Bakker, A.B. (2002), "The measurement of engagement and burnout: a two sample confirmatory factor analytic approach", *Journal of Happiness Studies*, **3**, 71–92.

Schulz, A. (2008), "Emotionen bei der Arbeit: Selbstgesteuerte Affektregulation bei der Arbeit und das Zusammenspiel mit Affekt, emotionaler Erschöpfung und Arbeitsengagement" (Emotions at work: self-controlled affect-regulation at work and the interplay with affect, emotional exhaustion and work engagement), unpublished Diploma thesis, University of Konstanz, Konstanz.

Sonnentag, S. (2003), "Recovery, work engagement, and proactive behavior: a new look at the interface between nonwork and work", *Journal of Applied Psychology*, **88**, 518–28.

Sonnentag, S., Binnewies, C. & Mojza, E.J. (2008), "'Did you have a nice evening?' A day-level study on recovery experiences, sleep and affect", *Journal of Applied Psychology*, **93**, 674–84.

Sonnentag, S., Dormann, C. & Demerouti, E. (2010), "Not all days are created equal: the concept of state work engagement", in A.B. Bakker & M.P. Leiter (eds), *Work Engagement: A Handbook of Essential Theory and Research*, London: Psychology Press, pp. 25–38.

Thayer, R.E., Newman, J.R. & McClain, T.M. (1994), "Self-regulation of mood: strategies for changing a bad mood, raising energy, and reducing tension", *Journal of Personality and Social Psychology*, **67**, 910–25.

Totterdell, P. & Parkinson, B. (1999), "Use and effectiveness of self-regulation strategies for improving mood in a group of trainee teachers", *Journal of Occupational Health Psychology*, **4**, 219–32.

Watson, D. (2000), *Mood and Temperament*, New York: Guilford Press.

Xanthopoulou, D., Bakker, A.B., Demerouti, E. & Schaufeli, W.B. (2007), "The role of personal resources in the job demands–resources model", *International Journal of Stress Management*, **14**, 121–41.

Xanthopoulou, D., Bakker, A.B., Demerouti, E. & Schaufeli, W.B. (2009), "Work engagement and financial returns: a diary study on the role of job and personal resources", *Journal of Occupational and Organizational Psychology*, **82**, 183–200.

21 More engagement is not necessarily better: the benefits of fluctuating levels of engagement

Jennifer M. George

Introduction

An implicit assumption in much of the work on employee engagement is the notion that "the more engagement the better" when it comes to work outcomes (George, 2009). This work tends to assume that high levels of sustained engagement are desirable for employees and their organizations and that engagement is synonymous with positive affective involvement in one's work. For example, in reviewing various definitions of engagement, Macey and Schneider (2008a, p. 4) indicate: "Common to these definitions is the notion that employee engagement is a desirable condition, has an organizational purpose, and connotes involvement, commitment, passion, enthusiasm, focused effort, and energy".

However, this work ignores a very sizeable literature which addresses the functionality and adaptability of nonconscious processes in everyday life. Active, conscious engagement is functional for certain kinds of work-related activities and tasks. Too much sustained conscious engagement can sometimes be dysfunctional. This work also ignores the benefits of negative affective states and the role of engagement that involves negative rather than positive affect. Furthermore, this work ignores the potential costs of high and sustained levels of engagement for employees.

Perhaps more fundamentally, work on employee engagement presupposes that conscious psychological engagement on the job leads to work behaviors. That is, if employees are positively and enthusiastically engaged in their work, they will perform better and engage in organizationally functional extra-role behaviors.

In this chapter, I discuss these issues by posing a series of questions for researchers to consider in the employee engagement domain. I propose that engagement may best be viewed as a dynamic process that fluctuates over time for a variety of reasons. Moreover, I suggest that fluctuations in levels of engagement may be beneficial for a variety of reasons and uniformly high levels of engagement may be detrimental (George, 2009).

Does conscious engagement lead to work behaviors?
In today's organizations facing a dynamic and complex environment, it is often thought that high levels of employee engagement are more important than ever before. As tasks and decisions become more complex, organizations are viewed as benefiting when their members are consciously engaged and involved, at high levels, in their work. Intuitively, one would be hard-pressed to dispute such a position. In fact, when one thinks about any activity in life that is purposive, it would seem that high levels of conscious engagement and involvement would be beneficial. And the logical progression is from global and conscious psychological engagement to actual behavior (ibid.).

The purported benefits of psychological engagement hinge around an implicit assumption dominant in the organizational behavior literature. That is, the field tends to implicitly assume that the majority of behaviors performed in organizations are the result of job holders' conscious forethought and will (ibid.).

While people tend to think that their own behavior is a function of their conscious will (and personal engagement), an extensive body of literature suggests that most day-to-day behaviors are performed automatically and are driven by nonconscious thoughts and feelings (for example, Uleman & Bargh, 1989; Wegner & Wheatley, 1999; Hassin et al., 2005; Bargh, 2007). Automatic thought occurs when cognitive processes take place without conscious control, effort, awareness, or intention (Bargh, 1989, 1994; Andersen et al., 2007). Perception is an automatic process and upon perception, automatic categorization into knowledge structures takes place; knowledge structures that are automatically primed via perception produce behavior typically without a conscious choice or intention (Bargh & Chartrand, 1999). Upon behaving, people think that their conscious will and decisions determined their behavior but this is more often than not an illusion (Norretranders, 1998; Wegner & Wheatley, 1999; George, 2009). Thus, it is not so much that people choose to behave based on global psychological reactions such as being engaged at work but rather that their work-related behaviors are driven by automatic responses to local cues (George, 2009). Around the time that behavior occurs, so too does the perception of having chosen the behavior and the experience of will (Wegner & Wheatley, 1999; George, 2009). As Wegner and Wheatley (1999, p. 490) indicate, "Believing that our conscious thoughts cause our actions is an error based on the illusory experience of will".

While the kinds of behavior that engagement is most beneficial for are likely goal-oriented behaviors, goals also are represented in knowledge structures that are automatically activated and pursued (Bargh, 1990, 1997; Kruglanski, 1996; Bargh & Chartrand, 1999; Dijksterhuis et al.,

2007). Goals can be nonconsciously activated and when activated, guide behavior in ways similar to the ways that goals consciously selected guide behavior (Bargh et al., 2001). More generally, as Dijksterhuis et al. (2007, p. 55) suggest,

> The fact that behavior starts unconsciously is important for our understanding of automaticity. It follows that we should treat the fact that behavior is unconscious as the default. This in turn means that there really are two kinds of behaviors. First, there are behaviors of which we are never consciously aware . . . Second, there are behaviors of which we do become aware (once or more often), somewhere between initiation and final completion.

Hence, while people can be consciously aware of their goal-directed behavior, the behavior itself is often automatically initiated by nonconscious processes (Wilson, 2002).

Automatic thought is adaptive in that at any moment in time, people are exposed to vast amounts of sensory information that could never be processed by consciousness alone, which has very limited capacity (Norretranders, 1998; Wilson, 2002). Likewise, in the unconscious mind, people have accumulated an extensive array of knowledge structures (for example, schemas, scripts, needs, goals, predispositions, and desires) and just a small fraction of this knowledge is available in consciousness at any one point in time (Glaser & Kihlstrom, 2005; George, 2009). As Glaser and Kihlstrom (2005, pp. 171–72) indicate, "After nearly three decades of research on automaticity and construct activation, it is increasingly clear that much of human mental life operates without awareness or intent . . . Arguments that the unconscious is complex and wide ranging have been made compellingly, and with increasing empirical support, for several decades".

Work engagement theory and research, on the other hand, seems to accord conscious thoughts and feelings a major role in the etiology of workplace behaviors (for example, Kahn, 1990; Bakker et al., 2006). Given the automaticity of much of everyday life and the dominant role that nonconscious processes play in determining behavior (Bargh & Chartrand, 1999; Wegner & Wheatley, 1999; Andersen et al., 2007), perhaps work engagement researchers should consider whether their assumption that conscious engagement precedes work behavior bears reconsideration.

Is more conscious engagement better?

An extensive and growing body of literature on nonconscious processes suggests that while high and sustained conscious engagement is beneficial for certain kinds of activities such as learning new skills or acquiring new knowledge and information (Ouellette & Wood, 1998; Wegner & Bargh,

1998), it may be less beneficial for other activities characterized by high uncertainty, ambiguity, the need for creative responses, the processing of large amounts of information, and the use of existing knowledge (Wilson & Schooler, 1991; Wilson, 2002; Dijksterhuis & Nordgren, 2006; George, 2009). Why is this the case? Principally because of differences in the conscious and nonconscious mind.

The conscious mind processes information in a convergent manner, is limited in terms of its processing capacity, and can typically take into account and recall about seven things at any one point in time (Miller, 1956; Norretranders, 1998; Wilson, 2002; Dijksterhuis et al., 2005; Dijksterhuis & Nordgren, 2006; Dijksterhuis & van Olden, 2006). In contrast, the nonconscious mind has far greater capacity, has access to vast amounts of accumulated knowledge and experience, operates in a more divergent and bottom-up fashion, can integrate and weigh different pieces of information, and is a relatively accurate pattern detector (Norretranders, 1998; Wilson, 2002; Dijksterhuis et al., 2005; Dijksterhuis & Nordgren, 2006; Dijksterhuis & van Olden, 2006; Bos et al., 2008).

When employees are trying to learn new skills or acquire new knowledge, high levels of engagement are likely to be desirable (Ouellette & Wood, 1998; Wegner & Bargh, 1998). On the other hand, when employees are actually relying on their existing bank of knowledge, skills, and experiences to come up with solutions to problems, be creative, and make judgments based on complex inputs and information, it may be the case that high and sustained levels of conscious engagement are disadvantageous, and alternating levels of high and low levels of engagement may lead to more desirable outcomes (Wilson & Schooler, 1991; Wilson, 2002; Dijksterhuis & Meurs, 2006; Dijksterhuis & Nordgren, 2006; Dijksterhuis & van Olden, 2006; Bos et al., 2008; George, 2009).

When facing difficult decisions, for example, it would seem that the more carefully engaged and involved in the decision-making process the decision maker was, the better. Such engagement might involve, for example, the careful listing of pros and cons of different decision alternatives. Does high conscious engagement in the decision-making process lead to better decisions? Research conducted by Wilson and colleagues suggests not. More specifically, in laboratory studies, Wilson and colleagues have shown that when making decisions ranging from judging jams, selecting art posters, and estimating how long an ongoing personal relationship will endure to choosing college classes, participants tended to make better decisions when they relied on their "gut" feelings, and tended to make less advantageous judgments when they were told to consider or list the reasons for their decisions (Wilson et al., 1984, 1993; Wilson & Schooler, 1991; Wilson & Kraft, 1993; Wilson, 2002). Wilson (2002) suggests that listing and analyzing reasons leads to inferior judgments because participants rely on incomplete or flawed information such as what their personal theories lead them to believe should go into such judgments, what comes easiest to mind, or what can be put into words. Those relying on gut feelings perhaps are able to access more inclusive and accurate information from their unconscious relevant to the judgment at hand (Wilson, 2002; George, 2009).

Nonetheless, this information has to be available in the unconscious to be accessed. Hence, high levels of engagement are necessary to acquire the knowledge and information relevant to decisions and judgments that come up on a job. When actually making complex decisions and judgments, perhaps, too much engagement and weighing of pros and cons may be dysfunctional at a certain point and decision makers might be better off relying on their gut feelings (George, 2009). As Wilson (2002, pp. 171–2) indicates,

> It is important to distinguish between informed and uninformed gut feelings. We should gather as much information as possible, to allow our adaptive unconscious to make a stable, informed evaluation rather than an ill-informed one . . . The trick is to gather enough information to develop an informed gut feeling and then not analyze that feeling too much . . . we should not analyze the information in an overly deliberate, conscious manner, constantly making explicit lists of pluses and minuses. We should let our adaptive unconscious do the job of forming reliable feelings and then trust those feelings, even if we cannot explain them fully.

Thus, fluctuating levels of conscious engagement might be beneficial with high engagement involved in acquiring knowledge, information, and expertise and less conscious engagement involved in using that expertise to make decisions.

Theorizing and research on intuition leads to similar conclusions. Dane and Pratt (2007, p. 40) define intuitions as "affectively charged judgments that arise through rapid, nonconscious, and holistic associations". Intuitive decision making is contrasted with analytical decision making which involves conscious and systematic consideration of the costs and benefits of different alternatives (Dane & Pratt, 2009). Dane and Pratt (2007, 2009) suggest that intuitive decision making may be advantageous when decision makers have relevant knowledge and expertise and the task involves complex judgments with no objective right or wrong solution.

From a somewhat different perspective, Elsbach and Hargadon's (2006) approach to job design for hard-working professionals also appears to advocate fluctuating levels of engagement rather than sustained levels of high engagement. In particular, Elsbach and Hargadon suggest that periods of "mindless work" that is low in difficulty and pressure yet important for effectiveness should be scheduled into the workdays of professionals who find their work dominated by difficult and complex work with a lot of pressure. Elsbach and Hargadon suggest that periods of mindless work provide the time for professionals to be creative.

Work on incubation and unconscious-thought theory (Dijksterhuis & Nordgren, 2006; Sio & Ormerod, 2009) also attests to the benefits of alternating levels of engagement rather than high sustained levels of conscious engagement. On a mundane level, we are all probably familiar with how sometimes putting aside a difficult problem or task for a while and then going back to it can lead to better outcomes than sustained engagement on the task and the sudden insights that arise when taking a walk or doing the dishes (George, 2008). Stories of creative geniuses also point to the role of incubation in their discoveries (Ghiselin, 1985; Claxton, 1997). In essence, this work suggests that when working on difficult problems in need of creative solutions, breaks or shifting conscious attention away from the task can be beneficial as the mind continues to work on the problem without conscious awareness (Csikszentmihalyi & Sawyer, 1995; Leonard & Swap, 1999; Jett & George, 2003; Dijksterhuis & Meurs, 2006).

Unconscious-thought theory suggests that while conscious attention can be focused on one task or activity, unconscious thought can be focused on something else (Dijksterhuis, 2004; Dijksterhuis & Meurs, 2006; Dijksterhuis & Nordgren, 2006). The theory suggests that "whereas unconscious thought works 'bottom up' and can integrate large amounts of information, conscious thought is very limited in its capacity and works 'top down' . . . This limited capacity of consciousness had led to the hypothesis that conscious thought often leads to relatively poor decisions" (Dijsksterhuis & van Olden, 2006, p. 628). Thus, according to this theory, when facing complex or difficult decisions with many parameters, decision makers might be advised to consciously consider all the information at hand and then take a break or distract themselves prior to making the decision in order to allow the unconscious time to process the information (Dijksterhuis & van Olden, 2006). From a series of laboratory experiments, Bos et al. (2008) concluded that unconscious thought is goal dependent and focuses on information that is to be used for some subsequent purpose. This suggests that unconscious thought does not proceed in an indiscriminant manner processing all the information that people encounter each day, but rather focuses on information that is relevant to ongoing goals (ibid.).

What about negative engagement?
A common premise in the engagement literature is that engagement entails positive affect (Macey & Schneider, 2008a). However, this work ignores

the fact that some of the conditions under which engagement might be especially important may precisely be those conditions in which negative emotions and moods are experienced (Frese, 2008). That is, negative emotions and affective reactions (both conscious and nonconscious) are important and adaptive signals that indicate that there are problems that need to be addressed and that can quickly change behavior in functional ways (Frijda, 1988; Damasio, 1999; Bechara & Damasio, 2005; George, 2009). Positive emotions and affective reactions signal that things are going well (George & Zhou, 2007). It would seem to be especially important for employees to be engaged at work when there are real problems and the need for improvements and change.

More generally, there is a tendency in the organizational behavior literature to focus on the benefits of positive affective reactions and a corresponding need to improve or repair negative affective reactions (George, 2009). However, negative affective reactions often occur because there are real problems, and these reactions are adaptive in focusing attention on problems and the need to improve the current situation. While no one likes to feel badly and clearly, in organizations, negative affective states should not be promoted, they are likely to be experienced nonetheless when problems occur, and this is functional and adaptive as they signal that there are problems and prompt people to work to address them and improve the current situation (George & Zhou, 2007).

What about the costs of high engagement for employees?

A common theme in the engagement literature is the organizational benefits of high levels of employee engagement. From an employee perspective, however, high engagement does not come without its costs. As Macey and Schneider (2008b, p. 80) note, "people cannot expend their energy at the highest levels all the time – there is a need for recovery to ensure continued employee well-being". In an era when many employees are facing competing demands on their time, whether it be from taking care of their children or their ailing parents, and in an era of frequent layoffs, high job insecurity, and economic uncertainty, pushing for higher and higher levels of employee engagement seems to ignore the costs that might accrue to highly engaged employees such as diminished time and energy available for engagement outside of work. For example, highly engaged employees may make sacrifices in other parts of their lives to sustain their high levels of engagement, and these sacrifices may entail considerable costs. For employees bearing these costs, job loss may be especially painful as so much of the self has been engaged in an ultimately punishing workplace, and sacrifices made in other parts of life may appear to have been made for naught. Of course, while these are ultimately empirical questions, the managerial orientation of much of the work on employee engagement tends to ignore the implications of high engagement for those so engaged and/or paint an overly rosy picture of high engagement which fails to consider the reality that many employees actually face in today's environment.

What are the potential implications of these questions?
In this chapter, I have raised four questions for employee engagement researchers to consider as they continue to study this interesting and important topic. In raising these questions, I by no means intended to downplay the important contributions and insights that have been made in this topical domain. Rather, I was hoping to expand the range of issues considered in the employee engagement realm. As such, and in conclusion, below I present some potential implications that these questions might have for future work in this area.

First, acknowledging that much of work behavior is likely performed in an automatic fashion and driven by nonconscious processes, suggests that perhaps more attention should be focused on contextual cues in organizations as it is these cues which likely prime or activate accessible knowledge structures that initiate behavior without conscious intent (Bargh & Chartrand, 1999; Andersen et al., 2007; George, 2009). That is, local cues and the local context are likely key determinants of behavior on the job and global evaluations and perceptions may be less influential than commonly thought (George, 2009).

Second, exploring the potential implications of fluctuating levels of engagement suggests that engagement should be considered over time (ibid.). For example, Dalal et al. (2008) advocate a within-person approach to engagement which explores individual variation in levels of engagement over time.

Third, consistent with recent research exploring the consequences of positive and negative mood at work (George & Zhou, 2002, 2007), taking into account the fact that engagement can involve negative affective reactions suggests that rather than viewing negative affective reactions as always detrimental and in need of repair, the very real and adaptive function of negative emotions and moods bears consideration (George, 2009). Often, when major fiascoes occur, it is discovered after the fact that certain key players may have had misgivings and negative reactions to ongoing events and initiatives related to the causes of the major problems (ibid.). Perhaps rather than suppressing these negative reactions (concerning matters seemingly large or small), they should be treated as important and adaptive signals of an undesirable state of affairs.

Lastly, engagement research should consider the effects of engagement on multiple stakeholders, including employees and their families, and track these effects over time. While a one-shot, cross-sectional view of engagement might suggest that it has primarily positive consequences, longitudinal research might paint a different picture, especially when employees are viewed as whole people with lives outside the workplace. Additionally, it would be useful to explore how reactions to adverse organizational events (for example, layoffs) differ, depending upon whether employees were highly engaged in their job prior to the event.

Clearly, there are many unanswered questions in the study of employee engagement. I hope that this chapter has spurred interest in trying to find answers to at least a few of these questions.

References

Andersen, S.M., Moskowitz, G.B., Blair, I.V. & Nosek, B.A. (2007), "Automatic thought", in A.W. Kruglanski & E.T. Higgins (eds), *Social Psychology: Handbook of Basic Principles*, 2nd edn, New York: Guilford Press, pp. 138–75.

Bakker, A.B., Van Emmerik, H. & Euwema, M.C. (2006), "Crossover of burnout and engagement in work teams", *Work and Occupations*, **33**, 464–89.

Bargh, J.A. (1989), "Conditional automaticity: varieties of automatic influence in social perception and cognition", in Uleman & Bargh (eds), pp. 3–51.

Bargh, J.A. (1990), "Auto-motives: preconscious determinants of social interaction", in E.T. Higgins & R.M. Sorrentino (eds), *Handbook of Motivation and Cognition*, Vol. 2, New York: Guilford, pp. 93–130.

Bargh, J.A. (1994), "The four horseman of automaticity: awareness, efficiency, intention, and control in social cognition", in R.S. Wyer, Jr. & T.K. Srull (eds), *Handbook of Social Cognition*, 2nd edn, Hillsdale, NJ: Erlbaum, pp. 1–40.

Bargh, J.A. (1997), "The automaticity of everyday life", in R.S. Wyer, Jr. (ed.), *The Automaticity of Everyday Life: Advances in Social Cognition*, Vol. 10, Mahwah, NJ: Erlbaum, pp. 1–61.

Bargh, J.A. (2007), *Social Psychology and the Unconscious: The Automaticity of Higher Mental Processes*, New York: Psychology Press.

Bargh, J.A. & Chartrand, T.L. (1999), "The unbearable automaticity of being", *American Psychologist*, **54**, 462–79.

Bargh, J.A., Gollwitzer, P.M., Lee-Chai, A., Barndollar, K. & Trotschel, R. (2001), "An automated will: nonconscious activation and pursuit of behavioral goals", *Journal of Personality and Social Psychology*, **81**, 1014–27.

Bechara, A. & Damasio, A.R. (2005), "The somatic marker hypothesis: a neural theory of economic decision", *Games and Economic Behavior*, **52**, 336–72.

Bos, M.W., Dijksterhuis, A. & van Baaren, R.B. (2008), "On the goal dependency of unconscious thought", *Journal of Experimental Social Psychology*, **44**, 1114–20.

Claxton, G. (1997), *Hare Brain Tortoise Mind: Why Intelligence Increases When You Think Less*, London: Fourth Estate.

Csikszentmihalyi, M. & Sawyer, K. (1995), "Creative insight: the social dimension of a solitary moment", in R.J. Sternberg & J.E. Davidson (eds), *The Nature of Insight*, Cambridge, MA: MIT Press, pp. 329–63.

Dalal, R.S., Brummel, B.J., Wee, S. & Thomas, L.L. (2008), "Defining employee engagement for productive research and practice", *Industrial and Organizational Psychology*, **1**, 52–5.

Damasio, A. (1999), *The Feeling of What Happens*, San Diego, CA: Harcourt.

Dane, E. & Pratt, M.G. (2007), "Exploring intuition and its role in managerial decision making", *Academy of Management Review*, **32**, 33–54.

Dane, E. & Pratt, M.G., (2009), "Conceptualizing and measuring intuition: a review of recent trends", in G.P. Hodgkinson & J.K. Ford (eds), *International Review of Industrial and Organizational Psychology*, **24**, 1–40.

Dijksterhuis, A. (2004), "Think different: the merits of unconscious thought in preference development and decision making", *Journal of Personality and Social Psychology*, **87**, 586–98.

Dijksterhuis, A., Aarts, H. & Smith, P.K. (2005), "The power of the subliminal: on subliminal persuasion and other potential applications", in Hassin et al. (eds), pp. 77–106.

Dijksterhuis, A., Chartrand, T.L. & Aarts, H. (2007), "Effects of priming and perception on social behavior and goal pursuit", in Bargh (ed.), pp. 51–131.

Dijksterhuis, A. & Meurs, T. (2006), "Where creativity resides: the generative power of unconscious thought", *Consciousness and Cognition*, **15**, 135–46.

Dijksterhuis, A. & Nordgren, L.R. (2006), "A theory of unconscious thought", *Perspectives on Psychological Science*, **1**, 95–109.

Dijksterhuis, A. & van Olden, Z. (2006), "On the benefits of thinking unconsciously: unconscious thought can increase post-choice satisfaction", *Journal of Experimental Social Psychology*, **42**, 627–31.

Elsbach, K.D. & Hargadon, A.B. (2006), "Enhancing creativity through 'mindless' work: a framework of workday design", *Organization Science*, **17**, 470–83.

Frese, M. (2008), "The word is out: we need an active performance concept for modern workplaces", *Industrial and Organizational Psychology*, **1**, 67–9.

Frijda, N.H. (1988), "The laws of emotion", *American Psychologist*, **43**, 349–58.

George, J.M. (2008), "Creativity in organizations", in J.P. Walsh & A.P. Brief (eds), *Annals of the Academy of Management*, **1**, 439–77.

George, J.M. (2009), "The illusion of will in organizational behavior research: nonconscious processes and job design", *Journal of Management*, **35**, 318–39.

George, J.M. & Zhou, J. (2002), "Understanding when bad moods foster creativity and good ones don't: the role of context and clarity of feelings", *Journal of Applied Psychology*, **87**, 687–97.

George, J.M. & Zhou, J. (2007), "Dual tuning in a supportive context: joint contributions of positive mood, negative mood, and supervisory behaviors to employee creativity", *Academy of Management Journal*, **50**, 605–22.

Ghiselin, B. (1985), *The Creative Process: A Symposium*, Berkeley, CA: University of California Press.

Glaser, J. & Kihlstrom, J.F. (2005), "Compensatory automaticity: unconscious volition is not an oxymoron", in Hassin et al. (eds), pp. 171–95.

Hassin, R.R., Uleman, J.S. & Bargh, J.A. (2005), *The New Unconscious*, Oxford: Oxford University Press.

Jett, Q.R. & George, J.M. (2003), "Time interrupted: a closer look at the role of interruptions in organizational life", *Academy of Management Review*, **28**, 494–507.

Kahn, W.A. (1990), "Psychological conditions of personal engagement and disengagement at work", *Academy of Management Journal*, **33**, 692–724.

Kruglanski, A.W. (1996), "Goals as knowledge structures", in P.M. Gollwitzer & J.A. Bargh (eds), *The Psychology of Action*, New York: Guilford, pp. 599–618.

Leonard, D. & Swap, W. (1999), *When Sparks Fly: Igniting Creativity in Groups*. Boston, MA: Harvard Business School Press.

Macey, W.H. & Schneider, B. (2008a), "The meaning of employee engagement", *Industrial and Organizational Psychology*, **1**, 3–30.

Macey, W.H. & Schneider, B. (2008b), "Engaged in engagement: we are delighted we did it", *Industrial and Organizational Psychology*, **1**, 76–83.

Miller, G.A. (1956), "The magical number seven, plus or minus two", *Psychological Review*, **63**, 81–7.

Norretranders, T. (1998), *The User Illusion*, J. Sydenham, trans., New York: Penguin Books.

Ouellette, J.A. & Wood, W. (1998), "Habit and intention in everyday life: the multiple processes by which past behavior predicts future behavior", *Psychological Bulletin*, **124**, 54–74.

Sio, U.N. & Ormerod, T.C. (2009), "Does incubation enhance problem solving? A meta-analytic review", *Psychological Bulletin*, **135**, 94–120.

Uleman, J.S. & Bargh, J.A. (eds) (1989), *Unintended Thought*, New York: Guilford Press.

Wegner, D.M. & Bargh, J.A. (1998), "Control and automaticity in everyday life", in D. Gilbert, S.T. Fiske & G. Lindzey (eds), *Handbook of Social Psychology*, 4th edn, New York: McGraw-Hill, pp. 446–96.

Wegner, D.M. & Wheatley, T. (1999), "Apparent mental causation: sources of the experience of will", *American Psychologist*, **54**, 480–92.

Wilson, T.D. (2002), *Strangers to Ourselves: Discovering the Adaptive Unconscious*, Cambridge, MA: Belknap Press of Harvard University Press.

Wilson, T.D., Dunn, D.S., Bybee, J.A., Hyman, D.B. & Rotundo, J.A. (1984), "Effects of analyzing reasons on attitude–behavior consistency", *Journal of Personality and Social Psychology*, **47**, 5–16.

Wilson, T.D. & Kraft, D. (1993), "Why do I love thee? Effects of repeated introspection on attitudes toward the relationship", *Personality and Social Psychology Bulletin*, **19**, 409–18.

Wilson, T.D., Lisle, D., Schooler, J., Hodges, S.D., Klaaren, K.J. & LaFleur, S.J. (1993), "Introspecting about reasons can reduce post-choice satisfaction", *Personality and Social Psychology Bulletin*, **19**, 331–9.

Wilson, T.D. & Schooler, J.W. (1991), "Thinking too much: introspection can reduce the quality of preferences and decision", *Journal of Personality and Social Psychology*, **60**, 181–92.

22 Passion for work: work engagement versus workaholism
Marjan J. Gorgievski and Arnold B. Bakker

Introduction

> Nothing great in the world has been accomplished without passion.
> Georg Wilhelm Friedrich Hegel (1770–1831)

Is passion needed for excellent performance? The question of what predicts outstanding performance at work remains timely and relevant. The term "passion for work" emerged from qualitative research on entrepreneurs' motivation, and has been defined as a selfish, passionate love for the work (Shane et al., 2003). Passion for work has been proposed as key to understanding entrepreneurial behavior and performance. Passion is "the enthusiasm, joy, and even zeal that come from the energetic and unflagging pursuit of a worthy, challenging and uplifting purpose" (Smilor, 1997, p. 342[1]). However, few attempts have been made so far as to operationalize the construct, let alone relate it to entrepreneurial behavior.

The current chapter aims to fill this void, by focusing on work engagement and workaholism as two motivational concepts indicating "passion for work". In doing so, we follow a dualistic approach analogous to that of Vallerand and his colleagues (Vallerand et al., 2003; Vallerand, 2008), who studied the psychology of passion toward activities in other life domains such as sports and gambling. We shall first clarify the concepts of work engagement and workaholism, and summarize new empirical evidence on the relationship between work engagement, workaholism and job performance among self-employed individuals versus salaried employees. Finally, we shall outline implications for future research and practice.

Work engagement versus workaholism

Passion towards activities has been defined as a strong inclination toward an activity that people like, find important and in which they spend time and energy on a regular basis (Vallerand, 2008). Two forms of passion have been identified: "harmonious passion" and "obsessive passion". In the case of harmonious passion, the person controls the activity, and the activity occupies a significant, but not overpowering space in people's lives. In contrast, in the case of obsessive passion, the activity controls

the person, because of which this activity eventually takes dispropor-
tionate space in the person's identity and causes conflicts with other life
domains.

In the context of work, two motivational concepts have recently been
introduced that bear strong similarities to these two forms of passion.
The first concept is work engagement, which is theoretically linked to
harmonious passion. Work engagement is defined as "a positive, fulfilling,
work-related state of mind that is characterized by vigor, dedication, and
absorption" (Schaufeli et al., 2006, p. 195). Engaged employees have a
sense of energetic and effective connection with work activities. They work
hard (vigor), are involved with a feeling of significance, enthusiasm, inspiration, pride and challenge (are dedicated), and feel happily engrossed
(absorbed) in their work. Engaged employees exercise influence over
events that affect their lives – they are self-efficacious.

The second concept is workaholism, which can be conceptually linked
to obsessive passion. Many conceptualizations of workaholism exist (see,
for example, McMillan & O'Driscoll, 2004). In the present chapter, we
follow Scott et al. (1997), who summarized three features of workaholism.
The first feature is a behavioral component: workaholics are excessively
hard workers who spend a great deal of time doing work-related activities.
The second feature is a more private behavioral process: workaholics find
it difficult to disengage from work, and persistently and frequently think
about work when they are not at work. Third, workaholics follow an inner
drive, a compulsion, because of which their behavior is quite consistent
across situations. The third component can be considered a qualification
of the first two (see Schaufeli et al., 2006). We therefore distinguish two
aspects of workaholism based on these criteria: excessive working and
compulsive working.

Two recent studies provided evidence for the empirical distinction
between work engagement and workaholism (Taris et al., 2008, 2010).
Confirmatory factor analyses showed that work engagement, working
compulsively and working excessively can be distinguished as three separate factors. Moreover, both studies indicated that work engagement and
workaholism may relate to an innate tendency to excessively allocate
time and thoughts to work and get fully immersed. However, the crucial
difference between workaholism and work engagement is that workaholism lacks the positive affective (fun) component of work engagement.
In contrast, work engagement does not include the compulsive drive of
workaholism.

There are several parallels between, on the one hand, harmonious and
obsessive passion, and on the other hand, engagement and workaholism
(see Vallerand et al., 2003). For example, people who have developed a

harmonious passion for an activity will likely feel positive affect before, during as well as after performing the activity. In contrast, people who have developed an obsessive passion will likely experience negative emotions during and after performing the activity – guilt or feeling hassled – and frustration and agitation when prevented from engaging in the activity. This would imply that engaged employees experience positive emotions during work, whereas workaholics experience negative emotions.

Work engagement, workaholism and job performance

The concept of work engagement has been coined quite recently in occupational psychology (see Bakker & Leiter, 2010). In addition, although expanding, literature on workaholism to date still predominantly deals with its conceptualization and operationalization (Taris et al., 2008). Hence, studies that provide insight into the relationships between work engagement, workaholism and job performance in an integrated manner are still scarce. Theoretically, there are several reasons why work engagement fosters excellent job performance (Bakker & Leiter, 2010). We mention two explanations here (see also Bakker, ch. 19, this volume). The first explanation relates to positive affect and emotions accompanying work engagement, which have been related to a broader scope of attention and an ability to build up one's resources. Thus, engaged business owners and employees may be more open to new opportunities, and may be better able to build social networks and personal resources than individuals low in engagement. Second, work engagement has been found to predict good health (see Bakker & Leiter, 2010). In turn, good mental and physical health has been found to predict employee performance (Demerouti & Bakker, 2006), and long-term financial business performance for the self-employed (for example, Gorgievski et al., 2000, 2009).

Some studies have indeed shown that engaged employees perform better than their less engaged colleagues (for an overview, see Gorgievski et al., 2010). For example, several studies related general work engagement to both higher self-reported task and contextual performance, and service quality as perceived by customers in the service industry. Furthermore, in a diary study, daily engagement had a positive effect on same and next day's objective financial returns of a fast-food restaurant.

Concerning workaholism, results are more equivocal (see Schaufeli et al., 2006; Taris et al., 2008). According to some authors, workaholics are extremely productive. However, other researchers have claimed that workaholics' performance would not necessarily be good and may even be poor, and comes at a high price for both the individual and the organization. For example, workaholics would have a tendency to make projects larger and more complex than necessary. In addition, they may suffer from perfectionism, rigidity and inflexibility, and as a consequence would not delegate and potentially create conflicts and difficulties for their co-workers.

Unfortunately, virtually no empirical research has been carried out on the relationship between workaholism and job performance. In a qualitative study, Machlowitz (1980) found workaholics to be both satisfied and productive. In contrast, Burke (2001) found that workaholic behaviors were *not* associated with salary increases. It has been proposed that the conflicting findings can be attributed to differential effects of the two workaholism components (Schaufeli et al., 2006). Whereas working excessively may facilitate performance, working compulsively may impair performance – particularly performance influenced by positive emotions.

Two recent studies investigated relationships between work engagement, workaholism and job performance simultaneously.[2] The first study compared results of 1,900 Dutch employees and 262 Dutch self-employed individuals (Gorgievski et al., 2010). Study two replicated study one among 295 salaried employees and 196 self-employed individuals in Spain (Gorgievski, 2010). Both studies convincingly showed that work engagement relates positively to self-reported work performance. Using multigroup structural equation modeling, Study 1 showed positive associations of work engagement with task performance ($\beta = 0.39$, $p < 0.05$), contextual performance ($\beta = 0.42$, $p < 0.05$) and innovativeness ($\beta = 0.33$, $p<0.05$) for Dutch salaried employees, and with task performance ($\beta = 0.44$, $p<0.05$) and innovativeness ($\beta = 0.24$, $p<0.05$), for the Dutch self-employed subsample. Using regression analyses, study 2 showed work engagement predicted task performance, contextual performance and innovativeness for Spanish salaried employees (respectively $\beta = 0.42$; $\beta = 0.37$; and $\beta = 0.33$, all $p < 0.001$) and self-employed individuals (respectively $\beta = 0.42$; $\beta = 0.37$; and $\beta = 0.33$, all $p < 0.001$).

Results concerning workaholism were more equivocal. For Dutch salaried employees, a positive association was found between working excessively and innovativeness ($\beta = 0.39$, $p <0.05$). However, a negative suppressor effect of working compulsively was found at the same time ($\beta = -0.13$, $p < 0.05$). For the Dutch self-employed, similar patterns of working excessively and working compulsively were found concerning contextual performance ($\beta = 0.63$ versus $\beta = -0.47$, $p < 0.05$) and innovativeness ($\beta = 0.53$ versus $\beta = -0.40$, $p < 0.05$). For Spanish salaried employees, excessive working positively related to contextual performance ($\beta = 0.25$, $p < 0.001$). For Spanish self-employed, workers working compulsively positively related to task performance ($\beta = 0.25$, $p < 0.05$), which was completely suppressed by working excessively ($\beta = -0.23$, $p < 0.05$). Working excessively was positively associated with innovativeness ($\beta = 0.17$, $p < 0.05$).

Future research agenda

From previous research it can be concluded that work engagement overall relates positively to work performance. In contrast, results for workaholism are still highly equivocal. If we want to further our understanding of work engagement versus workaholism and their link to performance, it is crucial to theorize and empirically investigate *how* and *why* they are related.

The role of affect and emotions

One key discriminating element of work engagement versus workaholism is positive versus negative affect. An interesting avenue for future research would therefore be to investigate the differential effects of engagement versus workaholism on different performance criteria that have been shown to depend on affect and emotions, and investigate possible mediation processes. Research could, for example, focus on the role that work engagement and workaholism play in the way people perform specific tasks which prior research has shown to be influenced by affect, such as decision-making strategies (for example, Forgas & George, 2001). Different pathways from work engagement versus workaholism to similar outcomes could be investigated as well, such as the dual pathway to creative performance, one involving positive valence of affect through cognitive fluency, and another involving a negative activation component of affect through persistence (De Dreu et al., 2008).

The role of recovery

Workaholics are willing to make many sacrifices to derive satisfaction from their work. They work excessively long hours, continue in the evenings, during weekends and on holidays. Hence, workaholics may have insufficient time for recovery and suffer poor relationship quality (see Bakker et al., 2010). This lines up with results that have been found for obsessive and harmonious passion. Whereas in case of harmonious passion, people will quit their passionate activities when the costs become too high, people with an obsessive passion will continue at all costs, and will not shift their focus towards recuperation. Indeed, a recent diary study (ibid.) indicated that employees who scored highest on workaholism were most likely to work in the evening, whereas at the same time, they showed the strongest negative relationship between time spent on working in the evening and vigor, recovery, and happiness. Not surprisingly, in several studies, workaholism has been found predictive of ill-health among self-employed individuals (Taris et al., 2008) and employees (Burke, 2001; Burke & Matthiesen, 2004). As already mentioned, poor health may predict poor performance.

Reversed causation

Finally, recursive processes would be an interesting avenue for further research. For example, based on the cognitive activation theory of stress (Andreassen et al., 2007) it can be proposed that "enthusiastic" workaholism (comparable to work engagement) versus "non-enthusiastic" workaholism results from high versus low performance expectancies, which may be based on feedback concerning current performance. Propositions concerning reversed causation could also build on conservation of resources theory (Gorgievski & Hobfoll, 2008), which would typically focus on explanations centered on resource gains and losses. Positive gain spirals of work engagement and resources have been identified. Good job performance can be expected to be part of such self-enhancing gain spirals, because it may predict the gain of significant job and personal resources. Whether similar processes might occur involving workaholism remains tentative. The crucial issue may be that over a longer period of time, workaholics can be expected to persist longer in their work activities, despite prevailing evidence of performance deficiencies, than engaged workers do. Hence, they may get more deeply entrenched into negative spirals of poor work performance and resource loss in other domains. As a consequence, highly significant resources of belonging and self-esteem may become more and more dependent on their achievements in the work domain, which may be further ground for more severe workaholism.

Implications for research designs

Investigating processes demands the use of longitudinal designs. Excellent tools for studying daily processes centered on cognitions, affect and behavior on- and off-work would be diary studies and the day reconstruction method (Kahneman et al., 2004). This could be combined with a longer-term follow-up measurement of performance or ultimate goal attainment. Concerning possible reversed causal effects of performance on work engagement, both diary studies and long-term follow-up studies of a few months have proved useful, because such effects may occur both simultaneously and over longer time lags. Similar research designs might prove useful to investigate relationships between workaholism and job performance. However, because workaholism may be far more stable over time than work engagement, longer time lags of several years may be necessary in order to investigate whether work performance plays a role in how people develop workaholism. Researchers interested in investigating how workaholism develops may also wish to focus on specific samples, such as adolescents and people just entering the labor market.

Practical implications

To conclude, research on the relationship between work engagement, workaholism and performance to date shows that work engagement is indeed key to excellent performance. In contrast, there is no evidence showing that workaholism would improve (organizational) performance at all. Hence, for both employees and self-employed workers it is important not only to increase work engagement (see Bakker, ch. 19, this volume), but also to prevent workaholism. Interventions aimed at preventing workaholism are typically individual level. For example, in order to prevent negative feelings when not working, predictability and controllability may be increased through planning of activities. Workaholics may especially benefit from actively planning recovery activities, such as engaging in sports after work hours.

Notes

1. In order to keep the article short we have included a minimum number of references. A complete reference list can be obtained from the first author.
2. Details of both studies can be obtained from the first author.

References

Andreassen, C.S., Ursin, H. & Eriksen, H.R. (2007), "The relationship between strong motivation to work, workaholism and health", *Psychology and Health*, **22**, 615–29.
Bakker, A.B., Demerouti, E., Oerlemans, W. & Sonnentag, S. (2010), "Daily recovery among workaholics: A day reconstruction study of leisure activities", manuscript submitted for publication.
Bakker, A.B. & Leiter, M.P. (eds) (2010), *Work Engagement: A Handbook of Essential Theory and Research*, New York: Psychology Press.
Burke, R.J. (2001), "Workaholism components, job satisfaction, and career progress", *Journal of Applied Social Psychology*, 31, 2339–56.
Burke, R.J. & Matthiesen, S.B. (2004), "Workaholism among Norwegian journalists: antecedents and consequences", *Stress and Health*, **20**, 301–8.
De Dreu, C.K.W., Baas, M. & Nijstad, B.A. (2008), "Hedonic tone and activation level in the mood-creativity link: toward a dual pathway to creativity model", *Journal of Personality and Social Psychology*, **94**, 739–56.
Demerouti, E. & Bakker, A.B. (2006), "Employee well-being and job performance: where we stand and where we should go", in S. McIntyre & J. Houdmont (eds), *Occupational Health Psychology: European Perspectives on Research, Education and Practice*, Vol. 1, Maia, Portugal: ISMAI Publications, pp. 83–111.
Forgas, J.P. & George, J.M. (2001), "Affective influences on judgements and behavior in organizations: an information processing perspective", *Organizational Behavior and Human Decision Processes*, **86**, 3–34.
Gorgievski, M.J. (2010), "Entrepreneurial motivation: independence, money, self-realization and passion for work", in M. Luker & M. Laguna (eds), *Entrepreneurship: A Psychological Approach*, Prague: Oeconomica.
Gorgievski, M., Bakker, A.B. & Schaufeli, W.B. (2010), "Work engagement and workaholism: comparing the self-employed and employees on payroll", *Journal of Positive Psychology*, **5**, 83–86.
Gorgievski, M.J., Bakker, A.B., Schaufeli, W.B., Van der Veen, H.B. & Giessen, C.W.M. (2009), "Financial problems and psychological distress: Investigating reciprocal effects

among business owners", *Journal of Organizational and Occupational Psychology*, appeared online: 25 April 2009.

Gorgievski, M.J., Giesen, C.W.M., & Bakker, A.B. (2000). "Financial problems and health complaints among farm-couples: results of a ten-year follow-up study", *Journal of Occupational Health Psychology*, 5, 359–73.

Gorgievski, M.J. & Hobfoll, S.E. (2008), "Work can burn us out and fire us up", in J.R.B. Halbesleben (ed.), *Handbook of Stress and Burnout in Health Care*, Hauppauge, NY: Nova Publishers, pp. 7–22.

Kahneman, D., Krueger, A.B., Schkade, D., Schwarz, N. & Stone, A.A. (2004), "A survey method for characterizing daily life experience: the day reconstruction method", *Science*, **306**, 1776–80.

Machlowitz, M. (1980), *Workaholics: Living with Them, Working with Them*, New York: Simon & Schuster.

McMillan, L.H.W. & O'Driscoll, M.P. (2004), "Workaholism and health: implications for organizations", *Organizational Change Management*, **17**, 509–19.

Schaufeli, W.B., Taris, T.W. & Bakker, A.B. (2006), "Dr Jekyll or Mr Hyde? On the differences between work engagement and workaholism", in R J. Burke (ed.), *Research Companion to Working Time and Work Addiction*, Cheltenham, UK and Northampton, MA, USA: Edward Elgar, pp. 193–217.

Scott, K.S., Moore, K.S. & Miceli, M.P. (1997), "An exploration of the meaning and consequences of workaholism", *Human Relations*, **50**, 287–314.

Shane, S., Locke, E.A. & Collins, C.J. (2003), "Entrepreneurial motivation", *Human Resource Management Review*, **13**, 257–79.

Smilor, R.W. (1997), "Entrepreneurship, reflections on a subversive activity", *Journal of Business Venturing*, **12**, 341–6.

Taris, T.W., Geurts, S.A.E., Schaufeli, W.B., Blonk, R.W.B. & Lagerveld, S. (2008), "All day and all of the night: the relative contribution of workaholism components to well-being among self-employed workers", *Work and Stress*, **22**, 153–65.

Taris, T.W., Schaufeli, W.B. & Shimazu, A. (2010), "The push and pull of work: the differences between workaholism and work engagement", in Bakker & Leiter (eds), pp. 39–53.

Vallerand, R.J. (2008), "On the psychology of passion: in search of what makes people's lives most worth living", *Canadian Psychology*, **49**, 1–13.

Vallerand, R.J., Blanchard, C., Mageau, G.A., Koestner, R., Ratelle, C., Léonard, M. & Gagné, M. (2003), "Les passions de l'âme: on obsessive and harmonious passion", *Journal of Personality and Social Psychology*, **85**, 756–67.

23 Flow in work as a function of trait intrinsic motivation, opportunity for creativity in the job, and work engagement
Giovanni B. Moneta

Introduction

In the past decade or so, creativity has become increasingly important for organizations (Bharadwaj & Menon, 2000; Amabile & Khaire, 2008). Organizational creativity refers to the generation of novel and useful ideas or products within an organization, including processes, procedures and services (for example, Woodman et al., 1993). Individual and team creativity are at the heart of entrepreneurial business whenever a new enterprise is launched or an established business seeks expansion into a new and competitive market (for example, Amabile & Khaire, 2008), and foster other facets of performance such as product quality and financial gain (for example, Huth, 2008).

Despite the practical relevance of organizational creativity, managers have been somewhat reluctant in considering the maximization of employees' creativity as a managerial target. This might be due to three complementary reasons. First, managers tend to believe that employees' creativity is essentially unmanageable (Amabile & Khaire, 2008). Second, both managers and employees tend to have limited insight into the psychology of creative processes. Finally, managers tend to be concerned with the negative facets of employees' subjective experience – such as work stress and burnout – while neglecting positive facets – such as flow in work and work engagement – that are key to creative achievement.

In the early 1990s, Csikszentmihalyi (1996) investigated through interviews the experiences that 91 outstanding individuals had prior to conceiving novel ideas and seeing them recognized by peers as innovations. Intense and recurrent flow in work emerged as the main theme underlying each innovation across the domains of science, art and business. Flow is a state of profound task-absorption, enhanced cognitive efficiency, and deep intrinsic enjoyment that makes a person feel at one with the activity. Contrary to popular belief, flow is a state of concentration rather than one of happiness; this is because task-absorption reduces the rate by which emotions gain access to consciousness, and in some of the purer instances of flow the reduction is so drastic that high levels of hedonic tone cannot be experienced (Moneta & Csikszentmihalyi, 1999).

As Scott Cook, co-founder and CEO of Intuit, puts it "traditional management prioritizes projects and assigns people to them. But increasingly, managers are not the source of the idea" (as cited in Society for Human Resource Management, 2009, p. 3). In this juncture, because flow appears to be the single most important psychological factor behind the generation and development of novel ideas, employees' ability and opportunity to experience flow when engaged in work activities becomes a primary management target. The goal of this chapter is to propose a simple psychological model of flow in work that both managers and employees can use for probing new ways of fostering flow in work.

A model of flow in work

The social psychology of creativity (Amabile, 1996; Csikszentmihalyi, 1996) has consistently highlighted the importance of two factors contributing to flow in work and hence creative achievement: a personality trait (intrinsic motivation) and a work environment characteristic (opportunity for creativity in the job). Work or employee engagement has emerged more recently as an additional factor. The proposed model of flow in work includes all three factors as explanatory variables.

Intrinsic motivation is the tendency to engage in tasks because one finds them interesting, challenging, and enjoyable, whereas extrinsic motivation is the tendency to engage in tasks because of task-unrelated factors such as anticipation of rewards, surveillance, and competition (Deci & Ryan, 1985). Experimental manipulations have shown that intrinsic and extrinsic motivations are states that can rapidly change. Factors that can turn off intrinsic motivation and promote extrinsic motivation include surveillance and competition. Classic experimental studies have shown that, after inducing temporary states of extrinsic motivation, participants exhibit poorer concept attainment, impaired problem solving, and lower creative output (see review by Deci & Ryan).

Amabile et al. (1994) have later defined and operationalized intrinsic and extrinsic motivation as independent traits to be driven either by the engagement of work or by a means to some end that is external to the work itself. Self-determination theory characterizes flow as the marker of intrinsically motivated behavior (Deci & Ryan, 1985, p. 29). As such, trait intrinsic motivation should foster flow. Therefore, the following hypothesis is posited:

H1: Trait intrinsic motivation will be positively associated with the probability of experiencing flow in work.

McClelland (1985) argued that motivation promotes preferential behaviors and tunes affective reactions towards motivation-specific contexts of activity; thus, certain contexts are congenial to the expression of a type of motivation and hence strengthen the relationship between that motivation and performance. In particular, intrinsic motivation should be more conducive to flow and in turn to creativity if the task is 'heuristic' rather than 'algorithmic', that is, if discovering the steps for completing the task is part of the task itself (Amabile, 1996). Jobs differ in the extent to which they provide heuristic tasks, or opportunity for creativity to employees. As such, trait intrinsic motivation should foster flow in work only if a job offers sufficient opportunity for creativity. Therefore, the following hypothesis is posited:

H2: Opportunity for creativity in the job will moderate the positive relationship between trait intrinsic motivation and the probability of experiencing flow in work.

Work engagement is a pervasive and proactive dedication to work that is energized by positive emotions such as interest and vigor; it can be viewed as a relatively stable state of intrinsic motivation when engaging in work activities (for example, Salanova, & Schaufeli, 2008) that is influenced by both personal dispositions and work environment characteristics. Because of the positive emotions it fosters, work engagement is likely to facilitate flow in work over and beyond the effects of personal and environmental characteristics. Fredrickson's (1998; Fredrickson & Branigan, 2005) "broaden-and-build" model posits that positive emotions lead to a broadening of attentional focus and behavioral repertoire, as well as to enhanced cognitive flexibility and ability to process information that may threaten self-esteem, such as slow progress towards goals and risk of failure. As such, work engagement should promote adaptive forms of cognitive restructuring that in turn foster flow in work. Therefore, the following hypothesis is posited:

H3: Work engagement will be positively associated with the probability of experiencing flow in work.

Test of the model
The model was tested on an opportunity sample of 220 British workers, of which 116 were males, 98 females, and the remaining six of unknown gender. They were aged 21–65 years ($X = 35.0$, SD = 9.1) and came from a wide range of occupations including as main groups health specialists (27.3 percent) and managers (22.7 percent). All participants had earned an undergraduate degree and 203 also had a postgraduate degree.

Participants completed an electronic and expanded version of the Flow Questionnaire (Csikszentmihalyi, 2000) including: (a) a flow section for assessing whether participants experience flow and, if so, whether they experience it more intensely in work or leisure, (b) an open-ended description of job and main responsibilities for assessing opportunity for creativity in the job, (c) the Work Preference Inventory (Amabile et al., 1994) containing a 15-item, 4-point scale for measuring trait intrinsic motivation, and (d) a 7-item, 9-point scale (for example, "I enjoy the experience and the use of my skills" and "I get involved") for measuring work engagement.

Flow was assessed by providing participants with three flow quotations (for example, "I am so involved in what I am doing . . . I don't see myself as separate from what I am doing"), asking if they ever felt similar experiences, and what activities (up to five) they were engaged in when they had such experiences. Participants who reported flow activities were asked to select the activity which best represented the experience described in the quotations. Finally, two independent judges coded the selected activity as either "work" or "leisure" reaching 98 percent agreement and easily resolving the remaining differences.

Opportunity for creativity in the job, relative to the other jobs in the set, was assessed by four independent judges on a 5-point scale with anchors of 1 (low) and 5 (high). The consistency among raters was assessed using the intraclass correlation coefficient ($r = 0.80$). The opportunity score for each participant was calculated as the mean of the scores provided by the four judges.

The scale scores of trait intrinsic motivation and work engagement were calculated by averaging the scores of their constituent items. The internal consistency of the scales was assessed using Cronbach's alpha coefficient ($\alpha = 0.77$ and 0.90, respectively).

Seventy-four (33.6 percent) participants reported never having experienced flow, 87 (39.5 percent) reported having the most representative flow experience in a leisure activity, and the remaining 59 (26.8 percent) reported having the most representative flow experience in a work activity. Of those 87 who reported having the most representative flow experience in a leisure activity, only 29 (33.3 percent) reported at least one work activity in which they experienced flow. Unexpectedly, intrinsic motivation and opportunity for creativity were nearly uncorrelated ($r = 0.10$), whereas, as expected, work engagement correlated positively with both intrinsic motivation ($r = 0.28$) and opportunity ($r = 0.25$).

Multinomial logistic regression of "flow in work" versus "no flow" and "flow in leisure", respectively, revealed significant ($p < 0.001$) main effects of work engagement and intrinsic motivation, and a significant ($p < 0.017$)

intrinsic motivation by opportunity interaction. The estimated odds ratios indicated that work engagement is the main predictor of flow in work (OR = 1.9 per unit increment of work engagement for "flow in work" versus "no flow", and OR = 2.42 per unit increment of work engagement for "flow in work" versus "flow in leisure"). Figure 23.1 shows the estimated intrinsic motivation by opportunity interaction graphs. Opportunity moderates the positive relationship between intrinsic motivation and the probability of experiencing flow in work, in such a way that intrinsic motivation is associated with flow for high opportunity, and is either not associated or even negatively associated with flow for low opportunity. These findings provide preliminary support to each hypothesis and the model as a whole, and suggest directions for further study and applications.

Applications

Only two of five employees reported having flow in a work activity, and only one in four reported having the most representative flow experience in a work activity. As such, there seems to be a need to manage flow. In an ongoing study Maier et al. (2008) administered the Flow Questionnaire as a priming technique for an interview to a mixed sample of 13 employees and managers in the same company, and found that both employees and managers experience flow in work mostly on weekends, late at night, on the way to or from work, or when working from home. How can managers – who have a hard time managing their own flow – manage for their subordinates' flow? Two findings suggest pathways to solutions.

Trait intrinsic motivation was a predictor of flow only if the job offered sufficient opportunity for creativity. The implication of this finding is that if flow in work fosters creativity, then both employees and employers would suffer from a mismatch between motivation and opportunity. In particular, other things being equal (for example, expertise), employees high in intrinsic motivation should look for heuristic jobs, and managers should give heuristic jobs to employees who are high in intrinsic motivation. However, there was no correlation between intrinsic motivation and flow. This finding suggests that – because of constraints and/or lack of awareness – neither managers nor employees seek matching intrinsic motivation with opportunity for creativity. However, both managers and employees should do so, through mentoring, explicit target setting, and selective assignment of employees to jobs and tasks that offer the appropriate level of opportunity for creativity.

Work engagement was the best predictor of flow in work. This finding suggests that work engagement fosters flow in work, albeit a reverse effect is also possible. The main implication is that the antecedents of work engagement – such as the work environment characteristics assessed by

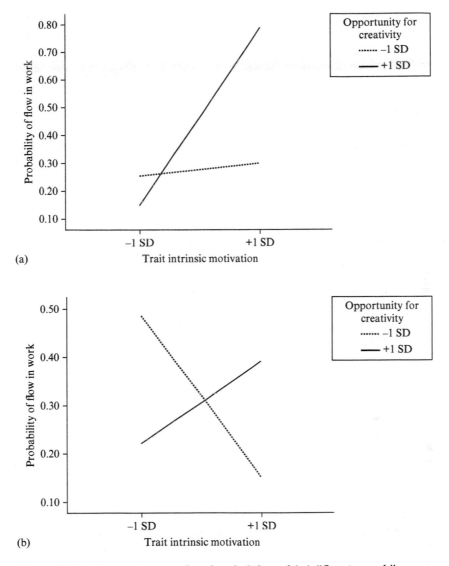

Figure 23.1 *Interaction graphs of probability of (a) "flow in work" vs. "no flow" and (b) "flow in work" vs. "flow in leisure" as a function of trait intrinsic motivation and opportunity for creativity in the job estimated using multinomial logistic regression*

the Q12 questionnaire (Gallup Organization, 1992–1999) – may also foster flow in work either directly or through the mediation of work engagement. As such, management strategies that enhance work engagement may also make flow in work more frequent and intense, and result in increased creativity.

Conclusions

The proposed model shows the relevance of work engagement, trait intrinsic motivation, and opportunity for creativity in fostering flow in work, and suggests directions for intervention. Managing for flow may prove expensive. Is it worth doing it?

On the one hand, skeptics may argue that flow is relevant only to those global companies that are at the forefront of innovation and hence badly need organizational creativity. On the other hand, creativity scholars have recently highlighted the importance of 'mini-c' creativity, a process-oriented concept of creativity as a learning process that energizes individual behavior even when it falls short of producing an output that would be appraised as creative by experts (for example, Beghetto & Kaufman, 2007), and organizational scholars have highlighted the pervasive contribution of 'mini-c' creativity to work (for example, Moneta et al., 2010). Moreover, it appears that job resources are both antecedents and consequences of flow in work (Salanova et al., 2006). Therefore, managing for flow is likely to climb the management agenda in the near future. Managing for engagement will need to be a key focus in this agenda.

References

Amabile, T.M. (1996), *Creativity in Context*, Boulder, CO: Westview Press.
Amabile, T.M., Hill, K.G., Hennessey, B.A. & Tighe, E. (1994), "The work preference inventory: assessing intrinsic and extrinsic motivational orientation", *Journal of Personality and Social Psychology*, 66, 950–67.
Amabile, T.M. & Khaire, M. (2008), "Creativity and the role of the leader", *Harvard Business Review*, 86, 100–109.
Beghetto, R.A. & Kaufman, J.C. (2007), "Toward a broader conception of creativity: a case for 'mini-c' creativity", *Psychology of Aesthetics, Creativity, and the Arts*, 2, 73–9.
Bharadwaj, S. & Menon, A. (2000), "Making innovation happen in organizations: individual creativity mechanisms, organizational creativity mechanisms or both?", *Journal of Product Innovation Management*, 17, 424–34.
Csikszentmihalyi, M. (1996), *Creativity: Flow and the Psychology of Discovery and Invention*, New York: Harper & Collins.
Csikszentmihalyi, M. (2000), *Beyond Boredom and Anxiety: Experiencing Flow in Work and Play*, 2nd edn, San Francisco, CA: Jossey-Bass.
Deci, E.L. & Ryan, R.M. (1985), *Intrinsic Motivation and Self-determination in Human Behavior*, New York: Plenum Press.
Fredrickson, B.L. (1998), "What good are positive emotions?", *Review of General Psychology*, 2, 300–319.
Fredrickson, B.L. & Branigan, C.A. (2005), "Positive emotions broaden the scope of attention and thought: action repertoires", *Cognition and Emotion*, 19, 313–32.

Gallup Organization (1992–1999), *Q12 Engagement Questionnaire,* Princeton, NJ: Gallup Organization.

Huth, T. (2008), *Organizing Cross-functional New Product Development Projects: The Phase-specific Effects of Organizational Antecedents*, Wiesbaden: Gabler.

Maier, E., Altman, Y. & Moneta, G.B. (2008), "Flow experiences at work: the relevance of context", London Metropolitan University.

McClelland, D.C. (1985), *Human Motivation*, Glenview, IL: Scott, Foresman.

Moneta, G.B., Amabile, T.M., Schatzel, E. & Kramer, S.J. (2010), "Multi-rater assessment of individual creative contributions to team projects in organizations", *European Journal of Work and Organizational Psychology*, **19**, 150–76.

Moneta, G.B. & Csikszentmihalyi, M. (1999), "Models of concentration in natural environments: A comparative approach based on streams of experiential data", *Social Behavior and Personality*, **27**, 603–37.

Salanova, M., Bakker, A.B. & Llorens, S. (2006), "Flow at work: evidence for an upward spiral of personal and organizational resources", *Journal of Happiness Studies*, **7**, 1–22.

Salanova, M. & Schaufeli, W.B. (2008), "A cross-national study of work engagement as a mediator between job resources and proactive behavior: a cross-national study", *International Journal of Human Resources Management*, **19**, 226–31.

Society for Human Resource Management (2009), "Innovative work teams in a challenging business environment", *Workplace Visions*, **1**, 1–6.

Woodman, R.W., Sawyer, J.E. & Griffin, R.W. (1993), "Toward a theory of organizational creativity", *Academy of Management Review*, **18**, 293–321.

PART IV

MANAGEMENT AND HR SYSTEMS, PRACTICES, AND PROCESSES: LEADERSHIP, TEAMS AND EMPOWERMENT

24 Engaging HR strategists: do the logics match the realities?

Paul Sparrow and Shashi Balain

Introduction

Our fundamental purpose in this chapter is to deconstruct the ideas behind engagement, and then put them back together again in to what we believe is a better human resources (HR) strategy, and one that will endure for several years to come. Specifically, we:

- present three ways in which engagement thinking is typically used by organizations;
- review what is meant by engagement in the practitioner and academic literature, noting that it is generally treated as an attitude;
- review evidence on the causes and consequences of engagement;
- ask whether, given its complexity and the existence of different employee segments, engagement can reasonably be managed;
- argue that it can be, but to do so needs the HR profession to much better understand the complexity of service models and the operational performance recipes that exist;
- argue that engagement is itself an outcome (that results in other outcomes such as satisfaction and commitment); and
- conclude that our understanding about engagement has advanced sufficiently now for organizations to identify *what* it is they want people to engage with. We develop the construct of performance beliefs to do this.

Three strategic uses of engagement

Our research inside organizations in the UK (Balain & Sparrow, 2009) shows that there are three streams of management thinking that have led to the importance of employee engagement as both an idea, and as a basis for HR strategy.

The first stream of engagement thinking is focused on internal marketing. The underpinning HR strategy targets specific communications, identified to resonate with key communities of employees, to develop a shared mental model of what is required of both the organization and the employee. The HR function then assesses the extent to which both sides appear to be delivering this "deal". Typically, an engagement survey is deployed as an employee feedback mechanism, and a management control device, to assess how well the organization seems to be doing and to see how the employees (as internal customers) feel about the proposition.

The second stream of engagement thinking is focused on process improvement. The underpinning HR strategy assumes that motivated employees, when also encouraged to act as good citizens, will self-manage, thereby taking initiative to improve on processes. Engagement is seen as part of a quid pro quo exchange relationship, a blanket of trust that can be put in place, whereby motivated employees pay back the investments made by the organization to motivate them by taking care in turn of the organization and its customers. While no claims are made by managers that this engagement strategy necessarily improves bottom-line perform-ance, engagement is seen as a necessary ingredient for – or precursor of – subsequent performance.

The third stream of engagement thinking assumes that engagement is predictive of corporate performance. This approach draws strongly on the customer services literature, which in turn draws upon models of emo-tional contagion and service climate. It suggests that there is a direct and causal engagement–service–profit chain such that more employee engage-ment means more business unit performance. The idea is that certain HR management (HRM) practices have the power to positively influence employee behaviour which in turn will lead to improved organizational performance.

In practice, organizations, or the people made responsible for manag-ing engagement strategies, often see a little of each of the above three purposes within their HR strategy. This is understandable, yet we argue also dangerous. The danger is that each of the three purposes outlined above makes very different assumptions about what needs to be measured under the label "engagement", what the consequence of positive or nega-tive scores on such measurement will be, and what remedial action by the organization needs to make dependent on that measurement.

In all too many businesses, engagement strategies are based more on acts of faith rather than any sound evidence. Is engagement a future-proof HR strategy? We argue that it is, but we must be far more critical about the construct and develop much better insight into how it influences organizational performance. We argue that HR strategists have taken far too much on trust.

Clarifying our terms
The concept of engagement has been understood, defined and used by prac-titioners, researchers and organizations in different ways. For example,

many practitioners draw upon the Gallup Workplace Audit (GWA, also popularly known as the Q12) to define and measure engagement. Gallup define engagement as the individual's involvement and satisfaction with as well as enthusiasm for work (Krueger & Killham, 2006). The Q12 has been found to have a highly significant relation to unit-level measures of company performance. A number of other well-known applied research and consultancy organizations have defined engagement along similar lines, often emphasizing the importance of discretionary effort as the key outcome or distinguishing feature of an engaged employee (Robinson et al., 2004). Such practitioner and consultancy views on engagement are largely driven from their respective survey databases, designed for problem description, tracking and benchmarking; and are based on an empirical model. However, there are three major problems with this approach:

1. Most survey-based research tends to infer causality in a way that suggests that it is the answers to the engagement items that can be presumed to "cause" performance, not merely correlate with it. However, there is very little support from their research designs that in reality enables them to make such a strong assertion.
2. There is little "construct validity" behind the items being clubbed under a single name of "engagement". The scale items are not embedded in any validated theory, so it is unclear exactly *how* they enable and deliver performance. Performance cannot always be predicted. If you do not know *how* a measure delivers its assumed outcome, you cannot manage the use of it.
3. Perhaps reflecting this, although all the major consultancies use different items in their measures, they all label it as "engagement".

Therefore, although much good work has been done by the consultancies on behalf of HR in bringing the issue of engagement to the attention of line managers, in the absence of a theoretical model explaining why a given set of items (that make up their definition of engagement) should improve organizational performance, we argue that there is no way organizations can design an evidence-based intervention to improve employee engagement. Furthermore academic researchers are not necessarily further advanced than practitioners in devising operational definitions of engagement that clearly differentiate the construct from other similar constructs. Academics are still debating some basic principles about engagement:

- Is engagement primarily a psychological reaction to job design and role, readily switched on or off?
- Is engagement the opposite of burnout?

● Is engagement more like an attitude (having the three components of cognition, affect and behaviour and therefore similar to the concept of job satisfaction) or is it a state of motivation (that is, a heightened state of goal-directed behaviour as in "vigor")?
● How is engagement any different to related ideas, such as job involvement, job commitment, and organizational citizenship behaviour?

The fact that we still have to ask such fundamental questions suggests that many organizations may be pursuing an HR strategy about which they know less than they think. While definitional debates are addressed elsewhere in this volume, for our purposes of deconstructing HR strategies, we need to recognize that most academic definitions of engagement generally do not clearly distinguish it from a number of other similar concepts – such as job involvement, job commitment, and organizational citizenship behaviour. There is ongoing debate in the academic literature as to the nature, dimensionality and measurement of engagement.

Causes and antecedents of engagement at the individual level
To understand what really causes engagement, and what it causes in turn, we need to embed the idea in a well-founded theory. We draw on social exchange theory (Saks, 2006, 2008), which sees feelings of loyalty, commitment and discretionary effort as all being forms of social reciprocation by employees to a good employer, to propose a "hearts and minds" way of thinking about engagement.

According to Saks, employee engagement is not the same thing as job satisfaction or organizational commitment; rather it is best thought of as an antecedent cause for these intermediate performance outcomes. Sparrow and Cooper (2003) noted that psychologists have tended to focus on five key antecedents. The five factors are: justice perceptions (Greenberg, 1990; Cropanzano, 1993); perceived organizational support (Eisenberger et al., 1986); support received from the supervisory relationship often measured using the concept of leader–member exchange (Settoon et al., 1996); the level of trust that exists in the employment relationship (Clark & Payne, 1997); and the existence of sound job characteristics and designs that provide employees with the necessary job variety and challenge, autonomy, control and power to deliver the strategy the organization wants them to engage with (Hackman & Oldham, 1980). These five factors establish the social climate, which in turn determines whether any significant engagement between the individual and the organization is likely to be developed subsequently, or if currently present, is likely to be maintained.

Once the appropriate social climate is in place, a number of key organization–individual linkages must be established (what we shall call "bonds"). Four bonds appear to be important at the individual level (Pierce et al., 2001). First, people need to have a motivation and incentive to bond – a reason and a desire for social membership (with the organization), which includes feelings and beliefs regarding the reasons why they want to maintain a relationship with, or their membership of the organization. Then there needs to be some organizational identification – whereby people use the characteristics of the organization they work for to define themselves. Then there has to be a process of internalization – the personal learning, internal recognition and personal adoption of the values and goals of the organization. Finally, there has to be a sense of psychological ownership – an attitudinal state of mind involving feelings of being psychologically tied to an object and a sense of responsibility and obligation that comes from the feeling of ownership. We argue that such bonds should be included in definitions and measures of engagement and that in practical terms, to reverse engineer performance, HR directors will need to know which specific, or bundle, of HR practices create these bonds which, in turn, improve intermediate performance factors. Collectively, according to Saks (2006, 2008), these bonds may create two conditions: job engagement (specific to the role task an employee is principally hired to perform) and organizational engagement (a more diffuse concept referring to other roles that an employee plays as a part of the larger organization). Each predicts different intermediate performance outcomes, such as job satisfaction (how content an individual is with his or her job), motivation (a state of arousal and reason to act towards a desired goal), discretionary effort, and job and organizational commitment (being bound intellectually or emotionally to a course of action and displaying sincere and steadfast purpose).

Can individual engagement be managed?
In our research (Balain & Sparrow, 2009) we found that in many organizations, HR directors have to consider survey results that are very difficult to interpret, with for example scores high in one part of the organization but low in another (even though both units may be performing acceptably), or some survey items linked with performance in some units but a different set of "high scores" on survey items predicting performance in another. In explaining the problem to us, one leading provider firm confided that when they analysed data for one of their major clients, there were as many as 20 different models of engagement inside the one organization.

From an academic perspective, too, there are sound reasons to argue that in terms of intermediate performance level outcomes, the answer to the question "does engagement predict performance" must be "it depends". We argue that:

1. Sometimes being in a good performing unit makes employees engaged, not the other way round. There is some reverse causation. Research on the link between job satisfaction and performance showed that organizational performance predicted as much job satisfaction as job satisfaction did performance.
2. The idea that employees are either engaged or not, and that once engaged, the impact on performance is linear (a bit more engagement equals just that bit more performance) is overly simple. Sometimes performance effects only begin at very extreme levels of engagement and this level of "sensitivity" may also change over time.
3. Sometimes engagement works through intermediate outcomes that can be measured at the individual level – being satisfied, committed, loyal. Other times it works through long causal chains where it takes only one or two events outside the influence of HR to break the whole chain, so good work on employee attitudes can soon get dissipated.
4. Sometimes engagement works only when it creates a collective capability – employees as a team display certain behaviours and emotions and understand how to correct their unit's performance. One unhappy person among a group of happy people can destroy unit performance, so average engagement benchmarks are problematic.
5. Different employees respond differently to the same work context and conditions, with such differences reflected in the way they answer survey questions. Similarly, the extent to which behavioural and survey responses will subsequently predict performance will depend on many other characteristics, such as tenure, age, gender, hours of work and pay patterns, what country they work in, whether they work for a core or a more peripheral organizational unit (for example, one that is outsourced), or whether they come from a particular organizational constituency (often important when an organization has developed through acquisitions). Such demographics can be direct causes of outcomes and performance. For example, new recruits might have a more positive perception of organizational life (because there is a novelty effect) while those with longer service may systematically be predisposed to more cynical assessments.

We argue that when analysed at the individual level, engagement is just too complex and too big a concept to be able to consistently and reliably explain much organizational performance. Organizations are measuring the symptoms of performance, not the causes.

Does engagement predict corporate performance (distal performance outcomes)?

If HR functions are to know how best to leverage employee engagement, they need to become expert in the "performance recipes" that bring together employee performance and important aspects of organizational performance. The link between employee engagement and organizational performance is then the last piece of the jigsaw that we need to consider.

Many HR functions fall back upon the service–profit chain to argue a link between engagement and performance. There are three broad models used to explain the service–profit chain: emotional contagion theory (Hatfield et al., 1993); service–profit chain theory (Heskett et al., 1997); and service climate theory (Schneider, 1990).

Taking service–profit chain thinking as the dominant model, we briefly restate the basic tenets and assumptions of the theory. It is considered that there is a clear link between employees' work experiences and financial performance in the service sector, with customer satisfaction acting as a critical intervening variable, based on a series of presumed causal links:

1. An association between employee and customer satisfaction (Heskett et al., 1997; Rucci et al., 1998; Schneider et al., 2000).
2. An association between employee perceptions of organization climate (especially its focus on service) and customer satisfaction levels; followed by an association between favourable climates and levels of employee satisfaction and commitment and generalizable relationships large enough to have substantial practical value between unit-level employee *satisfaction engagement* and these business-unit outcomes (Schmit & Allscheid, 1995; Johnson, 1996; Schneider et al., 1998; Harter et al., 2002; Ostroff et al., 2002).
3. An association between customer satisfaction and financial performance. By the mid-1990s, marketing research argued that levels of customer satisfaction and intentions to purchase were linked, although by the late 1990s, more mixed evidence began to emerge, with the link to intended purchases broadly supported but the link to actual purchases more uncertain (Zeithaml et al., 1996; Hennig-Thurau & Klee, 1997; Bolton, 1998; Verhoef et al., 2002).

The early empirical evidence therefore suggested that the service–profit chain is generally supported at the business-unit level, but the evidence is somewhat piecemeal and not as robust as we would like. As noted above, a number of longitudinal studies have found significant reverse causation between attitudes and performance, that is, it is the performance of the organization that may be feeding back to cause positive employee attitudes (Schneider et al., 2005; van Veldhoven, 2005).

Studies therefore also point to a long chain of events that occur between employee attitudes and organizational performance. A study of the service–profit chain in the retail banking sector (Gelade & Young, 2005) examined data for 1,407 branches in four retail banks. Although the service–profit chain was found to operate in the same way for all four banks, and customer satisfaction was found to mediate the relationship between commitment and sales achievement, the effect size was relatively small, with there being a more powerful direct impact of employee commitment on sales achievement. A range of climate factors (team climate, job enablers and supportive climate) were very predictive of employee commitment (predicting 83 percent of commitment) but this employee commitment predicted only 4 percent of customer satisfaction, and 8 percent of sales achievement. The problem with such long causal chains is also that it takes only one or two events outside the influence of HR to break the whole chain, so good work on employee attitudes can soon get dissipated.

Moreover, more recent research also shows that organizations are building complex service models that attempt to bring together a range of performance factors, such as internal service quality, customer expectations, organizational image or brand, perceived product or service quality, external service value, customer satisfaction, customer loyalty, customer advocacy, and so forth. Should a general relationship be assumed between employee satisfaction and customer satisfaction? Is there any difference in the sensitivity or influence that employee engagement has over organization performance when organizations operate to different service (industry) models? Why should we expect the same impact across all service (and indeed less service-orientated) settings?

There are a number of different service business models, and it has long been argued that the potential contribution that employee engagement should make to organizational performance must differ across these models: personal service versus non-personal or possession services (Lovelock, 1983); encounter/transactional versus relationship models (Gutek et al., 1999); collaborative, team-based and interdependence service versus single customer interface models (Ostroff & Harrison, 1992); and business-to-consumer (B2C) versus business-to-business (B2B) models, with the latter determined more by personal networks and reputation attributes than any emotional contagion (Ping, 2003).

A recent meta-analysis of 28 studies across these service models (Brown & Lam, 2008), found that employee satisfaction explains on average 6.3 percent of customer satisfaction and 8.4 percent of perceived service quality.

The relationship was stronger in personal service versus non-personal services – 16.8 percent in personal service business models. Therefore the answer to the question "How do employee attitudes (and the various measures we have noted that might reflect these) create each and every type of customer measure?" may well be different for each organization – part of a unique and competitive strategy – rather than something that is open to analytics that assess employee engagement as a construct that can be measured as a generic state that exists across organizations.

Once more controlled designs are used, measuring a wider range of individual-level attitudes and associated segment variables (such as demographics), then the link can become a lot clearer, but we argue that we should be very circumspect in overstating the impact that individual-level engagement can have on corporate performance measures. There is, we believe, a more fruitful way forward.

Conclusion: understanding organizational performance recipes and eliciting performance beliefs

Despite this evident complexity, we believe that HR directors have a powerful opportunity to step into the void that currently exists. We have argued that engagement can have positive impacts on distal performance outcomes – but that these effects are not as large as often claimed, and they work through complex dynamics and sets of causal processes. Relying on simple models that are assumed to apply across all business and service models and across all groups of employees, whatever their talent or strategic centrality, seems naive.

Managers have in their mind a "theory of action" that suggests the specific business performance outcomes that only result from engaged employees – what we call a "performance recipe". Some of these presumed links between employees and organizational-level performance outcomes may be misguided, and not eventually supported by data, but in other cases their knowledge and theories of action are extremely insightful. HR professionals need to help line managers understand the complex business performance benchmarks that they report to, and how these performance outcomes are best engineered through people management.

Given the three strategic uses of employee engagement as the basis of HR strategy outlined at the beginning of the chapter, we believe that if engagement is to be a meaningful concept for HR directors, then it has to be designed to work at the level of strategic business units or the team. It has to work at this level – business unit rather than individual – because HR directors need to "reverse engineer" the sorts of performance that are required by the particular service model that their organization pursues. They need to understand the logic that suggests why a particular range of employee attributes (whether you call them engagement or not) must serve a central purpose in delivering that type of performance.

Although most existing research still presents employee engagement as a fuzzy concept, arguably by drawing lessons across this research we do now have a useful understanding (if not a manageable one) of *how* engagement works as a psychological process. But from a strategic perspective, engagement is a rather sterile concept unless we know what it is that employees are expected to engage *with*.

By drawing upon some of the customer service literature we have shown that there is much to learn from other disciplines that have been working on similar concepts for a long time but in a different context. Given that some organizations treat the concept of engagement as an internal communication strategy, engagement implies that their employees must understand what the organization stands for, what the organization expects from them as employees, and what it is ready to provide them as employees in order to deliver the desired goals. This is more than just a very business-orientated psychological contract. It is a very performance-led understanding of engagement. In short, from the top to the bottom, engagement is intended to ensure that the organization shares a common corporate goal. When employees understand this objective, and live up to their organization's expectation, then that organization considers that it has an engaged workforce.

Moreover, when engagement is used by organizations as an integral part of their business strategy, it becomes much more of a two-way process. A wide range of activities become important for HR when they put in place the capability to be able to manage the process of engagement – a capability that shapes how the organization sends and receives signals to employees, how they interpret what those signals are telling them, and how they redirect strategic performance accordingly.

The time has come for the HR profession to de-layer the concept of engagement, as we have done in this chapter, and then rebuild it in a more meaningful way. In rebuilding it, there are two separate strategic needs:

1. Organizations need a two-way process to match their strategy with the way that their employees think, feel and act. Despite the conceptual limitations we have argued, many organizations will undoubtedly continue to use bellwether engagement surveys to check on these employee attitudes, unfortunately using a hotchpotch of multiple constructs comprising cognitions, affect, and behaviour. So, one important agenda is to improve and sharpen up this measurement in ways that we explained throughout this chapter.
2. From an applied perspective, however, the most fruitful way to think

about engagement is to look much more carefully at how attitudes are formed and how they get translated into real behaviour – and to take engagement back to its fundamental roots. The key question to ask is: what exactly is it the organization needs its workforce to engage with?

It is this second agenda that we believe is the most strategic, and the one to which HR functions should now turn their attention. HRM should ask what do they expect from an engaged workforce? The answer to this question will be different for different organizations and in fact may be quite different within an organization for its different business units.

If engagement is thought of as an attitude, which we have shown is the dominant way that it has been treated, then HR practitioners should apply what we know about how attitudes operate. Psychologists point out that there is a sequence through which any attitude (remembering that job satisfaction, commitment, or engagement are attitudes) ends up influencing behaviours. Fishbein and Ajzen (1974) made some important and useful distinctions in this area. Attitudes themselves are influenced by prior beliefs – it is beliefs that cause attitudes. In arriving at a belief, employees are coming to a subjective probability that there is a relationship between the object of their belief, and some other object, value, concept or attribute. What this means is that with regard to organizational performance, employees make a judgement about the ability of their organization to be able to deliver this. These beliefs then shape the specific attitudes that they hold. If we really want to know how good HR has been in delivering an engaged workforce, we need to measure the subjective probabilities that employees give to their organization's ability to deliver important aspects of the strategy and the necessary type of performance.

In short, we argue that when HR deals with engagement, it needs to separate out the cause from the effect. By measuring things such as how much do employees understand organizational goals, their emotional attachment to such goals, and willingness to provide discretionary effort, all one can know is the absence or presence of these employee attributes. Everything that is measured in the existing scales of engagement are outcomes – but these only really result from some underlying belief that employees have about certain work-related factors.

The results could be much better, much more robust, if we measured the causes of engagement. It would be far better if HR directs its measurement to what we call the "performance belief". This is a shared belief of a team that it has the required ability, resources, goal clarity and leadership attributes to achieve the desired performance outcomes. The performance belief is the cause, and being engaged to perform is the effect. As a strategic function, HR should be most concerned about how it needs to manage engagement – how it gets employees to believe in the vision of performance the organization offers. The inescapable reality, however, is that in shifting attention to how engagement is managed, it becomes clear that what you measure also has to change!

We argue that in thinking about engagement – especially when it is being used to manage performance – it makes far more sense to:

- measure and manage the beliefs about the underlying performance logic, and how that prescription of performance has been associated with the strategy. HR functions need to articulate whatever it is that they want their employees to engage with; and
- ask the harder questions – do employees believe in the strategy and the assumptions that the organization makes about the necessary performance? What are the probabilities of success on which their beliefs are based?

If such performance beliefs are to be assessed, then such assessment would need to look at:

- whether there is an understanding of the performance logic that underlies the operations of a given business unit among employees;
- how this performance logic can best be managed to deliver the strategy, that is, how people contribute value to the strategy;
- a belief that the unit has within its control the ability to deliver the performance recipe (this is a sort of collective efficacy – a shared belief in the team's ability);
- a belief that the business unit has the resources, capabilities to deliver this performance (that the unit they work in has a sense of agency);
- and finally, a belief that the immediate leadership has the right attributes to encourage and promote all the above stated beliefs. A belief in supportive leadership will be the key ingredient for employees to have a performance belief. If that is missing, nothing else will work.

In the final analysis, the concept of engagement would be better served if its cause is better understood, measured and managed. Unravelling performance beliefs, especially in organizations looking at employee engagement as a strategy to enhance organizational-level performance, should provide a much clearer line of sight between the individual, his or her engagement, and organizational performance. It is time the debate on engagement moves on to what lies beneath it, so that the HR function has the right measures to manage and can establish a construct that is directly related to an organization's performance and effectiveness.

References

Balain, S. & Sparrow, P.R. (2009), "Engaged to perform: a new perspective on employee engagement", Centre for Performance-led HR White Paper 09/04, Lancaster University Management School, Lancaster.

Bolton, R.N. (1998), "A dynamic model of the duration of the customer's relationship with a continuous service provider: the role of satisfaction", *Marketing Science*, **17**, 45–65.

Brown, S.P. & Lam, S.K. (2008), "A meta-analysis of relationships linking employee satisfaction to customer responses", *Journal of Retailing*, **84** (3), 243–55.

Clark, M.C. & Payne, R.L. (1997), "The nature and structure of workers' trust in management", *Journal of Organizational Behavior*, **18** (3), 205–24.

Cropanzano, R. (1993), *Justice in the Workplace: Approaching Fairness in Human Resource Management*, Hillsdale, NJ: Erlbaum.

Eisenberger, R., Huntington, R., Hutchison, S. & Sowa, D. (1986), "Perceived organizational support", *Journal of Applied Psychology*, **71** (3), 500–507.

Fishbein, M. & Ajzen, I. (1974), "Attitudes towards objects as predictors of single and multiple behavioral criteria", *Psychological Review*, **81**, 29–74.

Gelade, G.A. & Young, S. (2005), "Test of a service profit chain model in the retail banking sector", *Journal of Occupational and Organizational Psychology*, **78** (1), 1–22.

Greenberg, J. (1990), "Organizational justice: yesterday, today and tomorrow", *Journal of Management*, **16**, 399–432.

Gutek, B.A., Bhappu, A.D., Liao-Troth, M.A. & Cherry, B. (1999), "Distinguishing between service relationships and encounters", *Journal of Applied Psychology*, **84** (2), 218–33.

Hackman, J.R., & Oldham, G.R. (1980), *Work Redesign*, Reading, MA: Addison-Wesley.

Harter, J.K., Schmidt, F.L. & Hayes, T.L. (2002), "Business-unit-level relationship between employee satisfaction, employee engagement, and business outcomes: a meta-analysis", *Journal of Applied Psychology*, **87**, 268–79.

Hatfield, E., Cacioppo, J.T. & Rapson, R.L. (1993), "Emotional contagion", *Current Directions in Psychological Science*, **2** (3), 96–9.

Hennig-Thurau, T. & Klee, A. (1997), "The impact of customer satisfaction and relationship quality on customer retention: a critical reassessment and model development", *Psychology and Marketing*, **14**, 737–64.

Heskett, J.L., Sasser, W.E. & Schlesinger, L.A. (1997), *The Service Profit Chain*, New York: Free Press.

Johnson, J.W. (1996), "Linking employee perceptions of service climate to customer satisfaction", *Personnel Psychology*, **49**, 831–51.

Krueger, J. & Killham, E. (2006), "Why Dilbert is right?", *Gallup Management Journal*, March, 9.

Lovelock, C.H. (1983), "Classifying services to gain strategic marketing insights", *Journal of Marketing*, **47** (3), 9–20.

Ostroff, C. & Harrison, D.A. (1992), "The relationship between satisfaction, attitudes and performance: an organizational level analysis", *Journal of Applied Psychology*, **77** (6), 963–74.

Ostroff, C., Klinicki, A.J. & Clark, M.A. (2002), "Substantive and operational issues of response bias across levels of analysis: an example of climate–satisfaction relationships", *Journal of Applied Psychology*, **87**, 355–68.

Pierce, J.L., Kostova, T. & Dirks, K.T. (2001), "Toward a theory of psychological ownership in organizations", *Academy of Management Review*, **26** (2), 298–310.

Ping, R.A. (2003), "Antecedents of satisfaction in a marketing channel", *Journal of Retailing*, **79**(4), 249–58.

Robinson, D., Perryman, S. & Hayday, S. (2004), "The drivers of employee engagement", Institute of Employment Studies Report No. 408, IES, Brighton.

Rucci, A.J., Kirn, S.P. & Quinn, R.T. (1998), "The employee-customer-profit chain at Sears", *Harvard Business Review*, January–February, 83–97.

Saks, A.M. (2006), "Antecedents and consequences of employee engagement", *Journal of Managerial Psychology*, 21(6), 600–619.

Saks, A.M. (2008), "The meaning and bleeding of employee engagement: how muddy is the water?", *Industrial and Organizational Psychology*, 1, 40–43.

Schmit, M.J. & Allscheid, S.P. (1995), "Employee attitudes and customer satisfaction: making theoretical and empirical connections", *Personnel Psychology*, 48, 521–35.

Schneider, B. (1990), *Organizational Climate and Culture*, San Francisco, CA: Jossey-Bass.

Schneider, B., Bowen, D.E., Ehrhart, M.G. & Holcombe, K.M. (2000), "The climate for service", in N.M. Ashkanasy, C.P.M. Wilderom & M.F. Peterson (eds), *Handbook of Organizational Culture and Climate*, Thousand Oaks, CA: Sage, pp. 1–36.

Schneider, B., Ehrhart, M.G., Mayer, D.M., Saltz, J.L. & Niles-Jolly, K. (2005), "Understanding organization-customer links in service settings", *Academy of Management Journal*, 48, 1017–32.

Schneider, B., White, A. & Paul, M. (1998), "Linking service climate and customer perceptions of service quality: test of a causal model", *Journal of Applied Psychology*, 83, 150–63.

Settoon, R.P., Bennett, N. & Liden, R.C. (1996), "Social exchange in organizations: perceived organizational support, leader-member exchange and employee reciprocity", *Journal of Applied Psychology*, 81, 219–27.

Sparrow, P.R. & Cooper, C.L. (2003), *The Employment Relationship: Key Challenges for HR*, London: Butterworth-Heinemann.

van Veldhoven, M. (2005), "Financial performance and the long-term link with HR practices, work climate and job stress", *Human Resource Management Journal*, 15(4), 30–53.

Verhoef, P.C., Franses, P.H. & Hoekstra, J. (2002), "The effect of relational constructs on customer referrals and number of services purchased from a multi-service provider: does age of relationship matter?", *Journal of the Academy of Marketing Science*, 30, 202–16.

Zeithaml, V.A., Berry, L.L. & Parasuraman, A. (1996), "The behavioural consequences of service quality", *Journal of Marketing*, 60, 31–46.

25 Organizational socialization and newcomer engagement
Alan M. Saks and Jamie A. Gruman

Introduction

Employee engagement has received a great deal of attention in the last five years, especially in the popular press and among consulting firms. It has often been touted as the key to an organization's success and competitiveness. Numerous writers have sung the praises of engagement as a key driver of individual attitudes, behavior, and performance as well as organizational performance, productivity, retention, financial performance, and even shareholder return (Harter et al., 2002; Bates, 2004; Baumruk, 2004; Richman, 2006). It has also been reported that employee engagement is on the decline and there is a deepening disengagement among employees today (Bates, 2004; Richman, 2006). For example, roughly half of all Americans in the workforce are not fully engaged or they are disengaged, leading to what has been referred to as an "engagement gap" that is costing US businesses $300 billion a year in lost productivity (Kowalski, 2003; Bates, 2004; Johnson, 2004).

Given the importance of employee engagement to organizations, combined with the deepening disengagement among workers today, a key issue is how to promote the engagement of employees. As noted by May et al. (2004), "Engagement is important for managers to cultivate given that disengagement, or alienation, is central to the problem of workers' lack of commitment and motivation" (p. 13). In this chapter, we argue that organizations should begin to cultivate employee engagement as soon as a new hire joins an organization and that the socialization process represents an especially opportune time for getting employees engaged. Along these lines, we offer a new approach to organizational socialization – "socialization resources theory" – that provides a framework for socializing new hires with a focus on engagement.

Employee engagement

According to Kahn (1990), engagement refers to "the harnessing of organization members' selves to their work roles; in engagement, people employ and express themselves physically, cognitively, and emotionally during role performances" (p. 694). It is the "simultaneous employment and expression of a person's 'preferred self' in task behaviors that promote connections to work and to others, personal presence (physical, cognitive, and emotional), and active, full role performance" (p. 700). On the other hand, personal disengagement refers to "the uncoupling of selves from work roles; in disengagement, people withdraw and defend themselves physically, cognitively, or emotionally during role performances" (p. 694).

More generally, engagement means to be psychologically present when occupying and performing an organizational role (Kahn, 1990, 1992). When people are psychologically present they are attentive, connected, integrated, and focused in their role performances (Kahn, 1992). People vary in the extent to which they draw on themselves in the performance of their roles or what Kahn (1990) refers to as "self-in-role". Thus, when people are engaged they keep their selves within the role they are performing.

In his ethnographic study, Kahn (ibid.) found that a person's degree of engagement was a function of the experience of three psychological conditions of self-in-role: psychological meaningfulness, psychological safety, and psychological availability.

"Psychological meaningfulness" involves the extent to which people derive meaning from their work and feel that they are receiving a return on investments of self-in-role performances. People experience meaningfulness when they feel worthwhile, useful, and valuable and when they are not taken for granted. Workplaces that offer incentives for investments of self-in-role are more likely to lead to psychological meaningfulness.

"Psychological safety" has to do with being able to employ and express one's true self without fear of negative consequences to one's self-image, status, or career (ibid.). According to Kahn, social systems that are predictable, consistent, and non-threatening provide a greater sense of psychological safety.

"Psychological availability" refers to the belief that one has the physical, emotional, and psychological resources required to invest one's self in the performance of a role. Workplaces that provide employees with physical, emotional, and psychological resources necessary for role performances will have employees who are more engaged. In addition, Kahn found that individuals were more available to place themselves fully into their roles when they were able to cope with work and non-work demands.

May et al. (2004) investigated Kahn's (1990) three psychological conditions and found that meaningfulness, safety, and availability were significantly related to engagement. They also found that job enrichment and role fit were positive predictors of meaningfulness; rewarding co-worker and supportive supervisor relations were positive predictors of safety while adherence to co-worker norms and self-consciousness were negative predictors; and resources available was a positive predictor of psychological availability while participation in outside activities was a negative predictor.

Although much has been written about employee engagement, there has been little attention paid to the engagement of new hires in either the engagement or the socialization literature. In fact, as described in the next section, socialization research has focused primarily on knowledge acquisition and learning.

Organizational socialization
Organizational socialization "is the process by which an individual comes to appreciate the values, abilities, expected behaviors, and social knowledge essential for assuming an organizational role and for participating as an organizational member" (Louis, 1980, pp. 229–30). Given the increased mobility of the workforce over the last decade, organizational socialization has become more important than ever. According to Bauer et al. (2007), "new employee socialization or 'onboarding' is a key issue for organizations and newcomers alike as individuals undergo socialization more often in their careers and organizations deal with newcomers more often because of elastic personnel needs" (p. 707).

However, organizational socialization has been viewed mainly, and narrowly, as a cognitive sense-making process that involves information and knowledge acquisition. In fact, early reviews of organizational socialization described it as primarily a learning process (Fisher, 1986). In their review, Saks and Ashforth (1997) presented a multilevel process model of organizational socialization in which information and learning was at the core of the model. The most recent review described learning as the heart of socialization (Ashforth et al., 2007).

Although socialization research has studied the extent to which newcomers are knowledgeable of their roles, there has been little consideration of the degree to which newcomers occupy or fully engage in their roles. Furthermore, the evidence suggests that most organizations use an informational approach to orienting new hires and managers view the on-boarding process primarily as a means of providing newcomers with information (Rollag et al., 2005).

However, organizations today are facing an array of challenges like never before – global competition, new technology, economic uncertainty and a volatile economy, labor shortages, internal restructuring, and the recruitment and retention of talent. Today's fast-paced and competitive environment means that socialization programs have to do more than provide newcomers with exhaustive amounts of information (ibid.). In the remainder of this chapter, we describe a new, broader approach to organizational socialization that focuses on socialization resources which can foster newcomer engagement.

Organizational socialization and newcomer engagement

Kahn's (1990) research has some important implications for the engagement of newcomers. As indicated earlier, he found that three psychological conditions – meaningfulness, safety, and availability – predicted employee engagement. These three conditions seem especially important for newcomers. That is, given their vulnerability and uncertainty, newcomers need to feel worthwhile, useful, valuable and not taken for granted (meaningfulness); they need to feel that they can express themselves fully and be themselves without fear of negative consequences to their self-image, status, or career (safety); and they need to have the physical, emotional, and psychological resources to be available to perform their job and roles and to cope with work and non-work demands (availability). Given the high levels of uncertainty and anxiety generally associated with the organizational entry process, these three psychological conditions seem especially relevant for the engagement of newcomers.

Socialization practices that might lead to the three psychological conditions can be organized according to the job demands–resources (JD–R) model. According to the JD–R model, the work environment can be divided into demands and resources. "Job demands" refer to physical, psychological, social, or organizational features of a job that require sustained physical and/or psychological effort from an employee that can result in physiological and/or psychological costs. Common job demands include work overload, job insecurity, role ambiguity, and role conflict. "Job resources" refer to physical, psychological, social, or organizational features of a job that are functional in that they help achieve work goals, reduce job demands, and stimulate personal growth, learning, and development. Job resources can come from the organization (for example, pay, career opportunties, job security), interpersonal and social relations (supervisor and co-worker support, team climate), the organization of work (role clarity, participation in decision making), and from the task itself (skill variety, task identify, task significance, autonomy, performance feedback) (Bakker & Demerouti, 2007).

The basic premise of the JD–R model is that high job demands exhaust employees' physical and mental resources and lead to a depletion of energy and health problems. Job resources are motivational and can lead to positive attitudes, behavior, and well-being (ibid., 2007). The motivational

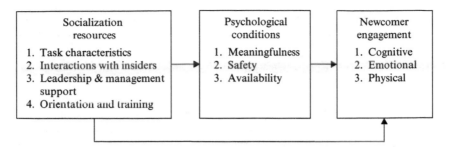

*Figure 25.1   Socialization resources, psychological conditions, and
newcomer engagement*

potential of job resources can be intrinsic because they facilitate growth, learning, and development, or extrinsic because they are instrumental for achieving work goals (ibid.). Job resources are also important because they help individuals cope with job demands and have been found to buffer the effect of job demands on job strain (ibid., 2008).

Research on the JD–R model has found that job demands are related to burnout and health problems while job resources predict work engagement, extra-role performance, and organizational commitment (Bakker & Demerouti, 2007). Along these lines, we argue that socialization programs should provide resources to newcomers that will lead to Kahn's (1990) three psychological conditions and engagement. We refer to this approach to organizational socialization as "socialization resources theory" (SRT). Figure 25.1 presents a model of the relationships between socialization resources, psychological conditions, and newcomer engagement.

SRT and newcomer engagement
In this section, we describe socialization resources for developing the three psychological conditions and newcomer engagement. Although our focus is on providing newcomers with resources, it is important to recognize that minimizing job demands is also important. As noted by Kahn (1990), individuals are more available to become engaged when they can cope with work and non-work demands. In the socialization literature, various job and role demands such as role ambiguity, role conflict, role overload, work/home conflict, and unmet expectations have been found to be negatively related to socialization outcomes (Saks & Ashforth, 2000). Thus, to the extent that newcomers experience these demands, they are less likely to be psychologically available or engaged. However, by providing newcomers with socialization resources, they are more likely to experience the psychological conditions and to cope with job demands.

Task characteristics
Task characteristics from Hackman and Oldham's (1980) job characteristics model have been found to be important job resources. For example, Bakker and Demerouti (2007) identified skill variety, task identity, task significance, autonomy, and performance feedback as job resources at the task level and several studies have found that autonomy/job control and performance feedback are related to positive work outcomes (Bakker et al., 2004, 2007; Schaufeli & Bakker, 2004). Similarly, Kahn (1990) found that task characteristics are important for the experience of psychological meaningfulness. In particular, work that is challenging, clearly delineated, varied, creative, and autonomous is most likely to be associated with the experience of psychological meaningfulness. In addition, people feel safer when they have some control over their work. Kahn (1992) also suggested that incentives are necessary to experience meaningfulness, and suggested that formal and informal reward systems must support the psychological conditions that produce engagement.

In the socialization literature, Katz (1980) noted that task significance and feedback are especially important for newcomers during the first three or four months, but by six months all of the job characteristics are important at least in terms of satisfaction and performance. Colarelli et al. (1987) found that autonomy and feedback were positively related to job attitudes and behaviors in a sample of newly hired entry-level accountants, and Feldman and Weitz (1990) found that job design characteristics were positively related to summer interns' job attitudes.

While each of the core job characteristics can aid in the development of engagement, it is important to recognize that the extent to which they are effective might depend on when they are provided during the entry-socialization period. Katz (1978, 1980) found that newcomers' receptivity to each of the job characteristics varies according to the stage of socialization, so it is possible that the influence of job characteristics on the psychological conditions and engagement might vary during the first six months of entry.

Interactions with insiders
Research on the JD–R model has found that social support from one's supervisor and co-workers is related to a number of positive work outcomes and negatively related to disengagement and burnout (Demerouti et al., 2001; Bakker et al., 2004; Schaufeli & Bakker, 2004). Supervisor support has also been found to buffer the negative effects of job demands (Bakker et al., 2007).

Kahn (1990) identified work interactions as important for psychological meaningfulness. In particular, individuals experienced meaningfulness when they had rewarding interpersonal interactions with co-workers and clients. He also argued that interpersonal relationships foster psychological safety when they are supportive and trusting. In addition, one can obtain emotional resources through interpersonal relationships with others which can enhance one's psychological availability.

In the socialization literature, organizational insiders play a key role in the socialization and adjustment of newcomers (Anakwe & Greenhaus, 1999) not only for the information they provide (see Ostroff & Kozlowski, 1992) but also as a main source of social support (Bauer et al., 1998). The importance of social support and interpersonal interactions with insiders has long been considered a critical factor in the socialization of newcomers (Katz, 1980; Fisher, 1985). In fact, it has been argued that interactions with insiders is "the primary vehicle through which initial socialization occurs" (Reichers, 1987, p. 278).

A study on the availability and helpfulness of socialization practices found that the three most important socialization aids reported by new hires were interaction with peers, supervisor, and senior co-workers (Louis et al., 1983). Fisher (1985) found that social support from co-workers and supervisors reduced the level of unmet expectations stress of newly hired nurses and predicted several adjustment outcomes. As well, positive relationships between newcomers and insiders are associated with a number of socialization outcomes (Bauer et al., 1998). Research on socialization tactics has found that social tactics are the strongest predictors of newcomer adjustment (Saks et al., 2007). Chatman (1991) found that attending firm-sponsored social events was positively related to person–organization fit, and Rollag et al. (2005) found that the development of a broad network of relationships with co-workers is a key factor for the rapid adjustment of newcomers.

Baker and Dutton (2007) suggested that socialization processes can be used to help newcomers develop high-quality connections with others through activities such as job rotation, mentoring programs, and special occasions designed for incumbent employees to meet new recruits. Many studies have shown that social support in the form of mentoring is related to positive outcomes among protégés including promotions, salary, job satisfaction, career satisfaction, organizational commitment, helping behavior, person–organization fit, and self-esteem (Chatman, 1991; Allen et al., 2004; Underhill, 2006; Eby et al., 2008; Kammeyer-Mueller & Judge, 2008). Meta-analyses demonstrate that mentoring is associated with individuals' perception of promotion opportunities (Underhill, 2006) and the belief that they will advance in their careers (Allen et al., 2004) – outcomes that are likely to result in higher levels of engagement.

Leadership and management support
Research on the JD–R model has found that managers can have a significant impact on the engagement of subordinates. For example, job resources including supervisory coaching and supervisory support have been shown to be related to subordinate engagement (Schaufeli and Bakker, 2004; Hakanen et al., 2006). Kahn (1990) identified management style and process as important for psychological safety. In particular, supportive, resilient, and clarifying management led to greater psychological safety. Supportive management allows individuals to try new things and to fail without the fear of negative consequences.

Leaders or the managers of newcomers are especially important for successful socialization. For example, Bauer and Green (1998) found that manager behavior predicted newcomer role clarity, performance efficacy, and feelings of acceptance, and Kammeyer-Mueller and Wanberg (2003) found that leader influence predicted newcomers' political knowledge and turnover.

Leaders can also play an important role in creating an environment in which newcomers experience meaningfulness and safety. Additionally, leaders can provide newcomers with resources that can enhance their availability. As suggested in the previous section, one of the most important resources that leaders provide newcomers is social support. Leaders can also develop engagement by providing assignments and experiences that are challenging, provide some control, autonomy, performance feedback, and allow for participation in decision making.

Orientation and training
Formal orientation and training are considered to be the main socialization process for many newcomers (Saks & Ashforth, 1997). Most organizations provide new hires with some form of formal orientation training (Wanous & Reichers, 2000). Although both orientation and training programs have been found to be associated with socialization outcomes (Saks, 1995; Klein & Weaver, 2000), they tend to focus solely or primarily on imparting information (Wanous & Reichers, 2000).

In the context of Kahn's (1990) psychological conditions, orientation and training are especially relevant for providing newcomers with resources that will make them feel available to fully engage in their roles (for example, knowledge and skills required to perform one's work tasks). Training can also make newcomers feel more secure about their ability to perform their job, thereby lowering their anxiety and increasing feelings of availability.

Orientation and training can be an important source of self-efficacy enhancing information. As described by Kahn (ibid.), individuals are more available when they feel secure, and an important dimension of security is self-efficacy. Saks (1995) found that a greater amount of entry training was related to the self-efficacy of newly hired entry-level accountants. Schaufeli and Salanova (2007) suggest that promoting self-efficacy is the cornerstone of fostering engagement through work training. Thus, orientation and training programs should incorporate the main sources of self-efficacy information (mastery experiences, vicarious learning, social persuasion, and physiological arousal) (Bandura, 1986).

Finally, orientation and training programs can be an important resource for preparing newcomers to cope with job demands. As described by Kahn (1990), individuals are more ready and available to engage in their roles when they can cope with various demands and when they have the ability to engage in coping strategies. In this respect, one type of orientation program that seems especially important is ROPES (realistic orientation programs for new employee stress). According to Wanous and Reichers (2000), ROPES are designed to teach coping skills for the most important stressors that newcomers will encounter. The basic principles for the design of ROPES involve: (i) realistic information that forewarns newcomers about typical disappointments to expect and possible adjustment problems, as well as how to cope by setting goals and taking action; (ii) general support and reassurance; (iii) the behavior modeling method of training; (iv) self-control of thoughts and feelings; and (v) targeting specific stressors for newcomers.

Preliminary research

We have begun to investigate relationships among socialization resources, Kahn's (1990) three psychological conditions, and newcomer engagement in a study of 111 newly-hired co-op students. These newcomers completed an online survey of their early employment experiences approximately three months after beginning their new job. To assess the socialization resources we asked them to indicate to what extent their early experiences included the following: control over the timing of their work (job control – timing), control over the methods used in executing their work (job control – methods), feedback received from superiors and co-workers (feedback), support from their supervisors (perceived supervisor support), the ability to participate in and influence organizational decisions (participative decision making), and the ability to receive rewards for good performance (rewards). We also assessed Kahn's three psychological conditions and engagement.

Correlation analyses indicated that all of the socialization resources were related to at least two of the psychological conditions, while feedback and perceived supervisor support were related to all three psychological conditions. In addition, all three psychological conditions were related to engagement with meaningfulness being the most strongly related (r = 0.77, p < 0.01). Further, all of the socialization resources were related to engagement, with correlations ranging from 0.29 to 0.52. These findings provide some preliminary evidence for the linkages between socialization resources, psychological conditions, and newcomer engagement.

Implications for practice

SRT offers organizations a new way to think about the socialization of newcomers. Rather than thinking about what new hires need to know and overwhelming them with information, they should think about what resources newcomers need to experience meaningfulness, safety, and availability. Along these lines, managers should ask three questions when socializing newcomers: (i) What do newcomers need to experience *meaningfulness*? (ii) What do newcomers need to feel *safe*? and (iii) What do newcomers need to feel *available* to perform their job? The answers to these questions can identify socialization resources that new hires need to become engaged.

In addition, a socialization resource audit can be conducted to identify the extent to which the socialization resources are being provided and where there is a need for additional resources. This might lead to changes in the tasks and jobs that newcomers are assigned, the amount and type of social support available for them, the actions and involvement of co-workers and supervisors in the socialization process, and the content of orientation and training programs.

Conclusion

We have argued that one of the most opportune times to develop employee engagement is during organizational socialization. Given the importance of engagement for individuals and organizations, socialization programs can no longer just involve providing newcomers with large amounts of information. Socialization programs should focus on the resources newcomers need to experience meaningfulness, safety, and availability, and to fully engage themselves in their new job and role. Socialization programs designed along these lines offer organizations the opportunity to foster employee engagement from the first day new recruits begin their jobs.

References

Allen, T.D., Eby, L.T., Poteet, M.L., Lentz, E. & Lima, L. (2004), "Career benefits associated with mentoring for protégés: a meta-analysis", *Journal of Applied Psychology*, **89**, 127–36.

Anakwe, U.P. & Greenhaus, J.H. (1999), "Effective socialization of employees: socialization content perspective", *Journal of Managerial Issues*, **11**, 315–29.

Ashforth, B.E., Sluss, D.M. & Harrison, S.H. (2007), "Socialization in organizational contexts", in G.P. Hodgkinson & J.K. Ford (eds), *International Review of Industrial and Organizational Psychology*, Chichester, UK: Wiley, pp. 1–70.

Baker, W. & Dutton, J.E. (2007), "Enabling positive social capital in organizations", in J. Dutton & B.R. Ragins (eds), *Exploring Positive Relationships at Work*, New York: Lawrence Erlbaum, pp. 325–45.

Bakker, A.B. & Demerouti, E. (2007), "The job demands–resources model: state of the art", *Journal of Managerial Psychology*, **22**, 309–28.

Bakker, A.B. & Demerouti, E. (2008), "Towards a model of work engagement", *Career Development International*, **13**, 209–23.

Bakker, A.B., Demerouti, E. & Verbeke, W. (2004), "Using the job demands–resources model to predict burnout and performance", *Human Resource Management*, **43**, 83–104.

Bakker, A.B., Hakanen, J.J., Demerouti, E. & Xanthopoulou, D. (2007), "Job resources boost work engagement, particularly when job demands are high", *Journal of Applied Psychology*, **99**, 274 84.

Bandura, A. (1986), *Social Foundations of Thought and Action: A Social Cognitive Theory*, Englewood Cliffs, NJ: Prentice-Hall.

Bates, S. (2004), "Getting engaged", *HR Magazine*, **49**(2), February, 44–51.

Bauer, T.N., Bodner, T., Erdogan, B., Truxillo, D.M. & Tucker, J.S. (2007), "Newcomer adjustment during organizational socialization: a meta-analytic review of antecedents, outcomes, and methods", *Journal of Applied Psychology*, **92**, 707–21.

Bauer, T.N. & Green, S.G. (1998), "Testing the combined effects of newcomer information seeking and manager behavior on socialization", *Journal of Applied Psychology*, **83**, 72–83.

Bauer, T.N., Morrison, E.W. & Callister, R.R. (1998), "Organizational socialization: a review and directions for future research", in G.R. Ferris (ed.), *Research in Personnel and Human Resources Management*, Vol. 16, Greenwich CT: JAI Press, pp. 149–214.

Baumruk, R. (2004), "The missing link: the role of employee engagement in business success", *Workspan*, **47**, 48–52.

Chatman, J.A. (1991), "Matching people and organizations: selection and socialization in public accounting firms", *Administrative Science Quarterly*, **36**, 459–84.

Colarelli, S.M., Dean, R.A. & Konstans, C. (1987), "Comparative effects of personal and situational influences on job outcomes of new professionals", *Journal of Applied Psychology*, **72**, 558–66.

Demerouti, E., Bakker, A.B., Nachreiner, F. & Schaufeli, W.B. (2001), "The job demands–resources model of burnout", *Journal of Applied Psychology*, **86**, 499–512.

Eby, L.T., Allen, T.D., Evans, S.C., Ng, T. & DuBois, D.L. (2008), "Does mentoring matter? A multidisciplinary meta-analysis comparing mentored and non-mentored individuals", *Journal of Vocational Behavior*, **72**, 254–67.

Feldman, D.C., & Weitz, B.A. (1990), "Summer interns: factors contributing to positive developmental experiences", *Journal of Vocational Behavior*, **37**, 267–84.

Fisher, C.D. (1985), "Social support and adjustment to work: a longitudinal study", *Journal of Management*, **11**, 39–53.

Fisher, C.D. (1986), "Organizational socialization: an integrative review", in K.M. Rowland & G.R. Ferris (eds), *Research in Personnel and Human Resources Management*, Vol. 4, Greenwich, CT: JAI Press, pp. 101–45.

Hackman, J.R. & Oldham, G.R. (1980), *Work Redesign*, Reading, MA: Addison-Wesley.

Hakanen, J.J., Bakker, A.B. & Schaufeli, W.B. (2006), "Burnout and work engagement among teachers", *Journal of School Psychology*, **43**, 495–513.

Harter, J.K., Schmidt, F.L. & Hayes, T.L. (2002), "Business-unit level relationship between employee satisfaction, employee engagement, and business outcomes: a meta-analysis", *Journal of Applied Psychology*, **87**, 268–79.

Johnson, G. (2004), "Otherwise engaged", *Training*, **41**(10), 4.

Kahn, W.A. (1990), "Psychological conditions of personal engagement and disengagement at work", *Academy of Management Journal*, **33**, 692–724.

Kahn, W.A. (1992), "To be full there: psychological presence at work", *Human Relations*, **45**, 321–49.

Kammeyer-Mueller, J.D. & Judge, T.A. (2008), "A quantitative review of mentoring research: test of a model", *Journal of Vocational Behavior*, **72**, 269–83.

Kammeyer-Mueller, J.D. & Wanberg, C.R. (2003), "Unwrapping the organizational entry process: disentangling multiple antecedents and their pathways to adjustment", *Journal of Applied Psychology*, **88**, 779–94.

Katz, R. (1978), "Job longevity as a situational factor in job satisfaction", *Administrative Science Quarterly*, **23**, 204–23.

Katz, R. (1980), "Time and work: toward an integrative perspective", in B. Staw and L.L. Cummings (eds), *Research in Organizational Behavior*, Vol. 2, Greenwich, CT: JAI Press, pp. 81–127.

Klein, H.J. & Weaver, N.A. (2000), "The effectiveness of an organizational-level orientation training program in the socialization of new hires", *Personnel Psychology*, **53**, 47–66.

Kowalski, B. (2003), "The engagement gap", *Training*, **40**(4), 62.

Louis, M.R. (1980), "Surprise and sense making: what newcomers experience in entering unfamiliar organizational settings", *Administrative Science Quarterly*, **64**, 226–51.

Louis, M.R., Posner, B.Z. & Powell, G.N. (1983), "The availability and helpfulness of socialization practices", *Personnel Psychology*, **36**, 857–66.

May, D.R., Gilson, R.L. & Harter, L.M. (2004), "The psychological conditions of meaningfulness, safety and availability and the engagement of the human spirit at work", *Journal of Occupational and Organizational Psychology*, **77**, 11–37.

Ostroff, C. & Kozlowski, S.W.J. (1992), "Organizational socialization as a learning process: the role of information acquisition", *Personnel Psychology*, **45**, 849–74.

Reichers, A.E. (1987), "An interactionist perspective on newcomer socialization rates", *Academy of Management Review*, **12**, 278–87.

Richman, A. (2006), "Everyone wants an engaged workforce, how can you create it?", *Workspan*, **49**, 36–9.

Rollag, K., Parise, S. & Cross, R. (2005), "Getting new hires up to speed quickly", *MIT Sloan Management Review*, **46**, 35–41.

Saks, A.M. (1995), "Longitudinal field investigation of the moderating and mediating effects of self-efficacy on the relationship between training and newcomer adjustment", *Journal of Applied Psychology*, **80**, 211–25.

Saks, A.M. & Ashforth, B.E. (1997), "Organizational socialization: making sense of the past and present as a prologue for the future", *Journal of Vocational Behavior*, **51**, 234–79.

Saks, A.M. & Ashforth, B.E. (2000), "The role of dispositions, entry stressors, and behavioral plasticity theory in predicting newcomers' adjustment to work", *Journal of Organizational Behavior*, **21**, 43–62.

Saks, A.M., Uggerslev, K.L. & Fassina, N.E. (2007), "Socialization tactics and newcomer adjustment: a meta-analytic review and test of a model", *Journal of Vocational Behavior*, **70**, 413–46.

Schaufeli, W.B. & Bakker, A.B. (2004), "Job demands, job resources, and their relationship with burnout and engagement: a multi-sample study", *Journal of Organizational Behavior*, **25**, 293–315.

Schaufeli, W.B. & Salanova, M. (2007), "Work engagement: an emerging psychological concept and its implications for organizations", in S.W. Gilliland, D.D. Steiner & D.P. Skarlicki (eds), *Managing Social and Ethical Issues in Organizations*, Greenwich, CT: Information Age Publishing, pp. 135–77.

Underhill, C.M. (2006), "The effectiveness of mentoring programs in corporate settings: a meta-analytic review of the literature", *Journal of Vocational Behavior*, **68**, 292–307.

Wanous, J.P. & Reichers, A.E. (2000), "New employee orientation programs", *Human Resource Management Review*, **10**, 435–51.

26 Staff nurse work engagement in Canadian hospital settings: the influence of workplace empowerment and six areas of worklife

Heather K.S. Laschinger

Introduction

Employee engagement is an important concept for human resources practitioners charged with creating fulfilling work environments that contribute to organizational productivity (Maslach & Leiter, 1997, 2008; Schaufeli & Bakker, 2004; Bakker & Demerouti, 2008). Engagement has been found to be related to important organizational outcomes, including in-role and extra-role behavior (Bakker et al., 2004), better mental and physical health (Schaufeli & Bakker, 2004; Hakanen et al., 2006), and organizational performance (Xanthopoulou et al., 2009). Clearly, work engagement is a worthy goal in any organization. However, creating work environments that promote employee engagement is challenging in today's constrained economic climate.

Members of Canada's workforce find themselves in dramatically changed working conditions after more than a decade of organizational restructuring and recent economic challenges. The healthcare sector in Canada, particularly nurses, the largest occupational health provider group, has been hard hit by these conditions. Increased job insecurity, job stress and job dissatisfaction resulting from heavy workloads and increased overtime hours have had negative effects on nurses' workplace health and well-being. Nurses experience the highest number of sick days of any occupation in Canada (O'Brien-Pallas et al., 2004) and an international study of nurses in five countries revealed that almost a third of nurses were dissatisfied with their working conditions (Aiken et al., 2002). These conditions hamper efforts to recruit and retain qualified nurses. Nursing is facing a severe shortage, estimated to reach 113,000 nurses by 2011, with many nurses nearing retirement in the next 5 years and fewer people choosing nursing as a profession (Canadian Nurses Association, 2002). Research has shown that workplaces that empower employees to accomplish work goals in meaningful ways result in more positive psychological relationships with work and lower burnout (Cho et al., 2006).

Burnout is a major cause of nurse job dissatisfaction and turnover (Hayes et al., 2006), whereas work engagement has the opposite effect, resulting in lower turnover intentions (Schaufeli & Bakker, 2004) and greater organizational commitment (Hakanen et al., 2006). Thus, it is imperative for management to find ways to create empowered work environments that promote greater work engagement to retain nurses currently in the system and to attract newcomers to the profession (Laschinger et al., 2003).

Maslach and Leiter (1997) argued that a mismatch between people and their work settings in some or all of six areas of worklife (workload, control, reward, community, fairness, values) results in burnout. The link between these six areas of worklife and burnout has been established in several studies (Maslach & Leiter, 2008). However, the relationship of these areas of worklife to Schaufeli and Bakker's (2004) notion of work engagement, characterized by vigor, dedication, and absorption, and the role of workplace empowerment in the process has not been established. An examination of these relationships is appropriate in light of the current focus of positive organizational psychology on building strengths rather than preventing deficits in organizations. Management can play an important role in creating empowering work environments that engage nurses in their work and promote retention.

Kanter's theory of structural power in organizations is a useful theoretical framework for guiding managers' efforts to create empowering work conditions that engage employees in their work. According to Kanter (1979, 1993), power is derived from the ability to access and mobilize the support, information, and resources required to accomplish work in a meaningful way; and from having access to opportunities to learn and grow in the organization. Employee empowerment depends on the extent to which they have access to these sources of empowerment within the organization (Kanter, 1979).

It is reasonable to expect that when employees are empowered to accomplish their work in meaningful ways, they are more likely to experience a fit between their expectations and their actual working conditions. In terms of Maslach and Leiter's (1997) six areas of worklife, they will feel that they have reasonable workloads, control over their work, have good working relationships, are treated fairly, are rewarded for their contributions, and that their values are congruent with organizational values. As a result, they are more likely to be more engaged in their work.

The purpose of this study was to test a model derived from Kanter's (1977, 1993) work empowerment theory that links staff nurses' perceptions of structural empowerment to their perceived fit with six key areas of worklife, and work engagement in acute care hospitals across Ontario. The model integrated Kanter's structural empowerment theory, Maslach and Leiter's (1997) worklife model, and Schaufeli and Bakker's (2004) conceptualization of work engagement.

Theoretical framework
According to Kanter, power is the ability to mobilize resources "to get things done" (1977, p. 66). This view of power differs from the notion of power as dominance or coercion. Power comes from formal and informal power systems within the organization (Kanter, 1977, 1993). Formal power results from jobs that are visible, support discretion, and are central to organizational goal accomplishment. Informal power refers to the personal relationships or alliances within the organization, such as with sponsors, peers, and other co-workers.

Kanter (1977, 1993) contended that both formal and informal power provide access to two organizational structures that create an empowering workplace. First, the structure of opportunity, which entails opportunities to move in the organization and/or opportunities to learn and grow, is important to employee engagement with work and influences employee commitment (Kanter, 1979). Employees lacking opportunity are less motivated to succeed and less productive. The structure of power in the workplace comes from three main sources or "lines" (ibid., p. 66). These "power lines" consist of information, support, and resources necessary for realizing organizational goals. Together, these structures influence employees' ability to meaningfully accomplish their work (structural empowerment). Without access to these structures, employees experience powerlessness (Kanter, 1977, 1993). Kanter argued that managers are key to ensuring employee access to these sources of structural empowerment in the work settings.

Related research

Empowerment
Kanter's theory has been tested extensively in nursing settings. Empowerment has been linked to important outcomes such as job satisfaction (Laschinger et al., 2001), commitment (Laschinger et al., 2000), burnout (Cho et al., 2006), perceptions of respect and fairness (Laschinger & Finegan, 2005a), and turnover intentions (Nedd, 2006). Leadership has been shown to be a strong predictor of structural empowerment in nursing settings (Upenieks, 2002; Greco et al., 2006). Laschinger et al. (1999) found that leader empowering behaviors and workplace empowerment together were predictive of greater work effectiveness. Thus, structural empowerment has been shown to be an important element in nurses' relationships with their work.

Six areas of worklife model of engagement/burnout

Maslach and Leiter (1997) suggested that person/job match in six areas of worklife is an organizational antecedent of burnout/work engagement. "Workload" refers to the relationship of work demands with time and resources (ibid.). Increasing workload is consistently related to higher emotional exhaustion. "Control" refers to role clarity within the organization that provides a clear understanding of expectations and responsibilities, and leads to efficiency, decreased stress, and autonomy in the work setting (ibid.). "Reward" refers to recognition associated with time invested in the work setting. "Community" includes the quality of social relationships within the organization. "Fairness" in the workplace involves trust, openness, and respect, and managerial support (Leiter & Harvie, 1997). Finally, "values", refers to the congruence between organizational goals and expectations and those of its employees (Maslach & Leiter, 1997). According to Leiter and Maslach (2004), a mismatch in one or more of these areas of worklife can result in burnout, beginning with emotional exhaustion, and subsequently cynicism and feelings of inefficacy. Maslach and Leiter (1997) argued that management must address areas of mismatch to promote work engagement.

Using data from 6,815 employees, Leiter and Maslach (2004) found that mismatched areas of worklife most strongly related to emotional exhaustion were workload, fairness, and control, whereas cynicism was most strongly related to a mismatch between values and fairness. Personal efficacy was most strongly related to control and values. Laschinger and Finegan (2005b) found that staff nurse empowerment had a direct effect on all areas of worklife, which in turn, influenced physical and mental health through burnout.

Work engagement

Schaufeli and Bakker (2004) defined "engagement" as "a positive, fulfilling, work-related state of mind that is characterized by vigor, dedication, and absorption" (p. 295). "Vigor" is defined as high levels of energy and mental resilience at work, manifested by high effort and persistence when difficulty arises. "Dedication" refers to "a sense of significance, enthusiasm, inspiration, pride, and challenge" (ibid., p. 295). "Absorption" refers to a state of being completely immersed in one's work, such that awareness of time disappears, and there is a reluctance to detach oneself from work. Engagement results from access to job resources in the workplace, such as, supportive supervision and development opportunities. Engagement serves as a motivational factor for employee performance, and subsequently leads to greater work satisfaction and organizational commitment. On the other hand, burnout results from heavy job demands in the presence of insufficient resources to meet these demands.

Schaufeli and colleagues have linked work engagement to important work outcomes in a variety of occupational groups, such as job satisfaction (Demerouti et al., 2001), organizational commitment and performance (Salanova et al., 2003), lower absenteeism, and turnover intentions (Schaufeli & Bakker, 2004). Also, working conditions similar to structural empowerment have been found to be significant predictors of work engagement. For instance, organizational resources, such as supportive supervision, performance feedback, and job autonomy are predictive of work engagement (Demerouti et al., 2001). In nursing, lack of decisional involvement, rewards, job autonomy, supportive management, and feedback on performance have been significantly associated with low levels of engagement (Demerouti et al., 2000). Numerous studies have shown that engagement is a mediating mechanism between organizational conditions and job performance and work behaviors, such as proactive work behaviors and extra-role behaviors (Salanova et al., 2003).

Hypothesized model
A model linking structural empowerment to work engagement through Maslach and Leiter's (1997) six areas of worklife model was tested (see Figure 26.1). Higher levels of empowerment were hypothesized to result in greater fit within the six areas of worklife, which, in turn, would lead to greater work engagement. Empowered staff nurses are better able to meet the challenges that confront them in their workplace (Kanter, 1993), which would logically result in greater perceptions of fit between their expectations of their workplace and actual conditions. In other words, they would

Figure 26.1 Hypothesized model

be more likely to experience a sense of control over their workload, feel rewarded for their accomplishments, experience a sense of community with their peers, feel that they are treated fairly within the organization, and that their personal values are aligned with those of the organization. Consequently, employees experience higher levels of engagement because they are more able to mobilize resources and create their own jobs (Bakker & Demerouti, 2008).

Method

Design and sample
A cross-sectional survey design was used to test the hypothesized model. A provincial registry list was used to obtain a random sample of 500 Registered Nurses (RNs) working full- or part-time in acute-care hospitals in Ontario. Of these, 35 did not meet the study inclusion criteria and were removed. The final sample consisted of 322 useable questionnaires (69 percent response rate).

The majority of the respondents were female (97.2 percent), averaging 42 years of age, 18 years of nursing experience, and 10 years of employment in their current workplace. Most nurses were married (74.5 percent), employed full-time (68.4 percent) and were diploma prepared (79 percent). Most (46.7 percent) worked in medical–surgical units.

Instruments
The Conditions of Work Effectiveness Questionnaire-II (CWEQ-II) measures the six components of structural empowerment (opportunity, information, support, resources, formal power, and informal power). Items are rated on a 5-point Likert scale ranging from 1 (none) to 5 (a lot). A total empowerment score is obtained by summing the six subscales (score range: 6–30). Reported subscale reliability coefficients range from 0.67 to 0.95 (Laschinger et al., 2001).

The Areas of Worklife Scale (AWS) measures the six areas of worklife (Maslach & Leiter, 1997) and consists of 29 items measured on a 5-point Likert scale which respondents rate from 1 (strongly disagree) to 5 (strongly agree). Job–person match is reflected by a score > 3.0 (Leiter & Maslach, 2004). Subscale reliability coefficients range from 0.70 to 0.82 (ibid.).

The short form of the Utrecht Work Engagement Scale (UWES) (Schaufeli et al., 2002) was used to measure the three components of work engagement: vigor (3 items), dedication (3 items), and absorption (3 items). Items are rated on a 5-point Likert scale. Schaufeli and Bakker (2004) reported evidence of convergent and divergent validity for the original UWES.

Data collection
Data were collected by mail survey using strategies advocated by Dillman (2000) to maximize return rate. Three mailings were carried out. Three weeks after the first mailing, a reminder letter was sent, followed by a second questionnaire three weeks later. Questionnaire packages included a gift certificate as a token of appreciation. The return rate was (69 percent).

Data analysis
Structural equation modeling techniques were used to test the hypothesized model using AMOS 16.0 (Arbuckle, 2007). The following fit criteria were used to evaluate fit of the model: the chi-square (χ^2), the comparative fit index (CFI), the incremental fit index (IFI), the normed fit index (NFI), and the root mean square error of approximation (RMSEA).

Results

Descriptive statistics
The means and standard deviations of the major study variables are presented in Table 26.1. Overall, staff nurses perceived their work setting to be only somewhat empowering, with greatest access to opportunity and least access to formal power. Community, value congruence, and rewards had the most highly rated degree of match in the six areas of worklife. The greatest degree of mismatch in the areas of worklife were workload, fairness, and control, respectively.

Nurses' engagement scores were highest for dedication, followed by vigor and absorption. This level of engagement is somewhat lower than previous research with dentists (Hakanen et al., 2005). Hakanen et al. (2006) also found that the dedication component of engagement was highest in their study of Finnish teachers, a profession often compared to nursing in terms of its demographic profile and work demands.

Testing the hypothesized model
The initial hypothesized model did not meet conventional criteria suggested by Hu and Bentler (1999) for a good fit with the data (χ^2 = 135.3, df = 13, NFI = 0.83, IFI = 0.84, CFI = 0.84, RMSEA = 0.15). The modification indices suggested additional theoretically defensible paths among the six areas of worklife. The final model revealed a good fit (χ^2 = 23.87, df = 12, NFI = 0.97, IFI = 0.99, CFI = 0.98, RMSEA = 0.05). As can be seen in Figure 26.2, overall structural empowerment was significantly and positively related to all six areas of worklife. The strongest relationships were with feeling rewarded for one's contributions (0.51) and a

Table 26.1 Means, standard deviations, Cronbach's alphas, and correlations of variables

Variable	M	SD	Alpha	1	2	3	4	5	6	7	8	9	10	11
1 Empowerment	18.43	3.44	0.89	—										
2 Workload	2.73	0.69	0.73	0.322*	—									
3 Control	2.99	0.76	0.62	0.525*	0.305*	—								
4 Reward	3.19	0.77	0.76	0.519*	0.316*	0.428*	—							
5 Community	3.57	0.77	0.84	0.348*	0.160*	0.359*	0.312*	—						
6 Fairness	2.71	0.68	0.70	0.524*	0.246*	0.495*	0.409*	0.295*	—					
7 Values	3.21	0.93	0.75	0.500*	0.321*	0.388*	0.368*	0.258*	0.481*	—				
8 Engagement	3.90	0.79	0.90	0.454*	0.222*	0.430*	0.480*	0.370*	0.318*	0.431*	—			
9 Vigor	3.72	0.87	0.78	0.354*	0.338*	0.396*	0.432*	0.315*	0.268*	0.420*	0.889*	—		
10 Dedication	4.36	0.95	0.85	0.529*	0.220*	0.428*	0.459*	0.425*	0.341*	0.443*	0.885*	0.680*	—	
11 Absorption	3.61	0.86	0.72	0.305*	0.024	0.307*	0.376*	0.229*	0.226*	0.269*	0.870*	0.678*	0.638*	—

Note: *$p < 0.05$.

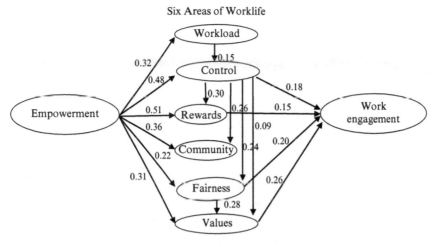

Note: χ² = 23.87; IFI= 0.99; CFI = 0.98; RMSEA = 0.05.

Figure 26.2   Final model

sense of control over one's work (0.48). Among the AWS subscales, the control scale played an important role in both directly and indirectly influencing engagement. Beyond directly predicting engagement, control was also predictive of greater rewards, better relationships with peers, a greater sense of fairness in the organization, and person–organization value congruence. Additionally, rewards, fairness and value congruence had a direct influence on work engagement. In sum, four of the six areas of worklife were shown to mediate the influence of empowerment on engagement. Furthermore, beyond directly influencing work engagement rewards, fairness and value congruence partially mediated the influence of control on engagement. Empowerment was also significantly related to manageable workload which in turn was related to control. Although influenced by empowerment, neither workload nor community directly influenced engagement.

Discussion
The findings support Kanter's (1977, 1993) contention that organizational structures within the workplace are essential in shaping and enhancing the worklife of employees. The analysis suggests that the impact of empowerment on engagement was partially mediated by perceived fit with various areas of worklife described in Maslach and Leiter's model. That is, empowerment influenced nurses' engagement through its effect on their psychological relationships with their work. These results support

Kanter's theory (1977, 1993), as well as those of Maslach and Leiter (1997) and Schaufeli and Bakker (2004), and highlight the key role of access to empowering work structures in creating positive responses to work and work engagement.

The findings suggest that when managers create organizational structures that empower nurses to carry out their job in optimal ways, they foster a greater sense of fit between nurses' expectations of worklife quality and organizational goals and processes, thereby promoting greater work engagement. Management must explore new evidence-based leadership strategies in today's radically changed workplace. Structural empowerment is an important leadership strategy for shaping positive work environments that engage nurses. In this study, having access to empowerment structures was important for nurses' feelings that they had control over their work and that their contributions to organizational goals were recognized. These factors have been shown to be important for nurse retention (Irvine & Evans, 1995). The findings are consistent with those of Greco et al. (2006), who found that staff nurses felt more empowered when their leaders promoted autonomy and shared decision making, and had confidence in employees. Fairness also was strongly related to empowerment in this study. These findings also corroborate previous results that linked empowerment to respect, trust, and organizational justice (Laschinger & Finegan, 2005a). The link in the current study between empowerment and work engagement is important, in light of issues currently facing the nursing profession: nurse recruitment and retention, job dissatisfaction, and high rates of absenteeism.

Control was a key area of worklife in this study, having a direct effect on four other aspects of nurses' relationships with work, as well as being related to the extent to which nurses perceived that their workload was manageable. This is consistent with Leiter's (2008) suggestion that control plays a foundational role in the dual process model of burnout/engagement. The direct effects of control on fairness and value congruence in this study are consistent with the values process described in Leiter's dual process model. In his study, Leiter found that the values process was predictive of the cynicism and efficacy components of burnout. According to Leiter, when employees have little or no control, they are limited in their ability to work according to their personal standards and experience distress. This is particularly the case in the nursing profession, where the ability to meet professional standards is important to nurses' work satisfaction and sense of personal accomplishment (Irvine & Evans, 1995). In this study, control was also positively related to feelings of having their work valued and rewarded and to a positive sense of community among their co-workers. These factors are also important for nurses' job satisfaction and organizational commitment (Kovner et al., 2006). This study demonstrated the importance of control over work as a mechanism through which workplace empowerment influenced work engagement.

Four areas of worklife had a direct effect on work engagement: control, fairness, rewards, and value congruence. The effects of these areas of worklife on work engagement are consistent with expectations in Schaufeli and Bakker's (2004) model of work engagement. Control had both direct and indirect effects on engagement. Control is an important job resource that is a driver of work engagement (Bakker & Demerouti, 2008), as are social support and performance feedback. When employees feel that they are supported in their workplace through fair treatment, they are more likely to be motivated at work and be more engaged in their work. Moliner et al. (2008) found that procedural and interactional justice were significant predictors of work engagement (vigor and dedication) in their study of Spanish service workers. Similarly, when employees feel that their contributions to the organization are appropriately rewarded, they are likely to be more engaged at work and motivated to pursue organizational goals. Bakker and Demerouti (2007) found that appreciation of work contributions acted as a buffer between stressful work demands and Finnish teachers' work engagement. Koyuncu et al. (2006) found that control, recognition, and values congruence were significantly related to work engagement of Turkish bankers, a finding replicated in this study.

Values congruence had the strongest influence on work engagement in this study. When employees' personal values matched those of the organization, they were more likely to be engaged at work. When asked to engage in work activities that contradict their values, employees experience discomfort and if prolonged, they are likely to withdraw from their work rather than engage. While the Schaufeli and Bakker (2004) model of engagement does not specifically address the notion of values congruence as a job resource, it is intuitively reasonable to expect that when workplace norms violate personal standards, individuals will be less dedicated, have less energy at work, and not experience a sense of flow or absorption due to the tension experienced by the values discrepancy. Ultimately, these conditions may lead to withdrawal, either mentally or physically. Maslach and Leiter (2008) have shown that value incongruence is a key factor in burnout, often considered the opposite of engagement. Thus, this result is not surprising.

Limitations
The findings of this study must be viewed with caution because the cross-sectional design precludes strong statements of cause and effect (Pedhazur

& Schmelkin, 1991). Method variance is a concern since the same subject completed all measures, although Spector (2006) argued that the negative effects of common method variance (CMV) have been overstated and reminds us that cross-sectional survey designs have similar biases to lab studies. He also argued that method variance is less of a problem when validated scales are used. Considering the documented reliability and validity of the measures used in this study, problems with CMV should be attenuated to some extent.

Conclusion

The results of this study provided support for an integrated model derived from three theoretical frameworks: Kanter's (1977) theory of organizational empowerment, Maslach and Leiter's (1997) areas of worklife model, and Schaufeli et al.'s (2002) theory of work engagement. The results reinforce the importance of workplace empowerment in creating engaging workplaces for employees. Nursing is currently facing a severe shortage of nurses and nurse managers. It is crucial to ensure that work environments allow both nurses and nurse managers to feel empowered to do their work in optimal ways that engage them personally and professionally. Nurse managers will need to learn new ways of leading that will empower staff nurses to engage in their work and to be motivated to provide high-quality care. Engaged professional nurses are critical to preserving the quality of healthcare and the health of their clients.

References

Aiken, L.H., Clarke, S.P., Sloane, D.M., Sochalski, J. & Silber, J.H. (2002), "Hospital nurse staffing and patient mortality, nurse burnout, and job dissatisfaction", *Journal of the American Medical Association*, **288**(16), 1987–93.

Arbuckle, J.L. (2007), *Amos User's Guide, Version 16*, Chicago, IL: SPSS.

Bakker, A.B. & Demerouti, E. (2007), "The job demands–resources model: state of the art", *Journal of Managerial Psychology*, **22**(3), 309–28.

Bakker, A.B. & Demerouti, E. (2008), "Towards a model of work engagement", *Career Development International*, **13**(3), 209–23.

Bakker, A.B., Demerouti, E. & Verbeke, W. (2004), "Using the job demands–resources model to predict burnout and performance", *Human Resource Management*, **43**(1), 83–104.

Canadian Nurses Association (2002), *Planning for the Future: Nursing Human Resource Projections*, Ottawa, ON: Canadian Nurses Association.

Cho, J., Laschinger, H.K.S. & Wong, C. (2006), "Workplace empowerment, work engagement and organizational commitment of new graduate nurses", *Canadian Journal of Nursing Leadership*, **19**(3), 43–60.

Demerouti, E., Bakker, A.B., Janssen, P.P.M. & Schaufeli, W.B. (2001), "Burnout and engagement at work as a function of demands and control", *Scandinavian Journal of Work, Environment and Health*, **27**, 279–86.

Demerouti, E., Bakker, A.B., Nachreiner, F. & Schaufeli, W.B. (2000), "A model of burnout and life satisfaction among nurses", *Journal of Advanced Nursing*, **32**, 454–64.

Dillman, D.A. (2000), *Mail and Internet Surveys: The Tailored Design Method*, 2nd edn, New York: Wiley.

Greco, P., Laschinger, H.K.S. & Wong, C. (2006), "Leader empowering behaviours, staff nurse empowerment and work engagement/burnout", *Nursing Leadership*, **19**(4), 41–56.

Hakanen, J.J., Bakker, A.B. & Demerouti, E. (2005), "How dentists cope with their job demands and stay engaged: the moderating role of job resources", *European Journal of Oral Sciences*, **113**(6), 479–87.

Hakanen, J.J., Bakker, A.B. & Schaufeli, W. (2006), "Burnout and work engagement among teachers", *Journal of School Psychology*, **43**, 495–513.

Hayes, L.J., O'Brien-Pallas, L., Duffield, C., Shamian, J., Buchan, J., Hughes, F., Laschinger, H.K.S., North, N. & Stone, P.W. (2006), "Nurse turnover: a literature review", *International Journal of Nursing Studies*, **43**(2), 237–63.

Hu, L. & Bentler, P.M. (1999), "Cutoff criteria for fit indexes in covariance structure analysis: conventional criteria versus new alternatives", *Structural Equation Modeling*, **6**(1), 1–55.

Irvine, D.M. & Evans, M.G. (1995), "Job satisfaction and turnover among nurses: integrating research findings across studies", *Nursing Research*, **44**, 246–53.

Kanter, R.M. (1977), *Men and Women of the Corporation*, New York: Basic Books.

Kanter R.M. (1979), "Power failure in management circuits", *Harvard Business Review*, **57**(4), 65–75.

Kanter, R.M. (1993), *Men and Women of the Corporation*, 2nd edn, New York: Basic Books.

Kovner, C., Brewer, C., Wu, Y.W., Cheng, Y. & Suzuki, M. (2006), "Factors associated with work satisfaction of registered nurses", *Journal of Nursing Scholarship*, **38**(1), 71–9.

Koyuncu, M., Burke, R.J. & Fiksenbaum, L. (2006), "Work engagement among women managers and professionals in a Turkish bank: potential antecedents and consequences", *Equal Opportunities International*, **25**(4), 299–310.

Laschinger, H.K.S., Almost, J. & Tuer-Hodes, D. (2003), "Workplace empowerment and magnet hospital characteristics: making the link", *Journal of Nursing Administration*, **33**(7/8), 410–22.

Laschinger, H.K.S. & Finegan, J. (2005a), "Empowering nurses for work engagement and health in hospital settings", *Journal of Nursing Administration*, **35**, 439–49.

Laschinger, H.K.S. & Finegan, J. (2005b), "Using empowerment to build trust and respect in the workplace: a strategy for addressing the nursing shortage", *Nursing Economics*, **23**(1), 6–12.

Laschinger, H.K.S., Finegan, J. Shamian, J. & Casier, S. (2000), "Organizational trust and empowerment in restructured healthcare settings: effects on staff nurse commitment", *Journal of Nursing Administration*, **30**(9), 413–25.

Laschinger, H.K.S., Finegan, J., Shamian, J. & Wilk, P. (2001), "Impact of structural and pschological empowerment on job strain in nursing work settings", *Journal of Nursing Administration*, **31**(5), 260–72.

Laschinger, H.K.S., Wong, C., McMahon, L. & Kaufmann, C. (1999), "Leader behavior, impact behavior impact on staff nurse empowerment, job tension, and work effectiveness", *Journal of Nursing Administration*, **29**(5), 28–39.

Leiter, M.P. (2008), "A two process model of burnout and work engagement: distinct implications of demands and values", *Giornale Italiano di Medicina del Lavoro ed Ergonomia*, **30**(1), A52–A58.

Leiter, M.P. & Harvie, P. (1997), "Correspondence of supervisor and subordinate perspectives during major organizational change", *Journal of Occupational Health Psychology*, **2**(4), 343–52.

Leiter, M.P. & Maslach, C. (2004), "Areas of worklife: a structured approach to organizational predictors of job burnout", in P.L. Perrewe & D.C. Ganster (eds), *Research in Occupational Stress and Well-being*, Oxford: JAI Press/Elsevier Science, pp. 91–134.

Maslach, C. & Leiter, M.P. (1997), *The Truth about Burnout*, San Francisco, CA: Jossey-Bass.

Maslach, C. & Leiter, M.P. (2008), "Early predictors of job burnout and engagement", *Journal of Applied Psychology*, **93**, 498–512.

Moliner, C., Martinez-Tur, V., Ramos, J., Peiró, J.M. & Cropanzano, R. (2008),

"Organizational justice and extrarole customer service: the mediating role of well-being at work", *European Journal of Work and Organizational Psychology*, **17**, 327–48.

Nedd, N. (2006), "Perceptions of empowerment and intent to stay", *Nursing Economics*, **24**(1), 13–18.

O'Brien-Pallas, L., Thomson, D., McGillis Hall, L., Pink, G., Kerr, M., Wang, S., Li, X. & Meyer, R. (2004), "Evidenced-based standards for measuring nurse staffing and performance", Final Report, Canadian Health Services Research Foundation, Toronto.

Pedhazur, E.J. & Schmelkin, L.P. (1991), *Measurement, Design, and Analysis: An Integrated Approach*, Hillsdale, NJ: Lawrence Erlbaum.

Salanova, M., Llorens, S., Cifre, E., Martínez, I.M. & Schaufeli, W.B. (2003), "Perceived collective efficacy, subjective well-being and task performance among electronic work groups: an experimental study", *Small Group Research*, **34**(1), 43–73.

Schaufeli, W.B. & Bakker, A.B. (2004), "Job demands, job resources, and their relationship with burnout and engagement: a multi-sample study", *Journal of Organizational Behavior*, **25**, 293–315.

Schaufeli, W.B., Salanova, M., González-Romá, V. & Bakker, A.B. (2002), "The measurement of engagement and burnout and a confirmatory analytic approach", *Journal of Happiness Studies*, **3**, 71–92.

Spector, P.E. (2006), "Method variance in organizational research: truth or urban legend?", *Organizational Research Methods*, **9**, 221–32.

Upenieks, V.V. (2002), "Assessing differences in job satisfaction of nurses in magnet and nonmagnet hospitals", *Journal of Nursing Administration*, **32**(11), 564–76.

Xanthopoulou, D., Bakker, A.B., Demerouti, E. & Schaufeli, W.B. (2009), "Work engagement and financial returns: a diary study on the role of job and personal resources", *Journal of Occupational and Organizational Psychology*, **82**(1), 183–200.

27 Engaged work teams
Joanne Richardson and Michael A. West

Introduction

At its best, teamwork offers a way of synthesizing individuals' knowledge, skills and abilities in order to achieve exceptional creativity, innovation and productivity. Through combining the efforts of individuals within a team the aggregate of individuals' contributions can be surpassed (West et al., 1998). As a result, team-based organizations have the unique collaborative capability to integrate a diverse range of skills and expertise, execute complex tasks and accomplish challenging goals in a timely and adaptive fashion (see Salas et al., 2009).

However, the intuitively appealing premise that teams can offer synergistic outcomes very often goes unrealized when teamwork is not designed, implemented and supported properly. Further, when team working goes wrong, there are detrimental consequences for team members and their organizations. So why do some teams flourish and other teams fail? Why do some teams have a passion for their work and contribute beyond expectations, when others lack enthusiasm, choose to procrastinate and exert only minimum effort? In this chapter, we argue that team engagement is the key to creating effective, positive team-based organizations. We explore two bodies of literature; work engagement and team effectiveness, to develop a conceptual model of team engagement which we hope provides a fresh insight into understanding team working.

Engagement as a team-level phenomenon

Engagement has recently been proposed as a powerful antecedent of performance outcomes in organizations (Salanova et al., 2005). Therefore it is conceivable that work engagement is not only an individual-level construct, but is also a unit- or team-level phenomenon (Little & Little, 2006). However, the level of analysis which the construct represents remains unclear. Given that the vast majority of work to date has only considered engagement as an individual-level variable, we aim to extend the engagement construct to the team level of analysis. Multilevel theory suggests that higher-level phenomena, in this instance team engagement, can emerge from the social interactions, behaviours, affects and cognitions of individuals (Kozlowski & Klein, 2000). Together, team members share knowledge and information, communicate their moods and emotions, exchange ideas, work closely to perform acts and execute tasks, and share their opinions. Over time, these interaction dynamics stabilize and team members develop similar and compatible cognitive representations of their teams (Kozlowksi et al., 1996). These cognitive representations combine in a complementary way, whereby the whole is greater than the sum of its parts. These synergistic outcomes are the essence of teamwork.

So what is team engagement? We shall begin by first defining engagement at the individual level. Although a number of different perspectives on engagement have emerged in the literature over recent years (for example, Kahn, 1990), the work of Schaufeli and colleagues has received the most empirical attention in Europe. They define work engagement as a positive affective–emotional state of fulfilment, characterized by "vigor", "dedication" and "absorption" (Schaufeli & Bakker, 2004). We argue that these three key dimensions of work engagement also hold substantially at the team level, and can be collectively experienced and displayed by a group of individuals working interdependently together towards a common goal.

Team engagement emerges bottom-up from the combined pattern of team members' resource allocations and interaction processes towards the team task and objectives. Thus, we conceptualize team engagement as an emergent collective construct whereby a team experiences a heightened positive affective–motivational state characterized by a sense of vigor, absorption and determination. Vigor is reflected in a team's high level of physical liveliness, cognitive alertness, and interpersonal energy and can facilitate goal-directed behaviours (Carver & Scheier, 1990). Dedication is characterized by high levels of team identification to a vision, strong commitment to tasks and roles, and persistence in times of challenge and adversity. Absorption characterizes a team which is fully focused and immersed in its work whereby time flies by unnoticeably and the team finds it difficult to detach itself from its tasks. An example of an engaged team is a dance team where the CD skips but the team continues to dance through the change without anyone noticing. Indeed, team engagement may manifest itself particularly in non-routine tasks or crises. For example, when there are high challenges but the team's resources, experience of working together and task-cycle knowledge enable them to bring their capabilities together in a coherent, coordinated and appropriate way to meet the current challenges. The passion and enthusiasm that team engagement fosters motivates the team to initiate and carry out adaptive processes which are directed towards the achievement of the team's tasks and goals. Such processes, we argue, are a manifestation of an engaged team in action, and so go beyond what is typical or "status quo" in teamwork, serving to motivate change, adaptability and improvement in the team.

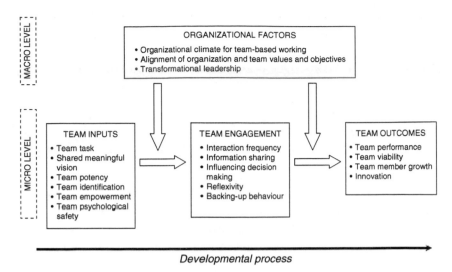

Figure 27.1   The team engagement model

Team engagement and its related behavioural process are depicted in the centre of the team engagement model presented above (see Figure 27.1). The model is fundamentally based on an input–mediator–outcome (IMO) framework (Ilgen et al., 2005), with the general premise that team processes mediate input–outcome relationships. Our model also acknowledges the critical role that temporal dynamics play in the emergence of team engagement. The developmental line beneath the model illustrates how teams qualitatively change over time, and are differentially influenced by micro- and macro-level factors as they mature (Kozlowski et al., 1999).

The remainder of this chapter is organized as follows. Focusing at the centre of the team engagement model, we first consider what engaged teams look like in practice by describing how team engagement manifests in five key team processes. We shall then consider a number of key engagement conditions, or inputs, before describing four important outcomes of team engagement. Moderating effects of macro-level variables on the IMO framework will then be discussed, before turning to some practical guidelines for implementing the model. Finally, the chapter will turn to a future agenda for research on team engagement.

Processes: what does team engagement look like in practice?

The following section discusses what team engagement looks like when manifested in five important team processes.

Interaction frequency

Engaged work teams will strive to interact as much as possible, with high levels of vigor creating a need for frequent interpersonal exchanges between team members. These social interactions provide a mechanism through which team members can share information and form close working relationships. Interaction may occur as part of regular team meetings, during which other critical team processes such as reflexivity and backing-up behaviour can occur. However, engaged teams will also endeavour to interact frequently on an informal basis; making efforts to meet team members at lunchtime, calling in on one another during work hours, or keeping regular contact using virtual means of communication.

During early stages of team development, interactions provide an opportunity for sharing information about team member personalities, backgrounds and skills, allowing the team to learn about one another and build close interpersonal relationships (Katz, 1978). Such bonding fosters commitment to and integration with fellow teammates (Reade, 2003). Frequent interaction also allows team members to recognize the importance of satisfying individual members' needs (Moreland & Levine, 2001), and helps to build team attachment which is characterized by security and trust. High interaction frequency has recently been shown to be critical for the crossover of daily work engagement between team members (Bakker & Xanthopoulou, 2009), thus further enhancing a sense of energy, vigor and absorption via emotional contagion processes.

Information sharing

Information sharing is critical for task performance in teams. During social interaction, team members have the opportunity to combine their range of knowledge, skills and abilities (KSAs) in a collaborative manner, and learn from one another during the process. Given that a degree of diversity is an inherent feature of any work team, it is likely that each team member is able to contribute to the team task in a different way. However, the difference between an engaged team and an unengaged team is the team members' willingness to share their KSAs with their group. In unengaged teams, team members may behave defensively or competitively, choosing to withhold certain information and keep it to themselves at the expense of team performance. However, members of engaged teams will consider the team's goal to be as important as their own goals, and will therefore exert all of their effort and resources towards its achievement.

High levels of dedication to the team's task prompts team members to thoroughly and thoughtfully exchange information on a regular basis, using open styles of communication such as inclusive language and active listening to ensure high levels of team participation. Members of engaged teams will make extra efforts to clarify and extend their individual contributions, taking time to give their ideas significance and relevance, and expressing them with enthusiasm and energy. In turn, other team members will listen actively, reserving judgement and recognizing the value of individual contributions. This open flow of communication ensures that information can be frequently and effectively exchanged, thus allowing for a collaborative and coordinated team effort.

Influencing decision making

A fundamental argument for team-based working is that teams will make better decisions than individuals working in isolation, given that teams have access to a larger, more diverse pool of knowledge and information to draw from. However, under the conditions of vigor, dedication and absorption, highly engaged teams do not just make decisions, but extend and influence their decision making.

Research has highlighted the potential process losses evident in team interaction, whereby psychological phenomenon such as social conformity, groupthink and production blocking can have negative impacts on the quality and creativity of team decisions. Often these process losses occur as team members are overly concerned with maintaining agreement and solidity within the team. However, highly engaged teams will be dedicated to their task and will therefore demonstrate a focus on task excellence rather than a focus on cohesion. Instead of simply accepting the first or easiest solution to a problem before quickly moving on to something else, engaged teams, because of their high levels of vigor and absorption, will take time to give an idea more meaning, to really elaborate and build on suggestions, even those which are opposing or ambitious, thus allowing for an open evaluation of every possibility. Constructive controversy (Tjosvold, 1998) involves the open-minded discussion of divergent perspectives, allowing teams to critically examine and appraise information. A dedication to task excellence, as opposed to protecting cohesion, allows teams to engage in such controversy whereby team members feel able to openly disagree, question and search each other's perspectives and create new alternatives. As a result, engaged teams will make more rigorous, high-quality and mutually beneficial decisions on important team issues.

Reflexivity

Team reflexivity is defined as "the extent to which group members overtly reflect upon, and communicate about the group's objectives, strategies (e.g. decision making) and processes (e.g. communication), and adapt them to current or anticipated circumstances" (West et al., 1997, p. 296). Reflexive teams with high levels of vigor and absorption will take time to explore their divergent perspectives (De Dreu, 2002) and cross-fertilize their ideas to come up with novel solutions to problems. High levels of dedication will also ensure that engaged teams demonstrate careful planning, pay attention to both the short- and long-term consequences of their actions, and have a high awareness of the environment in which they operate. This means that they can plan ahead and adjust their strategies and goals to changing circumstances. Dedicating time for reflection during team meetings signifies that a team is engaged and committed to their task, and allows team members the regular opportunity to discuss and reflect upon progress, issues and problems related to both the task at hand, as well as coordination processes within the team without interruption or distraction from the wider organizational system.

Backing-up behaviour
Porter et al. (2003) defined backing up behaviour as "the discretionary provision of resources and task-related effort to another member of one's team that is intended to help that team member obtain the goals as defined by his or her role when it is apparent that the team member is failing to reach those goals" (pp. 391–2). Backing-up behaviour is essentially the extent to which team members effectively help each other perform their roles, and has been proposed as a critical aspect of teamwork (Dickinson & McIntyre, 1997). In order to demonstrate backing-up behaviour effectively, team members must not only have an understanding of each other's roles and tasks, but must also be willing to both seek support as well as provide assistance within their team (Porter, 2005). Team members are more likely to carry out such behaviours if they strongly identify with their team and view their task as meaningful. Indeed, backing-up behaviours are neither enforced nor elicited by formal work roles but are spontaneously and wilfully displayed by employees who have a high level of work engagement. This willingness to cooperate and reciprocate for the benefit of the team characterizes engaged work teams in action.

When engagement manifests itself in backing-up behaviour, team members readily help each other when workload surpasses an individual's work capacity. Given that in engaged teams, group success is perceived as equally important as individual success, team members are more likely to dedicate extra time, effort and resources towards the team task. Where possible this includes compensating for one another in times of absence, and picking up the extra workload for the sake of the team's performance. Such teams also encourage their members to ask for help when it is needed, emphasizing solution-focused activities and allowing team members to talk openly about errors, incidents and problems. This sincere concern and involvement in all aspects of the team's work is reciprocated throughout the team, creating a virtuous cycle of backing-up behaviour.

Inputs: what are the conditions for team engagement?
Team-level inputs, or team engagement conditions, form the next section of the micro-level facets in our IMO model. These inputs describe the factors which can form part of the structure and design properties of work teams in order to facilitate the emergence of team engagement and its related processes.

Team task
The design of a team task is a critical input for determining how team members must work together, including team member roles, workflow processes, collective goals and team member interactions (Kozlowski & Ilgen, 2006). Most crucially, the task itself must be sufficiently challenging and complex that it is best achieved by a team. Task interdependence defines the interconnections among the tasks of team members, reflecting the overall extent to which they depend on one another to accomplish their work (Van de Ven & Ferry, 1980) and tends to be explicitly acknowledged in task-related interactions and collective goals. Indeed, a collective goal will compel a team to formulate a unified work approach in which the need for collaboration is recognized and a mutual sense of responsibility is established (Wageman, 1995). Such a unified strategy is critical given that work teams are often involved in executing tasks that are too complex to be achieved by individuals working alone. Successful teams will be those which explicitly recognize the high level of task interdependence required and use their intense work interactions in positive and adaptive ways.

In order to facilitate team engagement, it is also crucial that the task is complete, whereby the team oversees their work from beginning to end, as a complete task increases opportunity to experience task identity and task significance (see Hackman & Oldham, 1980). Further, in designing a team task, it is important to ensure that a team has the appropriate composition, skills and resources necessary for accomplishing the specific task at hand. Aspects to consider include personalities of team members, expert knowledge, and social skills as well as material, administrative and technological requirements. Ensuring that these conditions are in place is fundamental in facilitating team engagement.

Shared meaningful vision
According to Frankl (1992), individuals have the innate propensity to seek meaning in their work. Research has also demonstrated the importance that experienced meaningfulness can have in the workplace (Hackman &

Oldham, 1980). The opportunity to carry out meaningful work can facilitate both intrinsic motivation and personal growth (Spreitzer et al., 1997). We argue that meaningfulness can be explicitly articulated in a clear and compelling team vision that helps team members to recognize the importance and value of their work contribution. Engaged teams thrive on the demanding and multifaceted nature of their task, and feel compelled by the meaningful value that their work has. By collectively recognizing the meaning in their work, teams are more likely to experience feelings of dedication, vigor and absorption.

A shared meaningful team vision should be underpinned by a number of clear and specific team objectives (West, 2004). Such shared goals are critical for engagement as they motivate the team to agree upon priorities and emphasize the desired outcome of the team task (Campion et al., 1993). Clear and inspiring team-level objectives also give team members the incentive to combine their efforts and collaborate closely in their work together (Weldon & Weingart, 1993). Agreement on the team's overall vision and goals is also critical to ensure that all team members are working in the same direction and are committed to the team's purpose. Indeed, such agreement motivates team members to participate in engaged team processes such as reflexivity and information sharing.

Team potency
Bandura (1997) coined the term "self-efficacy" to describe an individual's belief about how well he or she could deal with prospective situations. Extending this concept to the group level, Guzzo et al. (1993) defined group potency as the shared belief within a group that it can be effective. Research has demonstrated that group potency is positively related to team effectiveness (Campion et al., 1993). Here, we propose group potency as an important antecedent of team engagement, which in turn impacts on the outputs of the team.

High levels of potency are characterized by persistence and motivation towards task accomplishment and commitment to the team's vision. Indeed, at the individual level, Bandura (1997) demonstrated that high levels of efficacy are linked to the expansion of high levels of energy targeted towards task completion, as well as becoming absorbed in a task itself. Conversely, low levels of efficacy have been shown to predict burnout, a state which is often considered as the direct antipode of work engagement (González-Romá et al., 2006). We argue that the same such relationships hold at the team level, whereby potency spreads within the group via emotional contagion. Over time, the collective work approach of a team encourages team members to synchronize their behaviours, thoughts and feelings (Hackman, 1992). Research has demonstrated that groups can develop a shared affective tone (George, 1990) which emerges from the personal disposition of group members. Therefore, if one or two team members are convinced of the team's capability to successfully perform their task, their positive mood and optimism can cross over to other team members. Similarly, Barsade (2002) argued that as a group performs a task, affective states can be subtle yet continuously transferred between group members to form shared group emotions. Empirical research has supported this notion, demonstrating that the moods of teams of nurses and accountants were related to each other even after controlling for shared work problems (Totterdell et al., 1998). Bakker et al. (2006) also found that positive interactions within a team facilitated feelings of energy and enthusiasm in individual team members, independent of the demands and resources they were exposed to. Given that a shared team vision will encourage a team to work together closely and intensively, team members will have the opportunity for such mood convergence or emotional contagion. Thus, we propose that a high level of group potency will impact on team engagement by directly enhancing the team's overall vigor, dedication and absorption to their task.

Team identification
Social identity theory posits that people's understanding of who they are is shaped by the group to which they belong (Tajfel & Turner, 1979). Further, social psychological researchers have argued that social identity can explain why individuals engage with groups and organizations (Tyler & Blader, 2003). In group settings, a strong social identity prompts deindividuation, which in turn fosters the internalization of group norms and attributes (Blader & Tyler, 2009). Thus, if group norms prescribe high levels of endeavour and engagement during team tasks, then greater behavioural effort from the team is likely to follow (Haslam & Ellemers, 2005).

Teams with a strong team identity develop a sense of "entitativity", which defines the degree to which team members see themselves as belonging to one unit (Lickel et al., 2001). Team identification therefore creates a degree of social interdependence, or cohesion, which reflects the psychological bond and attraction between team members to one another, as well as to the team as a whole. Indeed, when measured as a mood state, work group cohesion has been shown to predict vigor (Terry et al., 2000). When team identity is strong, team members will develop an inherent concern about the needs of the group and will therefore be more willing to make psychological investments, such as demonstrating loyalty (Zdaniuk & Levine, 2001) and dedication to their team.

Team empowerment
Research has shown that team empowerment is positively related to team productivity and proactivity (Kirkman & Rosen, 1999). According to Mathieu et al. (2006), team empowerment consists of both a psychological and a structural component. Team psychological empowerment refers to a team's "collective belief that they have the authority to control their proximal work environment and are responsible for their team's functioning" (p. 98). The actual practice of assigning responsibility, exercising control and delegating authority is referred to as structural empowerment (see Arnold et al., 2000). We argue that both psychological and structural empowerment are important conditions for fostering team engagement.

The literature has long acknowledged the important role that resources, such as autonomy, play in fostering work engagement. Autonomy is also considered a key structural characteristic of teams (Campion et al., 1993) whereby autonomous teams are able to "own" their task. Empowered teams have the decision-making authority to determine their own course of action, which can heighten an overall sense of determination and internal motivation (Spreitzer, 1995). Empowered teams can also choose to dedicate time to learning processes, allowing them to improve their effectiveness via localized adaptation to changes in demands and the wider environment (Pearce & Ravlin, 1987). Such empowerment is critical if engaged teams are able to reap the full benefits of their vigor, dedication and absorption in their work and channel their engagement towards meaningful and valued outcomes for their organization.

Team psychological safety
Kahn (1990, p. 708) defined psychological safety as "feeling able to show and employ one's self without fear of negative consequences to self-image, status, or career". Under such conditions, Kahn argued that individuals feel safe and willing to participate in decision making and task execution without negative repercussions, and as a result, are more able to experience personal engagement at work. Following an array of empirical research, Edmondson (1999) subsequently introduced the group-level concept of team psychological safety. She established that perceptions of psychological safety tend to be shared among members of a team, given their salient collective experiences and shared work context.

Team psychological safety is important for facilitating engagement as it fosters an environment in which team members feel confident to be themselves, and speak openly and honestly without fear of being rejected, punished or embarrassed by the team (Edmondson & Roloff, 2009). Such a climate stems from high levels of mutual respect and interpersonal trust between team members (Edmondson, 1999). Shared goals are also important for fostering team psychological safety, as they shift attention away from the individual to a wider concern for the group. Rather than being concerned about self-protection, a shared sense of fate means that team members can focus on the task of the group, prompting them to reflect on team objectives and progress, and helping them to anticipate problems and challenges early. A climate of team psychological safety is crucial if members are to fully participate in their team, engage in adaptive behavioural processes and take personal risks for their team in their endeavour to achieve the highest possible outcome.

Outcomes: what are the consequences of team engagement?
The notion of team engagement has far-reaching implications for both the individuals within the team, as well as the organization to which they belong. Outputs are results or outcomes of a team which are valued by one or more constituencies (Mathieu et al., 2000). Wageman et al. (2005) defined team effectiveness using the following three dimensions, which will all be predicted by team engagement:

- the productive output of a team meets or exceeds that quality, quantity and timeliness defined by the people who review, receive and/or use the output (*team performance*);
- the social processes used by the team to carry out the task and how they enhance the team members' capabilities to work together interdependently in the future (*team viability*); and
- the positive contribution of the group experience to the learning, growth and well-being of individual team members (*team member growth*).

Further, due to the high levels of adaptive and creative behaviours inherent in engaged teams, we also propose that team engagement will predict team innovation. Each outcome will now be briefly discussed in turn.

Team performance
A number of studies have linked employee engagement with performance, both at the individual and business-unit level. Such relationships are reviewed elsewhere in this volume and we shall not reiterate them here.

We argue that the same such relationships can be found between team engagement and team performance. Research indicates that individuals' experiences in teams have a profound impact on their commitment to and performance in present and future teamwork (Lester et al., 2002). Teams which are highly engaged will be more motivated to strive towards a challenging meaningful goal, putting all of their effort into their work.

This passion and energy is manifested in adaptive team behaviours which enable the team to perform well at their job (see Beal et al., 2005).

Team viability
Team viability refers to a team's capability to continue functioning together effectively in the future. According to Hackman (1987), teams without long-term viability will suffer from a reluctance to work cooperatively, and will eventually burnout due to unresolved conflict. However, highly engaged teams are likely to have high levels of long-term viability due to their positive social interactions which foster trust and cooperation (Forsyth, 1990). Consequently, team engagement should be positively associated with long-term team viability.

Team member growth
Team member growth is a key social dimension of team working (West, 2004) and is vital for individual need fulfilment. The learning orientation and adaptive behaviours inherent in highly engaged teams allows for the personal growth and development of individual team members, as well as the team as a whole. Members of engaged teams not only have the opportunity to acquire new knowledge and share information about their work, but they are also able to develop close interpersonal attachments to their teammates. In turn, such nourishing, fulfilling relationships have a beneficial effect on individual health and psychological well-being (Heaphy & Dutton, 2008).

Innovation
Innovation is defined as the introduction of new ideas and new ways of doing things at work (West, 2002). In today's challenging business climate, their innovative capacity is critical to their effectiveness and survival. Team processes which occur in engaged teams, such as team reflexivity, have been empirically related to team effectiveness and innovation (Tjosvold et al., 2004). Given their enthusiasm and energy, engaged teams are likely to go beyond the usual or typical, persist at challenging tasks and problems, and as a result, are more likely to come up with novel and creative ideas. Combined with a high level of potency in a team, these ideas are more likely to be followed up and implemented by the team, resulting in high levels of team innovation.

Macro-level moderators of team engagement
Given that teams do not operate in an organizational vacuum (Hackman, 2002), multilevel theory suggests that the emergence of team-level phenomena is also constrained and moulded by higher-level contextual factors in

an organization. Organizations are social systems that serve as environments for teams and thus, to thoroughly understand teams, the complexities of the context in which they are embedded must be considered. In our IMO model, the three *macro*-level factors represent moderators on the relationships between inputs, engagement processes and outputs, each of which will now be briefly discussed.

Organizational climate for team-based working

It is important that team-based organizations reflect the belief that organizational goals will be largely achieved by teams of individuals working cooperatively together, rather than individuals working in isolation and competing with one another. In practice, organizations can foster such cooperative outcome interdependence by rewarding team performance, rather than individual performance (see Tjosvold, 1998). Organizations must also promote the development of shared objectives by involving all teams, encouraging the exchange of their ideas through constructive debate and providing them with a say over wider decisions. Where such cooperation and collaboration are encouraged and rewarded in organizations, both inter- and intra-team working is likely to be more engaged and effective.

Alignment of organization and team values and objectives

Team engagement thrives in settings where there is a close alignment between organization and team values and objectives. Each and every team within an organization must feel that they are valued and have a potentially crucial role to play in the organization's performance. If a team's task is considered equally as meaningful and important to both the team's and the organization's success, the energy and focus of the team will be further heightened. Such recognition is likely to enhance team engagement, and in turn, team effectiveness and performance. Therefore, senior managers must ensure that there is an alignment between team and organizational values, so that team efforts are directed towards the overall purpose and targets of the organization. In turn, the organization should fully support and encourage the team to achieve their objectives, thus enhancing team potency and empowerment.

Transformational leadership

The leadership literature has proposed that transformational leaders arouse the emotional state of their followers by exhibiting energizing emotions (Avolio, 1999). Such behaviours can energize teams, infusing them with self-efficacy and stimulating them to think creatively (Brief & Weiss, 2002). Guzzo et al. (1993) also argued that leadership is an important determinant of group potency, which we argue is an important condition for team engagement. Transformational leaders empower their followers, delegate autonomy, develop self-confidence and encourage learning behaviour. When a team observes their leader exhibiting vigor and determination to succeed, this positive mood and optimism will spread throughout the team via emotional contagion, and the team members will be motivated to dedicate their efforts towards heightened team performance.

Overall, we suggest that what is needed for team effectiveness is not only engaged work teams, but a supportive organizational context which reinforces the team-based structure, ensures the alignment of team and organizational values, and provides inspiring and transformational leadership for teams.

Implications for practice
Implications for practice have been discussed throughout this chapter. However, below are a number of specific practical guidelines for managers or practitioners who wish to implement and stimulate engaged teamwork in today's organizations:

- assign teams with a non-routine and meaningful task which is realistically achievable, yet challenging enough to stimulate interest and enthusiasm;
- ensure that the vision of the team is clearly articulated and communicated. Encourage the team to re-assess, and where appropriate, revise their team objectives on a regular basis in order to stimulate team engagement;
- provide teams with the support and resources they need to carry out their work. This includes: support for the team's vision from top management; sufficient time for team members to reflect on their work together; and sufficient autonomy for the team to determine their own course of action;
- manage team conflict. Maintaining trust and respect between team members is a critical ingredient for creating a climate of team psychological safety, in which team members feel safe to participate fully and openly. Therefore interpersonal conflict should be recognized and dealt with early on to avoid the erosion of team member relationships. The discussion of cynical and negative information should also be limited where possible (Bakker et al., 2006) to ensure that team efforts are channelled efficiently and positively towards the task at hand; and
- monitor levels of team engagement and try to allocate and re-deploy team membership accordingly. If low team engagement is apparent,

recruit enthusiastic new team members who may be able to bring renewed energy and vision to the team.

Future research

Research on team engagement is currently sparse and hard to come by. Although some promising advancements have been made on the cross-over of work engagement within teams (for example, Totterdell et al., 1998; Bakker et al., 2006), more empirical research is needed to establish the antecedents, processes and consequences of a team-level construct of work engagement, and how these might differ from the individual-level construct. Such findings will have profound implications for team-based organizations. Indeed, as they strive to create a competitive advantage, engaged work teams, equipped with energy, passion and dedication to their work will undoubtedly become their most precious resource in today's challenging business climate.

References

Arnold, J.A., Arad, S., Rhoades, J.A., & Drasgow, F. (2000), "The Empowering Leadership Questionnaire: the construction and validation of a new scale for measuring leader behaviors", *Journal of Organizational Behavior*, **21**, 249–69.

Avolio, B.J. (1999), *Full Leadership Development*, London: Sage.

Bakker, A.B., van Emmerik, H. & Euwema, M.C. (2006), "Crossover of burnout and engagement in work teams", *Work and Occupations*, **3**, 464–89.

Bakker, A.B. & Xanthopoulou, D. (2009), "The crossover of daily work engagement: test of an actor-partner interdependence model", *Journal of Applied Psychology*, **94** (6), 1562–71.

Bandura, A. (1997), *Self-efficacy: The Exercise of Control*, New York: Freeman.

Barsade, S.G. (2002), "The ripple effect: emotional contagion and its influence on group behavior", *Administrative Science Quarterly*, **47**, 644–75.

Beal, D.J., Weiss, H.M., Barros, E. & MacDermid, S.M. (2005), "An episodic process model of affective influences on performance", *Journal of Applied Psychology*, **90** (6), 1054–68.

Blader, S.L. & Tyler, T.R. (2009), "Testing and extending the group engagement model: linkages between social identity, procedural justice, economic outcomes and extrarole behaviour", *Journal of Applied Psychology*, **94**(2), 445–64.

Brief, A.P. & Weiss, H.M. (2002), "Organizational behaviour: affect in the workplace", *Annual Review of Psychology*, **53**, 279–307.

Campion, M.A., Medsker, G.J. & Higgs, C.A. (1993), "Relations between work group characteristics and effectiveness: implications for designing effective work groups", *Personnel Psychology*, **46**(4), 823–50.

Carver, C.S. & Scheier, M.F. (1990), "Origins and functions of positive and negative affect: a control-process view", *Psychological Review*, **97**, 19–35.

De Dreu, C. (2002), "Team innovation and team effectiveness: the importance of minority dissent and reflexivity", *European Journal of Work and Organizational Psychology*, **3**, 285–98.

Dickinson, T.L. & McIntyre, R.M. (1997), "A conceptual framework for teamwork measurement", in M.T. Brannick, E. Salas & C. Prince (eds), *Team Performance Assessment and Measurement: Theory, Methods, and Applications*, Mahwah, NJ: Erlbaum, pp. 19–43.

Edmondson, A.C. (1999), "Psychological safety and learning behavior in work teams", *Administrative Science Quarterly*, **44**, 350–83.

Edmondson, A.C. & Roloff, K.S. (2009), "Overcoming barriers to collaboration: psychological safety and learning in diverse teams", in Salas et al. (eds), pp. 183–208.

Forsyth, D.R. (1990), *Group Dynamics*, 2nd edn, Pacific Grove, CA: Brooks/Cole.
Frankl, V. (1992), *Man's Search for Meaning: An Introduction to Logotherapy*, Boston, MA: Beacon.
George, J.M. (1990), "Personality, affect, and behavior in groups", *Journal of Applied Psychology*, **75**, 107–16.
González-Romá, V., Schaufeli, W.B., Bakker, A.B. & Lloret, S. (2006), "Burnout and work engagement: independent factors or opposite poles?", *Journal of Vocational Behaviours*, **68**, 165–74.
Guzzo, R.A., Yost, P.R., Gampbell, R.J. & Shea, G.P. (1993), "Potency in groups: articulating a construct", *British Journal of Social Psychology*, **32**, 87–106.
Hackman, J.R. (1987), "The design of work teams", in J. Lorsch (ed.), *Handbook of Organizational Behavior*, Englewood Cliffs, NJ: Prentice-Hall, pp. 315–42.
Hackman, J.R. (1992). "Group influences on individuals in organizations", in M.D. Dunnette & L.M. Hough (eds), *Handbook of Industrial and Organizational Psychology*, 2nd edn, Palo Alto, CA: Consulting Psychologists Press, pp. 199–267.
Hackman, J.R. (2002), *Leading Teams: Setting the Stage for Great Performances*, Boston: MA: Harvard Business School Press.
Hackman, J.R., & Oldham, G.R. (1980), *Work Redesign*, Reading, MA: Addison-Wesley.
Haslam, S.A. & Ellemers, N. (2005), "Social identity in industrial and organizational psychology: concepts, controversies and contributions", in G.P. Hodgkinson (ed.), *International Review of Industrial and Organizational Psychology*, Vol. 20, Chichester: Wiley, pp. 39–118.
Heaphy, E.D. & Dutton, J.E. (2008), "Positive social interactions and the human body at work: linking organizations and physiology", *Academy of Management Review*, **33**(1), 137–62.
Ilgen, D.R., Hollenbeck, J.R., Johnson, M. & Jundt, D. (2005), "Teams in organizations: from input-process-output models to IMOI models", *Annual Review of Psychology*, **56**, 517–43.
Kahn, W.A. (1990), "Psychological conditions of personal engagement and disengagement at work", *Academy of Management Journal*, **33**(4), 692–724.
Katz, R. (1978), "Job longevity as a situational factor in job satisfaction", *Administrative Science Quarterly*, **23**(2), 204–23.
Kirkman, B.L. & Rosen, B. (1999), "Beyond self-management: antecedents and consequences of team empowerment", *Academy of Management Journal*, **42**, 58–74.
Kozlowski, S.W.J., Gully, S.M., Nason, E.R. & Smith, E.M. (1999), "Developing adaptive teams: a theory of compilation and performance across levels and time", in D.R. Ilgen & E.D. Pulakos (eds), *The Changing Nature of Work Performance: Implications for Staffing, Personnel Actions, and Development*, San Francisco, CA: Jossey-Bass, pp. 240–92.
Kozlowski, S.W.J., Gully, S.M., Salas, E. & Cannon-Bowers, J.A. (1996), "Team leadership and development: theory, principles, and guidelines for training leaders and teams", in M. Beyerlein, D. Johnson & S. Beyerlein (eds), *Advances in Interdisciplinary Studies of Work Teams: Team Leadership*, Vol. 3, Greenwich, CT: JAI Press, pp. 251–89.
Kozlowski, S.W.J. & Ilgen, D.R. (2006), "Enhancing the effectiveness of work groups and teams", *Psychological Science in the Public Interest*, **7**, 77–124.
Kozlowski, S.W.J. & Klein, K.J. (2000), "A multilevel approach to theory and research in organizations: contextual, temporal, and emergent processes", in Klein & Kozlowski (eds), *Multilevel Theory, Research, and Methods in Organizations*, San Francisco, CA: Jossey-Bass, pp. 512–56.
Lester, S.W., Meglino, B.M., & Korsgaard, M.A. (2002), "Antecedents and consequences of group potency: a longitudinal investigation of newly formed work groups", *Academy of Management Journal*, **45**(2), 352–68.
Lickel, B., Hamilton, D.L. & Sherman, S.J. (2001), "Elements of a lay theory of groups: types of groups, relational styles, and the perception of group entitativity", *Personality and Social Psychology Review*, **5**, 129–40.

Little, B. & Little, P. (2006), "Employee engagement: conceptual issues", *Journal of Organizational Culture, Communication and Conflict*, **10**, 111–20.

Mathieu, J.E., Gilson, L.L., & Ruddy, T.M. (2006), "Empowerment and team effectiveness: an empirical test of an integrated model", *Journal of Applied Psychology*, **91**, 97–108.

Mathieu, J.E., Heffner, T.S., Goodwin, G.F., Salas, E. & Cannon-Bowers, J.A. (2000), "The influence of shared mental models on team process and performance", *Journal of Applied Psychology*, **85**, 273–83.

Moreland, R.L. & Levine, J.M. (2001), "Socialization in organizations and work groups", in M.E. Turner (ed.), *Groups at Work: Theory and Research*, Mahwah, NJ: Lawrence Erlbaum, pp. 69–112.

Pearce, J.A., & Ravlin, E.C. (1987), "The design and activation of self-regulating work groups", *Human Relations*, **40**, 751–82.

Porter, C.O.L.H. (2005), "Goal orientation: effects on backing up behavior, performance, efficacy, and commitment in teams", *Journal of Applied Psychology*, **90**(4), 811–18.

Porter, C.O.L.H., Hollenbeck, J.R., Ilgen, D.R., Ellis, A.P.J., West, B.J. & Moon, H. (2003), "Backing up behaviors in teams: the role of personality and legitimacy", *Journal of Applied Psychology*, **88**, 391–403.

Reade, C. (2003), "Going the extra mile: local managers and global effort", *Journal of Managerial Psychology*, **18**(3), 208–28.

Salanova, M., Agut, S. & Peiró, J.M. (2005), "Linking organizational resources and work engagement to employee performance and customer loyalty: the mediation of service climate", *Journal of Applied Psychology*, **90**, 1217–27.

Salas, E., Goodwin, G.F. & Burke, C.S. (eds) (2009), *Team Effectiveness in Complex Organisations: Cross-disciplinary Perspectives and Approaches*, London: Routledge.

Schaufeli, W.B. & Bakker, A.B. (2004), "Job demands, job resources and their relationship with burnout and engagement: a multi-sample study", *Journal of Organisational Behaviour*, **25**, 293–315.

Spreitzer, G.M. (1995), "Psychological empowerment in the workplace: dimensions, measurement, and validation", *Academy of Management Journal*, **38**, 1442–65.

Spreitzer, G.M., Kizilos, M.A. & Nason, S.W. (1997), "A dimensional analysis of the relationship between psychological empowerment and effectiveness, satisfaction, and strain", *Journal of Management*, **23**, 679–704.

Tajfel, H. & Turner, J.C. (1979), "An integrative theory of intergroup conflict", in W. Austin & S. Worchel (eds), *The Social Psychology of Intergroup Relations*, Monterey, CA: Brooks, pp. 33–47.

Terry, P.C., Carron, A.V., Pink, M.J., Lane, A.M., Jones, G. & Hall, M. (2000), "Team cohesion and mood in sport", *Group Dynamics: Theory, Research and Practice*, **4**, 244–53.

Tjosvold, D. (1998), "Cooperative and competitive goal approach to conflict: accomplishments and challenges", *Applied Psychology: An International Review*, **47**, 285–342.

Tjosvold, D., Tang, M. & West, M.A. (2004), "Reflexivity for team innovation in China: the contribution of goal interdependence", *Group and Organization Management*, **29**, 540–59.

Totterdell, P., Kellett, S., Teuchman, K. & Briner, R.B. (1998), "Evidence of mood linkage in work groups", *Journal of Personality and Social Psychology*, **74**(6), 1504–15.

Tyler, T.R. & Blader, S.L. (2003), "The group engagement model: procedural justice, social identity, and cooperative behavior", *Personality and Social Psychology Review*, **7**, 349–61.

Van de Ven, A.H. & Ferry, D.L. (1980), *Measuring and Assessing Organizations*, New York: Wiley.

Wageman, R. (1995), "Interdependence and group effectiveness", *Administrative Science Quarterly*, **40**, 145–80.

Wageman, R., Hackman, J.R. & Lehman, E. (2005), "Team Diagnostic Survey: development of an instrument", *Journal of Applied Behavioural Science*, **41**(4), 373–98.

Weldon, E. & Weingart, L.R. (1993), "Group goals and group performance", *British Journal of Psychology*, **61**, 555–69.

West, M.A. (2002), "Sparkling fountains or stagnant ponds: An integrative model of creativity and innovation implementation in work groups", *Applied Psychology: An International Review*, **51**, 355–424.

West, M.A. (2004), *Effective Teamwork: Practical Lessons from Organizational Research*, Oxford: Blackwell/British Psychological Society.

West, M.A., Borrill, C.S. & Unsworth, K.L. (1998), "Team effectiveness in organisations", in C.L. Cooper & I.T. Robertson (eds), *International Review of Industrial and Organisational Psychology*, Vol. 13, Chichester: Wiley, pp. 1–48.

West, M.A., Garrod, S. & Carletta, J.C. (1997), "Group decision-making and effectiveness: unexplored boundaries", in C.L. Cooper and S. Jackson (eds), *Creating Tomorrow's Organizations: A Handbook for Future Research in Organizational Behavior*, Chichester: John Wiley, pp. 293–317.

Zdaniuk, B. & Levine, J.M. (2001), "Group loyalty: impact of members' identification and contributions", *Journal of Experimental Social Psychology*, **37**, 502–9.

28 Enhanced employee engagement through high-engagement teams: a top management challenge
George B. Graen

Introduction

Top management teams (TMTs) should prepare for the full impact of the onset of the knowledge era under which new knowledge utilization becomes the life-giving blood of corporations (Lafley & Charan, 2008). Knowledge-driven organizations, such as Procter & Gamble (P&G) and Walmart are establishing many new competitive weapons called game-changing designs. When ROI/quarter-driven corporations find themselves confronted by these innovations in corporate competition they often experience "shock and awe". As a matter of sustainability, corporations must show due diligence and develop or acquire "new toys" and managers to employ them effectively (Graen, 2009a).

How can top management teams contribute to enhancing the utility of the corporation's human resources to better compete in the vastly increased turbulence of the new knowledge-driven, game-changer's environment? What should you be doing now in terms of selecting the best people, and training and developing them to use the "new toys" as team members and team leaders? Your top management teams should use their executive coaches to both learn and promote the development of new problem-solving teams and networks on the formal side of the corporation (Graen, 2009b). This implies that additional problem-solving tools and skills will be supplied to employees who boldly go "beyond business as usual" (BBU). Knowledge era problems are likely to create or expose many new gaps in current corporate processes that can only be properly filled by specially trained problem-solving teams. Increasingly employees are stopped from doing their business as usual (BU) work by such gaps. When this happens, they either become disengaged and give up or turn to special problem-solving teams who go BBU to fill the troubling gaps. These special teams are linked to other like teams to form a special network. These network teams help solve more complex network problems. This part of the organization will need to be significantly augmented in the immediate future to give the corporation its required sustainability. "Work to rule" practices, whereby employees do only what their role strictly prescribes and nothing further, provides an example of the gap problem. They voluntarily shut down their gap-filling practices. The result is that the organization quickly grinds to a halt. Clearly, such gaps need to be filled.

How can a top management team make a difference?

Given what we know about the undercover work of informal emergent competence teams and networks (ibid.), top management teams can make a significant difference by filling the expected gaps with high-engagement, problem-solving teams that are (i) properly trained in emergent problem-solving teamwork by qualified executive coaches, (ii) motivated to make gap-filling contributions, (iii) trained to use protocols as maps that work, and (iv) trained to use the dynamics of gap-filling teams (Majchrzak et al., 2007). When working on one of the most difficult management tasks of implementing new and significant organizational changes, special high-engagement teams may be expected to operate such that intergroup conflict over changes that would probably overwhelm the less engaged would be managed properly.

Employees are compensated for emergent, problem-solving team or network activities by future placement in "fast-track" development programs. Such fast tracks also enrich the pool for managerial succession at all levels. Employees at all levels who agree to join high-engagement BBU teams are a highly valued human asset and become critical when the beehives hit the fans. They possess enhanced engagement to the corporation and commitment to its continued sustainability beyond the typical employee. This high engagement improves both retention and contribution. Next, we turn to a protocol for building high-engagement, problem-solving teams.

Candidates for high-engagement teams are selected carefully to undergo special gap-filling training and development. Corporate climate and support regarding proper development are critical to the training programs. Candidates for BBU teams, including leaders and members, are trained with proper tools for high-stress, problem-solving events (Grace, 2009). This produces BBU teams ready to react to emergencies. When the alarm bells sound, high-engagement teams spring into action to fill the gaps and return to normal conditions with new knowledge and a good deal of intrinsic pride. After the gaps are filled, the team smoothly slides back into the ongoing corporate processes.

How top management use such teams

Top management has as its mission to protect and serve the interests of the stakeholders with "due diligence". This mission requires executives to perform BBU when and where needed. For executives, BU is typically calm periods between dealing with new and often discontinuous and complex problems in need of immediate solutions. Recently, the calm periods have become much shorter and the problems more frequent and complex, often calling for more multidisciplinary teams to solve. In sum, knowledge is the new driver of corporations. It is truer than previously that ignorance or lack of knowledge is a dangerous condition for competitors. Executives increasingly need assistance from high-involvement teams and will need to know how to develop such teams.

How do executives motivate people engaged in BU behavior to also become fully engaged in problem-solving teams when and where appropriate? First of all, executives understand that their people may miss most of what their supervisors say and do when focusing on their own work. Managers must get their full attention through a tailored strategy over time. What normally attracts the most attention is the possibility of career progression and earning placement on the fast-track elevator to the executive suite. Top management on its board of directors need to sponsor human resource management (HRM) processes and practices which support such strategies. For those not upwardly mobile, what attracts their attention is documented recognition of their value to the corporation, a salary increase, and the implied job security. Again, top management or the board must demand and support HRM in implementing such recognition and reward processes and practices. The process of redirecting engagement from average to high levels may be done in many ways, but the recommended is cascading coaching of problem-solving teamwork, starting with top executives and rolling down the hierarchy. Those who do not buy in, unless they are critical specialists, may be passed by as the corporation becomes more knowledge driven. In the information age, HRM departments will be transformed into human capital functions built within flexible, cross-functional formal networks. Employees will be required to engage more of their personalities in making the processes adapt to problems of discontinuous changes. Executive coaches are in a unique position to help. As McKenna and Davis (2009, p. 249) point out: "It's about the working relationship stupid". Top management teams must focus more on finding the right talent, train and develop role players, and coach middle managers in developing special teams. Executive coaches need to teach executives how to develop their human assets from normal working relations to high-engagement teams. The protocol for executive development of this kind can be used by executives to coach their middle managers to develop new, high-engagement teams. Clearly, top management teams need to drive employee engagement down their hierarchies for the good of the organization.

The progress of leadership motivated excellence (LMX) teamwork can be tracked statistically and clinically employing the new LMX–SLX inventory© (Graen, 2010). The psychometric characteristics of the following 10-item agreement measure were assessed using item response theory (Scherbaum et al., 2007) and its validity was assessed using longitudinal importance analysis (Naidoo et al., 2008). Team members with strong LMX have been shown to endorse the following statements. My (colleague, supervisor, or subordinate) (1) is satisfied with my work, (2) will repay a favor, (3) will help me with my job problem, (4) will return my help, (5) has confidence in my ideas, (6) and I have a mutually helpful relationship, (7) has trust that I would carry my workload, (8) is one of my informal leaders, (9) has respect for my capabilities; and finally (10) I have an excellent working relationship with my (colleague, supervisor, or subordinate).

Top management executives develop BBU emergent network teams through leadership coaching. McKenna and Davis (2009) collected and documented decades of research on psychotherapy relevant to high-engagement team development. Employing these findings, executive coaching can make a contribution to developing high-engagement teams. Executives can be trained to become coaches of problem-solving teams composed of superiors, peers, subordinates, customers, suppliers, and shareholders. They need to be professionally trained in individual and social group health and be competent in diagnosing and correcting organizational problems. I have delivered such training as a consultant over an 18-month period for a management team of 60 executives (Graen, 2007) and the points that McKenna and Davis (2009) make can be usefully applied to building high-engagement teams with competent, trustworthy and dependable colleagues.

A list of the questions to be asked and acceptable responses are relevant to the development of excellent LMX team relations (ibid.). Applying these recommendations to the LMX process requires that the executive coached become in turn a coach for his/her target people. The potential targets should be all those whose work is interdependent with the executive's team. This leads to LMX excellence in intra- and inter-team relations (Graen et al., 2006). Once the LMX partnership process is mastered, it can be taught to others and future-oriented, game-changing designs for corporations become more feasible (Graen, 2009a).

Finally, let me briefly comment from an LMX shared-leadership perspective on each of the main questions about the target person (McKenna and Davis, 2009). In the following list, the question asked is followed by acceptable responses:

- Readiness for partnership is critical? . . .
  (Three strikes and out)

  T_1 no, T_2 no, T_3 yes, or quit.
  (T indicates time)

- What else is the target doing to change?
  . . .
  (If nothing suggest something)

  Find out.

- Do you believe it is about your interventions? . . .
  (Get attribution clear)

  No, it's interactive.

- Is target taking full responsibility for change? . . .
  (Target is doer)

  T_1 no, T_2 no, T_3 yes, or quit.

- Do you have a reliable alliance? . . .
  (Use tests)

  T_1 no, T_2 no, T_3 yes, or quit.

- Is it an LMX excellence relationship?
  (Measure it)

  T_1 no, T_2 no, T_3 yes, or quit.

- Is the alliance individualized? . . .
  (This is a strength)

  Make it so.

- Is the reality shared? . . .

  Make it so.

I especially recommend the sage advice offered by McKenna and Davis about the treatment of potential LMX partners, whether they are strangers or acquaintances.

With strangers:

- make building the LMX alliance a high priority right from the start;
- organize your thinking and interaction with the target around establishing the three elements of the alliance: goals, tasks, and bonds; and
- set the target's expectation that you will have regular conversations about the relationship itself and how it is working for them. Then follow up and ask them for their evaluation of the elements of the alliance.

With acquaintances:

- take stock of the quality and strength of your LMX alliances; ask yourself how the state of the alliance is affecting progress in each engagement and what you can do to improve each relationship;
- assess your own strengths and weaknesses in building target alliances; where are your opportunities for improvement? and

- recognize that you are half the equation in an alliance. You can't be effective when distracted, anxious, fatigued, or unprepared. Take care of yourself to be a more effective partner.

Clearly, this is no place for amateurs, and proper training and supervised practice should be required. When in doubt, refer to *LMX Leadership: The Series*, Graen (2009a) and Schiemann (2009).

Chief executive officers and TMTs of organizations who support the LMX team and network development process often do so as part of their game-changing designs (Graen, 2009a). These designs include strategies for developing adaptable, knowledge-driven corporations (Graen, 2010) with high-engagement teams at all levels. The process has been described by Graen (2009b) and others (Hannah et al., 2008).

Conclusion
Most executives understand based on their own careers that problem-solving teams can cope with almost any corporate challenge from inside or out. Most would give anything to be blessed with more of these special teams. However, many executives do not feel confident that they can personally develop such teams but hope that they emerge naturally to keep the company operating. Executive readings about self-organized teams typically celebrate their outstanding achievements, but seldom speculate on how such teams are constructed.

Ingredients of such teams are (a) talented people, who develop respect, trust and commitment with the coaches, other players, and the team, (b) coaches who develop reciprocal relationships with all of their team members, and (c) engagement opportunities to be challenged by real, potentially serious problems. Such problems are appearing more frequently on the desks of many top managers. Now that the tsunami alert has sounded, top management teams may either grab their golden parachute or become coaches of their middle managers and beyond. HRM executives need to retrofit to include problem-solving teams. BU teams require little engagement to do their job, but BBU teams do because it requires going the extra distance. Now is the time to prepare for the sharks that will follow the tsunami to your doors. High-engagement teams and networks with their shark-shockers will become necessary to protect the company. Predators are circling, waves are growing huge, and your boat is leaking. Now may be a good time to alert your new captains in waiting and turn loose your problem-solving teams to compete equally with the likes of P&G and Walmart in your markets.

References

Grace, M. (2009), "Development of design project teams and their supporting resource networks for the knowledge era", in G.B. Graen & J.A. Graen (eds), *Predator's Game-changing Designs: Research-based Tools. LMX Leadership: The Series*, Vol. VII, Charlotte, NC: Information Age Publishing, pp. 1–18.

Graen, G.B. (2007), *Jessica's Web: Women's Advantages in the Knowledge Era*, Charlotte NC: Information Age Publishing.

Graen, G.B. (2009a), "CEO summary: find-design-capture comparative advantage", in G.B. Graen & J.A. Graen (eds), *Predator's Game-changing Designs: Research-based Tools. LMX Leadership: The Series*, Vol. VII, Charlotte, NC: Information Age Publishing, pp. 209–27.

Graen, G.B. (2009b), "Strategic development of competence networks to implement adaptation", in G.B. Graen & J.A. Graen (eds), *Predator's Game-changing Designs: Research-based Tools. LMX Leadership: The Series*, Vol. VII, Charlotte, NC: Information Age Publishing, pp. 43–63.

Graen, G.B. (2010), "How do you motivate teamwork beyond business as usual?", in M.G. Rumsey (ed.), *The Many Sides of Leadership: A Handbook*, Oxford: Oxford University Press.

Graen, G.B., Hui, C. & Taylor, E.A. (2006), "Experience-based learning about LMX leadership and fairness in project teams: a dyadic directional approach", *Academy of Management Learning and Education*, **5**(4) 448–60.

Hannah, S.T., Eggers, J.T. & Jennings, P.L. (2008), "Complex adaptive leadership", in G.B. Graen and J.A. Graen (eds), *Knowledge Driven Corporation: Complex Creative Destruction. LMX Leadership: The Series*, Vol. VI, Charlotte, NC: Information Age Publishing, pp. 79–123.

Lafley, A.G. & Charan, R. (2008), *The Game Changer: How You Can Drive Revenue and Profit Growth with Innovation*, New York: Crown Publishing Group–Random House.

Majchrzak, A., Sirkka, L., Javenpaa, S.L. & Hollingshead, A.B. (2007), "Coordinating expertise among emergent groups responding to disasters", *Organizational Science*, **18**(1), 147–61.

McKenna, D.D. & Davis, S.L. (2009), "Hidden in plain sight: the active ingredients of executive coaching", *Journal of Industrial and Organizational Perspectives in Science and Practice*, **3**(3), 244–60.

Naidoo, L.J., Scherbaum, C.A. & Goldstein, H.W. (2008), "Examining the relative importance of leader–member exchange on group performance over time, knowledge driven corporation: a discontinuous model", in G.B. Graen and J.A. Graen (eds), *Knowledge Driven Corporation. LMX Leadership: The Series*, Vol. VI, Charlotte, NC: Information Age Publishing, pp. 211–30.

Scherbaum, C.A., Naidoo, L.J. & Ferreter, J.M. (2007), "Examining component measures of team leader–member exchange: using item response theory", in G.B. Graen & J.A. Graen (eds), *New Multinational Network Sharing. LMX Leadership: The Series*, Vol. V, Charlotte, NC: Information Age Publishing, pp. 129–56.

Schiemann, W.A. (2009). "Applying I-O tools to achieve strategic results: Metrus Group experience", paper presented at the 24th annual Society for Industrial and Organizational Psychology conference, New Orleans, April 3.

PART V

GLOBAL PERSPECTIVES ON EMPLOYEE ENGAGEMENT

29 Developing and validating a global model of employee engagement

Jack W. Wiley, Brenda J. Kowske and Anne E. Herman

Introduction

Most organizations today conducting employee surveys refer to their programs as "engagement surveys" or measure employee engagement as one of their survey topics. We estimate that 90 percent of our current global survey clients conduct employee engagement surveys. As others note (Macey & Schneider, 2008; Wefald & Downey, 2009), employee engagement, while a relatively new construct, has grown in popularity and acceptance, in large part because organizations believe that they can leverage employee engagement for positive organizational outcomes such as higher employee retention, greater customer satisfaction and improved financial performance (Harter et al., 2002).

We accomplish several objectives with this chapter. First, we provide a definition of employee engagement and a method for its measurement. Second, we rank the countries representing the world's 12 largest economies on our measure of employee engagement. Third, we identify the global drivers of employee engagement and compare and contrast these drivers with those derived from an analysis of country-level data. Fourth, we build an overall model of employee engagement and validate the model against organization-level measures of financial performance. Lastly, we suggest actions that organizations can take to drive employee engagement levels higher.

Definition and measurement

Literature reviews suggest that most definitions of employee engagement are similar in terms of their key components. These common components include enthusiasm for work, commitment, organizational pride, employee alignment with organizational goals, and a willingness to exert discretionary effort (ibid; Vance, 2006; Robinson, 2007; Schneider et al., 2009). Our definition is mainstream; we define employee engagement as: "The extent to which employees are motivated to contribute to organizational success, and are willing to apply discretionary effort to accomplishing tasks important to the achievement of organizational goals".

The literature acknowledges that there is no universally accepted way of measuring employee engagement. Organizations typically measure employee engagement using survey items addressing organizational antecedents and/or drivers of employee engagement, the engagement construct itself, behavioral outcomes of employee engagement, or some combination of all four. Vance (2006) provides a useful summary of the most common employee engagement measurement approaches.

Our approach to measuring employee engagement treats engagement as a desired state (Macey & Schneider, 2008), measured by an equally weighted combination of four individual elements: pride, satisfaction, advocacy and retention. The rationale is straightforward: an engaged workforce is one whose employees have pride in and are satisfied with their organization as a place to work, and who advocate for and intend to remain with their organization. In this conceptualization, employee engagement is a result of organizational policies and practices and leadership and managerial behaviors that precede the state of employee engagement, which itself precedes the display of discretionary effort that promotes heightened individual, team and organizational performance.

We measure employee engagement with the items presented below rated on a balanced five-point Likert agreement scale:

- I am proud to tell people I work for my organization;
- overall, I am extremely satisfied with my organization as a place to work;
- I would recommend this place to others as a good place to work; and
- I rarely think about looking for a new job with another organization.

These four items comprise the Kenexa Employee Engagement Index (EEI), typically reported as percent favorable, that is, the average level of agreement across the four items. EEI coefficient alpha, an internal consistency estimate of reliability, is quite high at 0.91.

Employee engagement country ranking
Prior to a review of global and country-level EEI scores, we must first describe the WorkTrends™ survey, which provides the data from which our findings are drawn. WorkTrends is a research program begun under the direction of the senior author in 1984. Originally, WorkTrends was administered only in the United States. In 2007, the survey program expanded to include several additional countries. The dataset used for the analyses presented here was collected in 2009 from workers in the following

countries: Brazil, Canada, China, France, Germany, India, Italy, Japan, Russia, Spain, the United Kingdom and the United States. While these are not the only countries covered by WorkTrends, they do represent the 12 largest economies as measured by gross domestic product (GDP), accounting for 73 percent of the world's GDP (IMF, 2009). In its current form, WorkTrends is a multi-topic survey completed online by a sample of workers screened to match a country's worker population in terms of industry mix, job type, gender, age and other key organizational and demographic variables. Those who work full-time in organizations of 100 employees or more are allowed to take the survey. The survey has 115 items that cover a wide range of workplace issues. In 2009, approximately 10,000 workers in the United States, 750 in Russia and 1,000 in all other listed countries completed the survey. For the analyses described below, a representative subsample of 1,000 US workers was drawn to equalize the impact of the US data on the determination of employee engagement drivers.

Measuring employee engagement as described above, the global average and 12-country ranking of EEI scores is presented in Figure 29.1. In absolute terms, the average EEI score across these 12 countries is 56 percent. Clearly, for the countries studied, workers feel engaged at their workplace in varying degrees. Organizations in certain countries are not inherently more or less likely to engage their employees, but we acknowledge that cultural dynamics might affect scores. In fact, the spread between countries is substantial. The EEI score for India, the top-ranked country, is slightly more than twice that of Japan, the lowest-ranked country. In

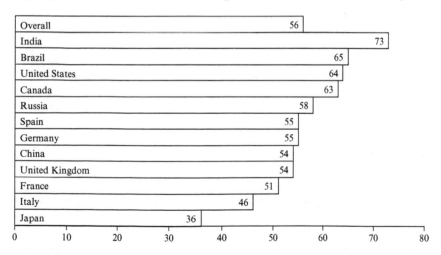

Figure 29.1   Country ranking on the Employee Engagement Index

general, North American countries score higher than Western European countries. India notably outpaces other Asian countries, perhaps due in part to its bright economic future and educated workforce. Among the fastest growth economies, Brazil ranks the highest; other fast-developing economies such as Russia and China rank lower, but their EEI scores could rise as their economies continue to grow and leadership and managerial practices strengthen.

Global drivers of employee engagement

Promoting employee engagement is at the top of many organizations' talent management agendas. The question becomes "how"? Relative weights analysis (RWA) is used to identify the key drivers of employee engagement (see Johnson, 2000; Lundby & Johnson, 2006, for a description of this advanced statistical procedure). The analysis reveals the top 10 global drivers:

1. confidence in the organization's future;
2. organization supports work/life balance;
3. excited about one's work;
4. promising future for one's self;
5. safety is a priority;
6. corporate responsibility efforts increase overall satisfaction;
7. opportunity to improve one's skills;
8. satisfied with recognition;
9. confidence in the organization's senior leaders; and
10. co-workers give their very best.

On reflection, this list can be further reduced. In broad terms, we believe that there are four "macro drivers" of employee engagement, or in other words, that employees are engaged by:

- leaders who inspire confidence in the future (drivers 1, 4 and 9);
- managers who recognize employees and mobilize their teams for peak performance (drivers 8 and 10);
- exciting work and the opportunity to improve their skills (drivers 3 and 7); and
- organizations that demonstrate a genuine responsibility to their employees and the communities in which they operate (drivers 2, 5 and 6).

Embedded in these macro drivers is the concept of the employees' future. Not only do employees need to do their current job well, they also need to feel secure about the future of the organization, as well as to be able to visualize their own future within the organization. An employee's trust in the future hinges on the competence and trustworthiness of senior leadership.

An employee's immediate manager influences his/her engagement and understandably so. The manager is the representative of the organization through which work, resources, support and communication flows. Two critical elements of a manager's job appear to have a special influence: giving recognition for a job well done and enabling his/her staff, through direction, resources and problem solving, to give their very best.

Management and leadership matters, but the work itself also plays a significant role. Beyond mastering the job's tasks, employees need to be enthusiastic about what they are doing, about meeting challenges and enjoying that sense of excitement when goals are achieved. Employees need to feel pride in what is being accomplished and they need to feel as if they are building their own skill set and becoming more capable of taking on new assignments.

Every organization has its own identity and goals. Employees care about the organization's mission and value working for an organization that is committed to serving others. Employees are more engaged when they feel that their organization is committed to its employees' livelihood and community, through both support of an employee's work/life balance as well as corporate responsibility efforts. These findings are intuitive; why would the employee care about the health of the organization if the organization does not care about him/her?

Three other observations about this list of 10 drivers deserve attention. The first is the noteworthy overlap between these drivers and Vance's (2006) listing of the 10 common themes for how organizations measure employee engagement. Three of Vance's themes correspond directly to how we measure employee engagement: pride, satisfaction and retention. Among the remaining seven on his list, six match directly or very closely to our list of drivers. The seventh, which deals with discretionary effort, is neither measured by the EEI nor a driver of the EEI, but is captured in our definition and assumed a consequence of an elevated state of employee engagement.

A second observation: our listing of employee engagement drivers reveals a pattern quite dissimilar from the observation of others who conclude that an EEI comprising items measuring pride, satisfaction, advocacy and retention is typically explained by job satisfaction, satisfaction with benefits and opportunities for promotion (Schneider et al., 2009). While those measures were included as potential drivers in our analysis, they failed to emerge as such. One could argue that job satisfaction and work excitement occupy the same explanatory space, but work excitement, even on the surface, reveals a much more nuanced sense of enthusiasm and passion about the work itself than does job satisfaction. In addition, not only did satisfaction with benefits and opportunities for promotion not appear as top three drivers, they failed to make the list of the top 10.

Finally, an observation about stability in the listing of drivers is warranted. Our 2008 WorkTrends study surveyed workers in 10 of the top 12 GDP economies; Spain and France were not included. When we compare the 2008 10-country RWA listing of drivers to the same 10-country RWA listing of drivers for 2009, the overlap is 100 percent. This reveals remarkable stability and demonstrates the reliability of conclusions drawn regarding the four underpinnings of employee engagement: leaders, managers, exciting work coupled with skill development and responsible organizations.

Country-level drivers of employee engagement: similarities and differences

Identifying the drivers of employee engagement across the world's 12 largest economies creates a generalized understanding of areas to leverage to push employee engagement levels higher. Are these findings generalizable across country borders? Recognizing a country's unique history and culture frame the broader context for organizational values, leadership styles and management–employee relations, how does this impact on employee engagement? Subjecting country-level data to the RWA procedure helps answer these questions. Commonalities among drivers are displayed in Figure 29.2.

The analysis reveals that the global drivers of employee engagement serve as an excellent predictor of the employee engagement drivers for any given country. In fact, for five of the 12 countries, the country-to-global

	Confidence in organization's future	Work/life balance	Excited about work	Promising future	Safety is a priority	Corporate responsibility	Opportunity to improve skills	Recognition	Confidence in senior leaders	Co-workers give their very best
Brazil	●	●		●	●	●	●	●	●	●
Canada	●	●		●	●	●	●	●	●	
China	●	●	●	●	●		●			●
France	●	●	●	●	●	●	●	●		
Germany	●	●	●	●		●	●	●	●	
India	●		●	●	●	●	●	●	●	●
Italy	●	●	●	●	●	●	●	●		
Japan	●	●	●	●	●		●	●	●	
Russia	●	●	●	●	●		●	●	●	
Spain	●	●	●	●	●	●		●		
UK	●	●	●	●	●		●	●	●	●
USA	●	●	●	●	●	●	●	●	●	

Figure 29.2   Commonality of country-level EEI drivers

employee engagement driver match is 90 percent; for another five countries, the match is 80 percent; and for just two countries, China and Spain, the match drops to 70 percent. On average, the country-to-global match of employee engagement drivers is 82.5 percent.

It is helpful to have an understanding of the drivers that emerge as universally important. The two drivers in the top 10 lists for all 12 countries are both future oriented: confidence in the organization's future and the belief that there is a promising future for one's self. A combination of important workplace practices, including support for work/life balance, placing a priority on safety, providing psychological recognition and opportunities for skill enhancement, are almost as common, emerging on the lists of 11 of 12 countries. Only one of the top 10 global drivers appears on the lists of fewer than eight countries: co-workers giving their best is a driver for just four countries.

Identifying each country's unique drivers is perhaps equally important to understanding the degree of commonality among employee engagement drivers across countries. They are summarized in Table 29.1. From patterns evident in the table, the following five observations seem noteworthy:

1. For workers in Canada and the United Kingdom, more so than for workers in other countries, the perceived effectiveness of their immediate manager is a key determinant of employee engagement.
2. For workers in China, their employee engagement level is more influenced by their perceptions of fair pay than by their satisfaction with recognition. This could be due to the speed of economic growth in their country and the resulting need for pay levels to keep pace with the cost of living, or it may be that for Chinese workers, to a greater degree than in other countries, pay is a primary mechanism for delivering recognition. Chinese workers are the only ones for whom pay appears as a top 10 driver.
3. For workers in Russia, employee engagement levels are somewhat uniquely driven by the emphasis their organization places on product quality and customer service.
4. For workers in France, Germany and Japan, employee engagement levels are influenced by the perceived organizational and leadership support for diversity in the workforce.
5. Of the drivers specific to a country's top 10, only one is common to at least three countries: their organization serves the interests of multiple stakeholders, including employees, customers, suppliers and financial stakeholders. The countries for which employee engagement is particularly influenced by this notion are Brazil, Canada and Italy.

Table 29.1   Specific country-level EEI drivers

Country	Country-specific drivers	Global list driver replaced
Brazil	Organization serves multiple stakeholders	Excited about work
Canada	Effectiveness of immediate manager	Co-workers give very best
	Organization serves multiple stakeholders	Excited about work
China	Concern for staff well-being	Corporate responsibility
	Fair pay	Recognition
	Communication open and two-way	Confidence in senior leaders
France	Communication open and two-way	Confidence in senior leaders
	Diverse enabled to excel	Co-workers give very best
Germany	Participation in decision making	Safety is a priority
	Co-workers display organization values	Co-workers give very best
India	Diverse enabled to excel	Support for work/life balance
Japan	Leaders committed to diversity	Co-workers give very best
Russia	Higher-quality products/services	Corporate responsibility
	Recognition for outstanding service	Co-workers give very best
Italy	Quality/improvement are top priorities	Co-workers give very best
	Organization serves multiple stakeholders	Confidence in senior leaders
Spain	Manager keeps commitments	Co-workers give very best
	Participation in decision making	Opportunity to improve skills
	Improving product/service quality	Confidence in senior leaders
UK	Effectiveness of immediate manager	Corporate responsibility
USA	Quality/improvement are top priorities	Co-workers give very best

Building and validating an overall employee engagement model

While some differences exist between countries on their respective lists of the top 10 drivers of employee engagement, the more important implication is that country-level drivers are much more similar than dissimilar. Further, each set of drivers by country tends to have distinct components dealing with the four macro drivers: the performance of leaders, the behavior of managers, the alignment of the individual to the work itself paired with the opportunity to grow further their skills, and the extent to which organizations demonstrate a sense of responsibility to their employees and the communities in which they operate.

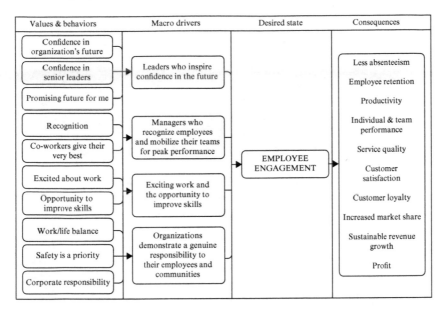

Figure 29.3   Prerequisites and outcomes of employee engagement

As a result, we propose the overall model of employee engagement presented in Figure 29.3. This model views employee engagement in "system" terms: there are unique inputs and outputs. Employees are compelled to engage by drivers that aggregate into the macro drivers. When the drivers of employee engagement are optimized, employee engagement itself increases dramatically. Beyond a sense of employee well-being, employee engagement predicates certain organizational outcomes, including talent retention, product/service improvement and organization-level financial success. Is this model valid? Below are the results of a study exploring the relationship of employee engagement to important financial metrics.

We combined EEI results from 139 organizations with two key financial metrics: diluted earnings per share (DEPS) and three-year total shareholder return (3-year TSR). The EEI scores were derived from employees participating in the 2009 WorkTrends study. To select organizations to include in this research, agreement statistics (R_{wg}) among raters within each organization with more than five employees were calculated. If the R_{wg} demonstrated low agreement (values greater than 1.0 and less than 0, James et al., 1984), the organization was excluded. The resultant sample represents all major industries including retail, banking and financial services, manufacturing, hospitality, healthcare and business services.

Eighty-five percent of the sample organizations are multinational with locations and employees in more than 100 countries; 80 percent employ more than 10,000 workers.

DEPS gauges an organization's profit margin and its quality. More specifically, it is a ratio of an organization's profit to the number of shares outstanding, and is often used by financial analysts when calculating the price to earnings ratio, which is referenced when classifying stock as buy, hold or sell. Total shareholder return is commonly used to compare the performance of organizations, and reflects a given organization's performance during a certain period by combining share price appreciation and dividends paid. Both metrics were collected in 2009 subsequent to the reporting of 2008 fiscal year results. For this study, DEPS is a metric of short-term recent performance, whereas 3-year TSR is a metric representing longer-term performance.

Results are presented in Figure 29.4. The correlations of EEI to both financial metrics are as expected, positive and significant. Clearly, those organizations in the top quartile of EEI scores outperform bottom quartile EEI organizations by substantial margins. While these results are correlational and conclusions about causation cannot be asserted, they demonstrate that attention paid to EEI drivers and to elevating EEI scores is associated with superior financial performance. In addition, these results are among the few that demonstrate linkage between employee survey

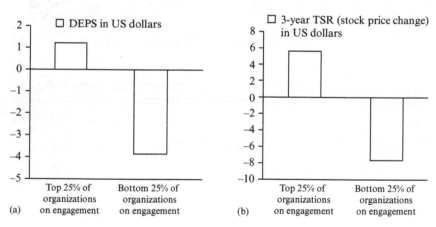

Notes:
(a)   One-tailed Pearson correlation: $r = 0.27$, $p < 0.01$.
(b)   One-tailed Pearson correlation: $r = 0.19$, $p < 0.01$; values have been mean-centered to aid interpretability.

Figure 29.4   Employee engagement, diluted earnings per share and total shareholder return

results and financial performance across organizations (Schneider et al., 2003). The generalizable nature of these results adds substantially to the potency of the conclusions drawn.

Driving employee engagement higher

Having established the relationship between employee engagement and organization-level financial performance, what can an organization do to drive employee engagement higher? Using the macro-driver framework, we believe there are several system-level actions that organizations can take (see Table 29.2).

By way of illustration, system-level influencers of "leaders who inspire confidence in the future" are several-fold and include: (i) how effectively organizations assess, select and promote executive talent; (ii) the quality of both strategic plans and their execution; (iii) the techniques utilized to develop leadership; (iv) very specifically, the communication abilities of leadership teams and the extent to which they communicate the key role

Table 29.2   Systemic-level influencers of employee engagement

Macro driver	Systemic influencers
Leaders who inspire confidence in the future	Executive assessment/selection
	Quality of strategic plan and execution
	Leadership development
	Communication abilities/employee orientation
	Balanced scorecard/performance management systems
Managers who recognize employees and mobilize their teams to peak performance	Management assessment/selection
	Management development/behavior modeling
	Performance and talent management systems
	Quality and improvement plan/initiatives
	Use of feedback systems: customers and employees
Exciting work and the opportunity to improve skills	Job–person match
	Employee involvement in decision making
	On-the-job training
	Stretch assignments/professional development
	Performance and talent management systems
Organizations genuinely responsible to employees and community	Safety procedures/training/compliance
	Work/life balance programs/support
	Genuine, consistent leadership/management support
	Corporate responsibility investment level
	Public relations and employee awareness

employees play in organizational success; and (v) how leaders themselves are evaluated and the extent to which their evaluation is a multifaceted view of performance (that is, contains employee, customer and financial components) versus a singular and narrow view of delivering financial results only. Each of the macro drivers can be viewed through the lens of systemic influencers.

Summary

In this chapter, we set out to present both a definition of, and a measurement technique for, employee engagement. Global drivers of employee engagement, reducible to four macro drivers (leaders, managers, job–person match and organizational values) have been identified. Employee engagement drivers for the countries representing the world's 12 largest economies have been compared and contrasted. Very importantly, the method of measuring employee engagement has been validated against both short- and longer-term independent measures of financial performance, using a seldom available cross-organization and cross-geography design. Finally, systemic influencers of employee engagement have been suggested for driving levels higher. This chapter has demonstrated that employee engagement can be measured, that drivers of employee engagement tend to be more universal than country specific and that higher levels of employee engagement are associated with stronger financial performance.

References

Harter, J.K., Schmidt, F.L. & Hayes, T.L. (2002), "Business-unit-level relationship between employee satisfaction, employee engagement, and business outcomes: a meta-analysis", *Journal of Applied Psychology*, **87**, 268–79.
International Monetary Fund (IMF) (2009), "World Economic Outlook Database" (datafile), available from IMF Website http://www.imf.org/external/data.htm.
James, L.R., Demaree, R.G. & Wolf, G. (1984), "Estimating within-group interrater reliability with and without response bias", *Journal of Applied Psychology*, **69**, 85–98.
Johnson, J.W. (2000), "A heuristic method for estimating the relative weight of predictor variables in multiple regression", *Multivariate Behavioral Research*, **35**, 1–19.
Lundby, K.M. & Johnson, J.W. (2006), "Relative weights of predictors: what is important when many forces are operating", in A.I. Kraut (ed.), *Getting Action for Organizational Surveys: New Concepts, Methods, and Applications*, San Francisco, CA: Jossey-Bass, pp. 326–51.
Macey, W.H. & Schneider, B. (2008), "The meaning of employee engagement", *Industrial and Organizational Psychology*, **1**, 3–30.
Robinson, D. (2007), "Engagement is marriage of various factors at work", *Employee Benefits*, **37**.
Schneider, B., Hanges, P.J., Smith, D.B. & Salvaggio, A.N. (2003), "Which comes first: employee attitudes and organizational financial and market performance?", *Journal of Applied Psychology*, **88**, 836–51.
Schneider, B., Macey, W.H., Barbera, K.M. & Martin, N. (2009), "Driving customer satisfaction and financial success through employee engagement", *People & Strategy*, **32**, 22–7.

Vance, R.J. (2006), *Employee Engagement and Commitment: A Guide to Understanding, Measuring and Increasing Engagement in Your Organization*, Alexandria, VA: SHRM Foundation.

Wefald, A.J. & Downey, R.G. (2009), "Job engagement in organizations: fad, fashion, or folderol?", *Journal of Organizational Behavior*, **30**, 141–5.

30 Work engagement from a cultural perspective
Akihito Shimazu, Daisuke Miyanaka and Wilmar B. Schaufeli

Introduction

In accordance with the expanding global economy, researchers in occupational health psychology have begun to conduct cross-cultural studies. This chapter focuses on work engagement from a cultural perspective and addresses basic measurement issues in cross-cultural research on work engagement.

Brief introduction of work engagement

Psychology has recently been criticized as being primarily dedicated to addressing mental illness rather than mental "wellness". Since the beginning of this century, however, increased attention is paid to what has been coined "positive psychology": the scientific study of human strengths and optimal functioning (Seligman & Csikszentmihalyi, 2000). This advocated positive turn is also relevant for occupational health psychology. It has been proposed that rather than focus on employees' poor functioning as a result of stress and burnout, what will be more beneficial for our understanding of individuals and organizations is to look at the role of a more positive state of mind, which is called "work engagement" (Schaufeli, 2004).

Work engagement is a psychological state assumed to be negatively related to burnout. While burnout is usually defined as a syndrome of exhaustion, cynicism, and reduced professional efficacy (Maslach et al., 2001), engagement is defined as a positive, fulfilling, work-related state of mind that is characterized by vigor, dedication, and absorption (Schaufeli et al., 2002b). That means that engaged employees have a sense of energetic and effective connection with their work activities. Vigor is characterized by high levels of energy and mental resilience while working. Dedication refers to being strongly involved in one's work and experiencing a sense of significance and pride. Finally, absorption is characterized by being fully concentrated and happily engrossed in one's work.

Measurement of work engagement

Work engagement is operationalized with the Utrecht Work Engagement Scale (UWES; Schaufeli & Bakker, 2003), a self-report instrument that includes the above three dimensions. The original UWES (UWES-17) includes 17 items (Schaufeli et al., 2002b): vigor (six items), dedication (five items), and absorption (six items). The UWES-17 has encouraging psychometric features. For instance, confirmatory factor analyses showed that the hypothesized three-factor structure of the UWES is superior to the one-factor model (for example, Schaufeli et al., 2002a; Schaufeli & Bakker, 2004), although the dimensions are highly related. In addition to the UWES-17, a shortened version of nine items (the UWES-9) – with three scales of three items each – shows similar encouraging psychometric features (Schaufeli et al., 2006). Hardly any systematic differences in work engagement were observed between men and women, or across age groups. In some occupational groups, engagement levels were found to be higher than in other groups (for example, executives versus blue-collar workers).

The UWES is now used especially in Western countries. Currently, 21 language versions are available (that is, Afrikaans, Brazilian, Chinese, Czech, Dutch, English, Estonian, Finnish, French, Italian, German, Greek, Japanese, Norwegian, Polish, Portuguese, Romanian, Russian, Spanish, Swedish, and Turkish) and an international database exists that currently includes engagement records of nearly 80,000 employees. For the 17-item version of the UWES, the three-factor model fits slightly better to the data than the one-factor model, at least as far as samples from Western countries such as Spain, Portugal, the Netherlands, and Greece are concerned (Llorens et al., 2006; Schaufeli et al., 2002a; Schaufeli & Bakker, 2003, 2004; Xanthopoulou et al., in press). In addition, a cross-national study that included samples from 10 mostly Western countries (that is, Australia, Belgium, Canada, Finland, France, Germany, the Netherlands, Norway, South Africa, and Spain) showed factorial invariance of the three-factor structure of the UWES-9 across samples from various countries (Schaufeli et al., 2006). Hence, the factor structure of the UWES is essentially similar and does not differ between countries. However, because the correlations between the three engagement dimensions are very high and the internal consistency of the 9-item scale is very good, the authors conclude that the total score can be used as an indicator of work engagement.

Culture and positive emotion

Because of the expanding global economy, researchers in occupational health have begun to conduct cross-cultural research. As far as work engagement is concerned, however, cross-cultural research has been

largely limited to Western countries with relatively small linguistic and cultural differences, such as Spain, Portugal and the Netherlands (Schaufeli et al., 2002a). Because the investigation of work engagement in other non-Western cultures, such as Japan, still stand out, it may contribute to our further understanding and to the generalizability of the concept of work engagement across different cultures. This is of special relevance, because previous cross-cultural studies showed that results obtained in Western samples cannot just be generalized to the Japanese context.

For instance, Scholz et al. (2002) showed the validity of generalized self-efficacy, the belief of being able to control challenging environmental demands by taking adaptive action (Bandura, 1997), applied in samples drawn from 25 different countries. However, they also showed that the mean scores of the general self-efficacy scale differed systematically among countries. The lowest means were found for the Japanese, followed by the Hong Kong Chinese; whereas highest values were found for the Costa Ricans, Danes, and French. Scholz et al. explained the low scores of self-efficacy among the Japanese as follows: "hard work and effort is more highly valued than ability in collectivistic cultures. Therefore, self-efficacy may be rated lower in collectivistic cultures than in individualistic cultures" (2002, p. 249).

Another example comes from Iwata et al. (1995), who examined cultural differences in responses to positive and negative items of the Center for Epidemiologic Studies Depression Scale (CES-D; Radloff, 1977) among American and Japanese adult workers. They found that responses to negatively worded items (for example, lonely, crying) were generally comparable in the two groups (mean scores 3.91 versus 3.52 for Japanese and US workers, respectively, $p > 0.10$), whereas the Japanese responses to positively worded items (for example, (not) hopeful, (not) happy) markedly differed from those of US workers (mean scores: 6.03 versus 1.83, respectively, $p < 0.001$: note that high scores mean high depressive symptoms). Iwata et al. (1995) explained their results in terms of the tendency to suppress positive affect expression among Japanese. According to Iwata et al., maintenance of social harmony is one of the most important values in Japanese society, and the Japanese have been taught since childhood to understate their own virtues and not to behave assertively. As a result, the Japanese may judge positive affect and affairs through a comparison with others (that is, relativistic judgment), which leads to suppression of positive affect expression. Kirmayer (1989) pointed out that in some cultures the suppression of distress could be a means of successful coping and, at the same time, might provide a mark of moral distinction. Likewise, the suppression of positive affect may represent a moral distinction and socially desirable behavior in Japanese society.

These examples suggest that a common bias exists in cross-cultural comparison of mental health and other psychosocial conditions due to the wording of the items: that is, particularly responses to positive items are likely to be biased among various ethnocultural groups.

International comparison of UWES scores

As mentioned in the previous section, in a collectivistic culture such as Japan, maintenance of social harmony is one of the most important values, which may result in suppression of positive affect expression (Iwata et al., 1995). This suggests that such a response tendency might negatively affect the psychometric properties of UWES, which consists of positively worded items. So, the following question emerges:

Is the score on the work engagement scale among Japanese lower than those among other samples?

To answer this question, scores of UWES-9 among Japanese employees were compared with those from employees from 15 other countries (that is, Australia, Belgium, Canada, China, the Czech Republic, Finland, France, Germany, Greece, Italy, the Netherlands, Norway, South Africa, Spain and Sweden) by use of an international database (see http://www.schaufeli.com/).

Figure 30.1 shows the scale scores of UWES-9 (Shimazu et al., 2005). Since multiple comparisons were made, the Bonferroni correction was applied to control for increased probability of Type 1 errors or spurious results. The alpha level was set at 0.001. As expected, Japanese employees scored significantly lower than the employees from any other country, suggesting that they are less engaged compared to employees from any other country. However, the relationships between engagement and country should be interpreted with caution since instead of using representative national samples, convenience samples have been used. Nevertheless, it is notable that Japanese employees had lower scores across any comparison and that the differences were rather large; that is, more than one standard deviation in eight out of 15 comparisons. Thus, these results may reflect "the Japanese tendency to suppress positive affect expression" (Iwata et al., 1995, p. 242).

Application of item response theory to UWES

Now we recognize that we should take into account the tendency to suppress the expression of positive affect among Japanese employees when comparing positive aspects of well-being, particularly with other Western countries, our second question is:

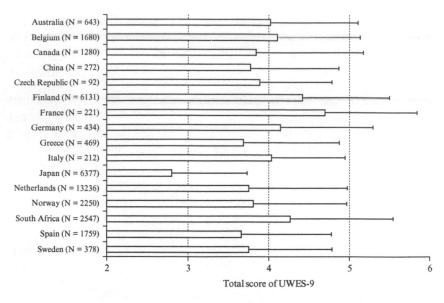

Australia (N = 643)
Belgium (N = 1680)
Canada (N = 1280)
China (N = 272)
Czech Republic (N = 92)
Finland (N = 6131)
France (N = 221)
Germany (N = 434)
Greece (N = 469)
Italy (N = 212)
Japan (N = 6377)
Netherlands (N = 13236)
Norway (N = 2250)
South Africa (N = 2547)
Spain (N = 1759)
Sweden (N = 378)

Total score of UWES-9

Note: All comparisons were significant at the 0.1% level (Bonferroni correction for multiple comparison was applied).

Figure 30.1   Comparison of UWES-9 scores between Japan and 15 countries

Is the UWES sensitive to change in the extent of work engagement among employees in non-Western countries like Japan?

To answer this question, an advanced psychometric scale analysis called item response theory (IRT; Emberson & Reise, 2000) was applied to our cross-cultural data. IRT is a model-based approach to understand the nonlinear relationships between individual characteristics (for example, traits), item characteristics (for example, difficulty), and individuals' response patterns. The use of IRT to study individual difference variables such as work engagement is advantageous for several reasons (Scherbaum et al., 2006; Oishi, 2007).

First, IRT analyses compute the standard error of measurement (SEM) at each level of the latent trait, which indicates the extent of measurement preciseness at each level of the trait. For instance, it may be the case that a measure may be more precise at particular levels (high versus low) of work engagement. Second, IRT analyses compute the amount of psychometric "information" about the latent trait at each level of the trait that is provided by each item, as well as the entire measure, using the item information functions (IIFs) and the test information function (TIF), respectively. The IIFs and the TIF are particularly useful because they indicate which items, and which levels of the latent trait, provide substantial information. For instance, it may be that some items or particular levels of the trait (for example, high versus low levels of work engagement) provide less information. Taken together, IRT can be used to evaluate measures in terms of how well the items and the entire measure assess a trait at different levels on the continuum for the trait (Lord, 1977; Hambleton et al., 1991).

By using IRT, we (Miyanaka, 2009) investigated (i) the measurement accuracy of the original (that is, Dutch) and the Japanese version of the 9-item short UWES and (ii) the comparability of the scale between the Netherlands (N = 13,406) and Japan (N = 2,339). Figure 30.2 shows the results of TIF and SEM among Dutch and Japanese samples, respectively (note that SEM equals the root square of 1/TIF), whereby the x-axis indicates the latent trait of the scale and the y-axis indicates measurement precision conditional on latent trait for the whole scale.

The TIF and SEM results showed that measurement accuracy of both versions was *not* similar. The amount of information in the Japanese version decreased sharply at the level of less than 2 (Figure 30.2b), meaning that the Japanese version had difficulty in differentiating respondents with extremely low work engagement. On the other hand, the amount of information in the original Dutch version decreased gradually at the level of more than 1 (Figure 30.2a), meaning that the original version had difficulty in differentiating respondents with high work engagement.

These results suggest that extremely low scores of the Japanese UWES-9 do *not* necessarily indicate low work engagement but might reflect decreased measurement accuracy of the scale in a Japanese sample. A possible cause of decreased measurement accuracy might be the tendency to suppress the expression of positive affect among Japanese people (Iwata et al., 1995). The results also suggest that (extremely) high scores of the original UWES-9 do *not* necessarily indicate high work engagement. The typical response tendency known as "self-enhancement", the general sensitivity to positive self-relevant information (Heine et al., 1997; Kitayama et al., 1997) might be a possible cause of decreased measurement accuracy. According to Kitayama et al. (1997), this tendency has positive social and psychological consequences within a cultural system that is organized to foster and promote the independence and the uniqueness of the self. Because self-enhancement maintains and enhances an overall evaluation of the self such as self-esteem, it could be a means of successful coping in Western countries.

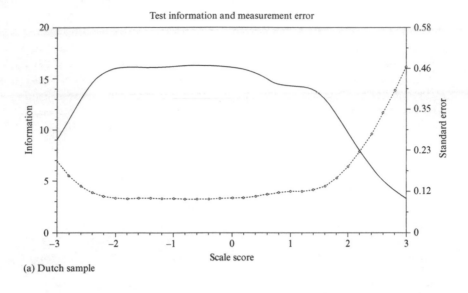

(a) Dutch sample

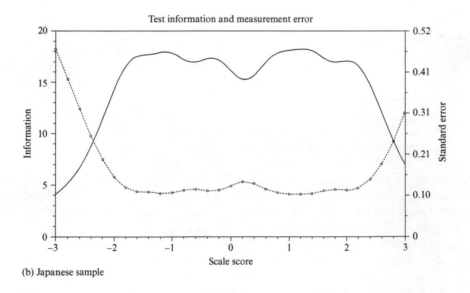

(b) Japanese sample

Note: TIF (solid line) is read from the left vertical axis; SEM (dotted line) is read from the right vertical axis.

Figure 30.2   TIF and SEM of UWES-9

Concluding remarks

With the globalization of occupational health psychology, more and more researchers are interested in applying employee well-being such as work engagement to diverse populations. This chapter addressed psychometric issues in conducting cross-cultural studies in the field of occupational health psychology. In comparing positive aspects of well-being such as work engagement between Western and Asian countries (at least Japan), we should take into account the tendency to suppress the expression of positive affect among Japanese as well as the tendency for self-enhancement among Westerners. Hence, for the time being, we should be cautious when interpreting low engagement scores among Japanese as well as high engagement scores among Western employees. Further psychometric studies are needed to differentiate respondents with low work engagement in Japan as well as to differentiate those with high work engagement in Western countries. Ultimately, accurate measurement contributes to our further understanding and to the generalizability of the concept of work engagement across different cultures.

References

Bandura, A. (1997), *Self-efficacy: The Exercise of Control*, New York: Freeman.

Emberson, S.E. & Reise, S.P. (2000), *Item Response Theory for Psychologists*, Mahwah, NJ: Erlbaum.

Hambleton, R.K., Swaminathan, H. & Rogers, H.J. (1991), *Fundamentals of Item Response Theory*, Newbury Park, CA: Sage.

Heine, S.J., Lehman, D.R., Markus, H.R. & Kitayama, S. (1997), "Is there a universal need for positive self-regard?", *Psychological Review*, **106**, 766–94.

Iwata, N., Roberts, C.R. & Kawakami, N. (1995), "Japan–U.S. comparison of responses to depression scale items among adult workers", *Psychiatry Research*, **58**, 237–45.

Kirmayer, L. (1989), "Cultural variations in the response to psychiatric disorders and emotional distress", *Social Science and Medicine*, **29**, 327–39.

Kitayama, S., Markus, H.R., Matsumoto, H. & Norasakkunkit, V. (1997), "Individual and collective processes in the construction of the self: self-enhancement in the United States and self-criticism in Japan", *Journal of Personality and Social Psychology*, **72**, 1245–67.

Llorens, S., Bakker, A.B., Schaufeli, W.B. & Salanova, M. (2006), "Testing the robustness of the job demands–resources model", *International Journal of Stress Management*, **13**, 378–91.

Lord, F. (1977), "Practical applications of item characteristic curve theory", *Journal of Educational Measurement*, **14**, 117–38.

Maslach, C., Schaufeli, W.B. & Leiter, M.P. (2001), "Job burnout", *Annual Review of Psychology*, **52**, 397–422.

Miyanaka, D. (2009), "An item response theory analysis of the Utrecht Work Engagement Scale among Dutch and Japanese workers", unpublished master's thesis, University of Tokyo, Japan.

Oishi, S. (2007), "The application of structural equation modeling and item response theory to cross-cultural positive psychology research", in A.D. Ong & M.H.M. Van Dulmen (eds), *Oxford Handbook of Methods in Positive Psychology*, New York: Oxford University Press, pp. 126–38.

Radloff, L.S. (1977), "The CES-D scale: a self-report depression scale for research in the general population", *Applied Psychological Measurement*, **1**, 385–401.

Schaufeli, W.B. (2004), "The future of occupational health psychology", *Applied Psychology: An International Review*, **53**, 502–17.

Schaufeli, W.B. & Bakker, A.B. (2003), *UWES – Utrecht Work Engagement Scale: Test Manual*, Utrecht: Utrecht University, Department of Psychology (http://www.schaufeli.com).

Schaufeli, W.B. & Bakker, A.B. (2004), "Job demands, job resources and their relationship with burnout and engagement: a multi-sample study", *Journal of Organizational Behavior*, **25**, 293–315.

Schaufeli, W.B., Bakker, A.B. & Salanova, M. (2006), "The measurement of work engagement with a short questionnaire: a cross-national study", *Educational and Psychological Measurement*, **66**, 701–16.

Schaufeli, W.B., Martínez, I., Marques-Pinto, A., Salanova, M. & Bakker, A.B. (2002a), "Burnout and engagement in university students: a cross national study", *Journal of Cross-Cultural Psychology*, **33**, 464–81.

Schaufeli, W.B., Salanova, M., González-Romá, V. & Bakker, A.B. (2002b), "The measurement of engagement and burnout: a confirmative analytic approach", *Journal of Happiness Studies*, **3**, 71–92.

Scherbaum, C.A., Cohen-Charash, Y. & Kern, M.J. (2006), "Measuring general self-efficacy: a comparison of three measures using item response theory", *Educational and Psychological Measurement*, **66**, 1047–63.

Scholz, U., Gutierrez-Dona, B., Sud, S. & Schwarzer, R. (2002), "Is general self-efficacy a universal construct? Psychometric findings from 25 countries", *European Journal of Psychological Assessment*, **18**, 242–51.

Seligman, M.E.P. & Csikszentmihalyi, M. (2000), "Positive psychology: an introduction", *American Psychologist*, **55**, 5–14.

Shimazu, A., Schaufeli, W.B., Kosugi, K., Kato, A., Sakamoto, M., Irimajiri, H. & Amano, S. (2005), "Development of the Japanese version of Utrecht Work Engagement Scale (UWES-J)", Abstracts – Second ICOH International Conference on Psychosocial Factors at Work, 64.

Xanthopoulou, D., Bakker, A.B., Kantas, A. & Demerouti, E. (in press), "The measurement of burnout and work engagement: a comparison of Greece and the Netherlands", *New Review of Social Psychology*.

PART VI

PERFORMANCE, OUTCOMES AND INTERVENTIONS: WHAT ENGAGEMENT INFLUENCES AND HOW TO DEVELOP IT

31 The nature and consequences of employee engagement: searching for a measure that maximizes the prediction of organizational outcomes

Peter H. Langford

Introduction

Despite organizations spending billions of dollars assessing employee engagement, there continues to be strong debate regarding the nature and consequences of employee engagement. To further inform this debate, this chapter has the following primary goals: (i) to better understand the nature of employee engagement by developing a theoretically grounded and empirically derived model that integrates the many characteristics that have been proposed to represent employee engagement; (ii) to derive from the model a broad, efficient, predictive measure of employee engagement; and finally, (iii) to better understand the potential return on investment from initiatives targeted at improving employee engagement. The chapter draws upon ongoing research at Voice Project, a research and consulting company founded and based at Macquarie University, Sydney, Australia.

Establishing the potential domain of employee engagement

With the goal of identifying a useful model and predictive measure of employee engagement, researchers at Voice Project designed a study in which we measured a broad range of constructs that various researchers and practitioners have proposed as representing employee engagement. We included long-standing, heavily researched constructs such as *job satisfaction* (for example, "Overall I am satisfied with my job"), *affective organization commitment* (modified from Allen & Meyer, 1990, for example, "I feel emotionally attached to this organization") and *intention to stay* (for example, "I am likely to still be working in this organization in two years' time"). One of the more commonly cited academic models of engagement is that of Schaufeli et al. (2006), so we included their measures of *vigor* (for example, "At my job I feel strong and vigorous"), *dedication* (for example, "I am enthusiastic about my job") and *absorption* (for example, "I get carried away when I am working"), all of which aggregate to their measure of engagement. In a series of articles led by Macey and Schneider (2008) a common theme was the relationship between engagement and positive affectivity, so we included a measure of *positive affectivity at work* (with items from the PANAS (Positive and Negative Affect Scale) by Watson et al., 1988, modified to refer to the work environment – for example, "I feel interested at work").

All of the above measures could be regarded as *attitudinal* given they all tap into thoughts, feelings or behavioural intentions. Given that some researchers have also argued that engagement comprises *behaviours*, we included measures associated with the self-report of the following behaviours: *discretionary effort* (Lloyd, 2003, for example, "I put in extra effort whenever necessary"), *citizenship behaviours* (directed towards both the organization and individuals; Morrison & Phelps, 1999, for example, "I keep abreast of changes in the organization" and "I help others who have work-related problems"), and items adapted from Griffin et al. (2007) assessing *in-role behaviour* (for example, "I carry out core parts of my job well"), *adaptivity* (for example, "I adapt well to changes in tasks"), and *proactivity* (for example, "I come up with ideas to improve the way tasks are done"). In total, the survey comprised 43 items representing short measures of each of the 13 above-mentioned attitudinal and behavioural constructs that have at various times been proposed to be representative of employee engagement.

Discriminant validity of employee engagement measures

To examine the relationships between all 13 measures, researchers at Voice Project collected data from 1,701 employees across 180 teams (for example, a department or work unit) with each team coming from a different organization, and with a broad range of industries and sectors being represented.

Wanting to better understand the pattern of relationships among all 13 engagement-related measures, we factor analysed all of the employee responses. The first strong finding was that a single factor explained around half of the variance across all of the measures. Second, there were numerous cross-loadings among the measures. While all of the original measures demonstrated good internal reliability, there was very poor discriminant validity among most of these constructs. These results strongly demonstrated an extensive overlap among all 13 engagement measures with team-level correlations ranging from 0.46 to 0.95 and averaging 0.76. Such findings have been highlighted elsewhere. Harrison et al. (2006) have previously demonstrated the presence of an overall job attitude factor. Similarly, Harter and Schmidt (2008) have argued that researchers and practitioners have poorly applied the fundamental scientific principle of

Occam's razor – the rule of parsimony that directs us to use the simplest explanation possible. Harter and Schmidt have criticized the proliferation of new constructs that may be conceptually different but which empirically show little or no advantage over previously researched constructs.

This finding of a single overarching factor provides the opportunity to label the factor as "employee engagement". Some researchers may feel that this decision hijacks the job attitude construct that could be argued to have scientific precedence. The term "employee engagement", however, is now extremely widely used among practitioners and increasingly researchers. As such, we are willing to yield ground to enormous momentum and use the label "employee engagement" to represent this overarching positivity or negativity of work attitudes and behaviours.

Of course, defining employee engagement as an overarching factor does not explain or negate a structure of subcategories within employee engagement. Desiring to explore this potential structure within, we searched for multiple lower-order factors and found empirical support for the model of employee engagement shown in Figure 31.1. The two most prominent factors to emerge within employee engagement closely mirrored the split between the attitudinal and the behavioural measures. That is, all measures that used items assessing attitudes (thoughts, feelings and intentions) tended to group together, and all the measures involving the self-report of one's own behaviours tended to group into a second factor.

These two higher-order factors in turn divided into the six lower-order categories shown in Figure 31.1. Two of the factors, intention to stay and proactivity, exactly mirrored the content of their original measures. We found that the original measures of positive affectivity, job satisfaction, and Schaufeli's measures of vigor, dedication and absorption tended to group into a single factor for which we have used the traditional label of "job satisfaction", capturing employees' level of positivity towards their job and work tasks. Another factor within the attitudinal half of the model, for which we have used the traditional label "organization commitment", contained content assessing the level of attachment and loyalty towards the organization. Bottom-centre in the behavioural half of the model is a factor represented by content from the original measures of in-role behaviour, adaptivity and organizational citizenship behaviours towards individuals. This factor, which we have labelled as "proficiency" following the lead of Griffin et al. (2007), appears to represent behaviours associated with doing one's primary job well, including adapting to required changes and helping others. The final factor, bottom-left, labelled "effort", was represented by items from the original measures for discretionary effort and citizenship behaviours towards the organization,

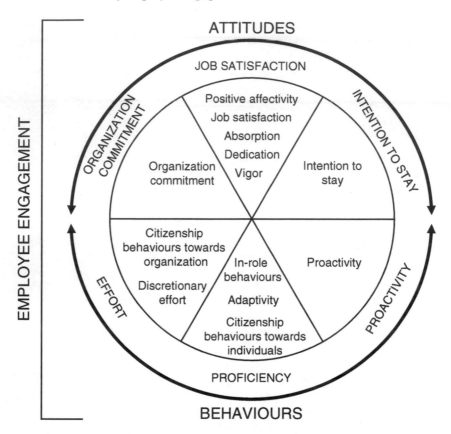

Figure 31.1   Modelling the structure within employee engagement

representing behaviours associated with working harder and longer than required or than is typical.

Developing a broad, efficient and predictive measure of employee engagement

The model in Figure 31.1 remains a theoretical plaything unless we can link its components to practically important organizational outcomes. To do that, we refined a measure from the original 43 items used to measure the original 13 constructs. The scope of this chapter prevents a detailed explanation of the process and results in developing the measure (contact the author for more information), but the final measure that we produced is shown in Box 31.1. We have labelled this measure the "Voice Engagement Survey" in reference to the researchers in Voice Project at Macquarie University who have developed the measure.

BOX 31.1   VOICE ENGAGEMENT SURVEY

Attitudes
Organization commitment
   I feel a sense of loyalty and commitment to this organization
   I am proud to tell people that I work for this organization
   I feel emotionally attached to this organization
Job satisfaction
   My work gives me a feeling of personal accomplishment
   I like the kind of work I do
   Overall I am satisfied with my job
Intention to stay
   I am likely to still be working in this organization in two years'
      time
   I would like to still be working in this organization in five years'
      time
   I can see a future for me in this organization

Behaviours
Effort
   When I work I really exert myself as much as I can
   I put in extra effort whenever necessary
   I work harder than is required
Proficiency
   I carry out core parts of my job well
   I cope with changes to the way I have to do tasks
   I complete tasks well using standard procedures
Proactivity
   I initiate better ways of doing tasks
   I come up with ideas to improve the way tasks are done
   I make changes to the way tasks are done

In order to cross-validate the measure shown in Box 31.1, we ran another study to confirm the above-mentioned findings and test the measure on a second set of data. In a similar style to the first study described above, we asked a further 1,186 employees from 193 different teams (with each team from a different organization) to self-report their employee engagement. We also gathered statistics for employee turnover (annual percentage of staff within the team) and absenteeism (days per employee) for these teams, and asked the managers of these business units to rate on a 1–5 rating scale their organization's productivity, safety, innovation, customer satisfaction, and the degree to which objectives were being achieved. By combining standardized scores for all these outcomes, we produced a single measure of composite performance for each team. The results are shown in Table 31.1.

One of the most notable findings is that the attitudinal measures outperformed the behavioural measures. Indeed, the measure of engagement attitudes (which was calculated by aggregating the scores from the three attitude scales of organization commitment, job satisfaction and intention to stay) outperformed the measure for engagement behaviours, and also outperformed the engagement overall measure. A possible explanation of these findings is that employees may see self-reports of attitudes as evaluating the job or organization, but may instead see self-reports of behaviours as evaluating one's own performance, resulting in biased and less accurate self-reporting of behaviours. One conclusion from these analyses is that the engagement attitudes measure may provide the best measure of employee engagement, given that it was more efficient (nine items, compared to 18 items for the full measure) and demonstrated the strongest association with many of the organizational outcomes. Indeed, in our ongoing research (for example, Parkes & Langford, 2008; Langford, 2009) and consulting work (for example, Langford, 2010; Mingo & Langford, under review) we have found it sufficient to measure only organization commitment, job satisfaction and intention to stay, aggregating these three scales into a measure of employee engagement.

The return on investment in employee engagement
The correlations between outcomes and employee engagement shown in Table 31.1 are not only statistically significant, but they are also practically important, against which dollar values can be estimated. For example, for an organization paying employees an average salary of A\$65,000, these correlations suggest a 5 percent higher score for employee engagement on a typical "percent favourable" scale equates to approximately A\$3,700 higher productivity output per employee, A\$1,500 lower turnover costs per employee, A\$150 lower absenteeism costs per employee, and A\$35 lower workers' compensation costs per employee, totalling almost A\$5,400 in increased revenue and reduced costs per employee (contact the author for details of the assumptions underlying these calculations). Further, these values are based on uncorrected correlations, and some researchers have demonstrated that true underlying correlations, based on statistical corrections for unreliability of measures and range restrictions, can be up to twice as strong as the original observed correlations (for

Table 31.1 Correlations between organizational outcomes and components of the Voice Engagement Survey

	M	SD	Composite performance	Turnover	Absenteeism	Productivity	Safety	Innovation	Customer satisfaction	Achieving objectives
M			0.00	16.02	6.31	4.20	4.30	3.97	4.34	4.31
SD			0.60	23.59	6.02	0.59	0.66	0.57	0.55	0.54
Engagement overall	4.08	0.40	0.45*	0.28*	0.16*	0.31*	0.30*	0.37*	0.18*	0.29*
Engagement attitudes	4.01	0.49	0.50*	0.25*	0.18*	0.36*	0.30*	0.39*	0.23*	0.35*
Engagement behaviours	4.19	0.35	0.27*	0.25*	0.09	0.15*	0.21*	0.27*	0.05	0.13*
Attitudes										
Organization commitment	4.07	0.51	0.46*	0.19*	0.12*	0.35*	0.29*	0.38*	0.21*	0.34*
Job satisfaction	4.13	0.46	0.46*	0.21*	0.12*	0.30*	0.28*	0.36*	0.27*	0.35*
Intention to stay	3.71	0.71	0.46*	0.26*	0.18*	0.35*	0.29*	0.33*	0.19*	0.30*
Behaviours										
Effort	4.19	0.36	0.24*	0.23*	0.15*	0.14*	0.16*	0.23*	0.03	0.06
Proficiency	4.31	0.38	0.25*	0.22*	0.04	0.10	0.22*	0.23*	0.06	0.17*
Proactivity	4.07	0.45	0.25*	0.21*	0.06	0.16*	0.19*	0.27*	0.04	0.11

Note: * $p < 0.05$, one-tailed.

example, Harter et al., 2002). Hence, it could be argued that these figures are underestimates.

An unfortunate limitation of our research and that of all other research-ers, however, is that all information linking employee engagement with organizational outcomes is correlational. What we do not know from existing research is the extent to which an improvement in employee engagement *causes* these financial outcomes. Research at Voice Project, and that of others, has shown a reciprocal relationship between employee engagement and organizational outcomes. For example, Langford and Demirian (2007) used an experimental design with hypothetical scenarios and found that improvements in customer satisfaction, innovation and achieving organization objectives resulted in employees subsequently reporting higher levels of engagement. Langford et al. (2006) used struc-tural modelling with correlational data from over 10,000 employees and found that models with engagement causing organizational outcomes, and models with organizational outcomes causing engagement, were equally plausible. Perhaps the safest assumption at this stage of our knowledge is that of a reciprocal causal relationship, in which higher employee engage-ment leads to desirable organizational outcomes, and improved organiza-tional outcomes also lead to higher employee engagement.

Conclusions and practical implications
The model and measure presented in this chapter have been designed to represent a broad domain of attitudes and behaviours that various researchers and practitioners have suggested are associated with employee engagement. The finding of a single overarching factor representing all of the attitudinal and behavioural constructs in Figure 31.1 provides firm grounds for using "employee engagement" as the label for this overarch-ing factor. Despite the inclusion of both attitudinal and behaviour content in our model of employee engagement, our research and consulting expe-rience suggests that an efficient measure of employee engagement need only assess the attitudinal components of employee engagement, and that the addition of behavioural content may have a neutral or even negative impact upon the ability to predict organizational outcomes. We have found that the nine attitudinal items in the top half of Box 31.1 provide a broad, efficient and predictive measure of employee engagement. These nine items also enable the calculation of specific subcategory scores for organization commitment, job satisfaction and intention to stay enabling comparison against decades of research into these constructs. Finally, higher levels of employee engagement are associated with tangible organizational out-comes that can be quantified in terms of dollar value. This chapter pre-sented estimates of such outcomes, but for organizations to make accurate

judgements of return on investment in employee engagement in their own unique circumstances, we argue that each organization should conduct its own internal linkage research. Such research would examine differences in employee engagement across different business units, and correlate such differences with tangible performance indicators for each business unit. Further, interventions to improve employee engagement can be costed and returns can be calculated, and we encourage researchers and practitioners to conduct such case-study analyses of organizational development efforts within organizations. It is only through such internal linkage research that organizations can make accurate decisions about how much to invest in the improvement of employee engagement, and what return on investment can be expected.

References

Allen, N.J. & Meyer, J.P. (1990), "The measurement and antecedents of affective, continuance and normative commitment to organizations", *Journal of Occupational Psychology*, **63**, 1–18.

Griffin, M.A., Neale, A., & Parker, S.K. (2007), "A new model of work role performance: positive behaviour in uncertain and interdependent contexts", *Academy of Management Journal*, **50**, 327–47.

Harrison, D.A., Newman, D.A. & Roth, P.L. (2006), "How important are job attitudes? Meta-analytic comparisons of integrative behavioral outcomes and time sequences", *Academy of Management Journal*, **49**, 305–25.

Harter, J.K. & Schmidt, F.L. (2008), "Conceptual versus empirical distinctions among constructs: implications for discriminant validity", *Industrial and Organizational Psychology*, **1**, 36–9.

Harter, J.K., Schmidt, F.L. & Hayes, T.L. (2002), "Business-unit-level relationship between employee satisfaction, employee engagement, and business outcomes: a meta-analysis", *Journal of Applied Psychology*, **87**, 268–79.

Langford, P.H. (2009), "Measuring organisational climate and employee engagement: evidence for a 7 Ps model of work practices and outcomes", *Australian Journal of Psychology*, **61**, 185–98.

Langford, P.H. (2010), "Benchmarking work practices and outcomes in Australian universities using an employee survey", *Journal of Higher Education Policy and Management*, **32**(1), 41–53.

Langford, P.H. & Demirian, S. (2007), "The effect of organisational performance on employee engagement", in M. Dollard, T. Winefield, M. Tuckey & P. Winwood (eds), *Proceedings of the 7th Industrial and Organisational Psychology Conference*, Melbourne: Australian Psychological Society, pp. 180–84.

Langford, P.H., Parkes, L.P. & Metcalf, L. (2006), "Developing a structural equation model of organisational performance and employee engagement", in M. Katsikitis (ed.), *Proceedings of the 2006 Joint Conference of the Australian Psychological Society and the New Zealand Psychological Society*, Melbourne: Australian Psychological Society, pp. 204–8.

Lloyd, R. (2003), "Discretionary effort in the workplace", unpublished doctoral dissertation, Macquarie University, Sydney, NSW.

Macey, W.H. & Schneider, B. (2008), "The meaning of employee engagement", *Industrial and Organizational Psychology*, **1**, 3–30.

Mingo, S. & Langford, P.H. (2009), "Revisiting the HR-performance link using longitudinal, business-unit level, multi-person, multi-item measures of HR practices and outcomes", manuscript submitted for publication.

Morrison, E.W. & Phelps, C.C. (1999), "Taking charge at work: extra-role efforts to initiate change at work", *Academy of Management Journal*, **42**, 403–19.
Parkes, L.P. & Langford, P.H. (2008), "Work–life balance or work–life alignment? A test of the importance of work–life balance for employee engagement and intention to stay in organisations", *Journal of Management and Organization*, **14**, 267–84.
Schaufeli, W.B., Bakker, A.B. & Salanova, M. (2006), "The measurement of work engagement with a short questionnaire: a cross-national study", *Educational and Psychological Measurement*, **66**, 701–16.
Watson, D., Clark, L.A. & Tellegen, A. (1988), "Development and validation of brief measures of positive and negative affect: the PANAS scales", *Journal of Personality and Social Psychology*, **54**, 1063–70.

32 Feeling good *and* performing well? Psychological engagement and positive behaviors at work
Uta K. Bindl and Sharon K. Parker

Introduction

In spite of its popularity in the practitioner and scientific literature, we know little about how feelings of engagement affect the way individuals perform at work. The aim of our chapter is to draw on theory, as well as empirical studies, to better understand the relationship between psychological engagement and positive behaviors at work.

While there have been many definitions of employee engagement, we focus here on psychological engagement and, more specifically, the feelings of activated positive affect. Schaufeli et al. (2002) identified vigor as one of the key elements of engagement, along with dedication and absorption, and Macey and Schneider (2008) identified feelings of energy, enthusiasm, alertness and pride as central to psychological engagement. Each of these feelings is characterized not only by their positive focus, but also by their high level of activation. As noted by Macey and Schneider, activated positive emotional states better capture the construct of engagement than low-activation emotional states, such as contentment and satisfaction.

In this chapter, we elaborate on how and why such activated positive emotional states might influence three different types of work role performance: proficiency, adaptivity, and proactivity (see Griffin et al., 2007). We conclude our chapter with suggestions for further research and practical implications to organizations. To set the foundation for our discussion, we first define affect and work performance.

Affect at work

Affect at work is usually distinguished into two related concepts: *moods* reflect the way employees temporarily feel when at work. For example, employees can feel energized and enthused at work. Employees are likely to interpret any events at work in the light of their current moods, and behave accordingly (Parkinson et al., 1996). In contrast, *emotions* are the feelings of an employee towards a specific event or issue (Brief & Weiss, 2002). For example, employees can feel frustrated about not

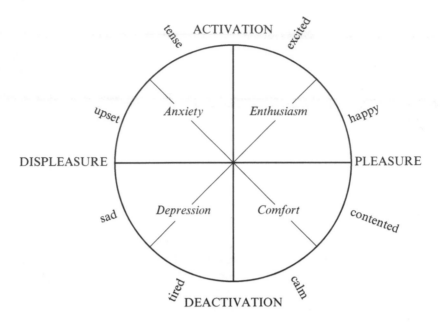

Source: Adapted from Russell (2003).

Figure 32.1 Circumplex model of affect

succeeding with a project, or proud about the feedback they receive from their supervisor.

When we speak of psychological engagement, we refer to moods, which tend to exist for longer time periods, rather than more short-lived emotions at work. Employees are said to be engaged at work when they experience activated positive feelings at work, such as energy and vigor. These and other types of feelings are represented in the *circumplex model of affect* (Russell, 2003). Russell distinguished between activation and deactivation, as well as between pleasure and displeasure, yielding in four different affect quadrants (see Figure 32.1). Employee engagement is best represented by the activated pleasure quadrant of affect, or feelings such as enthusiasm.

Positive work behaviors
For our review, we draw on the taxonomy of work performance introduced by Griffin et al. (2007), whereby work performance comprises three distinct types of positive work behaviors – proficiency, adaptivity, and proactivity.

Proficiency is characterized by the fulfillment of role requirements that can be clearly anticipated, such as a call-center agent who effectively answers incoming calls following formally prescribed guidelines. Such proficient behavior, which has received the most attention in the literature, was especially important in the past when the working environment was rather predictable, and job tasks were clearly defined. However, with increasing globalization, mergers, and dynamic changes in businesses it has become increasingly important for the viability of organizations to have employees who engage not only in proficient, but also in adaptive and proactive behaviors (Frohman, 1997; Campbell, 2000; Parker, 2000; Frese & Fay, 2001). *Adaptivity* refers to employees responding to changes at work, and *proactivity* relates to employees actively changing their work. For example, as well as answering calls (proficiency), a call-center agent can respond to changing customer requirements in an efficient manner (adaptivity), and suggest improved ways of dealing with customer queries (proactivity).

Importantly, Griffin et al. (2007) identified that each of these three types of individual work behaviors can be directed towards different levels. For example, employees can ensure that their tasks are completed properly (individual task proficiency), they can coordinate work with their co-workers (team member proficiency), or they can demonstrate loyalty to their organization by defending its reputation (organization member proficiency). Each of these three behaviors – completing one's tasks, coordination, and loyalty – are considered examples of proficiency because the need for them can be anticipated and prescribed. However, they vary in whether they contribute primarily to the individual's job, the team, or the organization. While there have been general arguments that employee engagement should promote positive work role behaviors, these lack theoretical precision, in part because distinctions have not been made between different types of performance.

Relationship between affect and positive work behaviors

There are theoretical reasons, as well as empirical evidence, to suggest that positive affect in general will promote each of the categories of positive work behavior. For example, positive affect leads people to focus on positive outcomes, which enhances their judgment that they will be able to perform the corresponding task, and thereby promotes greater effort towards achieving the task (proficiency). However, as described above, engagement is more specific, and involves activated positive affect, such as feelings of enthusiasm. In most of the research and theorizing on positive affect, it is not clear to what extent this affect must be "activated" to have the predicted effects on behavior. For example, laboratory-based research conducted in social psychology regularly speaks of "positive affect inductions" (for example, Isen & Reeve, 2005), and thus does not distinguish between activated or non-activated positive affect. Likewise, most organizational research relies on the PANAS (Positive and Negative Affect Scale) measure, which does not distinguish between activated and non-activated affect, although mainly captures activated affect (Tellegen et al., 1999).

In the following, we develop some initial propositions regarding how activated positive affect might influence positive work behaviors. We focus particularly on proactivity, for which there is the clearest evidence. We propose that activated positive affect will promote proactive behavior, albeit not for all individuals or in all situations. The positive element of engagement results in broadening and building of thought–action repertoires, and facilitates expected outcomes of actions; and the energized, activated aspect of it prompts the engagement in action and approach.

Although it is not the core focus of our chapter, we suggest that activated positive affect can also promote proficiency and adaptivity, however we suggest that boundary conditions exist for these associations.

Activated positive affect and its effect on proactivity
Proactivity at work has been defined as a special type of goal-directed behavior that it is self-starting, anticipatory and change oriented (Crant, 2000; Parker et al., 2006; Grant & Ashford, 2008; Bindl & Parker, in press). Employees can be proactive in initiating better ways of conducting their tasks (individual task proactivity), they can be proactive in developing methods to help their team perform better (team member proactivity), or they can actively suggest how to improve performance of the organization (organization member proactivity). Positive affect can broaden individuals' momentary action–thought repertoire (Fredrickson, 1998, 2001; Isen, 1999; Fredrickson & Joiner, 2002), thus encouraging engagement in generative, proactive behaviors. In support of this, positive affect has been shown to predict higher, and more challenging goals (Ilies & Judge, 2005), and to help individuals engage with a more problematic future (Oettingen et al., 2005). In this vein, a recent study by Foo et al. (2009) investigated entrepreneurs' daily behaviors and found that positive affect at work may prompt a more future-oriented focus, which then helps increase levels of effort into tasks that go beyond those immediately required. Finally, proactivity likely "rocks the boat", and is thus, although beneficial for the organization, not always welcomed by supervisors and colleagues (Frese & Fay, 2001). As Parker et al. (in press) suggest in their model of proactive motivation, the "energized-to" mechanism, that is, affective states, may promote proactivity at work via enhancing employees' expectations of success as well as the utility judgments of their proactive actions.

Several studies to date have focused on the relationship between employees' engagement, or activated positive affect, and proactivity at work. Salanova and Schaufeli (2008) found for managers of a telecom company in the Netherlands that there was a positive relationship between work engagement and self-reported personal initiative ($\beta = 0.64$, $p < 0.001$). Similarly, in an online study across professions in the Netherlands, work engagement was found to be positively related with self-reported innovative work behaviors ($\beta = 0.37$, $p < 0.001$; Schaufeli et al., 2006); and employees working in the healthcare sector reported increased levels of personal initiative at work if they were in an activated positive mood (Den Hartog & Belschak, 2007). These findings were supported in a longitudinal study of dentists which showed that individuals with high work engagement in the initial year of the study were more likely to indicate higher personal initiative three years later ($\beta = 0.13$, $p < 0.001$; Hakanen et al., 2008).

Longitudinal insights of more short-lived, daily processes also indicate a positive influence of engagement on proactivity at work. Sonnentag (2003) found over five consecutive days that day-level work engagement predicted higher levels of day-level self-initiative ($\gamma = 0.77$, $p < 0.001$) and pursuits of learning ($\gamma = 0.78$, $p < 0.001$). In an even more fine-grained level of investigation, Binnewies et al. (2009) showed that the feeling of being recovered and energized in the morning predicted higher levels of self-initiative during the same work day ($\gamma = 0.21$, $p < 0.001$).

The relationship between activated positive affect and proactivity holds not only for individual task proactivity but also for organization member proactivity. In a study of executive MBA students, individuals who indicated higher levels of activated positive affect also reported engaging in more strategic scanning (for example, anticipating needed changes in the organization) and issue selling; both behaviors directed at enhancing the organization's fit with its environment (Parker et al., 2008).

In sum, there is good evidence of the beneficial role of activated positive affect for proactive behaviors at work. We thus suggest:

Proposition 1: Activated positive affect promotes proactive behaviors at work.

Moderators

Individual and contextual contingencies may affect the relationship between activated affect and positive work role behaviors. First, prior evidence shows that the broadening effect of positive mood on cognitive processes only occurs if the task is judged to be important (Isen, 1999). This perception of importance is likely especially relevant for proactive behaviors at work, as they are self-initiated, without being imposed by others (Bindl & Parker, in press; Parker et al., in press). We thus suggest:

Proposition 2: The relationship between activated positive affect and proactivity at work is stronger if the situation or task is perceived as important.

Further, the actual control employees have over their tasks has been shown to affect the relationship between feelings of energy and recovery on the one hand and individual proactivity on the other. When employees perceive higher levels of job control, the positive relationship between state engagement and proactivity is stronger (Binnewies et al., 2009). These findings indicate that employees, in order to show proactivity at work, not only need to be engaged at work, but also need to be given a considerable amount of discretion over their tasks. We thus suggest:

Proposition 3: Activated positive affect promotes proactivity in a specific situation if the employee has control or influence over that situation.

Finally, Parker et al. (2008) showed that activated positive affect predicted the proactive behaviors of individual innovation and issue selling. This relationship, however, was sustained only if individuals did not possess a high performance orientation, that is, did not have a very strong desire to prove their competency in every situation. High levels of performance orientation appeared to overwhelm any value of activated positive affect for promoting proactivity. We thus suggest:

Proposition 4: Activated positive affect promotes proactivity if the employee does not have overarching dispositional orientations that discourage self-initiated and change-oriented behaviors at work.

Activated positive affect and its effect on adaptivity and proficiency

We argue that while general positive affect (that is, both the "enthusiasm" and "comfort" quadrants of affect in Figure 32.1) is beneficial for adapting to and complying with requirements within the work environment, there are several reasons why activated positive affect should be particularly helpful for some types of proficiency and adaptivity, albeit under some circumstances more than others.

Positive affect can increase performance at work by improving the efficiency by which employees process information, especially mood-congruent information (Matthews, 1992). When employees decide whether to behave in a positive work behavior, or not, the recall of positive past emotional experiences will signal to individuals that it is appropriate to engage in the planned action, thus promoting continued engagement in the action (Baumeister et al., 2007). Ultimately, individuals who are engaged in their work are thus more likely to be persistent at their tasks (Erez & Isen, 2002, Seo et al., 2004).

Empirical studies suggest the particular importance of activated positive affect in this respect. In a study of insurance sales agents, Tsai et al. (2007) showed that activated positive affect at work promoted self-efficacy and task persistence, and Totterdell (1999, 2000) showed that professional cricketers' feelings of energy, enthusiasm, and focus predicted higher performances in competitive games. In a similarly daily study design, Xanthopoulou et al. (2009) found that higher levels of daily engagement predicted higher levels of daily financial return by the respective service employee. These findings also appear to hold over a longer timeframe. Staw et al. (1994) showed that employees' experiences of positive affect at work predicted higher levels of supervisor-rated performance ($\beta = 0.31$, $p < 0.001$), as well as slight increases in wage ($\beta = 0.05$, $p < 0.01$), 18–20 months later. In sum, we argue:

Proposition 5: Activated positive affect is particularly important for facilitating proficient and adaptive behaviors where the situation requires persistence.

In addition, we propose:

Proposition 6: Positive affect will be especially important for promoting positive work behaviors that are oriented towards the team and the organization, such as team member proficiency and organization member proficiency.

Ample research suggests that positive affect promotes individuals to help other individuals. For example, Tsai et al. (2007) found that positive moods promote employees' helping colleagues ($\beta = 0.40$, $p < 0.01$), and Belschak and Den Hartog (2009) found partial support for a positive relationship between positive affect and intentions to engage in team member proficiency behaviors such as helping colleagues ($\beta = 0.12$, n.s.; $\beta = 0.52$, $p < 0.01$; $\beta = 0.16$, n.s., for study 1 (samples 1 and 2) and study 2, respectively). Likewise, studies support the facilitating role of activated positive affect for organization member proficiency. For example, salespeople who experience positive work-related mood were rated by their supervisors as engaging more in customer service-oriented work behaviors ($\beta = 0.17$, $p < 0.05$; George, 1991). Similarly, Belschak and Den Hartog (2009) showed that positive affect facilitates intentions to engage in citizenship behaviors that are directed towards the organization, such as active participation in organizational life and matters, and – with more inconsistent results – in citizenship behaviors that are directed towards the team. Similar effects have been found in studies focused on day-specific level of mood, although some studies have found stronger effects for behaviors directed at the organization rather than the work group (Dalal et al., 2009), whereas other studies (Lee & Allen, 2002) have shown that activated positive affect is most important for predicting citizenship behaviors that were directed at individuals, rather than the organization *per se*.

With regard to the facilitating effect of positive affect on adaptivity, Baron (2008) argued that positive affect may enhance an individual's capacity to respond effectively to dynamic situations, and to reach effective decisions under situational ambiguity. This is because individuals who experience activated positive affect are more likely to choose to engage in approach behaviors: they are likely to spend increased effort in the situation as opposed to deliberating and not engaging in action. For example, Salanova and Schaufeli (2008) investigated the relationship between engagement and employee behavior during technological changes in their company. More engaged employees were also more likely to indicate "When things are wrong, I search for a solution immediately" (p. 122; $\beta =$ 0.56, $p < 0.001$). We thus propose:

Proposition 7: Activated positive affect is particularly important for adaptivity in dynamic and ambiguous situations.

For employees to perform well on their job, help co-workers, or adjust efficiently to a changing situation in the organization, they need to be in the position to be able to do so (Blumberg & Pringle, 1982). In this vein, similar to the relationship between engagement and proactivity at work, job control appears to have a facilitating function for engaged employees to perform well in their job (individual proficiency) and to help co-workers (team member proficiency; Binnewies et al., 2009). These findings suggest that job control is an important facilitator for translating employee engagement into positive behaviors at work, leading us to suggest our final proposition:

Proposition 8: Activated positive affect promotes proficiency and adaptivity to the extent that employees perceive control over their tasks.

Theoretical implications and recommendations for research

We have discussed the relationship between psychological engagement, or activated positive affect, and its relationship with positive behaviors at work. Based on this discussion, we arrive at three main avenues for future research, which we shall outline in the following paragraphs.

1. *Measurement of state engagement:* As Macey and Schneider (2008) summarized, measures of employee engagement cover the activated emotional component to either a greater or a lesser extent. As we have argued, activated affect should be most relevant when predicting proactive behaviors at work, whereas for proficient and adaptive behaviors positive affect, regardless of activation, should be sufficient. Thus, using different types of measures will potentially yield conflicting or incoherent results. We call for a more explicit focus on activated positive affect when assessing state engagement, as well as the need to separate affect from distinct states such as absorption or dedication.

2. *Systematic studies:* We argued in our chapter that it is activated positive affect, rather than low activation positive affect, that is most important for promoting proactive behaviors at work. So far research in industrial and organizational psychology has mostly investigated activated positive affect because it mainly drew on the PANAS measure which has this as its sole focus. Systematic comparisons between activated versus non-activated, and positive versus negative, types of state affect and their relationships with different types of behaviors at work are lacking, as suggested in preliminary research by Warr and colleagues (Bindl et al., 2010).

3. *Context:* When studying the relationship between affect and behaviors, researchers need to incorporate contextual factors, such as job control, or task significance, as well as individual factors, such as learning versus performance orientation. As we summarized, these factors can act as contingencies in the relationship between affect and the way individuals perform at work. Therefore, not taking these factors into account can obscure existing relationships.

Practical implications

Our review shows that employee engagement can fluctuate not only between individuals but also within individuals over time, and that these fluctuations impact on performance. This means that, through enhancing engagement, organizations can influence the extent to which employees display positive work behaviors, such as proficiency, adaptivity, and proactivity. First, they can put in place practices to generate greater activated positive affect among their employees. Second they can ensure that engagement, and activated positive affect, among employees is "translated" into more positive behaviors at work.

What practices will generate greater positive affect or ensure its translation into performance? An initial and obvious strategy is to select individuals who typically experience high levels of positive affect at work (for example, George, 1989). However, since research shows that state positive affect likely affects performance at work to a greater extent than dispositional affect (George, 1991), it is just as important to consider the situation. Thus organizations, instead of only selecting engaged individuals, can promote feelings of engagement among their workforce by creating conducive work situations.

An important aspect of the work situation is the *work group* to which the employee belongs. For example, the larger the group size, the lower the group's affect tends to be. With increasing group size, the intensity of the relationship between group members decreases, and disagreement and tension become more common (George & Brief, 1992). Similarly, the affective tone of the work group, or the consistent affective reactions of group members, can influence individual positive affect. Thus if the team an employee works in experiences activated positive affect at work, this employee is also more likely to be able to experience activated positive affect themselves (Totterdell, 2000). For example, in a study with service employees, positive daily team climate predicted higher levels of individual employee engagement on the same day (Xanthopoulou et al., 2009). Organizations should therefore aim to pay attention to the moods of work groups. Interventions that improve teams' overall level of engagement will likely produce more sustained effects than targeting individuals only.

In addition to considering the work group, *features of the job* can influence individuals' positive affect at work. George and Brief (1992) focused on physical factors of the environment, such as pleasant office designs and good technological equipment (see also Salanova et al., 2005). Researchers have further identified task-related features as influences on positive affect at work. One of the most important is job control or autonomy, which has been shown to promote feelings of enthusiasm (see Warr, 2007). In addition, employees need control to execute positive behaviors at work. If the work is overly constrained, even if individuals feel positive, they will not have the latitude to engage in behaviors like proactivity (for example, Bindl & Parker, in press). A further important job feature is task variety. The greater the extent to which employees are involved in different types of tasks the more likely they will feel engaged. Being responsible for different tasks prevents feelings of monotony, and enables employees to feel stimulated in their job (Salanova & Schaufeli, 2008). With both job control and task variety, however, it is important to note that supports need to be in place. For example, if employees are expected to make decisions that they do not feel qualified to make, or have so much variety in their job that they feel overwhelmed, then well-being will be impaired (Warr, 1994).

A further important feature of the task environment for promoting engagement is feedback on job performance, either directly from the outcomes of the tasks or feedback from colleagues and supervisors. Feedback can also lead to employees realizing that their tasks are significant, such as by informing them on the consequences of their contribution to the end-beneficiary of the product or service. As noted in proposition 2 above, the more an individual sees his or her task as important, the more that positive affect is likely to result in positive work behaviors.

A further set of influencing factors is what George and Brief (1992) refer to as "motivational bases". An example is the internalization of organizational values: the more employees internalize and identify the values and goals of the organization they work in, the more likely they will feel engaged at work. Thus, organizational practices that effectively convey the values of the organization to all employees, and involve them with the goals of the organization, result in more engaged employees, and – ultimately – in more positive behaviors at work.

In sum, there is good evidence that engagement, and hence proficiency, adaptivity, and proactivity can be promoted through the design of more effective work situations.

Conclusion

When employees are engaged, they experience activated positive affect, such as feeling inspired and enthusiastic. We have proposed that such active and positive feelings promote employees' initiation of proactive behaviors at work (proposition 1), especially if the employee perceives the situation as important (proposition 2), experiences or can craft some control over the situation (proposition 3), and if the employee does not have a disposition against initiating change that overwhelms the value of the positive affect (proposition 4). We also proposed that activated positive affect is important for both proficient and adaptive forms of behavior, especially if these behaviors require considerable persistence (proposition 5), if these behaviors are directed toward the team and the organization (proposition 6), and if the adaptivity is required in a highly dynamic and ambiguous situation (proposition 7). Finally, for all types of performance, we have noted the importance of perceived control over one's tasks (propositions 3 and 8). Only if individuals feel able to exercise control, will the positive affect they experience translate into greater proficiency, adaptivity, or proactivity. In sum, there are good theoretical reasons, and accumulating evidence, to suggest that employees who feel positive in an activated way at work will *indeed* perform more effectively.

References

Baron, R.A. (2008), "The role of affect in the entrepreneurial process", *Academy of Management Review*, **33** (2), 328–40.
Baumeister, R.F., Vohs, K.D., DeWall, C.N. & Zhang, L. (2007), "How emotion shapes

behavior: feedback, anticipation, and reflection, rather than direct causation", *Personality and Social Psychology Review*, **11** (2), 167–203.

Belschak, F.D. & Den Hartog, D.N. (2009), "Consequences of positive and negative feedback: the impact on emotions and extra-role behaviors", *Applied Psychology*, **58** (2), 274–303.

Bindl, U.K. & Parker, S.K. (in press), "Proactive work behavior: forward-thinking and change-oriented action in organizations", in S. Zedeck (ed.), *APA Handbook of Industrial and Organizational Psychology*, Washington, DC: American Psychological Association.

Bindl, U.K., Warr, P.B., Parker, S.K. & Inceoglu, I. (2010), "Multiple patterns of affect-behavior associations", paper presented at the Annual Society for Industrial and Organizational Psychology (SIOP) Conference, Atlanta, GA, April.

Binnewies, C., Sonnentag, S. & Mojza, E.J. (2009), "Daily performance at work: feeling recovered in the morning as a predictor of day-level job performance", *Journal of Organizational Behavior*, **30** (1), 67–93.

Blumberg, M. & Pringle, C.D. (1982), "The missing opportunity in organizational research: some implications for a theory of work performance", *Academy of Management Review*, **7** (4), 560–69.

Brief, A.P. & Weiss, H.M. (2002), "Organizational behavior: affect in the workplace", *Annual Review of Psychology*, **53** (1), 279–307.

Campbell, D.J. (2000), "The proactive employee: managing workplace initiative", *Academy of Management Executive*, **14** (3), 52–66.

Crant, J.M. (2000), "Proactive behavior in organizations", *Journal of Management*, **26** (3), 435–62.

Dalal, R., Lam, H., Weiss, H.M., Welch, E.R. & Hulin, C.L. (2009), "A within-person approach to work behavior and performance: concurrent and lagged citizenship-counterproductivity associations, and dynamic relationships with affect and overall job performance", *Academy of Management Journal*, **52** (5), 1051–66.

Den Hartog, D.N. & Belschak, F.D. (2007), "Personal initiative, commitment and affect at work", *Journal of Occupational and Organizational Psychology*, **80** (4), 601–22.

Erez, A. & Isen, A.M. (2002), "The influence of positive affect on the components of expectancy motivation", *Journal of Applied Psychology*, **87** (6), 1055–67.

Foo, M.-D., Uy, M.A. & Baron, R.A. (2009), "How do feelings influence effort? An empirical study of entrepreneurs' affect and venture effort", *Journal of Applied Psychology*, **94** (4), 1086–94.

Fredrickson, B.L. (1998), "What good are positive emotions?", *Review of General Psychology*, **2** (3), 300–19.

Fredrickson, B.L. (2001), "The role of positive emotions in positive psychology: the broaden-and-build theory of positive emotions", *American Psychologist*, **56** (3), 218–26.

Fredrickson, B.L. & Joiner, T. (2002), "Positive emotions trigger upward spirals toward emotional well-being", *Psychological Science*, **13** (2), 172–5.

Frese, M. & Fay, D. (2001), "Personal initiative (PI): an active performance concept for work in the 21st century", *Research in Organizational Behavior*, **23**, 133–87.

Frohman, A.L. (1997), "Igniting organizational change from below: the power of personal initiative", *Organizational Dynamics*, **25**, 39–53.

George, J.M. (1989), "Mood and absence", *Journal of Applied Psychology*, **74** (2), 317–24.

George, J.M. (1991), "State or trait: effects of positive mood on prosocial behaviors at work", *Journal of Applied Psychology*, **76** (2), 299–307.

George, J.M. & Brief, A.P. (1992), "Feeling good–doing good: a conceptual analysis of the mood at work–organizational spontaneity relationship", *Psychological Bulletin*, **112** (2), 310–29.

Grant, A.M. & Ashford, S.J. (2008), "The dynamics of proactivity at work", *Research in Organizational Behavior*, **28**, 3–34.

Griffin, M.A., Neal, A. & Parker, S.K. (2007), "A new model of work role performance: positive behavior in uncertain and interdependent contexts", *Academy of Management Journal*, **50** (2), 327–47.

Hakanen, J.J., Perhoniemi, R. & Toppinen-Tanner, S. (2008), "Positive gain spirals at work: from job resources to work engagement, personal initiative and work-unit innovativeness", *Journal of Vocational Behavior*, **73** (1), 78–91.

Ilies, R. & Judge, T.A. (2005), "Goal regulation across time: the effects of feedback and affect", *Journal of Applied Psychology*, **90** (3), 453–67.

Isen, A.M. (1999), "On the relationship between affect and creative problem solving", in S. Russ (ed.), *Affect, Creative Experience, and Psychological Adjustment*, Philadelphia, PA: Taylor & Francis, pp. 3–17.

Isen, A.M. & Reeve, J. (2005), "The influence of positive affect on intrinsic and extrinsic motivation: facilitating enjoyment of play, responsible work behavior, and self control", *Motivation and Emotion*, **29** (4), 297–325.

Lee, K. & Allen, N.J. (2002), "Organizational citizenship behavior and workplace deviance: the role of affect and cognitions", *Journal of Applied Psychology*, **87** (1), 131–42.

Macey, W.H. & Schneider, B. (2008), "The meaning of employee engagement", *Industrial and Organizational Psychology*, **1**, 3–30.

Matthews, G. (1992), "Mood", in A.P. Smith & D.M. Jones (eds), *Handbook of Human Performance*, Vol. 3, London: Harcourt Brace Jovanovich, pp. 161–93.

Oettingen, G., Mayer, D., Thorpe, J.S., Janetzke, H. & Lorenz, S. (2005), "Turning fantasies about positive and negative futures into self-improvement goals", *Motivation and Emotion*, **29** (4), 237–67.

Parker, S.K. (2000), "From passive to proactive motivation: the importance of flexible role orientations and role breadth self-efficacy", *Applied Psychology: An International Review*, **49** (3), 447–69.

Parker, S.K., Bindl, U.K. & Strauss, K. (in press), "Making things happen: a model of proactive motivation", *Journal of Management*.

Parker, S.K., Collins, C.G. & Grant, A.M. (2008), "The role of positive affect in making things happen", paper presented at the Annual Society for Industrial and Organizational Psychology (SIOP) Conference, San Francisco, CA, April.

Parker, S.K., Williams, H.M. & Turner, N. (2006), "Modeling the antecedents of proactive behavior at work", *Journal of Applied Psychology*, **91** (3), 636–52.

Parkinson, B., Totterdell, P., Briner, R.B. & Reynolds, S. (1996), *Changing Moods: The Psychology of Mood and Mood Regulation*, London: Longman.

Russell, J.A. (2003), "Core affect and the psychological construction of emotion", *Psychological Review*, **110** (1), 145–72.

Salanova, M., Agut, S. & Peiró, J.M. (2005), "Linking organizational resources and work engagement to employee performance and customer loyalty: the mediation of service climate", *Journal of Applied Psychology*, **90** (6), 1217–27.

Salanova, M. & Schaufeli, W.B. (2008), "A cross-national study of work engagement as a mediator between job resources and proactive behaviour", *International Journal of Human Resource Management*, **19** (1), 116–31.

Schaufeli, W.B., Salanova, M., González-Romá, V. & Bakker, A.B. (2002), "The measurement of engagement and burnout: a two sample confirmatory factor analytic approach", *Journal of Happiness Studies*, **3** (1), 71–92.

Schaufeli, W.B., Taris, T. & Bakker, A.B. (2006), "Dr. Jekyll or Mr. Hyde: on the differences between work engagement and workaholism", in R. Burke (ed.), *Research Companion to Working Time and Work Addiction*, Cheltenham, UK and Northampton, MA, USA: Edward Elgar, pp. 193–217.

Seo, M.G., Barrett, L.F. & Bartunek, J.M. (2004), "The role of affective experience in work motivation", *Academy of Management Review*, **29** (3), 423–39.

Sonnentag, S. (2003), "Recovery, work engagement, and proactive behavior: a new look at the interface between nonwork and work", *Journal of Applied Psychology*, **88** (3), 518–28.

Staw, B.M., Sutton, R.I. & Pelled, L.H. (1994), "Employee positive emotion and favorable outcomes at the workplace", *Organization Science*, **5** (1), 51–71.

Tellegen, A., Watson, D. & Clark, L.A. (1999), "On the dimensional and hierarchical structure of affect", *Psychological Science*, **10** (4), 297–303.

Totterdell, P. (1999), "Mood scores: mood and performance in professional cricketers", *British Journal of Psychology*, **90** (3), 317–32.

Totterdell, P. (2000), "Catching moods and hitting runs: mood linkage and subjective performance in professional sport teams", *Journal of Applied Psychology*, **85** (6), 848–59.

Tsai, W.C., Chen, C.C. & Liu, H.L. (2007), "Test of a model linking employee positive moods and task performance", *Journal of Applied Psychology*, **92** (6), 1570–83.

Warr, P. (1994), "A conceptual framework for the study of work and mental health", *Work and Stress*, **8** (2), 84–97.

Warr, P.B. (2007), *Work, Happiness, and Unhappiness*, Mahwah, NJ: Lawrence Erlbaum.

Xanthopoulou, D., Bakker, A.B., Demerouti, E. & Schaufeli, W.B. (2009), "Work engagement and financial returns: a diary study on the role of job and personal resources", *Journal of Occupational and Organizational Psychology*, **82** (1), 183–200.

33 How to improve work engagement?
Wilmar B. Schaufeli and Marisa Salanova

Introduction: from treatment and prevention towards "amplition"

This chapter deals with how to enhance work engagement and other related, positive psychological states. In answering this question, we take an individual as well as an organizational perspective. So we rephrase the question in the title as: what can the employee do in order to flourish and thrive at work, and what can the organization do in order to promote a flourishing and thriving workforce? Before providing an overview of individual- and organization-based intervention strategies, we outline the broader positive psychological framework of these "positive" interventions.

Traditionally speaking, individual and organizational interventions in occupational health psychology are rooted in the so-called "medical disease" model. This means that interventions are carried out only when something is wrong or malfunctioning, and with the sole objective of fixing it. Essentially, a preventive approach operates according to the same logic of the medical model, albeit that the intervention focuses on future damage and damage control, rather than on momentary damage *per se*.

Currently it seems that we are entering into a novel phase of development that we would like to dub "amplition" (Latin, *amplio*; to enlarge, increase, or magnify). In contrast to treatment and prevention, amplition is not based on the maxim of the medical disease model – fix what is broken – but on the positive psychology principle of improvement or betterment (Seligman & Csikszentmihalyi, 2000). Amplition is about "positive" interventions that promote, increase and improve employee health and well-being, including work engagement. In a way this is a logical next step of widening the scope because treatment is – by definition – restricted to employees who suffer from an identified disease, whereas prevention is restricted to those who potentially may suffer from it. Amplition goes one step beyond to include the *entire* workforce because it is based on the belief that improving employee health and well-being – including work engagement – is a long-term mission that requires continuous and sustained effort. Instead of replacing one another, treatment, prevention and amplition supplement one another by widening the scope, not only from diseases via potential diseases to employee health and well-being, but also from individual sick or distressed employees, via particular groups at risk, to the entire workforce of the organization.

About "positive" interventions, happiness, and work engagement
Unfortunately, to date only very few interventions to improve work engagement exist and have been tested. The available interventions – particularly those that focus on the individual – are typically not targeted at the workplace and aim at increasing happiness in different life areas instead of engagement at work. For that reason we have to broaden our scope and include other positive psychological states, which are usually subsumed under the overarching and interchangeably used headings of "happiness" or "subjective well-being". Basically, happiness or subjective well-being refers to the preponderance of positive emotions such as joy, satisfaction, enthusiasm, and interest. These positive emotions partially overlap with our definition and operationalization of work engagement in terms of vigor, dedication and absorption. For instance, the Utrecht Work Engagement Scale includes items that explicitly refer to positive emotions, for example: "I am enthusiastic about my job" and "I feel happy when I am working intensely" (Schaufeli et al., 2002). The main difference between happiness and work engagement is that the former refers to a more general and context-free positive psychological state, whereas the latter is more specific and work related.

That happy employees are important for organizations is exemplified by a meta-analysis of Lyubomirsky et al. (2005) which showed that happy employees:

- are more likely to secure job interviews;
- obtain better jobs with more autonomy, meaning, and variety;
- are more positively evaluated by their superiors and by others;
- handle managerial jobs better;
- are less likely to show counterproductive and retaliatory workplace behaviors such as stealing, bullying, and sabotage;
- exhibit pro-social behavior at work, such as altruism, courteousness, and helping others;
- show less withdrawal behavior, such as turnover and absenteeism;
- are less likely to burn out;
- show more extra-role behavior ("going the extra mile"); and
- show superior performance and productivity.

This profile of happy employees is remarkably similar to that of engaged employees, who also work in challenging jobs, show personal initiative, pro-social behavior, extra-role behavior, less withdrawal behavior, lower burnout levels, better physical health, and superior academic and job performance (for an overview, see Schaufeli & Salanova, 2008; Salanova & Schaufeli, 2009). Taken together this suggests that it is viable to broaden our scope and to discuss positive individual interventions that promote happiness.

An overview of individual-based interventions

"Positive" interventions that aim at increasing the individual's level of happiness – including an employee's work engagement – may focus on changing the individual's behavior, on changing the individual's beliefs, or on changing the individual's goals and motives.

Behavioral strategies

Practicing virtues One of the basic principles of positive psychology is that sustained happiness – or work engagement, for that matter – is not fostered by the pursuit of pleasure (*hedonism*), but instead by leading a meaningful life (*eudiamonia*). That is, a virtuous life that is in accordance with one's own spirit or true self. Living an authentic life and fully realizing one's strengths, talents and potentials constitutes the key to sustained happiness (Ryan & Deci, 2001). Hence, identifying and developing one's unique personal strengths – so-called "signature strengths" – is crucial. Based on the Signature Strength Questionnaire (see: www.authentichappiness.org) one's signature strengths can be identified (Peterson & Seligman, 2004). An internet study in which respondents received individualized feedback about the top-five signature strengths and were encouraged to use them more often during the next week showed an increase in happiness, particularly when they were used *in a new and different way* every day of the week (Seligman et al., 2005). Similar positive results were found with the "Strengths-Finder" (Buckingham & Clifton, 2001) – which assesses 34 work-related strengths. Administering this tool and providing employees with follow-up activities to develop their dominant talents, significantly increased employee work engagement (Clifton & Harter, 2003).

Being kind to others Committing acts of kindness may boost happiness because such acts are likely to elicit positive feedback (for example, gratefulness, appreciation) and to stimulate reciprocation (for example, helping of others), and positive social interaction. Moreover, acts of kindness towards others may help the person to view him- or herself as altruistic, which may boost self-esteem and confidence. When participants were invited to practice acts of kindness (for example, holding the door open for a stranger, visiting an elderly relative, or donating blood) during a

10-week period, they felt happier than before (Boehm & Lyubomirsky, 2009). This positive effect was particularly strong for those who performed a *wide variety* of kindness acts and who concentrated their acts in a *short time period*. Acts of kindness can easily be committed at the workplace because social interactions with others (colleagues, supervisors, customers) are inherent to work. In order to be most effective, acts of kindness should be varied and committed in a short period, for instance at a designated "kindness day".

Expressing gratitude   Expressed gratitude promotes the savoring of positive life experiences instead of taking them for granted. Moreover, it bolsters self-worth, builds social bonds, and last but not least it is "an antidote to toxic workplace emotions" (Emmons, 2003, p. 90). In their internet study, Seligman et al. (2005) showed that writing and delivering a letter of gratitude to someone who had been especially kind or important increased happiness. Although writing gratitude letters at work might not seem immediately applicable, numerous occasions exist for expressing one's gratitude verbally.

Learning to forgive   Forgiveness involves suppressing or mitigating one's motivation for revenge and retaliation in response to an abuse such as an insult, an offence, a betrayal, or a desertion. As a result, negative emotions are replaced by more positive or benevolent attitudes, feelings, and behaviors. People who forgive are likely to be more happy, healthy, agreeable and serene, as well as less anxious, depressed and neurotic (McCullough, 2001). An intervention study with a group of elderly women who felt hurt by an abusive interpersonal experience and learned to forgive, showed that their level of anxiety decreased and their self-esteem increased (Hebl & Enright, 1993). At work, potentially threatening, harming or abusive events are plentiful, such as dismissal, reorganization, missed promotion opportunities, favoritism, violence and harassment by colleagues or customers, and negative performance feedback. It follows that there is great potential for acts of forgiveness at work. For instance, by writing a letter of forgiveness to someone who did wrong, by empathizing with an offender and granting him or her imaginary forgiveness, or by practicing empathy for the person who hurt you (Lyubomirsky, 2007).

Sharing good news   Research has shown compellingly that sharing good news or telling others about a positive experience increases the positive emotions (Gable et al., 2004). Moreover, it appeared that positive affect continues to increase with additional sharing of the good news, and that positive events that are shared are more likely to be remembered. It follows that celebrating one's successes at work together with other members of the team, such as having closed a lucrative business deal, seems an effective way to increase levels of work engagement. In addition, sharing good news might bolster the team spirit because indications have been found for the "contagiousness" of engagement in work teams (Bakker et al., 2006).

Nurturing social relationships   The most important function of social relations is that others provide support in times of distress. This social support comes in various ways, as practical help or assistance, as emotional support, or as information. Numerous studies have documented that social support at work is associated with better health and well-being. For instance, a meta-analysis including over 200 studies revealed that social support at work was associated with job satisfaction, self-reported health, less burnout and lower withdrawal intentions (Viswesvaran et al., 1999). In order to nurture social relationships at the workplace, employees could spend time together (for example, socialize during work breaks instead of isolating themselves), not only talk about work but also about personal matters, and be loyal and supportive helping others, listening to them, and giving them useful information.

Cognitive strategies

Counting one's blessings   This is about the savoring of positive life experiences instead of taking them for granted. One way of doing that is by keeping a journal in which daily three to five things are written down for which one is currently grateful. An internet study showed that keeping a journal like that increased participants' happiness levels up to a period of six months (Seligman et al., 2005). Another way to count one's blessings is to choose a fixed time and to simply *contemplate* each of the things for which one is grateful, and reflect on *why* one is grateful and *how* one's life has been enriched. A six-week intervention that used this contemplation method increased participants' happiness levels (Emmons & McCullough, 2003). Emmons (2003) argued for incorporating counting one's blessings into the everyday ethos of organizations. The reason is that – in addition to increasing happiness – gratitude serves a buffering role that allays embarrassment, shame or other negative emotions that undermine self-honesty.

Cultivating optimism   Generally speaking, optimism refers to the expectation that the future is bright and to the belief that one's goals can be accomplished. Because they feel confident that they will achieve their goals, optimists are likely to invest the necessary effort to succeed. Not surprisingly, optimism is associated with happiness, better mental and physical health, high self-regard, a sense of mastery, superior achievement (Peterson & Steen, 2002), and work engagement (Xanthopoulou et al., 2009a). Optimism can be cultivated by visualizing and writing about one's "best possible self", a mental exercise in which one focuses on one's best possible future self. It appeared that writing a narrative description of the "best possible future self" for four consecutive days increased happiness and decreased physical ailments in the five months after the writing sessions (King, 2001). Another strategy is to replace pessimistic explanations ("My boss did not speak to me today; he must not like me") – though using disputation ("What other evidence do I have that he doesn't like me?") – by more optimistic explanations ("He was probably too busy"). This boils down to unlearning a pessimistic and learning an optimistic attributional style (Seligman, 1991). Techniques such as writing about the best possible self or unlearning a pessimistic attributional style can be applied quite straightforwardly to the work situation.

Savoring This is about mindfully accentuating and sustaining pleasurable moments as they unfold, and about deliberately remembering experiences in ways that rekindle enjoyment. People who are inclined to savor life's joys are more self-confident, extraverted, and less hopeless and depressed (Bryant & Veroff, 2006). Various strategies have been suggested to foster savoring, such as reminiscence together with colleagues, replay happy days, be open to beauty and excellence, and take pleasure in the senses (Lyubomirsky, 2007). There is some empirical support for happiness increases as a result of these kinds of strategies. A remarkable finding is that *analyzing* positive experiences rather than *savoring* them seems to nullify the positive effect (Lyubomirsky et al., 2006). Since savoring involves stepping back, taking a time-out, and deliberately shifting one's attention to particular pleasurable events and experiences seems to be at odds with work. Nevertheless, work breaks may offer excellent opportunities for savoring, either alone (for example, enjoying one's coffee) or with one's colleagues (for example, looking back at a joint festivity).

Volitional strategies

Setting and pursuing personal goals Trying to achieve personal meaningful goals is important because it provides a sense of purpose and meaning, it bolsters self-esteem and efficacy beliefs, it adds structure and meaning to one's daily life, it structures time, and finally it encourages social contacts. It is easy to recognize the similarity with the psychological functions of work, which illustrates that work goals may act as very powerful personal goals. There are various ways to properly set and pursue personal meaningful goals that are intrinsic (gratifying in themselves), authentic (rooted in one's core interests) and harmonious (complementary rather than conflicting) (Lyubomirsky, 2007). For instance, in order to choose – or uncover – a proper long-term meaningful goal one may write down the personal legacy that one would leave after one had died. Or one may critically examine one's commitment to a particular goal; is one really committed to the goal with passion and zeal? Or break down a higher-level goal (for example, being promoted to supervisor) into smaller low-level goals (for example, enrol in a leadership training course and be a more active networker). The effectiveness of some of these strategies has recently been demonstrated in an intervention study by Sheldon et al. (2002) that focused on increasing goal identification, fostering intrinsic motivation and integrating the current goal into an overarching long-term goal. As expected, goal attainment led to enhanced well-being and personal growth, but only for those participants whose goals "fit" their interests and values. Another study demonstrated the effectiveness of a brief intervention that focused on developing goal-setting and planning skills (MacLeod et al., 2008). Participants either received collectively three one-hour weekly sessions or completed the program individually in their own time, using an instruction manual. In both cases an increase was observed in life satisfaction, efficacy beliefs and positive affect.

Increase resilience   A subset of people who, confronted with a major challenge that unsettles their personal foundations, report personal growth, strengthening or even thriving. They have a renewed belief in their ability to endure, their social relationships have been improved, and last but not least, they developed a deeper and more sophisticated and satisfying philosophy of life (Tedeschi & Calhoun, 2004). In short, these people are said to be resilient. Finding meaning in what has happened particularly fosters resilience. Numerous studies have shown that writing about one's deepest thoughts and feelings related to the negative event for about 15–30 minutes each day on three to five consecutive days leads to enhanced immune functioning and physical health, less depression, anxiety and distress, more life satisfaction, and also to less work absenteeism, and an increased likelihood of finding a new job after unemployment (Frattaroli, 2006). It seems that this positive effect is *not* caused by emotional catharsis but by the highly structured act of writing itself. Recently, resilience has also attracted the attention of organizational scholars. For instance, Sutcliffe and Vogus (2003) defined resilience as the maintenance of positive adjustment under challenging conditions; more specifically, the ability to bounce back from untoward events, to absorb strain and preserve or improve functioning despite the presence of adversity. According to Sutcliffe and Vogus, employee resilience – and with it personal growth and development, including work engagement – is fostered by adequate job resources (for example, colleague and supervisory support, job control) and mastery motivation (for example, optimism, self-efficacy). Recently, the effects were evaluated of a micro-intervention that aimed to increase not only the employees' resiliency, but also their self-efficacy, optimism and hope (Luthans et al., 2006). The combination of these four psychological states is dubbed "psychological capital" (PsyCap). A group-based intervention to increase employee's PsyCap consisted of: (i) formulating a specific work goal and being instructed how best to attain this (for example, by taking small steps, by having concrete and measurable end-points); (ii) specifying the pathway to be followed (that is, generating and discussing multiple pathways to the goal); and (iii) preparing to overcome obstacles (that is, building anticipatory abilities to overcome obstacles). Compared to the non-intervention control group, the intervention group showed a significant increase in PsyCap.

Applying individual interventions at the workplace
It is important to acknowledge that some of these individual interventions may be applied to the work situation but have a wider, more existential meaning. This relates to practicing virtues, setting and pursuing personal meaningful goals, and fostering resilience. These strategies involve the person's core values, interests and preferences; ultimately they are about knowing oneself. This not only implies that one is aware of one's talents, values and goals at work, but also how these fit into one's larger, existential scheme of things.

The most promising individual strategies focus on the interpersonal aspects of work and involve other people such as colleagues, supervisors and customers (that is, being kind to others, expressing gratitude, learning to forgive, sharing good news, and nursing social relationships). These strategies can easily be applied at work because communicating with other persons is inherent to most jobs. The reason why we believe that these strategies are particularly effective is twofold. First, they are likely to elicit positive reactions from others, which encourages the employee to continue with the positive behavior. As a result, this positive behavior is likely to be reciprocated by others in the form of smiling back, self-disclosure, kindness, and offering help and assistance. So, by using these interpersonal strategies at work, it is likely that the employee enters a self-perpetuating upward spiral (Salanova et al., 2010b). Second, these positive interpersonal strategies act as a double-edged sword. On the one hand they increase the employee's level of engagement, but on the other they also improve the social climate at work by fostering group cohesion, resolving conflicts, and increasing loyalty, team spirit, and pro-social behavior.

An overview of organizational-based interventions

The shift from the prevailing traditional, negative approach that focuses on sickness and unwell-being toward a more positive approach that focuses on health and wellness provides the opportunity for human resource management (HRM) and occupational health psychology (OHP) to join forces. After all, organizational health – the domain of HRM – and employee health – the domain of OHP – are co-dependent, meaning that increasing the former also increases the latter, and vice versa. This co-dependence is illustrated by the growing recognition that the organization's financial health correlates with investments in employee well-being (Goetzel et al., 2001). Hence, analogous to the classical adage "a healthy mind in a healthy body" one could formulate as common goal for OHP and HRM to promote healthy employees in healthy organizations.

In our opinion it is essential for building work engagement to initiate and to maintain so-called "gain spirals". Research suggests that upward spirals exist that are sparked by job resources and personal resources (that is, self-efficacy beliefs) and may result in various positive outcomes such as extra-role performance, via work engagement (see Salanova et al., 2010b for a review). In turn, these positive outcomes increase resources and foster high levels of engagement, and so on. Following the logic of these gain spirals, work engagement may be increased by stimulating each link of the spiral, be it resources or positive outcomes. Below it is outlined how this can be achieved, using strategies that focus on: (i) assessing and evaluating employees, (ii) designing and changing workplaces, (iii) enhancing transformational leadership, (iv) work training, and (v) career management.

Personnel assessment and evaluation

The ultimate purpose of personnel assessment and evaluation is to optimize the chance of having the right person in the right spot. That is, to create an optimal balance in terms of a good fit between personal values and goals, and those of the organization. More particularly, personnel assessment and evaluation is about increasing identification, motivation and commitment – from the perspective of the organization – as well as about personal and professional development – from the perspective of the employee. Work engagement plays a crucial role because, on the one hand it fosters employee identification, motivation and commitment, and on the other, it fosters employees' development; for instance by increasing the level of self-efficacy, which is an important prerequisite for organizational learning (Bandura, 2001). An essential tool for successful evaluation and appraisal on the job is systematic, tailor-made – preferably positive – feedback. The following three strategies can be distinguished that may enhance work engagement:

- *Establishing and monitoring the psychological contract* The psychological contract reflects the employees' subjective notion of reciprocity: the gains or outcomes from the organization (for example, salary, recognition) are expected to be proportional to one's own investments or inputs (for example, effort, loyalty). When the psychological contract is violated and reciprocity is corroded, this might lead to burnout (Schaufeli, 2006) and a host of other negative outcomes, including the intention to quit, turnover, job dissatisfaction, cynicism, poor organizational commitment, and absenteeism (for example, Rousseau, 1995; De Boer et al., 2002). Hence, a fair psychological contract should be established that reflects an optimal fit between employee and organization in terms of mutual expectations. This can be achieved by: (i) assessing the employee's values, preferences, and personal and professional goals; (ii) negotiating and drafting a written contract (Employee Development Agreement) that guarantees the necessary resources from the organization to achieve personal meaningful goals; and (iii) monitoring this written agreement periodically in terms of goal achievement.
- *Periodic work-wellness audits*   The aim of these audits is to inform individual employees, as well as the organizations they work for, about their levels of wellness, including engagement. This information is important for making decisions about measures for improvement that should be taken, either individually or organizationally. Based on the job demands–resources model (Bakker & Demerouti, 2007), work-wellness audits were developed in Spain (www.wont. uji.es) and in the Netherlands (www.c4ob.nl). These audits include job stressors (for example, work overload, conflicts, role problems, emotional demands, work–home interference), job resources (for example, variety, feedback, social support, job control, career development), burnout, engagement, negative personal and organizational outcomes (for example, depression, distress, absenteeism, turnover intention), and positive personal and organizational outcomes (for example, job satisfaction, organizational commitment, extra-role performance). In addition, personal and job information is included, as well as personal resources such as self-efficacy, and mental and emotional competencies.
- *Workshops on work engagement*   Workshops are structured group

meetings of employees to promote health and well-being, including work engagement, usually by means of augmenting personal resources. Workshops that aim to build engagement are similar to so-called "quality circles", except that they focus on the enhancement of personal resources, such as cognitive, behavioral and social skills (for example, positive thinking, goal-setting, time-management, and life-style improvement).

Job (re)design and work changes
The (re)designing of jobs serves two purposes: from an occupational health perspective it aims to reduce the exposure to psychosocial risks, whereas from an HRM perspective it aims at increasing employee motivation. It follows from the job demands–resources model (Bakker & Demerouti, 2007) that, in order to increase engagement, reducing the exposure to job stressors is not an option because this would also eliminate job challenge. Instead the motivating potential of job resources should be exploited because these stimulate personal growth, learning and development of employees. In contrast, the lack of organizational resources has a detrimental effect on workers' motivation and performance (Wong et al., 1998) since it precludes actual goal accomplishment, and undermines employees' learning opportunities (Kelly, 1992).

Another related strategy is to implement work changes. In doing so, job resources are not additionally provided or increased, but they are merely changed, for example, when jobs are rotated, when employees are temporarily assigned to carry out special projects, or when they are transferred to entirely different jobs. Based on qualitative research on engagement (Schaufeli et al., 2001) we may add that, most likely, changing work also increases work engagement. This will be particularly the case when employees feel challenged in their new job while at the same time they have the necessary competencies to meet the challenges (Salanova et al., 2002).

Transformational leadership
An important task of leaders is to optimize the emotional climate in their team. A good leader is able to enhance motivation and engagement. Research suggests that engagement is "contagious", it crosses over not only from partner to spouse, but also from one team member to another (Bakker et al., 2006). It also appears that engagement is a collective phenomenon, meaning that teams may feel "engaged" when their members closely collaborate to accomplish particular tasks (Salanova et al., 2003). Hence, team leaders may have a positive impact on levels of individual and collective engagement depending on the way they manage their work teams. For example, Aguilar and Salanova (2009) found that leaders who

were task oriented *and* supportive were more successful in increasing individual work engagement than those displaying other leadership behaviors. Such considerate leadership behaviors stimulate a favorable group climate that is characterized by fairness, trust, openness and constructive problem solving. In addition, considerate behaviors such as coaching and providing feedback and social support are important resources in and of themselves that may promote work engagement (Schaufeli et al., 2009).

According to Bass (1985), transformational leadership goes one step beyond this considerate, employee-centered leadership style by offering employees a purpose that transcends short-term goals and focuses on higher-order intrinsic needs. This kind of leadership is of special importance for today's organizations that go through profound changes and are therefore in need of charismatic, inspiring and visionary leaders, who are able to motivate employees and build engagement. Transformational leaders display conviction, take a stand, challenge followers with high standards, communicate optimism about future goal attainment, stimulate and encourage creativity and innovation, and listen to followers' concerns and needs (Avolio, 1999). Not surprisingly, this leadership style has a positive impact on followers' health and well-being (Nielsen et al., 2009), as well as on their performance and motivation (Salanova et al., 2010a). More particularly, the latter study showed that transformational leadership increased followers' work engagement, and in turn, also their extra-role performance.

Work training
Work training is a traditional HRM strategy that is used to enhance employees' levels of work engagement. In order to do so, work training programs should be particularly directed at personal growth and development instead of being exclusively content directed. In our view, building efficacy beliefs (that is, the power to believe that you can) is the cornerstone for the promotion of work engagement via work training.

According to social cognitive theory (SCT), self-efficacy lies at the core of human agency and is important because it influences employees' behavior, thinking, motivation, and feelings (Bandura, 2001). Research on work engagement has shown that it is related to high levels of self-efficacy (for example, Salanova et al., 2002, 2003, 2010a, 2010b). Even more so, research suggests an upward gain spiral in which self-efficacy boosts engagement, which in its turn, increases efficacy beliefs, and so on (for an overview, see Salanova et al., 2010b). This means that efficacy beliefs serve as a kind of self-motivating mechanism: as a consequence of evaluating their own competence, employees set new goals that motivate them to mobilize additional effort, focus on achieving these goals and being persistent in the face of difficulties. Engagement seems to fulfill two roles in this dynamic process, namely as an antecedent that fosters self-efficacy as well as a consequence associated with successful goal attainment.

But how can self-efficacy – and therefore work engagement – be enhanced? According to SCT, efficacy beliefs may be augmented by mastery experiences, vicarious experience, verbal persuasion, and positive emotional states (Bandura, 2001). Hence training programs should include, for instance, practical exercises to provide experiences of vocational success (mastery experiences), role models of good performance (vicarious experiences), coaching and encouragement (verbal persuasion), and reducing fear of rejection or failure (managing emotional states). According to SCT, mastery experiences are the most powerful tool for boosting efficacy beliefs. The best way to evoke mastery experiences in employees is therefore by tackling work problems in successive, attainable steps. In a similar vein, if people see similar others succeed by sustained effort, during work training, they come to believe that they also have the capability to succeed (vicarious experiences). Trainers and supervisors may also use social persuasion in order to influence employees that they have what it takes to succeed, and so they make more effort and are more likely to persevere if they have self-doubts when obstacles arise. Finally, employees' negative emotional states may be reduced by applying stress-management techniques. These principles to increase self-efficacy may also be applied by supervisors when coaching their employees.

Career management

Although most employees still favor lifelong job stability and vertical, upward mobility, current changes in organizational life make this perspective no longer a self-evident one. Hence, instead of a fixed career path, of which each step requires specific pre-defined experience and expertise, nowadays employees have to cope with a much more unstable job market. More than before, employees have to rely on their own initiative to continuously develop themselves professionally and personally in order to remain employable.

Employability also includes a high level of engagement because it makes employees more fit and able to do the job (Salanova & Llorens, 2008). However, following the upward gain spiral of work engagement, the reverse might also be true: by carefully planning one's career, that is, by successively selecting those jobs that provide ample opportunity for professional and personal development, it is likely that levels of engagement will remain high.

So the key issue for employees to remain engaged in their job is to keep developing themselves throughout their career. Some of the tools that have been introduced previously in this chapter can be used for career management. First, by completing a work-wellness audit periodically, the employee can monitor his or her level of engagement across time. Second, by including the development of specific skills and competencies in the Employee Development Agreement employability can be increased. Third, jobs can be re-designed, or work may be changed in such a way as to foster employee development. Finally, work training can be used to increase self-efficacy and hence work motivation. Taken together, these strategies are instrumental for keeping one's job challenging.

Conclusion

Improving work engagement is important for organizations and individuals alike. Given the vested interest of companies in a healthy, flourishing and thriving workforce they are well advised to advertise and promote work engagement. In order to survive and prosper in a continuously changing environment, modern organizations do not merely need "healthy" employees – that is, employees who are symptom free – but engaged employees, who are vigorous, dedicated, and absorbed in their work. This is in line with the basic tenet of Integral Health Management (IHM), a strategic approach to reduce employee sickness and promote their health and well-being, while at the same time fostering productivity (Zwetsloot & Pot, 2004). IHM posits that organizations have a legitimate business interest, not only to cure sick employees and to prevent others from becoming sick, but particularly to increase the well-being of the entire workforce. It seems that work engagement may play a crucial role in IHM because it links individual well-being with organizational performance (Harter et al., 2002; Salanova et al., 2005; Xanthopoulou et al., 2009b). Needless to say, the focus on promoting engagement (amplition) greatly benefits individual employees as well because they are encouraged to realize their full potential and flourish at work.

This chapter summarized 11 individual-based strategies and eight organizational-based strategies to improve work engagement. Although the former are targeted to the individual, they can be promoted by the organization. For example, online training or coaching programs can be offered to employees, for instance, to promote acts of kindness at work, to set personal goals, or to share good news with colleagues. Currently, we are developing and testing such programs. Ideally, these individual-based interventions are integrated into the usual work routine, such as regular team meetings. Also, like the reduction of absenteeism, the promotion of work engagement of employees may be included in leaders' job descriptions.

We believe that because it is an essential, positive element of employee health and well-being, the enhancement of work engagement may help to create synergy between positive outcomes for individual employees and for organizations. This is eloquently expressed by the slogan "Healthy employees working in healthy organizations".

References

Aguilar, A. & Salanova, M. (2009), "Leadership styles and its relationship with subordinate well-being" (manuscript submitted for publication).

Avolio, B.J. (1999). *Full Leadership Development: Building the Vital Forces in Organizations*, London: Sage.

Bakker, A.B. & Demerouti, E. (2007), "The job demands–resources model: state of the art", *Journal of Managerial Psychology*, **22**, 309–28.

Bakker, A.B., Van Emmerik, H. & Euwema, M.C. (2006), "Crossover of burnout and engagement in work teams", *Work & Occupations*, **33**, 464–89.

Bandura, A. (2001), "Social cognitive theory: an agentic perspective", *Annual Review of Psychology*, **52**, 1–26.

Bass, B.M. (1985), *Leadership and Performance beyond Expectations*, New York: Free Press.

Boehm, J.K. & Lyubomirsky, S. (2009), "The promise of sustainable happiness", in S.J. Lopez (ed.), *Handbook of Positive Psychology*, 2nd edn, Oxford: Oxford University Press, pp. 667–77.

Bryant, F.B. & Veroff, J. (2006), *Savoring: A New Model of Positive Experience*, Mahwah, NJ: Erlbaum.

Buckingham, M. & Clifton, D.O. (2001), *Now, Discover Your Strengths*, New York: Free Press.

Clifton, D.O & Harter, J.K. (2003), "Investing in strengths", in K.S. Dutton, J.E. Dutton & R.E. Quinn (eds), *Positive Organizational Scholarship*, San Francisco, CA: Berrett-Koehler, pp. 111–211.

De Boer, E.B., Bakker, A.B., Syroit, S. & Schaufeli, W.B. (2002), "Unfairness at work as a predictor of absenteeism", *Journal of Organizational Behavior*, **23**, 181–97.

Emmons, R.A. (2003), "Acts of gratitude in organizations", in K.S. Dutton, J.E. Dutton & R.E. Quinn (eds), *Positive Organizational Scholarship*, San Francisco, CA: Berrett-Koehler, pp. 81–93.

Emmons, R.A. & McCullough, M.E. (2003), "Counting blessings versus burdens: an experimental investigation of gratitude and subjective well-being in daily life", *Journal of Personality and Social Psychology*, **84**, 377–89.

Frattaroli, J. (2006), "Experimental disclosure and its moderators: a meta analysis", *Psychological Bulletin*, **132**, 823–65.

Gable, S.L., Reis, H.T., Impett, E.A. & Asher, E.R. (2004), "What do you do when things go right? The intrapersonal and interpersonal benefits of sharing positive events", *Journal of Personality and Social Psychology*, **87**, 228–45.

Goetzel, R.Z., Guindon, A.M., Turshen, I.J. & Ozminkowski, R.J. (2001), "Health and productivity management: establishing key performance measures, benchmarks, and best practices", *Journal of Occupational and Environmental Medicine*, **43**, 10–17.

Harter, J.K., Schmidt, F.L. & Hayes, T.L. (2002), "Business-unit-level relationship between employee satisfaction, employee engagement, and business outcomes: a meta-analysis", *Journal of Applied Psychology*, **87**, 268–79.

Hebl, J.H. & Enright, R.D. (1993), "Forgiveness as a psychotherapeutic goal with elderly females", *Psychotherapy: Theory, Research, Practice and Training*, **30**, 658–67.

Kelly, J.E. (1992), "Does job re-design theory explain job re-design outcomes?", *Human Relations*, **45**, 753–74.

King, L.A. (2001), "The health benefits of writing", *Personality and Social Psychology Bulletin*, **27**, 798–807.

Luthans, F., Avey, J.B., Avolio, B.J., Norman, S.M. & Combs, G.M. (2006), "Psychological capital development: towards a micro-intervention", *Journal of Organizational Behavior*, **27**, 387–93.

Lyubomirsky, S. (2007), *The How of Happiness: A Practical Guide to Getting the Life You Want*, London: Sphere.

Lyubomirsky, S., King, L. & Diener, E. (2005), "The benefits of frequent positive affect: does happiness lead to success?", *Psychological Bulletin*, **131**, 803–55.

Lyubomirsky, S., Sousa, L. & Dickerhoof, R. (2006), "The costs and benefits of writing, talking and thinking about life's triumphs and defeats", *Journal of Personality and Social Psychology*, **90**, 692–708.

MacLeod, A.K., Coates, E. & Hetherton, J. (2008), "Increasing well-being through teaching goal-setting and planning skills: results of a brief intervention", *Journal of Happiness Studies*, **9**, 185–96.

McCullough, M.E. (2001), "Forgiveness: who does it and how do they do it?", *Current Directions in Psychological Science*, **10**, 194–7.

Nielsen, K., Yarker, J., Randall, F. & Munir, R. (2009), "The mediating effects of team and self-efficacy on the relationship between transformational leadership, and job satisfaction and psychological well-being in healthcare professionals: a cross-sectional questionnaire survey", *International Journal of Nursing Studies*, **46**, 1236–44.

Peterson, C. & Seligman, M.E.P. (2004), *Character Strengths and Virtues: A Handbook and Classification*, New York: Oxford University Press.

Peterson, C., & Steen, T.A. (2002), "Optimistic explanatory style", in C.T. Snyder & S.J. Lopez (eds), *Handbook of Positive Psychology*, New York: Oxford University Press, pp. 244–56.

Rousseau, D.M. (1995), *Psychological c in Organizations: Understanding Written and Unwritten Agreements*, Thousand Oaks, CA: Sage.

Ryan, R.M. & Deci, E.L. (2001), "On happiness and human potentials: a review of research on hedonic and eudaimonic well-being", *Annual Review of Psychology*, **51**, 141–66.

Salanova, M., Agut, S. & Peiró, J.M. (2005), "Linking organizational resources and work engagement to employee performance and customer loyalty: the mediation of service climate", *Journal of Applied Psychology*, **90**, 1217–27.

Salanova, M. & Llorens, S. (2008), *Desarrollo de Recursos Humanos a Través del Aprendizaje para el Cambio* (Human resource development through learning for change), Madrid: Parthenon.

Salanova, M., Llorens, S., Cifre, E., Martínez, I.M. & Schaufeli, W.B. (2003), "Perceived collective efficacy, subjective well-being and task performance among electronic work groups: an experimental study", *Small Group Research*, **34**, 43–73.

Salanova, M., Lorente, L., Chambel, M.J. & Martínez, I.M. (2010a), "Linking transformational leadership to nurses' extra-role behavior: the mediating role of self-efficacy and work engagement", manuscript submitted for publication.

Salanova, M., Peiró, J.M & Schaufeli, W.B. (2002), "Self-efficacy specificity and burnout among information technology workers: an extension of the job demands control model", *European Journal of Work and Organizational Psychology*, **11**, 1–25.

Salanova, M. & Schaufeli, W.B. (2009), *El Engagement de los Empleados. Cuando el Trabajo se Convierte en Passion* (Work engagement: when work turns into passion), Madrid: Alianza Editorial.

Salanova, M., Schaufeli, W.B., Xanthopoulou, D. & Bakker, A.B. (2010b), "The gain spiral of resources and work engagement", in A.B. Bakker & M.P. Leiter (eds), *Work Engagement: A Handbook of Essential Theory and Research*, New York: Psychology Press, pp. 118–31.

Schaufeli, W.B. (2006), "The balance of give and take: toward a social exchange model of burnout", *International Review of Social Psychology*, **19**, 87–131.

Schaufeli, W.B., Bakker, A.B. & Van Rhenen, W. (2009), "How changes in job demands and resources predict burnout, work engagement, and sickness absenteeism", *Journal of Organizational Behavior*, **30**, 893–917.

Schaufeli, W.B. & Salanova, M. (2008), "Enhancing work engagement through the management of human resources", in K. Näswall, M. Sverke & J. Hellgren (eds), *The Individual in the Changing Working Life*, Cambridge: Cambridge University Press, pp. 380–404.

Schaufeli, W.B., Salanova, M., González-Romá, V. & Bakker, A.B. (2002), "The measurement of engagement and burnout: a confirmative analytic approach", *Journal of Happiness Studies*, **3**, 71–92.

Schaufeli, W.B., Taris, T., Le Blanc, P., Peeters, M., Bakker, A. & De Jonge, J. (2001), "Maakt arbeid gezond? Op zoek naar de bevlogen werknemer" (Does work make one healthy? In search of the engaged worker), *De Psycholoog*, **36**, 422–8.

Seligman, M.E.P. (1991), *Learned Optimism: How to Change Your Mind and Your Life*, New York: Simon & Schuster.

Seligman, M.E.P. & Csikszentmihalyi, M. (2000), "Positive psychology: an introduction", *American Psychologist*, **55**, 5–14.

Seligman, M.E.P., Steen, T.A., Park, N. & Peterson, C. (2005), "Positive psychology progress: empirical validation of interventions", *American Psychologist*, **60**, 410–21.

Sheldon, K.M., Kasser, T., Smith, K. & Share, T. (2002), "Personal goals and psychological growth: testing an intervention to enhance goal-attainment and personality integration", *Journal of Personality*, **70**, 5–31.

Sutcliffe, K.M. & Vogus, T.J. (2003), "Organizing for resilience", in K.S. Dutton, J.E. Dutton & R.E. Quinn (eds), *Positive Organizational Scholarship*, San Francisco, CA: Berrett-Koehler, pp. 94–110.

Tedeschi, R.G. & Calhoun, L.G. (2004), "Posttraumatic growth: conceptual foundations and empirical evidence", *Psychological Inquiry*, **15**, 1–18.

Viswesvaran, C., Sanchez, J.I. & Fischer, J. (1999), "The role of social support in the process of work stress: a meta-analysis", *Journal of Vocational Behavior*, **54**, 314–34.

Wong, C.S., Hui, C. & Law, K.S. (1998), "A longitudinal study of the job perception–job satisfaction relationship: a test of the three alternative specifications", *Journal of Occupational and Organizational Psychology*, **71**, 127–46.

Xanthopoulou, D., Bakker, A.B., Demerouti, E. & Schaufeli, W.B. (2009a), "Reciprocal relationships between job resources, personal resources and work engagement", *Journal of Vocational Behavior*, **74**, 235–44.

Xanthopoulou, D., Bakker, A.B., Demerouti, E. & Schaufeli, W.B. (2009b), "Work engagement and financial returns: a diary study on the role of job and personal resources", *Journal of Organizational and Occupational Psychology*, **82**, 183–200.

Zwetsloot, G. & Pot, F. (2004), "The business value of health management", *Journal of Business Ethics*, **55**, 115–24.

34 Using theatre-based interventions to increase employee self-efficacy and engagement
Richard Carter, Paul Nesbit and Miriam Joy

Introduction

In the simplest terms, employee engagement (also known as job engagement) can be thought of as the amount of "discretionary effort", in the form of extra time, brainpower or energy, that employees exhibit at work (Towers-Perrin, 2003). This definition implies that the more engaged employees are, the better they will perform at work and vice versa. This view is supported by research that shows that companies with high employee engagement substantially outperformed those with low engagement on a range of financial performance measures (Macey et al., 2009). Given these findings, increasing employee engagement is seen as highly desirable to organizations endeavouring to obtain competitive advantage from their human capital or even just to compete effectively. The challenge for organizations, therefore, is to find or develop programmes and interventions that create an environment where employees are willing to expend extra time, brainpower and energy at work.

Engagement and self-efficacy

Macey et al. (2009, p. 7) defined employee engagement as "an individual's sense of purpose and focused energy, evident to others in the display of personal initiative, adaptability, effort, and persistence directed toward organizational goals". This view overlaps Kanfer et al.'s (2008, p. 3) definition of work motivation as "the psychological processes that determine (or energize) the direction, intensity, and persistence of action within the continuing steam of experiences that characterize the person in relation to his or her work". The core focus of these constructs on the direction, intensity/effort and persistence that an individual displays at work suggests that employee engagement is clearly associated with the work motivation field.

Within the field of work motivation, constructs such as goal setting, feedback and coaching, and self-efficacy are factors that are seen to impact on individual behaviour and performance (Stajkovic & Luthans, 1998) and can be usefully explored for the development of engagement interventions.

The concept of self-efficacy, defined as "an individual's beliefs about their ability to organize and execute the courses of action required to produce given attainments" (Bandura, 1997, p. 3) is particularly relevant. In a recent meta-analysis self-efficacy was found to have high correlations (ranging from 0.71 to 0.76) with the three dimensions of engagement (vigor, dedication and absorption) as measured by the Utrecht Work Engagement Scale (UWES) (Christian & Slaughter, 2007). These high correlations suggest that self-efficacy and employee engagement are associated constructs and that interventions designed to improve employee self-efficacy are likely to increase employee engagement scores.

Given that engagement follows where employees believe that they have the capacity, reason or motivation, freedom and knowledge to engage (Macey et al., 2009), interventions designed to raise employee engagement scores must take these factors into account. By focusing on raising employee self-efficacy, three of these factors are directly addressed. First, increasing self-efficacy helps employees develop a greater sense of confidence in their competence to undertake their work responsibilities, effectively raising their capacity to be engaged in their work. Second, consistent with goal-setting theory (Locke et al., 1984), raising self-efficacy leads to the setting of more challenging goals and the motivation to reach those goals. Third, self-efficacy enhances personal agency and control and leads to employees perceiving they have more freedom to engage. In summary, the combination of confidence in one's competence, motivation via goal setting and sense of personal agency and control provide the platform for employees to become engaged. It is then the organization's responsibility to address the fourth factor (knowledge) by providing employees with the information they need so that they can clearly see how their work is aligned with the organization's strategy.

Job burnout and engagement

Besides the demonstrable relationship between employee engagement and self-efficacy, job engagement has also been characterized as the positive antithesis of job burnout (Maslach et al., 2001). Moving the focal point of study from the negative (job burnout) to the positive (job engagement) mirrors the broader aim of positive psychology to change the focus of psychology from preoccupation with repairing the worst things in life to building positive qualities (Seligman & Csikszentmihalyi, 2000). While the UWES's first two dimensions (vigor and dedication) are closely related to earlier definitions of employee engagement and work motivation with their focus on direction, intensity/effort and persistence, the third dimension (absorption) highlights the importance of self-efficacy with its focus on effectiveness and accomplishment. It is argued, therefore, that interventions designed to lift self-efficacy are likely to increase overall employee engagement scores, particularly through the absorption dimension.

Intervention techniques

Given self-efficacy's link with job engagement, interventions should focus on increasing the four principal sources of self-efficacy information: enactive mastery experiences; vicarious experiences; verbal persuasion and allied types of social influences; and physiological and affective states (Bandura, 1997). Enactive mastery refers to people's experience in successfully performing a task, and builds feelings of competency, in their perceived skill to perform a required task or function (Bandura, 2002). Vicarious experience allows people to learn by watching role models and then modelling their own behaviour on successful performance, while verbal persuasion uses a feedback and coaching process to address participants' perceptions of how the social environment impacts on their ability to achieve certain outcomes (Bandura, 1991). Finally, providing an environment where participants' physical and affective states are raised increases the likelihood that self-efficacy information will be transferred.

Although each of these four factors can independently assist in the process of increasing participant self-efficacy, the ideal intervention would incorporate all four in order to maximize participants' sense of their confidence in their competence to perform a challenging task and produce given attainments. An ideal intervention would also enhance participants' sense of their personal agency and control – their belief in their ability to be self-organizing, proactive, self-regulating, and self-reflecting, and not simply be an onlooker to their behaviour (Bandura, 2006). Overall, employees who feel confident, agentic and effective are more likely to be engaged. Given these requirements, three drama-based formats, Forum Theatre, Rehearse for Reality, and entertainment-education, offer significant potential as interventions to raise participant self-efficacy, particularly when used in combination.

Forum Theatre

Forum Theatre (Boal, 2000), originally called "Theatre of the Oppressed", is a form of simultaneous dramaturgy where participants ("spect-actors") watch a scripted performance and then participate in analysing the performance and coaching the actors on different ways of constructing it. The theory of second-order observation (Luhmann, 1998) provides insight into the observational and reflective processes undertaken by organization theatre audiences (Schreyögg, 2001). Rather than watching the actors perform a play, the audience actually observe the result of observations that others (that is, the actors and scriptwriters) have made about their organization. This process confronts the audience as it is likely to markedly differ from their usual perception of their reality. As a result, it brings about "reality duplication" (Luhmann, 1998) or a "splitting experience" (Schreyögg, 2001) as the audience observes the familiar from an unfamiliar angle, enabling them to view two different realities simultaneously and making the process *reflexive* (ibid.). Forum Theatre uses all three ways in which organizational theatre can be used: a *mirror* providing contrasting realities; a *window* showing hidden/overlooked scenes or potential future ones; and a *passage-like* form where the audience has the opportunity to participate on stage and craft new possibilities in an emergent rather than scripted setting (Meisiek & Barry, 2007). In summary, Forum Theatre confronts audiences with a different perspective of their familiar problem construction that in turn initiates a close examination of habituated behavioural patterns and established perceptual constructions (Schreyögg & Hapfl, 2004).

Forum Theatre features two key elements: a staged dialectic and a related dialogue. The staged dialectic denotes "conflict, contradiction, confrontation and defiance" in order to create an engaging analogy while at the same time reflecting the lived experience of the audience in order to generate change-related dialogue (Boal, 2000). Following on from the staged dialectic, the related dialogue component of Forum Theatre provides the opportunity for participants to explore their situation as equals as well as the possibilities associated with how things could be different. Consequently, Forum Theatre enhances participant self-efficacy in two ways. As observers, participants have the opportunity to learn vicariously by watching the actors perform scenes and then scrutinizing the interaction between the actors and spect-actors. To the extent that the actors and spect-actors are able to create and demonstrate appropriate new behaviours that achieve successful outcomes during the related dialogue stage, participants enhance their own self-efficacy by adjusting their behaviour to reflect the approaches used by these new role models. In addition, the conflict, contradiction, confrontation and defiance exhibited during the staged dialectic, stimulates participants' sense of their own personal agency. In effect, by mobilizing the audience's energy, Forum Theatre has a catalytic impact on personal agency and self-efficacy that sets it apart as a drama-based technology.

Rehearse for Reality (business simulation)
Rehearse for Reality is a variation of role playing where participants typically enter a dyadic role play with an actor while other participants watch. In some scenarios, the actor also plays a feedback and coaching role, while in others, a third person watches the interaction and provides feedback

and coaching to the participant. In contrast to role-play business simulations where learners take on the roles of specific characters in a contrived setting, Rehearse for Reality participants play themselves in a more realistic setting that could involve a range of situations such as a conversation with an employee, a presentation to a group or a team negotiation.

In Rehearse for Reality, a professional actor/coach gets the participant to describe in some detail the background, the conversation's purpose and personal characteristics of the individual the actor will play in the simulated conversation. Given their training in and skills at adopting a wide range of characters for theatre, the actor/coach is able to accurately portray the conversational partner for the participant from both a cognitive and an emotional perspective, making the conversation realistic and credible. Further, the actor is able to connect the emotion/motivation he/she displays in the conversation to a value or belief that the character he/she is playing holds and that participants need to address in order to achieve successful outcomes. As a result, participants experience a heightened physiological and affective state and engage in a realistic and genuine conversation where they directly gain enactive mastery practice at both managing the conversation's cognitive elements and its emotional context.

During the course of the conversation, the actor/coach will periodically call time out, give the participants the opportunity to reflect on their perception of their ability to reach their purpose in the conversation, provide feedback on how their behaviour in the conversation is affecting them as the character, and gain feedback from the group watching. Following this reflective practice, there is an opportunity for participants to experiment with different conversational approaches in the same way that Forum Theatre allows participants to suggest alternatives. In effect, the actor/coach helps the participants to enhance perceptions of their self-efficacy through a feedback and coaching process. Rehearse for Reality simulations are typically undertaken in small groups of 5–6 people where each person takes a turn at practising his/her skill while the rest of the group watch and provide feedback and support as appropriate. Each participant not only enhances his/her own self-efficacy through enactive mastery practice, feedback and coaching and through being in a heightened physiological and affective state but also through vicarious (observational) learning of other participants. Therefore, Rehearse for Reality offers a rich technology for enhancing participant self-efficacy.

Entertainment-education
Defined as the intentional placement of educational content in entertainment messages (Singhal & Rogers, 2002), entertainment-education (E-E)

has traditionally been used as a public health-oriented vehicle for mass market education, typically through radio or television serials. E-E has its theoretical roots in social learning (now social cognitive) theory with its focus on seeking to influence audience behavioural change by showing rather than describing positive and negative role models to the target audience (Singhal, 2004). As a non-participatory process, E-E relies primarily on enhancing individual self-efficacy through vicarious learning rather than enactive mastery practice or feedback and coaching as occurs in Forum Theatre and Rehearse for Reality. Nevertheless the parallels between E-E and Forum Theatre have been recognized with the prediction that future E-E interventions are likely to see more integration with participatory communication approaches for democratizing organizations (Singhal & Rogers, 2002). Given the difficulties faced by participants seeking to adopt new behaviours on challenging tasks, Bandura (personal communication, August 2, 2007) has suggested that E-E can be used as a self-efficacy reinforcement mechanism for interventions such as Forum Theatre until new behaviours become habitual. Therefore, E-E can perhaps best be described as a reflective narrative that acts as both a primary and a secondary behavioural change agent.

Intervention case study
Having established the theoretical underpinnings linking employee engagement with self-efficacy and described interventions designed to increase participant self-efficacy, the following case study shows the influence that these interventions have on employee engagement.

Research setting and participants
An independently branded retail business of an Australasian financial services organization had implemented a new customer relationship management (CRM) software program as part of a strategic push to deepen their relationship with customers as measured by the number of products held per customer. In order to achieve this objective, customer-facing employees were encouraged to use the software to identify eligible customers for a free financial "health check". The primary aim was to establish a regular dialogue with customers so that when the customer's circumstances required a new product, the organization would be firmly in the customer's consideration set to assist. The employee's task was to proactively ask the customer to make the appointment during a regular over-the-counter (OTC) transaction. Although the organization was seeing a general positive trend in the number of appointments being made by employees, budgets were not being met and the organization believed that employee self-efficacy (or lack thereof) in

approaching customers for an appointment, could be an underlying factor. In addition, this organization had embraced employee engagement as an important performance metric and was very interested in increasing its employee engagement scores. Twenty mid-sized, branches from a large city in Eastern Australia were selected to participate in the study. Pairs of branches were matched on a range of criteria and then randomly assigned to either the pilot group (who fully participated in the intervention) or the control group (who completed surveys only). Each branch typically had six employees: manager (1); supervisor (1); and frontline (4).

Intervention

The intervention was designed to increase participant task-specific self-efficacy (being proactive in customer conversations). Employees from the pilot group attended two half-day workshops (four weeks apart) that used Forum Theatre, visualization and personal action planning in the first workshop and Forum Theatre and Rehearse for Reality in the second. Three to four months after the second workshop, a version of E-E in the form of three short (six-minute) DVDs featuring characters created for the workshops were shown and discussed over a three-week period in a regularly scheduled weekly team meeting. In the intervention, Forum Theatre demonstrated proactive customer conversation issues, Rehearse for Reality gave participants practice at these conversations and E-E served to reinforce participant behavioural change. Engagement and performance was measured prior to the intervention and then eight months later.

Measures

The 9-item UWES (Schaufeli et al., 2006) incorporating a 7-point scale (0 = never to 6 = every day) was used to measure participant vigor, dedication and absorption and overall engagement. All scales and subscales showed Cronbach's alpha ranging from 0.70 to 0.83 for the pre-intervention survey and 0.85 to 0.87 for the post-intervention survey and are virtually identical to those reported in the literature (ibid.).

Results

Figure 34.1 shows that employee engagement scores for both the pilot and control groups decreased sharply between the pre- and post-intervention surveys with a significant main effect ($p = 0.000$). This decline was directly attributable to the announcement of a proposed corporate merger one week before the post-intervention survey was posted online. While engagement scores for both the pilot and control branches decreased,

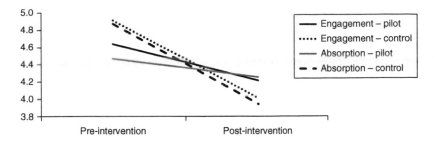

Figure 34.1   *Employee engagement and absorption – pre- and post-intervention*

the decrease for the pilot group was significantly lower ($p = 0.048$), suggesting that the pilot group's engagement score was "buffered" to some extent by the intervention. Analysis of the data indicated that this buffering effect was primarily caused by the highly significant difference in the rate of decline in the absorption dimension ($p = 0.01$) for the pilot group compared to the control group. In addition, although not quite statistically significant the vigor dimension ($p = 0.12$) appears to be a secondary buffering factor on the pilot group's relatively smaller decline in overall engagement compared to the control group. Given the relatively small number of employees responding to the post-intervention survey ($n = 53$ versus $n = 104$ for the pre-intervention survey) it is plausible that vigor would have had a statistically significant buffering influence if the merger had not been announced. Finally, the intervention had no buffering effect on the dedication dimension ($p = 0.46$). Overall the relatively smaller decline in the absorption and vigor dimensions buffered the pilot group's engagement scores compared to the control group. Although the merger announcement clearly had a profound influence on employee attitudes, the intervention mitigated the extent to which employee engagement was impacted upon.

With respect to performance, the number of appointments made by the pilot group increased sharply compared to the control group as a result of the intervention. Although the number of appointments being made by both groups had increased gradually since the CRM program was first introduced two years earlier, the number of appointments made by pilot group participants in the six months after the intervention increased at double (57.3 percent) the rate of the increase for participants from the control group (28.2 percent). Self-efficacy ratings for the pilot group improved relative to the control group as a result of the intervention, which clearly suggests that the increase in performance and engagement was a direct result of the intervention.

Conclusion

This chapter has shown the theoretical and practical connection between employee engagement and self-efficacy, and argues that employee engagement can be increased through self-efficacy-based interventions. The use of theatre technologies that act as catalysts to employee perceptions of their personal agency and control, provide comprehensive means to increase self-efficacy and build resilience to behavioural change has been shown. Overall, a focus on lifting employee self-efficacy increases both work-related performance and employee engagement.

References

Bandura, A. (1991), "Social cognitive theory of self-regulation", *Organizational Behavior and Human Decision Processes*, **50** (2), 248–87.

Bandura, A. (1997), *Self-efficacy: The Exercise of Control*, New York: W.H. Freeman.

Bandura, A. (2002), "Social cognitive theory in cultural context", *Applied Psychology: An International Review*, **51** (2), 269–90.

Bandura, A. (2006), "Toward a psychology of human agency", *Perspectives on Psychological Science*, **1** (2), 164–80.

Boal, A. (2000), *Theater of the Oppressed*, new edn, London: Pluto.

Christian, M.S. & Slaughter, J.E. (2007), "Work engagement: a meta-analytic review and directions for research in an emerging area", paper presented at the Proceedings of the Sixty-Sixth Annual Meeting of the Academy of Management, Philadelphia, PA, August 6.

Kanfer, R., Chen, G. & Pritchard, R.D. (2008), "The three C's of work motivation: content, context and change", in Kanfer, Chen & Pritchard (eds), *Work Motivation: Past, Present and Future*, New York: Taylor & Francis, pp. 1–16.

Locke, E.A., Frederick, E., Lee, C. & Bobko, P. (1984), "Effect of self-efficacy, goals, and task strategies on task performance", *Journal of Applied Psychology*, **69** (2), May, 241–51.

Luhmann, N. (1998), *Observations on Modernity*, Stanford, CA: Stanford University Press.

Macey, W.H., Schneider, B., Barbera, K.M. & Young, S.A. (2009), *Employee Engagement: Tools for Analysis, Practice, and Competitive Advantage*, Malden, MA: Wiley.

Maslach, C., Schaufeli, W.B. & Leiter, M.P. (2001), "Job burnout", *Annual Review of Psychology*, **52** (1), 397–422.

Meisiek, S. & Barry, D. (2007), "Through the looking glass of organizational theatre: analogically mediated inquiry in organizations", *Organization Studies*, **28** (12), 1805–27.

Schaufeli, W.B., Bakker, A.B. & Salanova, M. (2006), "The measurement of work engagement with a short questionnaire: a cross-national study", *Educational and Psychological Measurement*, **66** (4), 701–16.

Schreyögg, G. (2001), "Organizational theatre and organizational change", paper presented at the Academy of Management, Washington, DC, August 7.

Schreyögg, G. & Hapfl, H. (2004), "Theatre and organization: editorial introduction", *Organization Studies*, **25** (5), 691–704.

Seligman, M.E.P. & Csikszentmihalyi, M. (2000), "Positive psychology: an introduction", *American Psychologist*, **55** (1), 5–14.

Singhal, A. (2004), *Entertainment-education and Social Change: History, Research, and Practice*, Mahwah, NJ and London: Lawrence Erlbaum.

Singhal, A. & Rogers, E.M. (2002), "A theoretical agenda for entertainment-education", *Communication Theory*, **12** (2), 117–35.

Stajkovic, A.D. & Luthans, F. (1998), "Self-efficacy and work-related performance: a meta-analysis", *Psychological Bulletin*, **124** (2), 240–61.

Towers-Perrin (2003), *Working Today: Understanding What Drives Employee Engagement*, Stamford, CT: Towers-Perrin.

Index